THE SEVEN SACRAMENTS OF THE CATHOLIC CHURCH

ROMANUS CESSARIO, OP

Baker Academic
a division of Baker Publishing Group
Grand Rapids, Michigan

Published by Baker Academic
a division of Baker Publishing Group
Grand Rapids, Michigan
www.bakeracademic.com

Printed in the United States of America

Library of Congress Cataloging-in-Publication Data
Names: Cessario, Romanus, author.
Title: The seven sacraments of the Catholic church / Romanus Cessario, OP.
Description: Grand Rapids, Michigan : Baker Academic, a division of Baker Publishing Group, [2023] | Includes bibliographical references and index.
Identifiers: LCCN 2022043949 | ISBN 9781540962546 (cloth) | ISBN 9781493439997 (ebook) | ISBN 9781493440009 (pdf)
Subjects: LCSH: Sacraments—Catholic Church.
Classification: LCC BX2200 .C37 2023 | DDC 234/.16—dc23/eng/20221118
LC record available at https://lccn.loc.gov/2022043949

Baker Publishing Group publications use paper produced from sustainable forestry practices and post-consumer waste whenever possible.

23 24 25 26 27 28 29 7 6 5 4 3 2 1

For
Mr. Thomas S. Monaghan,
Chancellor, Ave Maria University
&
Dr. Roger W. Nutt,
Provost, Ave Maria University

Contents

Preface

The author acknowledges with gratitude Baker Academic for the invitation to write a book on the seven sacraments. I especially would like to thank Mr. Steve Ayers and Dr. R. David Nelson, who served to facilitate my communications with the press. These Christian gentlemen showed me extraordinary courtesy.

It happens that I completed the manuscript for this book at the close of 2021, the year in which I have observed the fiftieth anniversary of my priestly ordination. On May 27, 1971, the late archbishop of New York, Cardinal Terence Cooke, conferred on me the sacrament of Holy Orders at St. Vincent Ferrer Church on Manhattan's Upper East Side. As a member of the Order of Preachers (the Dominicans), most of my priestly ministry has transpired in classrooms, but the daily celebration of the Eucharist and the administration of the other sacraments, especially the sacrament of Penance and Reconciliation, have shaped my life for the past half century.

The final composition of this book occurred mainly at Ave Maria, Florida. In 2019, the authorities of Ave Maria University kindly offered me the Adam Cardinal Maida Chair of Theology. This post has afforded me the opportunity to serve as professor and priest to Catholics of both town and gown. Even after fifty years of priestly ministry, it edifies me to observe the devotion of these Ave Maria university students and parishioners to the sacraments of the Catholic Church. It would be difficult to imagine a more providential way for a Dominican priest to complete his service to the Church.

Romanus Cessario, OP
December 8, 2021
The Solemnity of the Immaculate Conception

Abbreviations

General

ad	reply to objection
arg.	objection
art.	article
ca.	circa
can(n).	canon(s)
chap(s).	chapter(s)
col(s).	column(s)
d.	died
dist.	distinction
lect.	lecture
no(s).	number(s)
q(q).	question(s)
§(§)	section(s)

Bibliographic

CCC	*Catechism of the Catholic Church*, 2nd ed. Libreria Editrice Vaticana. https://www.usccb.org/sites/default/files/flipbooks/catechism/IV/
CCL	*Code of Canon Law*. VRL. https://www.vatican.va/archive/cod-iuris-canonici/cic_index_en.html
DS	Denzinger, Heinrich. *Compendium of Creeds, Definitions, and Declarations on Matters of Faith and Morals*. 43rd ed. Edited by Peter Hünermann. San Francisco: Ignatius, 2012
EC2	Tanner, Norman P., SJ, ed. *Decrees of the Ecumenical Councils*. Vol. 2, *Trent–Vatican II*. Washington, DC: Georgetown University Press, 1990
PL	Patrologia Latina [= *Patrologiae Cursus Completus*. Series Latina]. Edited by Jacques-Paul Migne. 217 vols. Paris, 1844–64
Summa theologiae	Aquinas, Thomas. *Summa theologiae*. Blackfriars edition. Translated by Thomas Gilby et al. New York: McGraw-Hill, 1964–80
VRL	Vatican Resource Library. https://www.vatican.va/archive/index.htm

Vatican II Documents

Ad Gentes	Decree on the Church's Missionary Activity. December 7, 1965
Dei Verbum	Dogmatic Constitution on Divine Revelation. November 18, 1965
Gaudium et Spes	Pastoral Constitution on the Church in the Modern World. December 7, 1965
Lumen Gentium	Dogmatic Constitution on the Church. November 21, 1964
Perfectae Caritatis	Decree on the Appropriate Renewal of the Religious Life. October 28, 1965
Presbyterorum Ordinis	Decree on the Ministry and Life of Priests. December 7, 1965
Sacrosanctum Concilium	Constitution on the Sacred Liturgy. December 4, 1963
Unitatis Redintegratio	Decree on Ecumenism. November 21, 1964

Liturgical Sources

Roman Missal *The Roman Missal*, 3rd ed. International Commission on English in the Liturgy, 2010

Roman Ritual: The Order of Baptism of Children. International Commission on English in the Liturgy, 2017

Roman Ritual: The Order of Celebrating Matrimony. International Commission on English in the Liturgy, 2013

Roman Ritual: The Order of Confirmation. International Commission on English in the Liturgy, 2016

Roman Ritual: The Rite of Penance. International Commission on English in the Liturgy, 1975

Roman Ritual: The Rites of Anointing and Viaticum. International Commission on English in the Liturgy, 1982

Papal Documents

Unless otherwise indicated, quotations of the following papal documents have been taken from the Vatican Resource Library (VRL).

Francis

Amoris lætitia	Post-synodal Apostolic Exhortation on Love in the Family. March 19, 2016

Benedict XVI

Deus caritas est	Encyclical Letter on Christian Love. December 25, 2005
"Year for Priests"	"Letter Proclaiming a Year for Priests on the 150th Anniversary of the 'Dies Natalis' of the Curé of Ars." June 16, 2009

John Paul II

Christifideles laici	Post-synodal Apostolic Exhortation on the Vocation and the Mission of the Lay Faithful in the Church and in the World. December 30, 1988
Ecclesia de Eucharistia	Encyclical Letter on the Eucharist in Its Relationship to the Church. April 17, 2003
Familiaris consortio	Apostolic Exhortation on the Role of the Christian Family in the Modern World. November 22, 1981
Fidei depositum	Apostolic Constitution on the Publication of the Catechism of the Catholic Church Prepared Following the Second Vatican Ecumenical Council. October 11, 1992
Fides et ratio	Encyclical Letter on the Relationship between Faith and Reason. September 14, 1998
Magnum matrimonii sacramentum	Apostolic Constitution for the Definitive Juridical Form of the Pontifical Institute for Studies on Marriage and the Family. October 7, 1982
Ordinatio sacerdotalis	Apostolic Letter on Reserving Priestly Ordination to Men Alone. May 22, 1994
Pastores dabo vobis	Post-synodal Apostolic Exhortation on the Formation of Priests in the Circumstances of the Present Day. March 15, 1992
Reconciliatio et paenitentia	Post-synodal Apostolic Exhortation on Reconciliation and Penance in the Mission of the Church Today. December 2, 1984
Redemptor hominis	Encyclical Letter on the Redeemer of Man, to His Venerable Brothers in the Episcopate, the Priests, the Religious Families, the Sons and Daughters of the Church, and to All Men and Women of Good Will at the Beginning of His Papal Ministry. March 4, 1979
Veritatis splendor	Encyclical Letter on the Splendor of Truth and the Church's Moral Teaching. August 6, 1993
Vita consecrata	Post-synodal Apostolic Exhortation on the Consecrated Life and Its Mission in the Church and in the World. March 25, 1996

Paul VI

Divinae consortium naturae	Apostolic Constitution on the Sacrament of Confirmation. August 15, 1971
Ecclesiam suam	Encyclical Letter on the Church. August 6, 1964

Mysterium fidei	Encyclical Letter on the Holy Eucharist. September 3, 1965
Sacram unctione infirmorum	Apostolic Constitution on the Sacrament of Anointing of the Sick. November 30, 1972

Pius XII

Mystici corporis Christi	Encyclical Letter on the Mystical Body of Christ. June 29, 1943
Sacramentum Ordinis	Apostolic Constitution on the Sacrament of Order. November 30, 1947

Pius XI

Casti connubii	Encyclical Letter on Christian Marriage. December 31, 1930

Documents of the Roman Curia

Quotations of the following documents have been taken from the Vatican Resource Library (VRL).

Dominus Iesus	Congregation for the Doctrine of the Faith, *Declaration on the Unicity and Salvific Universality of Jesus Christ and the Church.* August 6, 2000
Donum veritatis	Congregation for the Doctrine of the Faith, *Instruction on the Ecclesial Vocation of the Theologian.* May 24, 1990
Ecclesiae de mysterio	Congregation for the Clergy, *Instruction on Certain Questions regarding the Collaboration of the Non-ordained Faithful in the Sacred Ministry of the Priest.* August 15, 1997
Inter insigniores	Congregation for the Doctrine of the Faith, *Declaration on the Question of Admission of Women to the Ministerial Priesthood.* October 15, 1976
Pastoralis actio	Congregation for the Doctrine of the Faith, *Instruction on Infant Baptism.* October 20, 1980
"Questions on Christology"	International Theological Commission, "Select Questions on Christology." 1979
"Reconciliation in the Current Pandemic"	Apostolic Penitentiary, "Note on the Sacrament of Reconciliation in the Current Pandemic." March 19, 2020
Social Doctrine	Pontifical Council for Justice and Peace, *Compendium of the Social Doctrine of the Church.* October 25, 2004

Introduction

This book aims to present Catholic teaching on the seven sacraments that the Catholic Church administers to both catechumens and her members. Truth to tell, the liturgical celebration of each of these sacraments forms the backbone of ordinary Catholic life. For instance, when a Catholic parent brings a newborn child to the church for Baptism, the event occasions in most cases not only a religious celebration but also a family one. Catholic parents host christening parties or receptions to mark this important moment in the life of an infant. Next, the Catholic child prepares to receive his or her First Holy Communion. Since a child must have attained the age at which he or she can distinguish the Eucharist from ordinary foodstuff, catechetical instruction is required to prepare children for this milestone in their Catholic lives. Again, in many places, the day when the child first receives the Eucharist reunites family members, especially grandparents, who share in some communal celebration. Next, in ordinary practice, the Catholic child prepares for Confirmation, the Catholic sacrament that completes the baptismal consecration. Religious instruction likewise precedes the reception of this sacrament, which, in order to show the young Catholic the breadth of Catholic life in a region, normally is administered by a diocesan bishop. At this point, the Catholic believer has received those sacraments called the Sacraments of Initiation. This means that a Catholic believer stands ready to take on the challenges involved in professing the Catholic religion in a public forum.

Catholic life, however, does not require only a sacramentalized initiation. The sacraments accompany the baptized Catholic all along the way of life. In the present state of the world, human life suffers from both moral and physical weaknesses and sins. Catholic faith is not required for anyone to acknowledge such a claim. Most people discover the signs of sinful disorder that affect the human race as a result of their involvement in everyday life. Secular remedies, of course, exist that aim to relieve the difficulties people experience in their pursuit of happiness. The Catholic Church offers a divine remedy that appears in the Sacraments of Healing.

The first of these, the sacrament of Penance and Reconciliation, many Catholics call *Confession*. Indeed, ordinary folks often indicate their intention to receive this sacrament by saying, "I'm going to Confession." Because of the secrecy that binds the priest confessor, this sacrament oftentimes attracts attention from the general public, especially from those who argue that some secrets should not enjoy such privilege. For her part, the Catholic Church vigorously defends the practice of the sacramental seal of Confession. She knows that divine healing works better than civil adjudication to cure a malefactor.

While various persons and institutions offer help for psychic disabilities, none can offer a remedy for death. God, however, confided to the Catholic Church a sacrament that aims to strengthen seriously ill and dying Catholics so that they can worthily meet Christ who comes as their judge. The sacrament of the Anointing of the Sick gains public notice at moments when priests administer this sacrament in high-profile circumstances, such as during battlefield combat, before capital punishment, and during times of pandemic. Priests also bring the so-called last rites to those who require them in whatever everyday circumstance they find themselves, often in hospital rooms but also in private homes and in nursing facilities.

The Catholic Church sanctifies certain states of life. She calls these sacraments the Sacraments at the Service of Communion. Because the Catholic Church values above all the supernatural life of divine grace in which human beings can be made participants, the first of these sacraments consecrates men for service as priests. The sacrament of Holy Orders establishes the hierarchy that teaches and governs and sanctifies God's holy people. The Catholic priest comes into a local community of believers as an irreplaceable and indispensable minister of Word and sacrament. As even most non-Catholics know, in order to fulfill these duties, the Roman Catholic priest normatively remains celibate. Childbearing, therefore, falls to other members of the Catholic community. These folks are called married couples, and their unique sacrament is called Matrimony. Husbands and wives together with their children form what the Catholic Church today emphasizes as the *domestic church*, a place where all that happens for the sanctification of human beings finds an exemplary environment. Priests serve the supernatural community of the Church, whereas married couples serve the natural but sanctified communion of the human race.

* * * *

Because the purpose of this book is to provide the Catholic view of the sacraments, the official documents of the Catholic Church make up the major portion of the documentation. No effort is made to recap the many different efforts at theological understanding that have appeared throughout the Christian centuries. The only theological disputes that receive mention serve to explain the evolution of some important sacramental doctrine, especially with respect to the sacraments of Baptism and the Eucharist. The sixteenth-century reform movements provided significant motivation for the Church to crystallize her teaching on the sacraments. This explains the several references to the Council of Trent that appear throughout the treatment of the individual sacraments.

In addition to doctrinal statements, the Catholic Church guards her spiritual treasure, the seven sacraments, with norms of both law and ritual. References, however, to the *Code of Canon Law* and to the various liturgical books and documents that regulate Catholic worship have been kept to a minimum. As a general rule, however, the reader may assume that what both Church law and ritual prescribe supports and finds its warrant in the doctrinal statements that together set forth what the Catholic Church holds about the sacred seven.

This book has been made easier to compose because of the publication in 1992 of the *Catechism of the Catholic Church*. References to this compendium of the Catholic faith appear on almost every page of the present work. This frequency of citation should come as no surprise, however. How else may one assure the benevolent reader, who has picked up this volume to find out what official Catholic Church teaching on the sacraments contains, of the trustworthiness of the account?

Although the reform movements of the sixteenth century figure prominently in the presentation of Catholic teaching on the sacraments, the phrase *Counter-Reformation* does not appear in the chapters that follow. Still, the sixteenth-century Protestant Reform provoked, in many ways, the formulation of what standard Catholic teaching advances about the seven sacraments of justification. So, I refer—after the suggestion of the late historian Guy-Thomas Bedouelle—to both Catholic and Protestant reforms that began in the sixteenth century. Only rarely do the names of those who took issue with the teachings of the Catholic Church appear in the text. This presentation of the Catholic understanding of the seven sacraments does not purport to serve apologetic purposes, at least as those endeavors played out during the period between the Council of Trent and the twentieth-century Second Vatican Council. Instead, the book aims to present, without apology, the seven sacraments from a Catholic point of view.

* * * *

The theological achievement of Saint Thomas Aquinas appears throughout this presentation. References to the works of Aquinas and to those commentators who followed him help to explain why the Catholic Church teaches what she does about the sacraments. The work of Father Colman O'Neill also figures prominently in this volume. There are three reasons for favoring the work of this late Irish theologian: First, he wrote during and after the Second Vatican Council. Second, O'Neill, a Dominican, possessed a deep grasp of Thomist thought and of the classical givens of Catholic theology. Third, because he held a university professorship in Fribourg, Switzerland, O'Neill engaged fully and frequently with theologians from both the Reformed and the Lutheran traditions. For these reasons, drawing on O'Neill's presentation of Thomist thought seems a prudent way to augment a presentation of Catholic teaching for a broad audience.

PART 1

CATHOLIC SACRAMENTAL THEOLOGY

1

Catholic Theology

In order to introduce well a treatment of Catholic teaching on the sacraments of the Church, one can find no better official text than the one from the start of the proceedings of the sixteenth-century Council of Trent. The fathers of the council located Catholic teaching on the sacraments within the Church's overall end or *telos*: "For the completion of the doctrine of salvation concerning justification which was promulgated at the immediately preceding session by the unanimous consent of the fathers, there was general agreement to treat the most holy sacraments of the church by means of which all true justness either begins, or once received gains strength, or if lost is restored."[1] In other words, the sacraments of the Church confer, strengthen, or restore holiness to the members of the human race. The twentieth-century Second Vatican Council then explained this divine purpose as follows: "God gathered together as one all those who in faith look upon Jesus as the author of salvation and the source of unity and peace, and established them as the Church that for each and all it may be the visible sacrament of this saving unity."[2] The seven sacraments of the Catholic Church communicate to those who receive them the salvation won by Christ.

Theologians of all stripes, it is true, may envisage other starting points than the Council of Trent for a study of the sacraments. Many inquirers would have thought that the Bible offers the best place to discover what God teaches about the sacraments of the New Law. Others of a more dialectical persuasion would

1. Council of Trent, Session 7, Decree on the Sacraments, *EC2* 684.
2. *Lumen Gentium*, no. 9 (VRL).

have begun with authentic texts from authors within the Christian tradition. Still others who may be well read in sociology or anthropology may have thought it necessary to examine the practices of other religious traditions outside the ambit of Christian revelation in order to give an account of the sacraments. Why, then, begin with a decree from a sixteenth-century Church council held in a somewhat out-of-the-way town in northern Italy? In order to appreciate why the Council of Trent offers the best starting place for treating the sacraments of the Church, one must first recall some principles that govern the production of Catholic theology.

What Is Catholic Theology?

In an address that the late cardinal Avery Dulles delivered on the occasion of the fiftieth-anniversary celebration of the Catholic Theological Society of America, one finds some key points that summarize the criteria that Catholic theologians must observe in order to accomplish their work well.[3] Above all, as the word *catholic* suggests, Catholic theology exhibits an inclusiveness or universal application. This means that what sound Catholic theologians teach holds true for the world's billion-plus Catholic believers. At the same time, Catholic theology enjoys a kind of specificity that derives from the fact that Catholic theologians draw their conclusions from the same principles and in a way that observes recognized patterns of visible mediation. The working of Catholic theology finds expression in the classic phrase *fides quaerens intellectum* (faith seeking understanding). Catholic theology finds its unity when a practitioner undertakes a disciplined reflection on what is held in faith by all Catholic believers.

At the same time, Catholic theology recognizes a distinction between *fides quae creditur* and *fides qua creditur*. These Latin expressions point to the difference between those things *that* (*quae*) faith holds or believes and the act of faith *by which* (*qua*) one assents to them. It is generally held that a theologian must assent to Catholic and divine truths in order to reflect successfully on them. Can someone who does not assent in an effective way to divine truth still do theology? While a scientific enterprise can be judged on its own merits based on rules, methods, and sources, Cardinal Dulles prefers to speak about a spiritual attunement. In other words, in order to penetrate deeply into the mysteries of the faith—as is the theologian's charge—he or she should demonstrate some sympathy with the divinely revealed truths (such as the Blessed Trinity and

3. The text was subsequently published in an issue of the English edition of the international Catholic journal *Communio*. See Avery Dulles, "Criteria of Catholic Theology," *Communio* 22, no. 2 (1995): 303–15.

the Incarnation) that the mysteries of the faith embody. So one may conclude that Catholic theology, while extending to a transnational and indeed universal humanity, also finds its lodestar in the particular mediation that Jesus Christ introduces into our world. In a word, what unites believers within the Catholic Church remains the belief that God bestows his gifts of grace only through Christ and the visible mediations that Christ establishes and bequeaths to his Church.

Another characteristic of Catholic theology involves the role that human thinking plays in the development of theology. Human reason operates within the structures of Christian faith. Human intelligence is not an enemy of Christian faith. First in the order of importance stands the knowability of God.[4] God possesses the perfection of all perfections. He can be known by human reasoning, and so there exist grounds for speaking about God without appeal to what divine faith holds. Catholic theology also defends the catholicity of Jesus Christ. The person of Jesus Christ remains central to both personal human existence and the order of the world. His divinity stands at the heart of the Christian confession of faith, and the union of both divine and human natures must be understood in ontological terms.

From the belief that Christ enjoys relevance for all human beings, the Church of Christ undertakes a worldwide mission. Missionary universalism proceeds on the basis of a faith conviction that no one is saved from sin and destined for eternal life apart from some union with the Incarnate Word. The normal mode of salvific union between a human being and the Savior, Jesus Christ, the Eternal Word of God "who was born of the Virgin Mary, suffered death and was buried, rose again from the dead, and is seated at the right hand of the Father," begins with Baptism.[5] The present treatment of the Church's sacraments will expose a particular instance of Catholic theology that shows all the earmarks of human thinking applied to what is held in faith about the seven sacraments both in general and with respect to each one.

Baptism of course introduces the ecclesial context within which Catholic theology operates. In short, Catholic theology finds its home within the ecclesial structures of the Catholic Church. In order to become a recognized part of Catholic theological thinking, theological work done outside these ecclesial structures requires scrutiny and approval. In fact, Catholic theology belongs to the Catholic Church in three ways: the Church communicates the truth, she

4. For a comprehensive and authoritative account of what the Catholic Church holds about the knowability of God and other truths often thought to be available only through faith, see John Paul II, *Fides et ratio*. For further discussion, see Romanus Cessario, "Duplex Ordo Cognitionis," in *Reason and the Reasons of Faith*, ed. Paul J. Griffiths and Reinhard Hütter (New York: T&T Clark, 2005).

5. *Roman Missal*, "Renewal of Baptismal Promises."

expresses the truth, and she first of all believes the truth. For this reason, Catholic theology cannot exist in servitude to academic or political authorities. The displacement of Catholic theology from its native place within the recognized structures of the Catholic Church—for instance, monasteries, seminaries, and some other Catholic educational institutions—to secular universities and other places unaffiliated with the Church's governance may come to be viewed as a self-defeating historical development.

To speak of theology under the aegis of ecclesial governance is to introduce another feature of Catholic theology. Catholic theology flourishes when its practitioners remain in communion with Rome—that is, with the Church of Jesus Christ as it subsists in the body of believers who are in communion with the Church of Rome.[6] The Bishop of Rome holds a place of supervision over the work of theology such that no one can come to a conclusion that he would not accept. Theology done outside this "communion" may manifest some aspects of superior intellectual qualities, but overall such theology also reflects the doctrinal suppositions of the particular ecclesial community from which it originates. This critique holds true for both positive theology, such as biblical studies and historical studies, and works of systematic theology.

Cardinal Dulles recognizes an obvious feature of the communion that sustains Catholic theology. He acknowledges what he calls a differentiated unity. The differentiation, however, can suffer assaults when theologians do not respect both elements of the expression—that is, *differentiated* and *unity*. Theological activism can produce one-sided presentations that effectively compromise the divine truths that the Catholic theologian commits to defending. For example, consider efforts made in some quarters to change the revealed names of persons of the Blessed Trinity. One should never achieve contextualism at the price of foreshortening the whole truth. Dulles further insists on what he calls the "synchronic" catholicity that sound Catholic theology should always exhibit. *Synchronic* in this usage means that the theologian needs to keep everything in mind simultaneously as he or she plies the craft of theology. To cite another example, one cannot consider only the sociological implications of an all-male priesthood and ignore the fact that the priesthood comes about, as Pope Saint John Paul II has reminded the Church, as both gift and mystery.[7]

Another kind of unity informs all legitimate Catholic theology. In a word, Catholic theology always stands in continuity with the Christian past, with the authorities that the Church recognizes and that date back to her earliest years.

6. See *Lumen Gentium*, no. 8. For further discussion, see also *Donum veritatis*.

7. See John Paul II, *Gift and Mystery: On the Fiftieth Anniversary of My Priestly Ordination* (New York: Doubleday, 1996).

Dulles calls this feature of Catholic theology "diachronic" catholicity. Diachronic unity does not mean that the Catholic theologian may only repeat what was said in some earlier period. Instead, Catholic theologians infuse their work with an active apostolicity, one that carries through in time and throughout time. This commitment to diachronic unity prohibits one from creating large-scale ruptures, whether in the patristic, medieval, or modern periods. Well-executed historical research will uncover the vast varieties of expression and approaches to divine truth that appear throughout the history of Catholic theology. At the same time, Catholic theologians will eschew a romantic archaeology—that is, they will not make the more primitive the de facto preference. In other words, Catholic theologians avoid the temptation to subject divine truth to the vagaries of historical development with the result that the communication of divine truth appears marked more by discontinuity than by diachronic catholicity.

In order to see the truthfulness of diachronic catholicity, one does not need to adopt a particular theory of history or of doctrines. It suffices to recite at Mass each Sunday the Niceno-Constantinopolitan Creed.[8] Sunday worship suggests another feature of Catholic theology that relates to both the sacraments and worship. A theological proposal that weakens the life of worship or draws people away from the path of holiness will be for that very reason theologically suspect. An ancient Christian rule of thumb argues that the rule of faith also supplies the norm for worship. The *Catechism of the Catholic Church* records "the ancient saying, *lex orandi, lex credendi*. . . . The law of prayer is the law of faith: the Church believes as she prays."[9] One may usefully note that styles of worship—for example, the choice of musical expression and the styles of artistic design used to create sacred objects and images—fall under the heading of differentiated unity. Tampering with the elements used for the sacraments—for example, to replace the wine and bread of the Eucharist with foodstuffs that may be more easily available in certain regions of the world—strikes at the catholicity that unites Catholic believers worldwide. The regulation of practices that seek to implement some form of inculturation falls to ecclesiastical authority. Still, the principle that sound Catholic theology respects the approved practices of Catholic worship remains a hallmark of the former's authenticity.

Other considerations present themselves. Dulles usefully distinguishes between a kind of laicism that intrudes into the divinely appointed structure of the Church and the rightful place that Christ's faithful hold in shaping the practice of the faith. He insists that the sense of the faithful (*sensus fidelium*) that has become a common feature of Catholic theology after the Second Vatican Council

8. See CCC no. 195.
9. CCC no. 1124.

(1962–65) flows from another principle that comes to us from the great saints, such as Ignatius Loyola—namely, *sentire cum Ecclesia*. Sometimes this expression is translated "to think with the Church." In fact, the meaning of the Latin *sentire* suggests a complete conformity of both mind and heart to what the Church says and does. The Catholic theologian, in any case, may never play the "rebel without a cause." While some reasonable revolutions in political and cultural settings may prove useful, mindless revolutions never serve the common good.

Catholic theology proceeds best when those who practice it commit themselves to an acceptance of authority.[10] Dulles reminds theologians that the Catholic Church affords them a place of spousal receptivity. This means, in short, that theologians and the faithful as a whole learn from her. Catholics do not treat ecclesiastical authority as if the Church or her pastors were foreign usurpers. The general rule of Christian living—namely, that God assures his grace to the humble of heart—applies also to professional theologians.

Catholic theologians read the Sacred Scriptures within a tradition. A traditional Catholic view of biblical interpretation seeks to maintain the integrity of the Word of God. As a result, the Catholic theologian watches carefully to avoid whatever leads to a fragmentation of the Scriptures. The best way to ensure that one reads the Scriptures in conformity with Catholic practice is to observe the rule set down in the *Catechism of the Catholic Church*: "It is clear therefore that, in the supremely wise arrangement of God, sacred Tradition, Sacred Scripture, and the Magisterium of the Church are so connected and associated that one of them cannot stand without the others. Working together, each in its own way, under the action of the one Holy Spirit, they all contribute effectively to the salvation of souls."[11]

Within this context, it is easy to understand why Cardinal Dulles made a point of encouraging his hearers to observe a fidelity to the Magisterium of the Church's Sacred Pastors. This encouragement holds good for Catholic theologians of every period. The Church does not admit of a parallel magisterium—that is, one that appears to offer guidance on matters of Catholic faith but diverts from what the Bishop of Rome and those who assist him set down. It is wrongheaded to interpret the obedience of faith as an act of submission to a distant absolutism. Absolute political authority enjoys the reputation of crushing personal liberty. The obedience of faith produces another kind of

10. The Church has delicately indicated the mode in which theologians may register their views before ecclesiastical authority. See *Donum veritatis*, no. 26: "In the dialogue, a two-fold rule should prevail. When there is a question of the communion of faith, the principle of the 'unity of truth' (*unitas veritatis*) applies. When it is a question of differences which do not jeopardize this communion, the 'unity of charity' (*unitas caritatis*) should be safeguarded."

11. CCC no. 95, quoting *Dei Verbum*, 10.

relationship, one that both liberates and gives life. Saint Cyprian of Carthage (d. 258) is quoted as saying, "No one can have God as Father who does not have the Church as Mother."[12]

Traditionally, Catholic theologians develop a collaborative association with the Magisterium. For her part, the Church often seeks a *consensus theologorum*, an overall consensus of what theologians hold. However, she also notes that it is possible to misconstrue what this consensus means and as a result cause damage to the spiritual well-being of the Church's members.[13]

Magisterium and Community

In an important article, "Communion and Magisterium: Teaching Authority and the Culture of Grace," published around the same time as that of Cardinal Dulles, Dominican theologian J. A. Di Noia explains the positive value of theology that is done within a collaborative relationship with Church authority.[14] The author suggests that we should recognize the limits that social analysis—for example, anthropology, sociology, psychology—imposes on ecclesial structures. Imagining that human science enjoys the ability to police, as it were, what God accomplishes in the world constitutes an odd reversal of values. Functional explanations of ecclesial structures cannot proceed without properly theological explanations. However, the temptation to implement the culture of management in ecclesial affairs without at the same time adverting to the culture of grace remains a strong one.[15]

12. Cyprian, *On the Unity of the Catholic Church* (*De catholicae ecclesiae unitate*) 6, as quoted in CCC no. 181. For the Latin text, see PL 4:519.

13. *Donum veritatis*, no. 39, explains this abusive use of consensus in this way:

> After the pattern of the members of the first community, all the baptized with their own proper charisms are to strive with sincere hearts for a harmonious unity in doctrine, life, and worship (cf. Acts 2:42). This is a rule which flows from the very being of the Church. For this reason, standards of conduct, appropriate to civil society or the workings of a democracy, cannot be purely and simply applied to the Church. Even less can relationships within the Church be inspired by the mentality of the world around it (cf. Rom 12:2). Polling public opinion to determine the proper thing to think or do, opposing the Magisterium by exerting the pressure of public opinion, making the excuse of a "consensus" among theologians, maintaining that the theologian is the prophetical spokesman of a "base" or autonomous community which would be the source of all truth, all this indicates a grave loss of the sense of truth and of the sense of the Church.

14. J. A. Di Noia, "Communion and Magisterium: Teaching Authority and the Culture of Grace," *Modern Theology* 9 (1993): 403–18.

15. Can philosophy's stepdaughters (sociology of religion and sociology of knowledge) help theology in the way that philosophy itself does? Can the human sciences, social studies, serve the same purpose as metaphysics? Probably not. The human sciences attempt to study the human reality under the aspect of a living organism. They make no claim to ultimate assertions about

Communion in the Church realizes a highly personal expression of intimacy with God. As a gift of grace, the Church cannot be understood apart from the mysteries of the Blessed Trinity, of Christ, and of the Blessed Virgin Mary. These sacred realities influence the Church in a real, causal way. They are not, as some suppose, file envelopes that require proper filing. Di Noia quotes the German theologian Walter Kasper, who affirms that the Church is the place of truth. Truth comes to us as a gift from God, not as an acquisition whose discovery and possession can be claimed as a human or even an ecclesial accomplishment. Thus, it is customary to affirm that the Church teaches what is true. Something, however, is not true because the Church teaches it.[16] The affirmation simply recognizes that all truth comes from God. As the catechism puts it, "God is Truth itself, whose words cannot deceive."[17]

Faith, then, is about God's truth. "Magisterium" remains instrumental with reference to divine truth. This relationship also influences in a causal way the shape that legitimate theological discourse takes. The Petrine office is itself a grace, a truth like the others. Why? The Holy Spirit remains at work in the Church. "Magisterium" simply provides a relatively modern way to express "authoritative teaching." Infallibility, rightly understood, reflects the importance that the Church attaches to ensuring that a place of truth be found in a secularized world. It should come as no surprise to discover that this pronouncement became especially necessary in the last quarter of the nineteenth century, when a number of scientific and other advances of human reason resulted in the distraction of large portions of the population. The ecclesial role of the theologian aims to give Catholic theologians an identity that the secular world otherwise would not bestow on them. Recall that the theological name for engaging in debate and dialogue is *pondering*. One distinguishes, then, *fides quaerens intellectum* from ordinary human inquiry. The work of Catholic theology is not the equivalent of what other disciplines, such as the science of religion, purport to be.

The circumstances of the modern world require some guarantee that a place for truth will be found in the world. Catholic theology done within the bosom of the Church makes bold to claim this place. The Magisterium of the Church's Sacred Pastors also ensures that those who occupy this place enjoy a communion of persons that affords mutual support in the truth. The concrete

---

how human beingness fits into being and other questions that philosophers dispute. Because the faith communicates God's truth to us, it requires a science that conceives of itself as an ultimate discourse.

16. The German Jesuit Karl Rahner (d. 1984) made a similar remark: The Catholic "believes in the authority of the teaching office because he already believes in God." See Karl Rahner, *Theological Investigations* (Baltimore: Helicon, 1961), 12:24.

17. CCC no. 215.

expression of this support appears within the Church of Christ as the seven sacraments. The following chapter provides an overview of Catholic teaching on the sacraments as it appears after the Second Vatican Council. The remainder of the book then includes discussions of the basic principles that govern the working of the seven sacraments as well as a brief introduction to each of the sacred seven. The Church governs the administration of the sacraments through juridical structures, including the *Code of Canon Law*. The celebration of the sacraments, on the other hand, observes, according to the mind of the Church, the approved liturgical norms set down in various documents.[18] The emphasis of the remainder of part 1, however, falls on the theological reasoning that underlies the various canonical and liturgical prescriptions.

18. See CCC no. 1125.

2

Sacramental Theology after the Council

The Second Vatican Council (1962–65) marked a shift of emphasis in the way that sacramental theology was taught. In fact, the council brought about changes in the way that Catholic theologians approached their métier. At the same time, as with each ecumenical council held in the Church, the Second Vatican Council marks a moment of continuity with the givens of the Catholic faith. In fact, the overall history of sacramental theology is best chronicled by an account of the controversies that have arisen over the centuries about individual sacraments and, on certain occasions, about some of the general principles that govern the working and administration of the sacraments.

The major controversies about and diverse opinions concerning the sacraments find notice in a series of textbooks produced in the twentieth century by the priest Emmanuel Doronzo, of the Missionary Oblates of Mary Immaculate, who taught at the Catholic University of America.[1] The volumes followed the scholastic style of textbook presentation that had been developed since the Middle Ages. Father Doronzo presents various theses that, in the main, were considered, before roughly 1965, as obligatory for seminary instruction. Then, in a manner reminiscent of the medieval practice, he enumerates opinions held

1. Emmanuel Doronzo, *Tractatus dogmaticus de sacramentis in genere* (Milwaukee: Bruce, 1946). The other textbooks include *Tractatus dogmaticus de Baptismo et Confirmatione* (1947); *Tractatus dogmaticus de Eucharistia* (2 vols., 1947–48); *Tractatus dogmaticus de Poenitentia* (3 vols., 1949–52); *Tractatus dogmaticus de Extrema unctione* (2 vols., 1954–55); *Tractatus dogmaticus de Ordine* (3 vols., 1957–62); and *De matrimonio* (1964).

by various authors on the given thesis. He concludes with what, in his view, represents the commonly held positions among the theologians of his day. He also refers to the major historical occurrences that have played a role over the centuries in the explication of Church doctrine.

Doronzo's thirteen hefty volumes of Latin prose give some indication of the challenge that composing a definitive history of sacramental theology entails. At the same time, the variety of views held over the centuries does not lead one to conclude that the Church offers no definitive instruction on the working of the sacraments or on the particulars of the seven different sacraments. Truth to tell, Doronzo carefully notes the propositions of faith that the Church declares to belong to the deposit of faith.[2] Today, the essential authoritative teachings of the Catholic Church find convenient expression in the *Catechism of the Catholic Church*.

Sacramental Theology in the 1950s

In the decade before the beginning of the Second Vatican Council, some of the themes that would shape the documents of the council were discussed among the largely clerical corps of professors who taught sacramental theology mainly to future priests in Roman Catholic seminaries. Consider the 1956 article by the Irish Jesuit priest Bernard Leeming, "Recent Trends in Sacramental Theology."[3] This article introduces the interested inquirer or student to some of the main issues that occupied sacramental theologians immediately before the Second Vatican Council. Father Leeming was an acknowledged expert in sacramental theology as distinguished from liturgical studies. The conflation of sacramental and liturgical studies that has taken place since the issuance of the Second Vatican Council's document *Sacrosanctum Concilium*, one may argue, has introduced a vacuum into an important area of Catholic theology—one especially noticeable in theology curricula. In short, a conciliar document that was meant to renew the liturgical practices and piety that flourished within the Catholic Church also had the, perhaps unintended, effect of directing the attention of theologians away from the classic themes in Catholic sacramental theology that, by and large, had achieved formulation during the periods after the sixteenth-century Council of Trent. The proper study of this development, however, belongs in the area of historical studies.[4]

2. See CCC nos. 84, 90.

3. Bernard Leeming, "Recent Trends in Sacramental Theology," *Irish Theological Quarterly* 23 (1956): 195–217.

4. For a discussion of the conciliar document that mainly concerns the celebration of the sacraments, see Romanus Cessario, "The Sacraments of the Church," in *Vatican II: Renewal within*

The Catholic Church preserves a sacramental theology. To point out one indication of the breadth of considerations that continues to form the substance of a Catholic theological treatment of the sacraments, one may conveniently note the material that Saint Thomas Aquinas sets forth in his account of Catholic sacramental theology. The last thirty questions of the *Summa theologiae* deal with the sacraments.[5] Aquinas's treatment of the sacraments, it should be noted, was cut short by his death in 1274. For this reason, the *Summa* contains questions on Baptism, Confirmation, and the Holy Eucharist and some questions on the sacrament of Penance. Aquinas, however, completed his treatment of the general principles of sacramental theology.

Among the reasons that argue for citing Aquinas as a recognized source for Catholic teaching on the sacraments, it is held that the work of Saint Thomas Aquinas influenced the theologians who helped to draft the documents of the Council of Trent.[6] This influence, it is further held, appears especially in the texts that treat of the seven sacraments. In fact, the treatment of the sacraments fell to the Spanish Dominicans from within the territories of the Hapsburg princes, whose civil policies impeded the spread of views advanced by the sixteenth-century reforming theologians.[7] These agents of a putative reform, as the anonymous anathemas of the Council of Trent suggested, demurred on much that traditional Catholic teaching on the sacraments had espoused.

To return to the decade before the Second Vatican Council: Father Leeming's article provides a glimpse of the state of standard Catholic theology on the sacraments as it was discussed in the mid-twentieth century. The composition of the Catholic theological academy prior to the Second Vatican Council was quite different than it is today. The principal participants were mainly drawn from the clerical state, seminary faculties, and even university faculties in those places where the Church oversaw faculties of theology. It would require a separate study to analyze, document, and interpret each factor that Leeming cites as

Tradition, ed. Matthew L. Lamb and Matthew Levering (Oxford: Oxford University Press, 2008), 129–46.

5. For the best information on Aquinas and his works, see Jean-Pierre Torrell, *Saint Thomas Aquinas*, vol. 1, *The Person and His Work*, rev. ed., trans. R. Royal (Washington, DC: Catholic University of America Press, 2005). Aquinas, of course, discusses the sacraments and principles of sacramental theology in other of his compositions.

6. For further discussion, see Romanus Cessario, "Sixteenth-Century Reception of Aquinas by the Council of Trent and Its Main Authors," in *The Oxford Handbook of the Reception of Aquinas*, ed. Matthew Levering and Marcus Plested (Oxford: Oxford University Press, 2021), 159–72.

7. See Reginald Lynch, *The Cleansing of the Heart: The Sacraments as Instrumental Causes in the Thomistic Tradition* (Washington, DC: Catholic University of America Press, 2017), 43n91, 50n107. See also Guy Bedouelle, *The Reform of Catholicism, 1480–1620*, trans. J. K. Farge, in *Catholic and Recusant Texts of the Late Medieval & Early Modern Periods*, Studies and Texts 161 (Toronto: Pontifical Institute of Medieval Studies, 2008), 83, 130.

characteristic of the evolution of Catholic sacramental theology. The following summary will serve, however, to indicate the main themes that were discussed shortly before the Second Vatican Council and so undoubtedly influenced the framers of what the council advanced as sacramental teachings.

Leeming first reports on various methods that theologians began to use to study the seven sacraments. As foremost among them, he identifies the renewal of biblical studies and the philosophical study of words and language. This trend does not mean that theologians of earlier periods, even the medieval masters, ignored the Bible. However, during the course of the twentieth century biblical exegesis took on new forms and even new purposes.[8] Likewise, Catholic theologians who treated the sacraments have always been attentive to the meaning of words. Spoken words, in fact, play an essential role in the confecting of each sacrament. At the same time, modern philosophy exhibits a predilection for the study of language that can eclipse some larger metaphysical themes that find their origins in classical antiquity.

One of the substantive issues that appears among Leeming's "recent trends" is discussion about the objective efficacy of the sacraments. Catholic theology holds firmly that the sacraments do something for the human person who properly receives them. This general affirmation leads to the need to explore further explanations that expose the efficacy of each of the seven sacraments.

Controversies about the efficacy of the sacraments date from the earliest Christian periods. The Donatist heresy, for example, included views about sacramental efficacy that heavily favored the subjective disposition of either the one who administers the sacrament or the one who receives it. The twentieth century brought its own questions about objective efficacy to light. These often arose within the context of changed outlooks on the ecclesial communions that sprang from the sixteenth-century reform—for example, the efficacy of their ritual actions.

In some ways, a related question that theologians have long debated concerns the nature of sacramental grace. Sacramental grace refers to the divine graces that each of the sacraments bestows on a worthy recipient. Among the better-known sacramental graces are those associated with the sacraments that consecrate mission in the Church. For example, married couples were and still are promised that their reception of the sacrament of Matrimony brings with it sacramental graces especially attuned to help them sustain the burdens of married life. Those who are not married do not receive these graces.

8. For further discussion of this somewhat controversial development, see Romanus Cessario, "Scripture as the Soul of Moral Theology: Reflections on Vatican II and *Ressourcement* Thomism," *The Thomist* 76 (2012): 165–88.

Over the course of the centuries, theologians debated how to separate sacramental graces from the general teaching on grace as sanctifying (habitual) and actual graces. Even today, the question remains a disputed one among various theological schools.[9] The *Catechism of the Catholic Church* identifies sacramental grace with the gifts of the Holy Spirit that help all baptized persons live out a Christian vocation.[10] In the mid-twentieth century, as Leeming indicates, theologians also debated how best to explain the working out of a sacramental grace. Among other values one can glean from these discussions, debates about how to speak of sacramental graces show that thc sacraments remain ordered to the actual living out of a Catholic life. They are not, as some have opined, empty rituals.

Another question that occupied theologians, especially after the sixteenth-century reform, deals with the manner of dominical institution. The Church holds that Christ instituted each of the seven sacraments. She also identifies biblical texts that support this faith assertion. However, some of the sacraments, such as Baptism and the Holy Eucharist, appear to qualify for dominical institution more than do others. These sacraments can appeal to certain texts of the New Testament that connect them to Christ's public life in a way that sacraments such as the Anointing of the Sick and Matrimony cannot. This circumstance leads to the question of how the Church finds grounds for affirming unequivocally that Christ instituted each of the sacraments of the New Law. The development of Scripture studies—which enjoyed something of a springtime after Pope Leo XIII's 1893 encyclical *Providentissimus Deus, On the Study of Holy Scripture*—provided an occasion for Catholic scholars to take up again the question of dominical institution.

Father Leeming's list of the topics that made up the theological discussion du jour in 1956 includes a question of sacramental theology that prompted considerable discussion during the post-Tridentine period. Sacraments are for the People of God and their sanctification. However, no one can administer a sacrament without the benefit of a minister, who most often appears in the form of a cleric. Because of its necessity for salvation, Baptism may be administered by any human being, even one who does not confess the Christian religion. The other six sacraments, however, require the participation of a priest. In order to avoid what may be thought of as the promotion

9. For further information, see Jean-Hervé Nicolas, "La grâce sacramentelle," *Revue Thomiste* 61 (1961): 165–92, 522–38.

10. See *CCC* nos. 1996, 2000, and—for a more basic consideration—654. The text itself avoids reference to the historical debates that are considered properly theological considerations though not direct expressions of revealed truth.

of superstitious rituals, Catholic theology stipulates conditions required in a minister. Foremost among them stands the personal intention of the minister. According to Catholic doctrine, this intention unites the minister of a sacrament to the saving intentions of Christ and the Church. Although other requirements in a qualified minister can be identified, the intention the minister brings to the performance of the sacramental action provides the default condition for sacramental efficacy.

In the case of sacramental actions that employ ordinary human activities, such as washing and eating and drinking, one may inquire about how to distinguish the sacramental action from the ordinary action. For example, What sets apart the baptismal bath from the ordinary physical cleansing of a child? The answer to this and other related questions involves various considerations. One indispensable distinguishing feature remains the intention that a minister forms when performing the required sacramental action. Still, mid-twentieth-century sacramental theologians wondered what it means for a minister to form an interior mental act that expresses purpose or intention. As a result, disputes arose during the course of the twentieth century.

There are other requirements that the Catholic Church stipulates for the valid administration of the sacraments. Even though the specifics concerning these requirements are usually set down in the authoritative texts that govern the Church's life, theologians still query these provisions and their applications.

Another challenge to sacramental theology concerns the structure of the Church. Under the influence of mainly modern biblical theology, a question arose early in the twentieth century concerning the proper way to explain the priesthood of all the faithful. In fact, Father Leeming reports that some theologians were content to present the common priesthood as a topic to be treated in mystical theology. That is, the layperson participated in Christ's priesthood by the practice of spiritual victimhood, an act of self-negation that one makes in the face of suffering, whether physical or spiritual. Many saints indeed referred to themselves as victims of their self-offering to Christ.

Other theologians preferred a less dramatic account of priesthood as applied to those who did not receive the sacrament of Holy Orders. They argued that the expression *priesthood of the faithful* can bear only a metaphorical meaning—that is, it is a kind of poetic way to express the unity of the faithful with Christ. Still others developed an account of a common priesthood that relied on the philosophical teaching on analogy. Theorizing about analogy enjoyed a prominent place in the Catholic theology of the preconciliar Church. The analogical option probably best describes the status of this theologoumenon after the reception that the common priesthood of the faithful received in the documents of the Second Vatican Council.[11]

The post–Second World War period witnessed a breakdown of the cultural ties to religious confessions. One may even speak of the secularization of Europe, which in the twentieth century supplied the major theological resources for the Catholic Church. In other words, the strict societal separation of Catholic from Protestant believers began to evaporate. The ecumenical movement was afoot among the Protestant denominations from the end of the nineteenth century. Catholic participation in this movement came along slowly, with some strong resistance from ecclesiastical authorities that dot the history of the ecumenical movement in the Catholic Church.

Because the break-off denominations that find their origin in the sixteenth-century Protestant Reform had developed diverse practices and beliefs concerning the sacraments, Catholic theologians had begun to wonder whether the right intention required in the minister suffered impairment from mistaken beliefs. This discussion raised practical concerns because, according to standard Catholic teaching (as mentioned above), when some factor causes a defect of intention, then the validity of the administered sacrament comes into question. Of the seven sacraments, Baptism gave rise to many of the questions that theologians posed about validity. Indeed, so much did ecumenical dialogues attract the attention of Catholic theologians that the very concept of the validity of the sacraments became debated within the context of the nascent ecumenical movement.

Finally, Leeming reports that theologians of the 1950s, especially those who worked closely with those charged with providing catechetical instruction, were discussing features of the Church's teaching on the sacrament of Confirmation. This discussion brought to the fore practical questions about the time and age suitable for the administration of Confirmation as well as questions about how to view this sacrament in relation to Baptism.

Leeming also reports on what he describes as wider trends that had begun to emerge, especially among European theologians. These wider trends would each receive an evaluation during the course of the Second Vatican Council. Some of them would shape the documents that the council produced, whereas others would fail to gain sufficient momentum to become permanent features of Catholic theology. The first trend that Leeming cites concerns the ways in which the Leonine revival of Aquinas, launched by the encyclical *Aeterni Patris* of Pope Leo XIII, had begun to suffer some setbacks. Indeed, one may speak of an antischolastic tendency that sought its theological wherewithal elsewhere

11. See *Lumen Gentium*, chap. 2, "On the People of God."

than in the standard scholastic manuals that had governed—with some noteworthy exceptions—Catholic theology since the fifteenth century.

During the twentieth century, the interest in historical theology gained momentum under the aegis of the well-known "return to the sources" movement and its flagship series Sources Chrétiennes.[12] Leeming describes as "inclusive" the trend that centered on the general heading of a return to the sources—in French, *ressourcement*. However, he points out a difficulty that he, being an accomplished scholastic theologian himself, recognized as early as the 1950s: "The trend is genial, but sometimes results in a lack of clearness and blunt facing of the problems."[13]

Another fashion of the day that flourished in some circles of sacramental theologians arose from the Southern German liturgical renewal, centered on the ancient Benedictine monastery of Maria Laach. One may signal many features of the Maria Laach history that may interest the Catholic theologian, but the specific piece of theology that Leeming cites concerns an explanation of sacramental efficacy that relies heavily on the proper execution of the Sacred Liturgy, an art for which Benedictine monks justly enjoy a strong reputation. The author of the teaching that Leeming considers was a German monk, Dom Odo Casel (1886–1948). His theory became known by its German name, *Mysterienlehre*, and was built on a theory that places the efficacy of the sacraments in what Dom Casel called *Mystery-Presence*. The Jesuit Leeming refrained from providing too enthusiastic an endorsement of Casel's innovative thoughts. "The word 'mystic,'" he wrote, "may perhaps sometimes be used to cover up poverty or confusion of thought."[14]

A discussion of the efficacy of the sacraments raises questions about how to best explain what the sacraments permanently accomplish in the life of the Christian believer. The tradition, especially by its refusal to allow the repetition of certain sacraments, points up that there abide lasting effects that mark the soul of the person who receives these sacraments, which include Baptism, Confirmation, and Holy Orders. The practice of recognizing the permanent validity of the sacraments in those who receive them, even when the beneficiaries of these graces fall away from an active participation in the spiritual life of the Church, raises the further question of the relationship of the sacraments to the Catholic Church herself. For example, Can one who has received the sacraments completely dissociate oneself from the effects that the sacraments create?

12. For some introductory remarks, see Romanus Cessario, "An Observation on Robert Lauder's Review of G. A. McCool, S.J.," *The Thomist* 56 (1992): 701–10.
13. Leeming, "Recent Trends," 204.
14. Leeming, "Recent Trends," 206.

The above discussion of questions that dominated Catholic theology of the mid-twentieth century serves to point up the continuity that marks sacramental practice and theology. Truth to tell, each of the issues in Father Leeming's list remains an active topic that sacramental theologians consider today. That is, these issues form part of classic Catholic sacramental theology that has developed over the centuries and that has achieved, as I have said, a certain recognizable and lasting form after the sixteenth-century Council of Trent. Of course, other issues that Leeming only broadly hints at have arisen after the Second Vatican Council, and these appear with a focus that may constitute a paradigmatic shift in Catholic thought. Such a shift, however, remains one of appearances. As I pointed out above, *Sacrosanctum Concilium* stands in continuity with the tradition, even though its emphasis on the renewal of sacramental celebrations introduces considerations that theretofore were not included in the standard manuals of sacramental theology.

Sacramental Theology after 1965

For a brief account of postconciliar sacramental issues, one may consult the periodical literature that appeared immediately after the publication of *Sacrosanctum Concilium*.[15] As with so much of the theology produced in the wake of the Second Vatican Council, the student of the twenty-first century must take into account the very salutary instruction that Pope Benedict XVI gave to the Church on the occasion of his Christmas message to the Roman Curia in 2005.[16] In this papal address, Pope Benedict explained how "the hermeneutic of discontinuity is countered by the hermeneutic of reform," which on the Pope's account finds its bona fides in the principal addresses given by Pope John XXIII at the start of the council and by Pope Paul VI at the council's conclusion.[17]

For example, many Catholic writers, theologians, journalists, popular authors, and practitioners of *haute vulgarisation*, sometimes known as popularizers, relied uncritically on the hermeneutic of discontinuity to publicize what they held to represent the authentic teaching of the council. This trend appeared prominently in the work done throughout the late 1960s and 1970s and, during the same period, became almost standard teaching in Catholic universities and seminaries. In short, many popular Catholic authors stressed the novelty

15. For example, see Matthew O'Connell, "New Perspectives in Sacramental Theology," *Worship* 39 (1965): 195–206.

16. The official text is "Ad Romanam Curiam ob omnia natalicia," *Acta Apostolicae Sedis*, vol. 98 (January 6, 2006), 40–50. An English translation can be found in Lamb and Levering, *Vatican II: Renewal within Tradition*, ix–xv.

17. Lamb and Levering, *Vatican II: Renewal within Tradition*, xi.

in Catholic teaching on the sacraments, which they argued or simply assumed emerged from the council's documents. Moreover, because of the dramatic changes that ordinary Catholic believers experienced in their liturgical celebrations, this claim was easy to defend rhetorically. The use of the vernacular language alone was sufficient to dispose people to believe that change in the Church's sacramental practices had become the order of the day.

Perhaps no theme better represents the practice of discontinuous sacramental theology than the claim that the Church under the direction of the Second Vatican Council had moved from interpretations of the sacraments by appeal to metaphysics or ontology to explanations that relied on the modern notion of encounter. The Flemish theologian Edward Schillebeeckx (d. 2009) gained international notice with the 1963 English publication of his book *Christ the Sacrament of the Encounter with God* at the well-known Catholic publishing house Sheed & Ward.[18] Others followed this initiative to interpret the sacraments as instruments of union with Christ, indeed of a concrete meeting with Christ.[19]

Of course, it is true that the sacraments of the Church do supply instruments of union with God and so may be thought of as moments of personal encounter with the person of Jesus Christ in whose name any minister of the sacraments acts. Both Edward Schillebeeckx and Colman O'Neill belonged to the Dominican Order. Both authors demonstrated a mastery of the scholastic categories that characterized the instruction given on the sacraments prior to the Second Vatican Council. O'Neill, however, understood the hermeneutics of reform as set forth by Pope John XXIII—namely, "to transmit the doctrine pure and integral, without any attenuation or distortion."[20] Edward Schillebeeckx, who, through his service to the Dutch bishops of the conciliar period, is said to have exercised influence on the drafting of certain of the council's documents, may have moved in other directions. The fact remains that his theological opinions, especially in the area of ecclesiology, gradually edged toward discontinuity. In fact, some of his later publications earned him a certain suspicion among the Roman authorities who exercised supervisory control over the Church's doctrines.[21]

18. Edward Schillebeeckx, *Christ the Sacrament of the Encounter with God* (New York: Sheed & Ward, 1963). The book was originally published as *Christus, Sacrament van de Godsontmoeting* (Bilthoven, Netherlands: H. Nelissen, 1960).

19. For example, the Irish theologian Colman O'Neill published his *Meeting Christ in the Sacraments* in 1964. A revised edition, edited by Romanus Cessario, appeared in 1991 (also from Alba House).

20. John XXIII, speech at the inauguration of the Second Vatican Council on October 11, 1962, quoted in Lamb and Levering, *Vatican II: Renewal within Tradition*, xi.

21. The Congregation for the Doctrine of the Faith, with the approval of Pope John Paul II, said that some of Father Schillebeeckx's views on the priesthood were "at variance with the teaching

Some of the other themes that emerged shortly after the issuance of *Sacrosanctum Concilium* led to the observation that many believed, perhaps in good faith, that the council had encouraged theologians to take a half step back from appeal to sign and cause when explaining how the sacraments work. The common textbook definition that the Church customarily used for each of the sacraments made of them visible signs that cause invisible grace. Instead, again as so many proposed, the council had urged theologians to place the sacraments within the larger context of the mysteries of Christ's life.

While such a suggestion enjoys merit, it oftentimes led theologians to undertake an approach that favored historical studies to determine the wider context of the sacraments within Christ's earthly ministry. In short, during the decades following the council, the view that there existed hitherto unexplored areas of sacramental theology gained ascendency. It was argued—for instance, by theologians who heavily favored the method of *ressourcement*—that the Catholic tradition, especially as it unfolds during the period of the Church fathers, requires that one treat sacramental theology within the context of the ensemble of topics that theology entertains. The connection of the sacraments to the Trinity, to the Church, to authentic accounts of divine grace, and to eschatology became areas of theological reflection. One could discover these emphases, of course, in the systematic accounts of the sacraments developed by the great theologians of the Middle Ages.

To give the movement a benign interpretation, one may argue that these appeals to the tradition afforded a subtle way to challenge the hegemony that the juridical side of Catholic theology had acquired in the modern period. It may come as a surprise to some to discover that oftentimes, if not frequently, instruction in the sacraments was confided, in seminaries at least, to professional canon lawyers. On the other hand, directing attention to the overarching themes within which the Church locates her sacramental instruction can also serve to distract theologians from the finer details that the tradition before the council safeguarded and that it perfected by a progressive refinement of thought.

Some Catechetical Distortions

The philosophical categories that had received a new impetus during the pontificate of Pope Leo XIII (1878–1903) suffered a certain eclipse in the wake of the Second Vatican Council. Instead, sacramental theologians took up themes such as how to establish a compatibility between relational ontology and the

of the Roman Catholic Church." So reported the *New York Times*. "Vatican Issues Rebuke to European Educator," *New York Times*, September 24, 1986, 15.

social sciences. To render an account of the metaphysical themes that had served the Church's teaching on the sacraments since the first millennium in a way that emphasizes the personal features of the sacramental system exemplifies sound theological method. Theses were written to show that metaphysical thought does not necessarily mean abstract and impersonal thought.[22] However, the popularization of themes in sacramental theology drawn from a potpourri of university disciplines produced the unwelcome result of making the sacraments appear as if they were readily recognizable features of ordinary human experience. This deflection from the tradition was especially felt in catechetical circles, where the sophisticated treatment of modern notions such as symbol, ritual, myth, metaphor, and language gave way to somewhat uncritical textbook discussions of these same topics.[23]

Children enrolled in Christian doctrine classes and adults who sought to enter into full communion with the Catholic Church (through a program officially recognized as the Rite of Christian Initiation of Adults) became the unknowing and unfortunate beneficiaries of some fairly deflated catechetical instruction about the sacramental life of the Church. For instance, confusion about how symbols work affords the best example of the mistaken notions that, one may argue, have weakened the actual practice of the sacraments. Take the familiar catechetical definition that describes the sacraments as "efficacious signs of grace."[24] It was not uncommon in the 1980s (and it may not be uncommon still, in some quarters) to hear remarks such as this: "[The sacraments] are not just ritual <u>acts</u> that give grace but opportunities for people already in GOD's grace to celebrate that fact through symbolic ritual."[25] A corollary to this assertion offers the following caution: "SACRAMENTS don't happen in <u>church</u> so much as they happen in <u>people</u> who come together as a church community to celebrate what has already been happening to them."

22. For example, see Romanus Cessario, *Christian Satisfaction in Aquinas* (Washington, DC: University Press of America, 1982). The author aimed to show that very personal significance of the satisfaction that Christ made on Calvary to make amends for the sins of the world. The book received warm reviews overall, and it saw a new edition in 2020: Romanus Cessario, *The Godly Image: Christian Satisfaction in Aquinas* (Washington, DC: Catholic University of America Press, 2020).

23. Of course, not every serious theological undertaking fell captive to these somewhat banal accounts of sacramental efficacy. For a survey of work done largely throughout the 1980s, see the series of articles published in *The Thomist*: Kevin Irwin, "Recent Sacramental Theology: A Review Discussion," *The Thomist* 47 (1983), 52 (1988), 53 (1989). A sampling of themes that became commonplace among Catholic theologians may also be found in David N. Power, Regis Duffy, and Kevin Irwin, "Sacramental Theology: A Review of Literature," *Theological Studies* 55 (1994): 657–705.

24. See CCC no. 1131.

25. Unpublished 1980s educational materials distributed to adult students at a prominent Catholic university (emphasis original).

Students of philosophy are familiar with the turn to the subject that marks the history of modern philosophy from the seventeenth century on. It does not require too much philosophical erudition, however, to see the weight of the anthropological turn actively shaping the way theologians and the religious educational world had begun to treat the workings of the sacraments. This movement finds confirmation when we consider the way that recourse to cultural or social anthropology became a means by which to explain the seven sacraments. Utterances such as the following also became commonplace among Catholics: "People have always had certain objects/actions/places/persons that are symbolic of some sacred reality; needed ritual to celebrate significant moments in life, such as birth/initiation/conversion/reconciliation/healing/unity/calling. For them [presumably such practitioners of these anthropological rituals], they [the rituals] are signs of GOD's presence in their lives."[26]

Remarks such as these raise a question that strikes squarely at the basic tenets of Catholic theology: Can the modern social sciences, such as cultural anthropology, do the same work as classical philosophy when it comes to elucidating the truths of faith? Although the answer to this question would require significant qualifications to take account of the fact that the Church does recognize a place for the disciplines that seek to give an account of human behavior, the concern that Pope John Paul II raises in his 1998 encyclical, *Fides et ratio*, merits close attention.

In the authoritative document *Fides et ratio*, the Pope warns against certain outlooks endemic to modern thought. One of these he calls "scientism." Scientism, he says, "is the philosophical notion which refuses to admit the validity of forms of knowledge other than those of the positive sciences; and it relegates religious, theological, ethical and aesthetic knowledge to the realm of mere fantasy."[27] How does the theologian guard against succumbing to the polyvalent influences of "scientism"? Again, it would be wrong to suggest that the answer to this question can be expressed in a simple phrase or concept. At the same time, it is important to recall an injunction that Pope John Paul II gives to all Catholic theologians: "A theology without a metaphysical horizon could not move beyond an analysis of religious experience, nor would it allow the *intellectus fidei* to give a coherent account of the universal and transcendent value of revealed truth."[28]

One wonders whether reductionist views of the sacraments, such as the one expressed in the statement "SACRAMENTS are special moments that can

26. Unpublished 1980s educational materials.
27. John Paul II, *Fides et ratio*, no. 88.
28. John Paul II, *Fides et ratio*, no. 83.

heighten our awareness of GOD's grace meeting us everywhere/changing us,"[29] actually include "a metaphysical horizon." One might argue that the absence of metaphysical considerations in accounts of the sacraments, as in many of the accounts given in the decades after the close of the Second Vatican Council, has left Catholic practice somewhat impoverished. The decline in sacramental practice that has been chronicled by recognized research agencies indicates that significant percentages of Catholics, many of them born after the Second Vatican Council, have not been given the benefit of instruction that moves beyond various accounts of human behavior or even of religious experience.[30]

The *Catechism of the Catholic Church*, published in 1992, has enjoyed a qualified success in counterbalancing the deleterious effects that hasty educational projects designed to make the Catholic faith easy for the modern person to grasp have left in many Catholic believers. The catechism devotes part 2 to "The Celebration of the Christian Mystery: The Sacraments and the Liturgy." In order to resist the gravitational pull that makes the sacraments expressions of human subjectivity instead of instruments of divine action, this solid instrument of instruction in the givens of Catholic and divine faith requires of its readers considerable theological knowledge, or an expert instructor. To return to the course outline used in a well-known Catholic university, it is not sufficient to say, "In SACRAMENTS, we gather to celebrate our belief in GOD/GOD's care in liturgical ritual."[31] The anthropological turn tends to reduce the Church's sacraments to human, and perhaps even religious, experiences. Of course, as the catechism holds, they remain divinely appointed instruments of salvation.[32]

Other Questions about the Sacraments

Sharing this evaluation of the state of Catholic sacramental theology at the end of the twentieth century does not require that one subscribes to conservative theories that decry the depreciation of Catholic orthodoxy. The recognition that sacramental theology requires some form of serious reappraisal appears in a short essay published in 2000 by the late Cardinal Godfried Danneels (d. 2019), "Current Challenges for Sacramental Theology."[33] The Belgian prelate raises

29. Unpublished 1980s educational materials.

30. See, for example, Mark M. Gray and Paul M. Perl, "Sacraments Today: Belief and Practice among U.S. Catholics" (report, Center for Applied Research in the Apostolate, Georgetown University, Washington, DC, April 2008).

31. Unpublished 1980s educational materials.

32. See CCC nos. 1127–29.

33. Godfried Danneels, "Current Challenges for Sacramental Theology," *Antiphon* 5, no. 2 (2000): 44–45.

ten issues that to his mind set an agenda for sacramental theologians to work on. Two of these issues express concerns that Leeming had discussed in 1956.

Danneels puts first on his list of tasks that require the attention of sacramental theologians in the twenty-first century the broad theological heading of the "Redemptive Incarnation." The sacraments, he reminds his readers, can be treated only within the overall framework of the logic of the Incarnation.[34] Specifically, the cardinal draws our attention to a familiar expression from the early church father Tertullian (d. 220): "caro cardo salutis."[35] This expression, which translates to "the flesh is the hinge of salvation,"[36] appears in Tertullian's *Apologia* (208), which defended the Church's teaching on the body.

Each of the sacraments, of course, entails some tangible reality. The tangible realities, however, point to unseen graces. Theologians, in Danneels's view, must confront candidly the difficulty that many modern folk experience when they try to grasp the reality of the immaterial and therefore invisible world. While the observation of this difficulty seems pertinent, the solution of course does not appear readily. Certain schools of philosophers, especially within the Thomist tradition, argue that a proper reading of Aristotle and of Aquinas reveals that it is possible to prove the existence of immaterial being.[37] Danneels raises a question that points to the indispensable role that metaphysics or a metascience plays in the theology of the sacraments.

Other questions that philosophers discuss also pose challenges for some folks of a certain modern mindset. For example, What does *real* mean? Likewise, philosophy provides answers for questions about causality. Efficacious signs do something. Danneels opines that this question, which formed such a central part of sacramental theology before 1965, has, at the dawn of the new millennium, been eclipsed in some quarters by other considerations. So Danneels inquires, What status do discussions of sacramental causality hold among sacramental theologians? One could even opine that some reflection is required to answer the question, What do the sacraments actually do?

The major considerations that directed sacramental theologians away from the classic treatments of causality include the attention paid to the broad category of symbol. Danneels faces this issue with a directness that evinces a certain boldness when one considers how much various accounts

34. The expression, at once both suggestive and useful, "logic of the Incarnation" appears in John Paul II, *Fides et ratio*, no. 94.

35. PL 2:852.

36. CCC no. 1015.

37. For a solid account of this philosophical inquiry, see Benedict M. Ashley, *The Way toward Wisdom: An Interdisciplinary and Intercultural Introduction to Metaphysics* (South Bend, IN: University of Notre Dame Press, 2006).

of symbolic action have begun to eclipse the scholastic category of efficient, instrumental causality. The question he raises asks whether research work is required to explain the nature of symbol and the role symbol plays in human development, or what one might call the "anthropology of the symbol." In other words, an inquiry into the function of symbols, so the author suggests, might help one answer the question of whether symbol is a useful concept for conveying the efficacious divine action present in the sacraments. Of course, an objector may ask whether talk about symbols, even with the help of a refined philosophical discourse, proves sufficient to carry the weight of sacramental efficacy.

Danneels continues his list of issues that face contemporary sacramental theology. He observes that, in order to explicate the Church's teaching on the sacraments, the postconciliar work in sacramental theology has introduced human sciences other than philosophy. The interdisciplinary character of sacramental theology requires a careful review to ensure that the use made of the human sciences does not distort the revealed truth about how the sacraments figure in the life of the Catholic believer.

The council's emphasis on the Church as a communion prompts Danneels to raise the question of the way that the sacramental rites figure in the lives of the members of the local community, especially the parish. Sometimes theologians place an emphasis on the practices of local communities that can lead to distortions of the Church's discipline of the sacraments. The psychology is fairly simple to explain. When the faithful are instructed repeatedly that the sacramental rituals can be altered to accommodate local preferences and practices, good-willed but uninformed deviations from what remains normative can occur.

At the same time, how much the Church's rituals can be accommodated to various cultural expressions and still keep their doctrinal integrity has been discussed at least since the sixteenth century. The Chinese Rites Controversy bears witness to the difficulties that inculturation can raise. The arguments for and against the Chinese efforts, made by the European Jesuit Matteo Ricci (d. 1610), are not easy to summarize. The debate lasted throughout the seventeenth and eighteenth centuries. Missionaries to China during that period, in fact, argued against Ricci's proposals. They felt that the common folk would not be able to recognize the difference between the Christian religion and traditional forms of Chinese religious practice. Opinion remains divided, however, about how to interpret the Chinese Rites Controversy and the more or less unfavorable reactions that the Holy See exhibited toward the proposals at various moments in the early history of evangelization in China.

Danneels continues his list of challenges by raising a vexing question that affects not only the sacraments but also the body of Christian doctrine and practice: How does one express the Christian faith in such a way that it becomes intelligible to those who are evangelized or catechized? The pursuit of ease of comprehension, however, cannot occur at the price of falsifying revealed truth or, what is more common, smoothing over the fact that all expressions of Christian faith make known realities that surpass the ability of any human mind to fathom.

Another issue deals with the place that "performative" language holds in explaining sacramental principles. Performative language is not to be confused with informative, narrative, or sapiential language. The work of J. L. Austin (d. 1960) and Jacques Derrida (d. 2004) develops the theory of performativity, which enjoys a place within modern philosophy, especially among those who focus almost exclusively on language as the ambit of philosophical reflection.

Finally, Danneels raises what one might describe as a sensitive pastoral question: Under what conditions should the Church admit to the sacraments those who seek them only as religious alternatives to secular rites? The issues active in this question involve what sometimes passes for cultural Catholicism, where Baptism, Matrimony, and funeral rites remain options even among those who have fallen away from the practice of the Christian faith. While some general guidelines can be established and put into practice, the fact remains that no easy answer to the question exists. Also, sadly, the first decades of the twenty-first century have demonstrated a sharp decline in those who may qualify for cultural Catholicism. Instead, the sociologists now speak about "former Catholics."

Appeal to Faith

One may conclude from the foregoing that the presentation of adequate teaching on the sacraments remains a challenge to both Catholic scholars and the Catholic faithful. The least that one may observe suggests that Catholic teaching on the sacraments requires appeal to authoritative statements. At the same time, it would be impossible to respond to every cultural, philosophical, and theological ambiguity that faces the Catholic sacramental theologian.

Of course, this circumstance does not create something new for the Church. Arianism threatened Catholic orthodoxy in the early centuries of the Church's existence. Neoplatonic themes that suffused the common cultural conceptions of that period made it easy to think of Christ as only somewhat divine. Then the Council of Nicaea in 325 adopted the term *homoousios* (consubstantial) as a description of the Christ's relation to God the Father.[38] Today, Catholics still confess with theological faith that the Lord Jesus Christ, the only begotten Son of God, is "consubstantial with the Father."[39] Something similar—a rule of faith, if you will—can apply to the sacraments of the Church.

38. See *CCC* no. 465.
39. *Roman Missal*, "Profession of Faith," The Niceno-Constantinopolitan Creed.

3

Some Preliminary Notions of Causality

The Sacraments as Causes

A basic axiom of Catholic theology holds that "the sacraments confer the grace they signify."[1] Shortly before the start of World War II, the French Dominican Albert Michel, one of the principal contributors to the *Dictionnaire de théologie catholique*, composed for the *Dictionnaire* an exhaustive treatment of Catholic sacramental theology.[2] The text includes a detailed analysis of the teaching of the Council of Trent. In terms of presenting an *ex professo* explanation of the sacraments, Trent still provides the basic dogmatic teachings that govern what the Catholic Church teaches about the sacraments. Michel devotes more than a few columns (cols. 577–624) to the question of sacramental causality.

It is generally held that the fathers of Trent consciously avoided using the term "cause" when they drafted the documents concerning the sacraments. Instead they preferred to use the verbs "to confer" or "to contain." It is also generally agreed that this conscious choice on the part of the fathers of Trent was made to avoid raising questions about the specific kind of causality at work in the seven sacraments of the New Law. Standard histories of medieval philosophy and theology show that sacramental causality became one of the most prominent topics disputed among the doctors (*disputata inter doctores*) of

1. CCC no. 1127.

2. Albert Michel, "Sacrements," in *Dictionnaire de théologie catholique*, vol. 14.1 (Paris: Librairie Letouzey et Ané, 1939), cols. 485–644.

the period. So rather than put forth authoritative teaching as an endorsement for a particular school of theological interpretation, the fathers chose instead to describe the causal action at work in the sacraments by a less partisan and charged expression.

The strict followers of Saint Thomas Aquinas have found the Tridentine compromise somewhat unpleasant. However, while Michel concedes that the word "cause" does not exist in the canons that treat of the sacraments in general, he does show that the word is used elsewhere in the official text.[3] For example, Michel notes that the word *cause*, even with the modification *instrumental*, appears in chapter 7 of the *Decree on Justification*, which treats of justification and Baptism.[4] So one may affirm that an authoritative text of the Church's Magisterium does describe the sacraments as instrumental causes of grace.

This text, then, leads Michel to conclude in his *Dictionnaire de théologie catholique* article that the word *cause* stands in conformity not only with the spirit of the Council of Trent but also with the letter of the conciliar declarations.[5] Michel's exegesis of the conciliar chapters no doubt owes a great deal to his own theological positions. He was a Dominican and a partisan of instrumental causality as employed by Aquinas in order to explain the double agency that operates in each of the seven sacraments. At the same time, Michel also captures what remains at the heart of a Catholic understanding of sacramental efficacy.

It would move this presentation beyond its established purposes to rehearse the debates about sacramental efficacy that have developed roughly since the thirteenth century. In what follows, the present exposition follows the Thomist school on instrumental causality.[6] Truth to tell, the scholastic debates, while they still display a great deal of sophistication and creativeness in articulating the cooperation between human willing and divine action, occurred by and large before the eighteenth century. The challenges that Enlightenment thinkers raised to the classical notions of causality pose a much greater threat to Catholic theology than the distinctions that exercised most of the earlier scholastic authors. However, as the best of Catholic thought shows, those who cavil with efficient causality find it difficult to explain even natural phenomena.[7]

3. Michel, "Sacrements," col. 613: "Le mot 'cause' n'existe pas dans les canons concernant les sacrements en général."

4. *DS* 1529: "The causes of this justification are the following: . . . The instrumental cause (is) the sacrament of baptism, which is the 'sacrament of faith.'"

5. Michel, "Sacrements," cols. 613–14.

6. The scholastic authors point, for example, to Aristotle's *Physics*, book 2, chap. 3, as a locus for his enumeration of the causes.

7. See the very compelling studies by William A. Wallace, *Causality and Scientific Explanation*, 2 vols. (Ann Arbor, MI: University of Michigan Press, 1972–74).

Some Distinctions

The classical instruction from which the mainline commentatorial positions were developed shared a common vision of how one thing depends on another. The following terminological and conceptual clarifications will help the student of sacramental theology locate the general area of philosophical inquiry that undergirds the Church's explanation of the sacraments.

In the first place, one must distinguish a principle from a cause. Philosophers define a *principle* as that from which something flows in any way whatsoever. The riverhead identifies the place where the river begins, its principle, without necessarily indicating the source or headwaters on which the river depends for its volume. *Cause*, on the other hand, includes an ontological reference to that from which it develops. The general definition of *cause* must include some reference to the being or existence of the effect for which it is a cause. Again, textbook definitions run something like this: a cause is a positive principle from whence something flows with dependence in being.[8] The phrase "dependence in being" provides the salient point of the definition. The standard philosophical discussions used by Catholic theologians to describe how causality works owe their inspiration and shape to the works of Aristotle.[9]

There are weaker explanations of factors that contribute to the coming-to-be of something other than itself. First among these, philosophers consider the conditions necessary for something to happen or to come about. Condition qualifies as a principle. However, even though a condition may be required for something to happen or come about, condition does not include the important qualification of "dependence in being." Light may serve as a condition for seeing, but it does not cause vision. Weaker still, one may point to the category of occasion. An occasion rises to the level of neither a cause nor a condition. Instead, an occasion refers to a principle that facilitates the production of an effect. For example, holidays provide occasion for festive meals and social gatherings.

As already mentioned, these distinctions arise from the general theory of causality that Aristotle discusses in his cosmological works.[10] The four causes that Aristotle identifies are material, formal, efficient, and final. Aquinas pro-

8. For example, see H. D. Gardeil, *Introduction to the Philosophy of St. Thomas Aquinas*, vol. 2, *Cosmology*, trans. John A. Otto (St. Louis: B. Herder, 1958), 63.

9. For further explanation, see William A. Wallace, "Cause and Effect: Temporal Relationships," in *From a Realist Point of View: Essays on the Philosophy of Science* (Washington, DC: University Press of America, 1979), 115–30.

10. For a contemporary explanation of causality in Aristotle, see the comprehensive summary of Thomist philosophy provided in Benedict M. Ashley, *The Way toward Wisdom: An Interdisciplinary*

vides a very instructive and brief summary of Aristotle's account of reality in *On the Principles of Nature*, a minor work of his that oftentimes goes unnoticed.[11] The philosophical working out of causality entails numerous distinctions that philosophers excel at making. One of the masters of twentieth-century Thomist thought, the Dominican H. D. Gardeil (d. 1974), provides a brief account of Aquinas's employment of the Aristotelian corpus with respect to causality. Gardeil, whose manuals were translated into several languages, summarizes the material well: "Broadly speaking, the Aristotelian notion of cause contains two essential notes. A cause is a *principle of being* and secondly, in the order of knowledge, a *principle of explanation*. Primarily, it is a principle of being, of concrete reality. Everything that is, save God, depends on something not only for its being but also for its becoming. This something, of whatever sort, is a cause. 'Those things are named causes,' says St. Thomas, 'on which other things depend for their existence or becoming': *causae autem dicuntur ex quibus res dependent secundum esse suum vel fieri*."[12]

Students of philosophy recognize easily the four causes and the example of the statue that Aristotle uses to illustrate the four causes. To limit our consideration to the line of efficient causality, the sculptor stands in relation to the statue he sculpts as efficient cause to its effect.

Gardeil further observes how the Aristotelian discussion of causes influenced Christian thought. Although one finds the word *cause* used in patristic discussions of the sacraments, causality enters into mainstream Christian theology in the scholastic period. "Aristotle's enumeration of causes," affirms Gardeil, "is universally accepted in the Aristotelian and the Scholastic tradition. 1) Material cause, 2) formal cause, 3) efficient cause, 4) final cause, these are the four causes. . . . The distinction of the four causes is . . . a distinction in kind or species."[13] So even though the Council of Trent for its own purposes suggests an alternative expression to describe what the sacraments do, each of the causes figures in the way that theologians explicate what the Church holds about the seven sacraments.

---

and Intercultural Introduction to Metaphysics (South Bend, IN: University of Notre Dame Press, 2006), esp. parts 2 and 3.

11. See the English translation by Vernon J. Bourke in Thomas Aquinas, *The Pocket Aquinas*, ed. Vernon J. Bourke (New York: Pocket Books, 1960), 61–77.

12. Gardeil, *Introduction to the Philosophy*, vol. 2, *Cosmology*, 61, quoting Aquinas, *Commentary on Aristotle's Physics*, book 1, lect. 1, no. 10.

13. Gardeil, *Introduction to the Philosophy*, vol. 2, *Cosmology*, 62. Aquinas's teaching on causality appears in his *Commentary on Aristotle's Physics*, trans. R. Blackwell et al. (New Haven, CT: Yale University Press, 1963), book 2, lect. 5: "Physics determines what the causes are and how many species of causes there are."

Efficient Causality

At this juncture in the discussion, however, consideration needs to be given especially to the category of efficient causality. Aristotle provides a definition for *efficient cause* that stresses the movement initiated by an efficient cause. In the *Physics*, he writes that an efficient cause is "the primary source of the change or coming to rest; e.g., the man who gave advice is a cause, the father is cause of the child."[14] As the examples suggest, agency, like finality, remains extrinsic to the effect produced, whereas matter and form are intrinsic causes of a thing produced.

The scholastic thinkers summarized Aristotle's teaching in this way: "Efficient cause is the principle from which motion primarily springs."[15] Efficient causality does not point to something passive, like a mechanical button that one pushes with the result that something, such as the engine of an automobile, begins to operate. The Thomist commentatorial tradition has stressed that an efficient cause exerts itself on its subject and so produces a real influx from agent to patient. When one considers how the *Catechism of the Catholic Church* describes the truth of the faith as solemnly defined at the Council of Trent, that "the sacraments confer the grace that they signify,"[16] it becomes clear why Aquinas and other theologians looked to the category of efficient cause to explicate the faith of the Church that stands behind the council's affirmation. The sacraments, says the present catechism, "are efficacious because in them Christ himself is at work; it is he who baptizes, he who acts in his sacraments in order to communicate the grace that each sacrament signifies."[17]

The reference to Christ and the sacraments requires a distinction that takes account of the double agency at work in the sacraments of the New Law. Theologians again discovered a philosophical discussion that perfectly fits the unique way that the sacraments work. When appeal is made to efficient causality, a distinction is drawn between a principal cause that acts through its own proper power and an instrumental cause that acts in virtue of a cause that stimulates its proper effect. Although at first glance the concept seems somewhat abstract and even removed from the evangelical good news that Christ saves a sinful humanity, truth to tell, Catholic theologians from the earliest centuries have discovered the usefulness of "instrument" to explain how God does save the world through Christ. In fact, instrumental causality has been invoked at least since the fourth century to describe the relationship of Christ's human nature

14. Aristotle, *Physics* 2.3.194b29–31.
15. Gardeil, *Introduction to the Philosophy*, vol. 2, *Cosmology*, 66.
16. CCC no. 1127.
17. CCC no. 1127.

to his divinity.[18] The same notion also ensures that the benefits of the Incarnation for the human race can trace their origin to God. How else would one talk about divinization, a theme so favored by the early Church fathers?

Because efficient causes, whether principal or instrumental, communicate something of their being to that which they cause, we speak about an assimilated effect. Hand-chopped vegetables turn out one way, whereas the same foodstuffs confided to a food processor come out differently. (Gourmet French chefs notice the difference, moreover.) The same agent may take up either a hammer or a saw; however, what has been hammered differs from what has been sawed. Other examples follow easily. Scholars attribute to Aquinas the application of the instrumentality of Christ's humanity to explain a central point of sacramental theology. Since the sacraments provide instruments of human salvation, how can one attribute this effect to a created reality such as the humanity of Christ? Aquinas returns to the theme of instrumental causality and, in the words of one author, offers an innovative solution: "Whereas the humanity of Christ is an instrument conjoined to his divinity, the sacraments are separated instruments—separated, this is to say, in space and time, but nevertheless still truly instruments" of what Saint Paul calls "a new creation" (2 Cor. 5:17).[19]

Another distinction that appears in discussions of sacramental theology distinguishes between physical and moral causalities. Broadly speaking, a physical cause produces its effect by its own action, whereas a moral cause moves another agent—for example, by offering counsel or by giving a command—to produce a given effect. The deployment of the word *physical* to describe the action of a sacrament may prima facie strike some persons as an awkward way to describe a spiritual reality. Albert Michel replies to the difficulty in a way that should relieve all those who find the expression alien to Christian understanding and sensibilities. The word *physical*, he writes, "is employed analogically to indicate simply that the sacraments receive from God, principal Cause of grace, a real power, however spiritual."[20] Nothing mechanical is suggested by use of the adjective *physical*. Commentators generally agree that Thomists like Thomas de Vio, known as Cardinal Cajetan (d. 1534), follow Aquinas on physical causality. The early Jesuit commentators on Aquinas, such as Francisco

18. For a discussion of the use that St. Athanasius makes of *instrument* to explain the relationship between the human body of Christ and the Logos, see Aloys Grillmeier, *Christ in Christian Tradition*, trans. J. Bowden, vol. 1, *From the Apostolic Age to Chalcedon (451)* (Atlanta: John Knox, 1975), 317–18.

19. David Bourke, *The Sacraments*, vol. 56 of the Blackfriars edition of *Summa theologiae*, by Thomas Aquinas (New York: McGraw-Hill, 1975), xxii.

20. Michel, "Sacrements," col. 617.

Suárez (d. 1617) and Robert Bellarmine (d. 1621), also found the description more than fitting to defend Catholic doctrine.[21]

In short, those who follow Aquinas on physical instrumental causality provide the best and most successful accounts of the "double agency" that stands at the heart of the sacramental system. They also, as the Spanish commentator Dominic Bañez (d. 1604) has illustrated well, have shown the importance of sacramental theology for ensuring right thinking about grace, potency, and anthropology.[22]

Alternative Explanations

Admittedly, other proponents of ways to explain how the sacraments work have made their mark in the long history of the Catholic theological enterprise. Various factors have influenced the thinking of those theologians who shy away altogether from talking about causality in a strong sense. For example, theologians influenced by nominalist philosophy tend to favor a weaker version of sacramental causality. They view the sacraments as so many occasions for God to impart his grace. Some proponents of occasional causality include the Dominican Durandus of Saint-Pourçain (d. 1334), the Franciscan William of Ockham (d. 1349), and the cathedral canon Gabriel Biel (d. 1495), whose work is said to have influenced Martin Luther (d. 1546).

The reform of the sixteenth century introduced considerations that moved not a few significant theologians to adopt some version of moral causality to explain the sacraments. Moral causality effectively reduces the work of the sacraments to something akin to moral persuasion. Proponents of moral causality include the Dominican Melchior Cano (d. 1560), the Jesuit Gabriel Vasquez (d. 1604), and some later Jesuits from the seventeenth through the nineteenth centuries.

Finally, historians of sacramental theology cite the theory of dispositive causality, which appears to assign the weakest ontological value to the sacraments' efficiency. This theory is found in the writing of some early Thomists and was revived, so it is said, in the nineteenth century by the Jesuit theologian Louis Billot (d. 1931) under the rubric of "intentional causality."[23]

21. For a recent overview of Thomist opinions, see Reginald Lynch, *The Cleansing of the Heart: The Sacraments as Instrumental Causes in the Thomistic Tradition* (Washington, DC: Catholic University of America Press, 2017), 10–66.

22. For an illuminating exposition of Bañez's defense of physical causality, see Reginald Lynch, "Domingo Bañez on Moral and Physical Causality: Christic Merit and Sacramental Realism," *Angelicum* 91 (2014): 105–25.

23. For further information on these theories and their authors, see the unparalleled exposition in Michel, "Sacrements," cols. 576–624.

Modern Challenges to Causality

Whatever school of thought one may find an attractive explanation of sacramental causality, it should become clear that the variety of explanations can be read to show that Catholic theologians as a whole and from the earliest period of scholasticism testify to the importance of the discussion for the Catholic faith. In other words, it is difficult to find an orthodox Catholic thinker who failed to recognize that the sacraments do something—that is, that they play a role in the drama of salvation that each Christian believer faces throughout his or her life.

The fate of sacramental efficacy in the proposals that emerged after the Second Vatican Council exhibits a certain discontinuity with this tradition. As already mentioned, Catholic sacramental theology faced certain challenges that were generated by those who had accepted the view that the council represented a period of rupture or discontinuity with the earlier Catholic theological tradition. For example, not a few Catholic thinkers came to identify the classical metaphysical infrastructure that laid out the principles of Catholic sacramental theology, such as efficient causality, with a legalism that these same thinkers felt the council's aggiornamento had set aside once and for all. Recall, again as mentioned above, that in order to ensure that each sacramental administration would receive a proper execution, it was common practice for canon lawyers to teach sacramental theology, especially in seminaries and other ecclesial educational settings.

This wrongheaded identification of metaphysics with legalism provoked in some quarters not only questionable sacramental practices but also some received scandal. The challenge of *ressourcement* theologians—that is, those who read the conciliar documents as a clarion call to Catholic theologians to return to the sources of the Christian tradition, mainly biblical and patristic—resulted in many Catholic theologians abandoning the preconciliar theological syntheses, such as those accomplished by the French Dominican Reginald Garrigou-Lagrange.[24]

Because it seemed that old scholastic models for the sacraments no longer fit the conciliar way of speaking about them, university-based theologians began to suggest diverse contexts of explanation for the sacraments, such as liturgiology (the study of comparative liturgies, both Christian and non-Christian), the sociology of religion and anthropology, and other philosophical studies of religion. A theory that developed a version of symbolic causality came about as a result of the German Jesuit Karl Rahner's attempt to make Aquinas a bedfellow with Hegel. Rahner's theorizing produced a notion of symbolic causality that required

24. See Reginald Garrigou-Lagrange, *De Eucharistia et Paenitentia* (Turin: Marietti, 1948).

more extensive exegesis than most of those who appealed to the concept were capable of undertaking. In general, one may safely generalize that the period immediately after the Second Vatican Council witnessed the eclipse of efficient causality in the several accounts of sacramental efficacy that were set forth.

Such an eclipse should not come as a surprise. The philosophical world provided many attractive alternatives. To point up a few of the broad philosophical movements that influenced Catholic theologians, one can point to the major figures of German philosophy. For example, commentators cite the critique of metaphysics undertaken by Immanuel Kant (1724–1804), in which God appears as a transcendental ideal though not as a universal cause. Or consider the experiential theology developed by the Protestant thinker Friedrich Schleiermacher (1768–1834), in which God becomes available as a "direct" object of consciousness. Then again, consider the important influence of idealist philosophy that originated with G. W. F. Hegel (1770–1831), which regards divine agency as a formal rather than an efficient principle.

This list of certain modern philosophical movements that have proven deleterious to classical metaphysics neither makes a judgment about the philosophical work of the modern thinkers themselves nor aims to dismiss their proposals out of hand. When, however, one examines the work in Catholic sacramental theology done during the final decades of the twentieth century, the diverse influences of thinkers such as Kant, Schleiermacher, and Hegel seem difficult to ignore. Other figures in modern philosophy may also merit a place among them, especially Ludwig Wittgenstein (1889–1951). In any event, the overall effort of sacramental theologians to substitute symbol for cause when it comes to explaining what the sacraments do produced no fruitful effects and, perhaps in some quarters, caused harm. As one prelate has observed, "The emphasis on the *meaning of the signs*, in itself wholly admirable, entirely neglected the issue of the *efficacy* of the signs, not to mention their double agency"; as a result, the bishop concludes, "God was left out."[25]

25. Private communication from an anonymous prelate of the Roman Curia (emphasis added).

4

Some Fresh Perspectives on the Sacramental Economy

Not a few Catholics of the postconciliar period have been persuaded that the efficacy of the sacraments depends on some form of communitarian symbolic activity. As is broadly suggested in the preceding chapter, a variety of factors have resulted in the eclipse of efficient causality as a way of explaining what the sacraments do for the individual who receives them. Instead, the assumption that underlies not only most popular opinion but also the instruction given in various venues holds that whatever the celebration of the sacraments accomplishes, it results from the combination of symbolic ritual actualized or—to use the more familiar expression—celebrated in a community setting. As has already been noted, this explanatory framework makes it difficult to insert the divine agency into the sacramental action. In short, as also has been previously observed, God gets left out as a cause of the sanctification that the sacraments are instituted to communicate to the human race. Despite this obviously deficient account of how the sacraments work, some version of communitarian symbolic activity has become the default explanation for sacramental efficacy among Catholics of the twenty-first century.

Contemporary Accounts of Sacramental Efficiency

Sacraments, it is true, do entail symbolic rituals duly celebrated within the context of the Church that forms a communion.[1] However, as Colman O'Neill

1. For a recent work that captures well the essentials of Catholic teaching on the sacraments and their working, see Roger W. Nutt, *General Principles of Sacramental Theology* (Washington, DC: Catholic University of America Press, 2017).

has argued, the appeal to symbolism in order to explain the sacramental system must itself be grounded in a particular theory or set of concepts that effectively accounts for how symbols work.[2]

Philosophers, of course, discuss signs and symbols. These discussions, for the most part, are limited today to setting forth theories of language and communication. The emphasis that classical sacramental theory places on efficient causality, with its reference to the coming about of something godly or the coming into existence of something supernatural, should give one pause, however. This pause appears opportune, especially in the face of proposals that appear all too limited by earthly realities such as a human community that finds a principle of cohesion in its members' common acceptance of shared religious symbols.

The fact of the matter remains that communitarian symbolic activity does not provide sufficient ontological weight to ensure a proper account of what the sacraments of the Church do. Why? Again, Father O'Neill puts it straightforwardly when he points out that without an ontological grounding, the category of *symbol* to explain what the sacraments do remains inadequate to communicate what the Church teaches about the efficacy and reality of the sacraments.[3]

One might observe a lesson from the history of theology. If the scholastic theologians had wanted to say that the sacraments work precisely because they amount to nothing more than enacted symbols, these same theologians would have made such a claim. The scholars of the scholastic periods possessed the intellectual wherewithal, moreover, to do so. Instead, the Catholic thinkers of yesteryear explained the sacraments by appeal to a philosophy of being. At this juncture, we turn to a useful reminder in Pope John Paul II's *Fides et ratio*: "Set within the Christian metaphysical tradition, the philosophy of being is a dynamic philosophy which views reality in its ontological, causal and communicative structures."[4] The phrase "communicative structures" points us back to the Church's creedal formulation about creation and the God who creates out of nothing. The *Catechism of the Catholic Church* wisely remarks on the relationship between the God who creates and the God who saves: "Since God could create everything out of nothing, he can also, through the Holy Spirit, give spiritual life to sinners by creating a pure heart in them and bodily life to the dead through the Resurrection."[5] No need to mention how much symbolism

2. O'Neill presents a case for a realist account of the sacraments that can explain the real effects of them. Colman E. O'Neill, *Sacramental Realism* (Chicago: Midwest Theological Forum, 1998), esp. 139–63.

3. O'Neill, *Sacramental Realism*, 203–18.

4. John Paul II, *Fides et ratio*, no. 97.

5. CCC no. 298.

in itself fails to capture the full causal explanations of these mysteries of both creation and salvation.

The descriptive phrase *sacramental realism* points to those explanations of the sacraments that take into account the full dimensions of all that authentic Christian religion promises to communicate to those who receive the sacraments fruitfully. What follows aims to illustrate what Pope John Paul II means when he invites theologians to "recover and express to the full the metaphysical dimension of truth."[6] The sacraments require considerable ecclesial governance. For each of the sacraments, provisions are made to govern their liturgical enactment and their canonical administration. Defects occur in nature and in art. The Church points out defective moral actions—namely, those that cause harm to the sinner, who should live in conformity to the truth about the good of the human person. The Church also warns about defective sacramental administrations and, when necessary, provides remedies for them.

The present volume, as mentioned above, does not offer a comprehensive analysis of the liturgical and canonical rules that govern the administration of the sacraments. Instead, this study seeks to ensure that the sacraments of the Church are properly understood in a correct theological presentation that enables the attentive reader to understand both the Church's liturgical practices and prayers and her canonical disciplines.

The Seven Sacraments and the One Church

From what has been said about the governance that the Church exercises over the sacraments, we can appreciate that the sacraments belong to the Church. They are "instituted by Christ and entrusted to the Church."[7] It follows, then, that many questions debated in the discipline of ecclesiology and even in that of ecumenical theology touch upon the sacraments.

The answers to such questions and the resolution of the debates that arise from the divisions within Christianity require separate discussions and arguments. One principle, however, merits attention in any attempt to answer the often complex questions of sacramental efficacy that arise from the valid administration of Baptism outside of the Catholic Church. This principle finds succinct expression in the 2000 declaration issued under the authority of Pope John Paul II, *Dominus Iesus*: "If it is true," the declaration says, "that the followers of other religions can receive divine grace, it is also certain that objectively speaking they are in a gravely deficient situation in comparison with those who,

6. John Paul II, *Fides et ratio*, no. 105.
7. *CCC* no. 1131.

in the Church, have the fullness of the means of salvation."[8] These means fall under the general headings of teaching, sanctifying, and governing.

It seems important to note that the footnote attached to this sentence refers the reader to an earlier, 1943, papal encyclical of Pope Pius XII—namely, *Mystici corporis Christi.* This papal document addresses questions pertinent to the salvation of those who "do not belong to the visible Body of the Catholic Church."[9] Pius XII's teaching, in brief, holds that such people should enter into Catholic unity. The reason for such a movement includes the aforementioned benefits found only in the Catholic Church. The seven sacraments, to be sure, fall under what Pope John Paul II calls the "means of salvation" and what Pope Pius XII in his aforementioned encyclical refers to as "the many heavenly gifts and helps that can only be enjoyed in the Catholic Church."[10]

There are many reasons why only those who remain in full communion with the Catholic Church may avail themselves of her sacraments. These reasons, though stipulated in the Church's legal documents, find their own grounding in the metaphysical dimension of truth. Take the case of Baptism. The Catholic Church teaches as true that "Baptism constitutes the foundation of communion among all Christians, including those who are not yet in full communion with the Catholic Church."[11] This principle (which today should find explication in courses on the theology of the Church) affords a good example of the metaphysical dimension of truth as realized in the sacraments of the Church. Just as the transcendentals that metaphysicians discuss embrace each concrete realization of, say, the true and the good, so Baptism embraces all those who themselves have been validly baptized in whatever Christian denomination this Baptism took place.[12] At the same time, those baptized outside of communion with the Catholic Church cannot ordinarily receive the other sacraments of salvation.[13]

In order to capture an overview of how sacramental realism and its wider theological considerations govern what the Catholic Church holds about the sacraments, one may usefully turn to the *Catechism of the Catholic Church.* The

8. *Dominus Iesus,* no. 22.

9. Pius XII, *Mystici corporis Christi,* no. 103, *DS* 3821.

10. *DS* 3821.

11. *CCC* no. 1271. The catechism quotes the Second Vatican Council's Decree on Ecumenism, *Unitatis Redintegratio,* no. 22: "Baptism therefore constitutes *the sacramental bond of unity* existing among all who through it are reborn" (emphasis original).

12. The *Code of Canon Law* in vigor in the Catholic Church includes a description of the essentials for validity: "Baptism, the gateway to the sacraments and necessary for salvation by actual reception or at least by desire, is validly conferred only by a washing of true water with the proper form of words. Through baptism men and women are freed from sin, are reborn as children of God, and, configured to Christ by an indelible character, are incorporated into the Church" (can. 849).

13. For extraordinary circumstances, see the *Code of Canon Law,* can. 844.

first thing that the text teaches about the sacraments appears in an image inspired by the Gospel of Mark. In Mark 5:25–34 we read of a miracle that Jesus worked on a hemorrhagic woman. This woman appears as depicted in an early fourth-century fresco found in one of the Roman catacombs, which portrays the miracle as reported in Mark's Gospel.

The painting shows the woman kneeling behind Jesus and reaching out to touch the bottom of his cloak. This image was chosen carefully, one assumes, to introduce the second part of the catechism, which treats the sacraments of the Church. The connection between sacrament and the woman cured of a flow of blood is found in the power that goes out from the person of Christ. The caption for the image states this axiom clearly: "The sacraments are as it were 'powers that go forth' from the Body of Christ to heal wounds of sin and to give us the new life of Christ."[14]

This text from the catechism makes a fundamental assertion about the sacraments that undergirds Catholic teaching. Indeed, the long-standing tradition that makes use of efficient causality to describe how the sacraments work finds one of its biblical warrants in this account of the miracle worked by Christ. In short, we learn that the sacraments continue the work that Christ performed during his earthly life.

Truth to tell, each sacrament, not only the Eucharist, provides a meeting place where the Catholic believer encounters Christ. This encounter, broadly speaking, results in the healing of sin's wounds and the bestowal of new life. These real effects of the sacraments apply analogically to each of the seven sacraments. When one considers how much the Church emphasizes intrinsic justification—that is, the transformation of the sinner, not only the new designation of the sinner—it becomes apparent that the full weight of causal efficacy with its ontological significance alone can offer an adequate account of what the sacraments do.

The Sacraments and Spiritual Healing

Each sacrament, not only Penance and Reconciliation, heals the wounds of sin. This divinely wrought work may be called the work of image-restoration.[15]

14. *CCC*, frontispiece for part 2, appearing in the print edition: *Catechism of the Catholic Church*, 2nd ed., by United States Catholic Conference, Inc. (Washington, DC: Libreria Editrice Vaticana, 1994, 1997).

15. For an extended discussion of the notions of image-restoration and image-perfection, expressions that find their origin in the Augustinian tradition, see Romanus Cessario, *The Godly Image: Christian Satisfaction in Aquinas* (Washington, DC: Catholic University of America Press, 2020).

Original sin and the sins we ourselves commit leave wounds in our individualized human natures. These wounds appear in the disordering of the human powers of action. Evidence of this disordering emerges when we choose what we should not choose, fear what we should not fear, and desire what we should not desire. Christ restores our natural powers to their proper ordering. This restoration does not happen all at once—at least as a matter of course. Gradually, however, those who receive fruitfully the sacraments experience a healing of sin's disorders.

Christ does more, however, than forgive sins and heal the wounds that they leave in the sinner. Christ also bestows a new life that comes from his own divinity. This means that the sacraments, beginning with Baptism, introduce the recipient into a new world of graced existence. In this earthly life, recipients of the sacraments are distinguished from those without the benefit of sacramental mediation by, among other things, their capacity to perform acts of faith in God, of hope in God, and of theological charity.[16] To believe in God, to hope in God, and to love as Christ loves requires abilities that do not come naturally to the human person. Each human being needs to receive these abilities, to become strengthened in these abilities, and, oftentimes, to find renewal of these abilities. To sum up, these supernatural endowments flow from the sacraments of the Church.

At the heart of each sacrament, the Church recognizes both a form or formula and a stipulated matter that is required for the valid administration of the sacrament. Under ordinary circumstances, the sacraments are celebrated publicly within stipulated liturgical services. This principle includes emergency administrations of sacraments, which follow their own foreshortened rubrics. However, the essence of the sacrament lies in the distinctive sign-action that each sacrament possesses. A Catholic's commitment to the Church's sacramental economy—that is, to the way that the Church distributes the powers that flow from the risen Christ—both ensures the Catholic's salvation and measures the Catholic's attachment to the Lord. Each Catholic recipient of a sacrament, like the woman with the flow of blood in Mark's Gospel, should repeat frequently, "If I but touch his clothes, I shall be cured" (Mark 5:28). The scholastic theologians gave extended treatment to the place that the Incarnate Word holds in the communication of divine grace that the sacraments effect. For the present, it suffices to observe that the sacraments of the New Law—that

16. See CCC no. 1129: "The Church affirms that for believers the sacraments of the New Covenant are *necessary for salvation*" (emphasis original). At the same time, CCC no. 1257 states, "*God has bound salvation to the sacrament of Baptism, but he himself is not bound by his sacraments*" (emphasis original).

is, the sacraments instituted by Christ—figure squarely in the overall economy of salvation that finds its highest expression in the life, death, and resurrection of Jesus Christ.

Before we address issues in theology that traditionally have been treated under the heading of sacramental theology, it makes pedagogical sense to locate the general teaching of the sacraments within coordinates that treat the immediately connected tenets of the faith that throw light on the sacraments. These topics include discussions that form part of treatments dedicated to Christian anthropology, soteriology, and the history of salvation. Because of the fragmentation that has invaded theological education since the end of the nineteenth century, it is easy for the student of theology to miss the overall context of divine instruction that earlier centuries sought to maintain.[17]

Saint Thomas Aquinas's *Summa theologiae*, along with the literary productions of other medieval summists, exemplifies these efforts. The following theological points capture the main elements of theology that one requires to approach a study of the Church's sacraments. While each of these elements has received extensive theological examination throughout the Christian centuries and, further, has generated a wide range of theological opinions that seek to interpret them, the basic tenets of the Christian faith concerning each element, in the eyes of the Catholic Church, at least, are contained in the *Catechism of the Catholic Church*. Pope John Paul II made this clear in the apostolic constitution *Fidei depositum*. The catechism, he says, "is a statement of the Church's faith and of catholic doctrine, attested to or illuminated by Sacred Scripture, the Apostolic Tradition, and the Church's Magisterium."[18]

Theological Topics Related to the Sacraments

The sacraments, as the adage runs, are for human beings—*sacramenta propter homines*.[19] Among the elements of Catholic doctrine that merit consideration as part of a presentation of the sacraments, the creation of the human person enjoys a prominent place.[20] Theological interest in the *creation of man* (an inclusive term used to express the common nature that men and women share) includes truths about the origin of the human person, the structure of the human person,

17. For an analysis of these developments, see Edward Farley, *Theologia: The Fragmentation and Unity of Theological Education* (Philadelphia: Fortress, 1983).

18. John Paul II, *Fidei depositum*, no. 2.

19. For a short account of the history of the expression, used by both sacramental and moral theologians, see René Brouillard, "Sacramenta propter homines," *Nouvelle revue théologique* 50, no. 9 (1923): 464–73.

20. See CCC nos. 355–61.

and the destiny of the human person. Scientific research and hypotheses about evolution, anthropological investigations, and philosophical debates about the immateriality of the human soul belong to other disciplines. At the same time, the Church welcomes empirical investigations that complement what one might call a biblical anthropology. Pope John Paul II made this point with special insistence in his encyclical *Fides et ratio*: "I cannot fail to note, especially in the context of this Encyclical Letter, that one chapter of the Constitution *Gaudium et Spes* amounts to a virtual compendium of the biblical anthropology from which philosophy too can draw inspiration. The chapter deals with the value of the human person created in the image of God, explains the dignity and superiority of the human being over the rest of creation, and declares the transcendent capacity of human reason."[21] From a theological viewpoint, creation forms the foundation for all that God intends to accomplish for our salvation and so may be regarded as the beginning of salvation history that finds its completion in Jesus Christ.[22]

Creation

There is another consideration about creation that illuminates Catholic teaching on the sacraments. Aquinas treats this aspect of creation in his *Summa theologiae* when he inquires "whether God is the efficient cause of all things."[23] While the sacraments belong squarely within the Christian tradition, their efficacy depends on the God who creates all things visible and invisible. O'Neill summarizes this indispensable feature of Catholic doctrine on the sacraments as follows. First, he states the incarnational principle and its metaphysical implications: "Because it is Christ who mediates the Spirit in virtue of his mission from the Father the unity of all flows from his unique person and this unity goes beyond that of the psychological order."[24] Then O'Neill points to the juncture that the hypostatic union—that is, the union of the human and divine natures of Christ in the single divine person of the Word—establishes for the Christian dispensation. Again referring to the "unity of all," O'Neill writes, "It is Christological, referring back beyond the humanity of Christ to the person of the divine Word who encompasses all that is created. It is, for this reason, ontological, belonging to the order of being that is the gift of the Father of creation."[25]

21. John Paul II, *Fides et ratio*, no. 60, citing *Gaudium et Spes*, nos. 14–15.
22. See CCC no. 280.
23. *Summa theologiae* I.44.1.
24. O'Neill, *Sacramental Realism*, 38.
25. O'Neill, *Sacramental Realism*, 38.

To return to the question that Aquinas addresses in his discussion of creation, we discover the principle that O'Neill refers to when he speaks of the "Father of creation." Aquinas's consideration of the whole of creation leads him to conclude "that all things other than God are not their own existence but share in existence."[26] Then he identifies that in which creation shares by pointing to the One who most perfectly exists (*perfectissime est*)—that is, the most perfect being. In the very words of Aquinas, "It follows strictly that all things which are diversified by their diverse sharing in existence . . . are caused by one first being which simply *is* in the fullest sense of the word."[27] Some Catholic thinkers find that this truth evokes Exodus 3:14: "God replied [to Moses], 'I am who am.'"[28]

In a remarkably concise expression of Catholic doctrine concerning what can be called continuing creation, the *Catechism of the Catholic Church* sets forth a truth that applies to the sacraments of the Church. Since the sacraments serve Christian believers of every generation and period of time, they figure in the way that God upholds and sustains creation. God is not a watchmaker who puts together an instrument that can run without the watchmaker's assistance. To express this truth in other terms, God does not abandon his creatures. "He not only gives them being and existence, but also, and at every moment, upholds and sustains them in being, enables them to act and brings them to their final end."[29]

This general metaphysical rule that governs everything that exists also applies to the sacramental economy. God did not abandon the human race after Adam's sin. The promise of rescue, according to Catholic exegesis, appears as early as in the book of Genesis when God promises to establish enmity between the serpent and the woman.[30] The fulfillment of that promise appears in the person of Jesus Christ, whose friendship brings blessings that even Adam did not experience. This explains why the Church solemnly proclaims at the Easter Vigil a phrase that can strike some hearers as paradoxical: "O happy fault that earned so great, so glorious a Redeemer."[31] What does this paschal exclamation mean? The Church holds that Christ brings graces to the human race that surpass whatever

26. *Summa theologiae* I.44.1.

27. *Summa theologiae* I.44.1.

28. See Etienne Gilson, *The Christian Philosophy of St. Thomas Aquinas,* trans. L. K. Shook (New York: Random House, 1966), 46–58.

29. *CCC* no. 301. God carries out his plan for creation and for the supernatural perfection of intelligent creatures infallibly. For the catechism's succinct but complete treatment of divine providence, see nos. 302–14.

30. See Gen. 3:15. For a short catechesis that addresses an objection often raised by those who fail to understand the proper relationship between the divine omnipotence and human freedom, see *CCC* nos. 410–12.

31. *Roman Missal,* "Easter Proclamation." Expanded: "O truly necessary sin of Adam, destroyed completely by the Death of Christ! O happy fault that earned so great, so glorious a Redeemer."

spiritual endowments were lost by Adam's sin. Indeed, nothing prevents God from raising human nature up to something greater than what man possessed at creation.[32] Were this not true, Christian salvation would indeed appear as a Band-Aid for an irreversibly broken human creature. Instead, the saints teach us that the justification of the sinner stands out as God's greatest work for his creatures. "Justification is the *most excellent work of God's love* made manifest in Christ Jesus and granted by the Holy Spirit."[33] In this work, the sacraments play an indispensable and irreplaceable role.

Imago Dei

Catholic truth regards each individual human being as made in the image of God. The Latin phrase *imago Dei* serves as a shorthand expression for a teaching that plays a central role in the unfolding of a Christian anthropology. The document that the Second Vatican Council issued on the Church, *Lumen Gentium*, begins with reference to the divine plan for the human creature. "The eternal Father, by a free and hidden plan of His own wisdom and goodness, created the whole world. His plan was to raise men to a participation of the divine life."[34]

Next, the document explains that the fall neither disqualifies human nature from participating in the divine life nor leaves the human race without some expectation of a Redeemer. Indeed, the positive account of the divine pedagogy that takes place during the period of the Old Testament indicates that, whereas the image of God in which man had been created suffered a certain besmirchment, the human person did not lose altogether the divine image of creation. The Dogmatic Constitution on the Church puts it this way: "Fallen in Adam, God the Father did not leave men to themselves, but ceaselessly offered helps to salvation, in view of Christ, the Redeemer 'who is the image of the invisible God, the firstborn of every creature'" (Col. 1:15).[35]

The same text puts emphasis on the immutability of the divine plan. It would provide an example of a very strange reversal indeed were a creature's sinning to have been allowed to effect in God a change of his eternal plan. Still, a sort of drama emerges from the fact that the human creature made to share an eternal inheritance with Christ finds himself after the original sin without the means to satisfy this desire for God. In short, after original sin, the human race remains unable to realize the high destiny of beatific communion with God. So while it is true that "all the elect, before time began, the Father 'foreknew and predestined

32. For one authority for this claim, see *Summa theologiae* III.1.3 ad 3.
33. *CCC* no. 1994 (emphasis original).
34. *Lumen Gentium*, no. 2 (VRL).
35. *Lumen Gentium*, no. 2 (VRL).

to become conformed to the image of His Son, that he should be the firstborn among many brethren'" (Rom. 8:29),[36] the actualization of this divine decree had to await an initiative that only God could take. This remedy appears to us when "in the sixth month, the angel Gabriel was sent from God to a town of Galilee called Nazareth, to a virgin betrothed to a man named Joseph, . . . and the virgin's name was Mary" (Luke 1:26–27).

The Council of Trent chose to describe the condition of the human race after the fall in terms that emphasize the privations, and indeed the punishments, that original sin introduces into the world. In the sixteenth-century council's "Decree on Original Sin," the Church anathematizes those who do not profess that by sinning Adam drew upon himself a "captivity in the power of him who henceforth 'has the power of death,' (Heb. 2:14) that is, the devil."[37] Historians suggest that tenets advanced by some of the sixteenth-century Protestant Reformers go a long way to explain this prefatory statement about the effects of original sin.[38] By contrast, the council fathers set down what authentic Catholic faith holds.

Additionally, they also venture to explain why such clarification about original sin is necessary—namely, because the devil ("the perpetual enemy of mankind"), who favors doctrinal confusion, "has stirred up among the many evils that beset the Church of God in this time of ours both new and old controversies about original sin and its remedy."[39] In any event, the Church today still holds that ignorance about the state of the human race under the reign of sin "gives rise to serious errors in the areas of education, politics, social action, and morals."[40] Catholic usage speaks about this circumstance of our humanity as "wounded nature," a condition that makes out of human life a hard battle to accomplish the good.

The early pages of the Old Testament, even on a casual reading, suggest the progressive alienation that the human person experiences under the reign of sin. Cain slays Abel (Gen. 4:8). The Tower of Babel (Gen. 11:1–9) makes

36. *Lumen Gentium*, no. 2 (VRL).

37. Council of Trent, Session 5, Decree on Original Sin, no. 1, *DS* 1511.

38. For further discussion, see A. Gaudel, "Péché Originel," in *Dictionnaire de théologie catholique*, tome 12 (Paris: Letouzey et Ané, 1933): cols. 510–27. One may also usefully consult the work of T. C. Obrien, *Original Sin*, vol. 20 of the Blackfriars edition of *Summa theologiae*, by Thomas Aquinas (New York: McGraw-Hill, 1964–81), especially Appendix 8, "Original Justice": "The meaning of original sin depends on the meaning of original justice which is its positive contrast. Original sin is its privation or lack, and thus is not pure privation but a 'corrupt habit of sorts.'" O'Brien also explains that "Luther's teaching on the total depravity of human nature was an extreme reaction against the optimism of nominalism" (p. 106).

39. Council of Trent, Session 5, Decree on Original Sin, introduction, *DS* 1510.

40. *CCC* no. 407.

common effort impossible. Noah builds his ark (Gen. 6:13–22). What may one conclude? Brother turns on brother. Neighbor becomes divided by language against neighbor. Creation itself threatens the existence of all living things. This sacred history all in all points up the fragility of wounded nature when it relies solely on those "truths naturally accessible to reason."[41] The Old Law marks a moment of divine intervention that helps the human person by laying the foundation for his or her vocation to live as an image of God. Saint Augustine summarizes the purpose of this divine intervention when he asserts that "God wrote on the tables of the Law what men did not read in their hearts."[42] Again, the Old Law, in the phrase of Saint Paul, served as a tutor for the human race, as a preparation for the gospel. "Like a tutor (Gal 3:24) it shows what must be done, but does not itself give the strength, the grace of the Spirit, to fulfill it."[43]

By contrast, the New Law, which Aquinas describes simply as the "grace of the Holy Spirit," both fulfills and surpasses the Old Law.[44] The Church accepts Aquinas's teaching and makes it her own when she states authoritatively that "the New Law is the grace of the Holy Spirit received by faith in Christ."[45] The perfection that the New Law of grace brings to the Old Law's dispensation appears in both instruction and the forms of mediation that God establishes to provide for the sanctification of the individual. The Christian tradition has established recognizable icons of these two forms of perfecting. Ancient Christian writers frequently compared the instruction given to Moses on Mount Sinai with that given by Christ in what has become known as the Lord's Sermon on the Mount.

Again, Christian authors, especially those who, like Origen (d. 254), favored allegorical interpretations of the Scriptures, drew many comparisons between the prescribed rituals of the Mosaic Law and the sacramental practices of the New Covenant. For his part, Aquinas captures this sentiment in his composition to honor the Blessed Sacrament of the Altar. In the Sequence (a hymn sung before the reading of the Gospel on solemn feast days) *Lauda Sion*, composed around 1264, Aquinas penned this strophe of Latin poetry:

> Hail! Bread of the Angels, broken,
> for us pilgrims food, and token
> of the promise by Christ spoken,

41. See *CCC* no. 1961.

42. Augustine, *Enarrationes in Psalmos*, 57, 1, as quoted in *CCC* no. 1962.

43. *CCC* no. 1963.

44. The phrase is found in his treatment of the New Law in *Summa theologiae* I-II.106.1 and is considered a principle of interpretation for everything that Aquinas writes about both morality and the sacraments: "Now it is the grace of the Holy Spirit, given through faith in Christ, which is predominant in the Law of the New Covenant, and that in which its whole power consists."

45. *CCC* no. 1983.

children's meat, to dogs denied!
Shown in Isaac's dedication,
in the Manna's preparation,
in the Paschal immolation,
in old types pre-signified.[46]

The relationship of the sacraments to the New Law of grace recalls the image of Christ healing the hemorrhagic woman (see Mark 5:25–34). The Church cherishes the image of this miracle inasmuch as it "symbolizes the divine and saving power of the Son of God who heals the whole man, soul and body, through the sacramental life."[47] The healing that the sacraments of the New Covenant bring involves the remission of sin and its effects as well as the bestowal of a share in the divine life.

Redemption

In a sermon he preached sometime in the fifth century, Pope Saint Leo I (d. 461), called Leo the Great, enunciated a principle that governs how the sacraments of the Church work their saving effects. At the ascension, the Pope recalled, Christ's visible presence had passed beyond the clouds of the sky (see Acts 1:9). Christian believers can take comfort from this mystery of Christ's life, for Pope Leo assures them that "what was visible in our Savior has passed over into his sacraments."[48] A complete account of Christian salvation must reckon with the fact that the justification of the sinner entails a twofold movement of grace. We are cleansed from our sins and we receive "'the righteousness of God through faith in Jesus Christ' and through Baptism."[49]

One traditional way to approach this mystery of justification that the sacraments accomplish in us includes reference to the satisfaction for sin that Christ accomplishes in a preeminent way on the cross. Under the Old Law, the satisfaction for sin available to sinners enjoyed only a relative efficacy based on its divinely sanctioned origin, such as one finds in the ritual prescriptions contained in the book of Leviticus. Aquinas—in a brilliantly differentiated answer

46. "*Lauda Sion*," Treasury of Latin Prayers, by Michael Martin, accessed July 29, 2022, https://www.preces-latinae.org/thesaurus/Hymni/LaudaSion.html. The Latin expresses the relationship of the Old Testament figures to the Eucharist, with explicit reference to the Eucharist as both sacrifice and meal: "Ecce Panis Angelorum, factus cibus viatorum: vere panis filiorum, non mittendus canibus. In figuris praesignatur, cum Isaac immolatur, agnus Paschae deputatur, datur manna patribus."

47. CCC, frontispiece for part 2.

48. Leo the Great, *Sermon* 74, 2 (*PL* 54:398A).

49. CCC no. 1987, quoting Rom. 3:22.

to the question "Had the ceremonies of the Old Law any power of imparting justification during the period of the Old Law?"—admits that "in the Old Law certain sacrifices were offered for sin; not that they cleansed from sin, but that they were a kind of profession of the faith which cleanses from sin."[50] At the same time, he refrains from assigning to the Old-Law sacrifices a saving power in themselves. On the contrary, Aquinas clearly affirms, "Since the mystery of Christ's incarnation and passion had not been enacted, those ceremonies of the Old Law could not have contained the power issuing therefrom, as do the sacraments of the New Law."[51] In short, the expectation of Christ that all the saints of the Old Testament entertained served to enliven the sacrificial and other rites of the Old Law with their relative efficacy.

The Happy Fault

The sacraments of the New Law enjoy an objective efficacy based on the supreme work of Christ. The word "objective" in this context points to the power of God at work in the sacramental action. The *Catechism of the Catholic Church* quotes Aquinas, who writes that "the sacrament is not wrought by the righteousness of either the celebrant or the recipient, but by the power of God."[52] Further clarifications are required in order to understand properly how the sacraments work, as it were, objectively. Obviously, any suggestion of magic or superstition remains out of place. Instead, the sacraments of the New Law figure in the work of image-restoration and image-perfection, categories that represent God's twofold justifying action in the sinner.[53]

Detachment from sin and the sanctification of the human person, both body and soul, requires that the Christian believer properly understand the providence of God as it pertains to the divine permission for man's sin. As with Adam's sin, the sins of his progeny always can become expressions of a *felix culpa* inasmuch as the sacraments of the New Law exist to restore people to friendship with Christ that not only exceeds, obviously, the state of sin but also exceeds whatever natural happiness a person may discover in this world.

50. *Summa theologiae* I-II.103.2.
51. *Summa theologiae* I-II.103.2.
52. CCC no. 1128, quoting *Summa theologiae* III.68.8.
53. For a summary of Catholic teaching on justification, see CCC nos. 1987–95.

5

The Saving Work of Christ

Saint Thomas Aquinas often ponders the mystery of what makes the passion and death of Jesus Christ the kind of salvific event that Catholic theology affirms. Indeed, the *Catechism of the Catholic Church* follows Aquinas's teaching on the motive for the Incarnation.[1] "The desire to embrace his Father's plan of redeeming love," the catechism explains, "inspired Jesus' whole life, for his redemptive passion was the very reason for his Incarnation."[2] The history of theology reveals that other theologians advance different reasons for why God becomes man. The question that remains asks how one can explain that the violent death of Jesus, which holds a central place in the mystery of God's plan, brings about the saving benefits it does for the whole world. Of course, a fundamental principle of Catholic theology holds that Christ died for all men without exception.[3] A complete answer to the question of how the death of Christ saves the world requires several considerations that appear in the third part of Aquinas's *Summa theologiae*.[4]

Modes of Redemption

Aquinas's treatment of the efficacy of the passion of Christ proceeds by identifying six modes or ways in which the passion of Christ produces, as it were,

1. The question of the motive for the Incarnation occupied Catholic theologians of the Middle Ages. For an introduction to this vexing question, see Jeremy Moiser, "Why Did the Son of God Become Man?," *The Thomist* 37 (1973): 288–305. For a presentation of the Franciscan position, see Juniper B. Carol, *Why Jesus Christ?* (Manassas, VA: Trinity Communications, 1987).
2. CCC no. 607.
3. See CCC no. 605.
4. See *Summa theologiae* III.48.1–6.

the effects that it does. It is important to realize that Aquinas distinguishes between how the effect was produced (*de modo efficiendi*) and the effect itself (*de ipse effectu*). Because, as we have already indicated, the sacraments of the Church draw their power from the passion and death of Christ, it is reasonable to assume that the various modes of efficiency discussed in *Summa theologiae* III.48 will also appear in the administration of the sacraments.

The first mode to consider returns us to the basic philosophical tenet of efficient causality. Because of the central place that double causality plays in the drama of Christian redemption, the reply in which Aquinas explains efficiency merits our attention.[5] He writes, "An efficient cause is twofold: principal and instrumental. God is the principal efficient cause of man's salvation. But since Christ's humanity is the instrument of his divinity, all Christ's acts and sufferings work instrumentally in virtue of his divinity in bringing about man's salvation. Thus Christ's passion causes the salvation of men as an efficient cause."[6]

The mode of efficient cause points ultimately to the Blessed Trinity as the principal cause of salvation. This accords with what Catholic teaching holds following a rule of faith—namely, that all the actions of the Trinity outside the Trinity, the so-called *ad extra* acts, result from "the common work of the three divine persons."[7] Were this not the case, each sacramental action would introduce division into the Godhead. So when the theologian discusses the divine agency, a way is sought to account for God's relationship with things outside himself. Within the Blessed Trinity, there are no causes but only principles—namely, the processions. In the sacraments, however, there operates a true divine causality. In other words, as has been emphasized throughout this treatment, God in the sacraments does something. Furthermore, the agency involves a twofold, coordinated movement.

While the principal cause remains the Blessed Trinity, the instrumental cause appears as the sign-action that each sacrament requires when celebrated duly in the Church. As has already been mentioned briefly, modern science's understanding of causes aims to explain the connections behind phenomena. Aquinas uses cause to express the effects' true dependence in being on that which brings the effect about in the real order. To refer to Aquinas's use of causal analysis does not simply express a preference for older rather than newer theories of explanation. The Christian religion requires some account of causality to preserve

5. The enumeration of the six modes does not follow that found in Aquinas's texts. The arrangement of modes has been constructed to help the modern reader grasp the profundity of Aquinas's reflections on the modes.

6. *Summa theologiae* III.48.6.

7. See CCC no. 258: "The whole divine economy is the common work of the three divine persons."

the divine transcendence. Were God not the cause of all that exists, in its very existence, some other explanation would be required for the world. Such explanations would likely look like various cosmogonic theories of the origin of the universe. Such theories, however, do not generally rely on a Creator of heaven and earth who creates from nothing.[8]

The second mode by which the passion of Christ works introduces the notion of merit. In brief, merit signifies that someone possesses a claim to receive a reward. In order to explain the work of image-perfection—that is, the ennobling of the human creature through the gift of divine grace—the theologian uses the category of merit to describe one aspect of the saving work of Christ. If sin did not exist in the world, the human creature would still need to merit the reward of eternal life and what leads up to it. For to participate in God's very own life is not something that any human creature can claim as his or her due. In other words, beatitude does not constitute a perfection perfectly proportionate to the resources of unaided human nature.

As many theological battles illustrate, discussions about condign and congruous merit aim to distinguish between a reward due in strict justice (*de condigno*) and one that comes to us through gracious liberality (*de congruo*). It remains Catholic doctrine that grace cannot be merited by purely natural works either condignly or congruously. Even when condign merit is employed to describe the actions of believers, the supposition is that this order of merit exists only because God has devised it, and that he has done so sheerly because of his infinite goodness.

The third mode provides a companion consideration to merit. Aquinas and other medieval theologians acknowledge the Christian tradition's early adoption of satisfaction to explain the effects of the passion and death of Christ. In order to refer to the penal aspect of reparation or expiation that attaches to the passion of Christ, early liturgical texts appeal to the satisfaction for sins that Christ and the saints make on behalf of a sinful humanity. In the eleventh century, Anselm of Canterbury (d. 1109) made satisfaction a permanent feature of Christian soteriology by his composition of *Cur Deus Homo?*, a treatise that aims to explain why Christ had to suffer and die. Because the world is marked not only by the evil of fault (*malum culpae*) but also by the evil of punishment (*malum poenae*), satisfaction remains an indispensable element in any account of Christian salvation.

Satisfaction describes how suffering figures in the plan of salvation: First, in Christ, who, though sinless, died for us; second, in the Christian, in whom satisfaction addresses the turning away from one's own disordered loves. In

8. See CCC nos. 296, 285.

short, it is the case that sinful disorders bring about their own punishments. However, the remedy for these disorders requires that one embrace what runs counter to one's own fallen inclinations. Think only of the difficulty that people experience turning away from pleasures that in reality cause them harm. Thus, satisfactions must entail something burdensome or painful. "In all men," writes Aquinas, "God loves the nature which he has made. What he hates in man is the sins which men commit against him."[9] Painless salvation, like bloodless crosses, proves an illusion.[10]

The fourth mode that Aquinas treats in question forty-eight of the third part of his *Summa* introduces the biblical term *redemption*. He devotes two articles to this mode: the first asks whether Christ's passion brings about our salvation by way (*per modum*) of redemption, and the second, whether it was proper that Christ be a redeemer. By singling out the theme of redemption from other themes in the New Testament that describe what Christ accomplishes by his passion, Aquinas emphasizes the sad lot in which original sin leaves the human race. Redemption, then, describes the state in which those for whom a superabundant satisfaction has been made find themselves. Aquinas puts it this way: "Christ offered satisfaction, not by the giving of money or anything like that, but by giving the greatest of all things, namely himself, for us. For that reason, the passion of Christ is said to be our redemption."[11] A further implication of redemption implies the liberation or freedom from whatever restricts that which those redeemed by Christ enjoy.

A Contemporary Appropriation

Although the most common way to speak about Christian salvation, the theme of redemption actually points to an effect of Christ's suffering and death on the cross. So the Christian Church celebrates the fact that the world has been redeemed—that is, substantially freed from the restrictions that sin imposes on a human creature. These restrictions are coincidental with the wounding to human nature that the Church holds derives from original sin: "Human nature . . . is wounded in the natural powers proper to it; subject to ignorance, suffering, and the dominion of death; and inclined to sin—an inclination to evil that is called 'concupiscence.'"[12]

9. *Summa theologiae* III.49.4 ad 1.

10. For a short treatment of the history of satisfaction in the theological tradition, see Romanus Cessario, *The Godly Image: Christian Satisfaction in Aquinas* (Washington, DC: Catholic University of America Press, 2020).

11. *Summa theologiae* III.48.4.

12. CCC no. 405.

From these punishments and others that original sin imposes, such as the loss of eternal beatitude, Christ emerges as our Redeemer. However, the drama of salvation points to causes beyond any historical event, even that of Good Friday. Aquinas summarizes the efficiency at work in the mode of redemption as follows: "Christ as man . . . is, properly speaking, the immediate Redeemer, although the actual redemption can be attributed to the entire Trinity as to its first cause."[13] It is a feature of sound Catholic theology always to return to the transcendent causes of whatever qualifies as supernatural.

The fifth mode by which Christ's passion is effective brings to the fore another biblical notion, that of sacrifice. Sacrifice applies, in the words of Saint Augustine, to "every work performed for the purpose of being united to God in holy fellowship."[14] Holy fellowship is another way of expressing the communion of divine charity (*koinonia*) or beatitude. This mode of efficacy includes the reconciliation with God that Christ's sacrifice on the cross brings about. Aquinas draws our attention to an important distinction that locates precisely the way that sacrifice works in the Christian mysteries. "When we say that Christ's passion reconciled us to God, we do not mean that God has begun anew to love us, for it is written that 'with age-old love I have loved you' (Jer. 31:3). Thanks to Christ's passion the cause for hatred has been removed, both because sin has been wiped away and because compensation has been made in the form of a more acceptable good."[15] The mode of sacrifice will find new expression in the sacrament of the Holy Eucharist. The communion that Holy Communion creates among those who worthily receive this sacrament comes about when sinful disorders have been remedied by the Catholic believer's sacramental union with Christ in the Eucharist. Obviously, deliberate persistence in serious sin becomes incompatible, not to mention counterintuitive, with a Catholic's physical reception of this sacrament.

Although there are many ways to envision the relationship of Christ's death on the cross to our salvation, the five modes that Thomas Aquinas has constructed allow us to think in terms of a basic plan. The International Theological Commission, a Vatican entity inaugurated after the Second Vatican Council, acknowledges, moreover, the usefulness of what Aquinas has accomplished. The commission identifies five main elements of the Church's soteriological reflection: (1) the Christ gives himself; (2) he takes our place in the mystery of salvation; (3) he frees us "from the wrath to come" and from all evil powers; (4) in so doing, he fulfills the salvific will of the Father; and (5) he wants

13. *Summa theologiae* III.48.5.

14. Augustine, *The City of God* (*De civitate Dei*) 10.6, as quoted in *Summa theologiae* III.43.3.

15. *Summa theologiae* III.49.4 ad 2.

to insert us into the life of the Trinity through participation in the grace of the Holy Spirit. Then the commission acknowledges the following: "It is the task of later theology to show how these elements fit together. Thomas Aquinas underlines five ways in which the work of redemption takes effect: merit, satisfaction, redemption, sacrifice, and efficient cause. Other ways can no doubt be added."[16] The list that the International Theological Commission composed finds parallel expression in what Aquinas treats in two places in his writings: in his discussion of the abovementioned modes of efficacy and in question 49 of his *Summa theologiae*, which treats the effects themselves that the passion of Christ introduces into the world.

In summary, the mode of efficiency establishes a connection between the passion of Christ and the work of the Blessed Trinity. The mode of merit, which establishes a claim to a reward, points to the human will of Christ whereby he endured in patience and charity his bloody sufferings and violent death. The mode of satisfaction relates to the very flesh of Christ wherein he suffered the agonies associated with the passion—agonies, moreover, that afflicted both his body and his human soul. The mode of redemption signals that the passion changes the lot of fallen human nature. Lastly comes the mode of sacrifice, which perfects the worship that the religious person offers to God.

Sacraments and the Pierced Heart of Christ

From the earliest centuries of Christian reflection on the passion of Christ, the Church's authoritative writers have recognized the intimate connection that exists between the passion of Christ and the sacraments of the Church. One of the best and representative examples of these texts finds its way into the official prayer of the Church, the *Liturgy of the Hours*. For the Office of Readings, formerly known as *matins* because the office was traditionally sung in the very early morning hours, the Church has chosen an excerpt from a catechetical writing of the fourth-century doctor of the Church Saint John Chrysostom. He writes, "The gospel records that when Christ was dead, but still hung on the cross, a soldier came and pierced his side with a lance and immediately there poured out water and blood. Now the water was a symbol of Baptism and the blood of the Holy Eucharist. . . . From these two sacraments the Church is born."[17]

16. "Questions on Christology," 4.4.

17. International Commission on English in the Liturgy, *The Liturgy of the Hours* (New York: Catholic Book, 1976), 2:474. The Chrysostom text that *The Liturgy of the Hours* is here quoting, "Catéchèse III" (Catechesis 3), can be found in full at Jean Chrysostome, *Catéchèses bapistmales 1–8*, Sources Chrétiennes 50bis, trans. Antoine Wenger (Paris: Cerf, 1957).

Another indication of the archetypal place that this image holds in the practice of the Christian religion appears in a text from the *Roman Missal*. The preface (a prayer that introduces the eucharistic prayer at each Mass) assigned to the Feast of the Most Sacred Heart of Jesus contains this explicit reference to the relationship between the pierced side of Christ and the sacraments of the Church:

> For raised up high on the Cross,
> he gave himself up for us with a wonderful love
> and poured out blood and water from his pierced side,
> the wellspring of the Church's Sacraments.[18]

The symbolic, even poetic, language used in these liturgical texts points to the accounts of efficient causality that remain indispensable for Catholic sacramental theology. Recall that when Aquinas asks whether God is the efficient cause of all things, he replies in the affirmative: "All things," he says, "are caused by one first being which simply *is* in the fullest sense of the word"[19]—in other words, by that which possesses being *perfectissime*, most perfectly. God, who is sheer existence subsisting of his very nature (*ipsum esse per se subsistens*), alone fits this description. This God both creates and saves.

The modern scholar T. C. O'Brien has said that Aquinas's commentary on 2 Corinthians captures how creation and salvation differ. The text provides a succinct instruction on the two divine actions that terminate in diverse realities—that is, creation and salvation: "God is in all things through his own action, namely conjoining himself to them as the cause creating and preserving them in being."[20] This presence of God to all that exists has been described in the early theological tradition as God being in all things by presence, power, and essence. Aquinas, however, continues: "[God] is in the sanctified through *their* own acts, whereby they reach God and in a certain sense take hold of him, i.e., they love him and know him."[21]

18. *Roman Missal*, "Preface for the Most Sacred Heart of Jesus, Celebrated on the Friday after the Second Sunday after Pentecost."

19. *Summa theologiae* I.44.1 (emphasis original).

20. Thomas Aquinas, *Commentary on 2 Corinthians*, chap. 6, lect. 3, as quoted in T. C. O'Brien, *Father, Son, and Holy Ghost*, vol. 7 of the Blackfriars edition of *Summa theologiae*, by Thomas Aquinas, 260.

21. Aquinas, *Commentary on 2 Corinthians*, chap. 6, lect. 3, as quoted in O'Brien, *Father, Son, and Holy Ghost*, 260.

6

The Sacramental Economy

Catholic theology recognizes progressive stages in the unfolding of the visible signs that God supplies for the purpose of saving a fallen human race. These stages correspond roughly to the theological periods of salvation history. These periods, in turn, are marked by the several divine interventions that serve to keep the human person fixed on the true God. In order to understand how the various sacred signs figure into the several periods of salvation history, it is necessary to recall the basic givens that define the relationship between the human creature and God from the moment of creation. The Church, for her part, teaches that the "first man was not only created good, but was also established in friendship with his Creator."[1] Because this friendship established a proper ordering within the human person and between Adam and Eve, the first couple, as well as between them and all of creation, it is customary to refer to the state of original holiness as a state of "original justice."[2]

Original Justice and Original Sin

The reference to the virtue of justice signals that the just person orders all things well. Within this well-ordered universe, the human person's relationship with God requires no mediation. Harmony was a given of man's original state. Still, it is important to recall, as explained above, that the act of creation and the act of elevating Adam to the state of friendship with God make up two distinct acts of the divine will. The distinction arises not because of multiplicity in God but because of the effects of the divine action in the human person. In other words,

1. CCC no. 374.
2. See CCC nos. 375–76.

to be created as a human creature in its integrity does not require the special endowment of becoming friends with God.

The creation of the human person indeed creates a relationship between the Creator and the creature. This relationship, however, develops into what we know as the moral virtue of religion. Friendship, on the other hand, does not form part of religion's obligations. Religion rather ensures that the creature exhibits the required honor and worship to the Creator. This explains why Saint Thomas Aquinas refuses to number religion among the theological virtues. Religion perfects the human person in what is proper to humanity—namely, the obligation to honor and to show reverence to, indeed to worship, the Creator God. Religious people, not God, find perfection in religion, because their minds are subjected to God.

On the other hand, the theological virtues—faith, hope, and charity—directly unite the Christian believer to the Godhead.[3] These virtues elevate human nature to a participation in the Godhead that exceeds subjection. It remains a matter of speculation what form the practice of the virtue of religion would have taken in the state of original justice—that is, in paradise. However, since, as Aquinas and all the saints hold, the internal acts of religion are principal and essential, one may assume that exterior acts of religion did not figure in the "Garden."[4]

Original sin changes one's position before God. In a word, "the harmony in which [Adam and Eve] had found themselves, thanks to original justice, is now destroyed."[5] The lack of harmony that original sin introduces into human life affects how fallen human beings relate to God. No longer a friend, God becomes to them an object of fear. Adam and Eve are left with a "distorted image—that of a God jealous of his prerogatives."[6]

Still, various created effects remind fallen men and women of God, even though a distorted image of God hinders them from interpreting such effects rightly. Nevertheless, these created indicators point beyond themselves. When Aquinas describes the progressive divine pedagogy that draws the human race back from its disordered state, he cites Saint Augustine's *Contra Faustum*, a work that deals with the errors of the Manichaeans.[7] Aquinas begins by stating the principle that governs Augustine's opinion on sacraments through the history of the world: "Just as different states of time are signified by different words, namely present, past, and future, so too different sacraments are appropriate

3. See *Summa theologiae* II-II.81.5.
4. For an explanation of the Garden, see *Summa theologiae* I.102.1.
5. CCC no. 400.
6. CCC no. 399, citing Gen. 3:5–10.
7. Augustine, *Contra Faustum* 19.16 (PL 42:356).

to different states of time."[8] The text continues: "Thus we may recall that there was a time when there was no formally explicated code of law and the condition men lived in was governed by the law of nature, so that it was their interior instincts alone that prompted them to worship God. And correspondingly at that time it was men's interior instincts likewise that determined which sensible things they should use in the worship of God."[9]

Perhaps the best illustration of what both Aquinas and Augustine have in mind comes from the account in Genesis of Cain and Abel: "In the course of time Cain brought an offering to the LORD from the fruit of the soil, while Abel, for his part, brought one of the best firstlings of his flock" (Gen. 4:3–4). Aquinas again reflects the general Christian tradition when he explains why the sons of Adam seemed moved to express properly their religious instincts. "Immediately after the Fall," he writes, "because of the knowledge of Adam who was fully instructed in divine matters, faith and natural reason still flourished in man to such an extent that it was not necessary to determine certain signs of faith and salvation for man; rather each one manifested his faith through signs which he thought best."[10] The fratricide that follows upon the brothers' offerings shows that reasonable religious instinct did not suffice for long to ensure morally right conduct.

The Old Dispensation

To continue with Aquinas's account of how sacred symbols became formalized brings us to "around the time of Abraham" when, as Aquinas contends, the biblical narrative reveals both a diminishment of faith and reports of idolatry. He explains this infelicitous turn of events by appeal to carnal concupiscence, even including sins against nature, which drew the human race from the true worship of God. The Christian tradition does recognize the sacraments of the Old Law. These sacraments are described in the Old Testament when it treats the ceremonial rituals prescribed by the Law of Moses, especially in the books of Leviticus and Numbers. Aquinas considers these prescribed ceremonies as ordained for the worship of God, whereas he says that the judicial precepts govern relations within the human community. In fact, he compares the ceremonial precepts with the juridical ones: "The ceremonial precepts are particular

8. The text is found in *Summa theologiae* III.60.5, where Aquinas treats of prescribed materials for the sacraments.

9. *Summa theologiae* III.60.5 ad 3.

10. *Summa theologiae* III.70.2 ad 1.

applications of the moral precepts relating to God, just as the judicial are applications of those relating to one's neighbor."[11]

All in all, the Catholic tradition looks back at the sacred rites of the Old Law with appreciation since, from a Christian point of view, they pointed toward the Christ who would come into the world. "The sacraments of the Old Law," writes Aquinas, once again reporting Saint Augustine's opinion on the matter, "were foretellings of the Christ who was to come. And for this reason the meaning of Christ which they conveyed was less explicit than in the sacraments of the New Law, which spring from Christ himself and which . . . bear a certain similarity [*similitudinem*] to him."[12] The remarkable insight that the sacraments of the New Law look like or resemble Christ finds a more philosophical expression in the causal relationship that each of the sacraments enjoys with the Christ, who has suffered for us (*Christus passus*). By contrast, the sacraments of the Old Law served as so many protestations that pointed to the Christ who would suffer (*Christus passurus*).

The New Dispensation

The new dispensation follows the piercing of Christ's side by the soldier's lance while Christ hung dead on the cross. For this reason, the sacraments of the Catholic Church are uniquely endowed spiritual realities that perfect those who receive them with the proper dispositions. This general description of a sacrament finds authentication in an important text from Aquinas's *Summa*. "The term 'sacrament' is properly applied," says Aquinas, "to that which is a sign of some sacred reality pertaining to men; or . . . it is applied to that which is a sign of a sacred reality inasmuch as it has the property of sanctifying men [*signum rei sacrae inquantum est sanctificans homines*]."[13] In light of this definition, one may set forth three basic principles that fall under the heading of sacramental realism.

The first principle holds that the sacraments exist as "separated instruments" of the Trinity. Colman O'Neill observes succinctly that "the Trinitarian sacrament is specified therefore by the historical mission of the incarnate Word and the mission of the Spirit that follows upon it."[14] The missions of the divine persons of the Trinity point to the ways that the Son and the Holy Spirit are active in the sanctification of the world. For his part, Aquinas distinguishes

11. *Summa theologiae* I-II.101.1.
12. *Summa theologiae* III.60.6 ad 3.
13. *Summa theologiae* III.60.2.
14. Colman E. O'Neill, *Sacramental Realism* (Chicago: Midwest Theological Forum, 1998), 69–70.

between a visible mission of a divine person and an invisible mission.[15] What is characteristic of the missions appears when theologians discuss how the divine persons are present to the souls of the justified. The consensus among Catholic theologians holds for an experiential knowledge that results from the indwelling of the divine persons.[16] There is an affective quality to the divine indwelling that the sacraments both initiate and sustain.

Emphasis, however, on the psychological description of the union should not distract one from the fact that this affective knowledge reaches its term in the divine, although without involving a composition in being of the divine with the created. The sanctification of those who receive the sacraments produces within them real relations with the persons of the indwelling Trinity.[17] When Aquinas points out the relationship between knowledge and love within the processions of the Trinity, he captures the origins of the affective knowledge that marks Christian holiness. "As for the Son," Aquinas reminds his readers, "he is a Word, yet not an ordinary word, but the one who breathes love."[18] The sacraments of the Church not only originate in the divine Trinity but also bring the worthy recipient back to Father, Son, and Holy Spirit.

The second principle concerns the sacraments as lived professions of faith. We find the model for this confessional principle in the Blessed Eucharist. In short, only those who assent in faith to the Real Presence—that is, the real, true, and substantial presence of Christ's body, blood, soul, and divinity in the Eucharist—may approach Holy Communion. The other sacraments also require of their recipients a faith that is proportionate to the person's state. For example, the faith of the catechumen about to be baptized differs from the full-blown theological faith of the baptized who wish to receive fruitfully the other sacraments. The *Catechism of the Catholic Church* offers a general statement of the relationship between faith and the sacraments when it explains why evangelization through preaching must precede the administration of the sacraments. "The mission to baptize, and so the sacramental mission, is implied in the mission to evangelize, because the sacrament is prepared for by *the word of God and by faith* which is assent to this word."[19] Because they nourish, strengthen, and express the faith of the Church, the sacraments may be described as sacraments of faith.

15. See *Summa theologiae* I.43.1–8.

16. For a discussion of this important feature of Catholic spiritual theology, see Walter Farrell and Dominic Hughes, *Swift Victory: Essays on the Gifts of the Holy Spirit* (New York: Sheed & Ward, 1955).

17. For further explanation, see William J. Hill, *Proper Relations to the Indwelling Divine Persons* (Washington, DC: Thomist, 1952).

18. *Summa theologiae* I.43.5 ad 2.

19. CCC no. 1122 (emphasis original).

One must exercise care, however, not to conflate the efficacy of the sacraments with the faith of the one who receives them, as if the sacraments were so many external protestations of graces received independently of them. Of course the preaching of the gospel, especially in its sole authoritative venue—from the pulpit within the liturgical celebration—possesses its own unique efficacy.[20] In short, this efficacy is measured by the reception that the preaching receives in a given soul. Still, some theologians argue that authoritative preaching possesses a quasi-sacramental efficaciousness.[21] Catholic theology holds that the divine agency at work in the preaching of the Word of God and the administration of the sacraments to those worthily prepared differs according to kind. The informed rhetoric of the preacher and the moved dispositions in the hearer combine to bring about some kind of assent in the one who hears the gospel.[22] In the sacraments celebrated in the Church, on the other hand, the Catholic Church, for instance at the Council of Trent, affirms that the sacraments act *ex opere operato* (literally, "by the very fact of the action's being performed").[23]

Colman O'Neill takes up this teaching in the context of the twentieth-century debates within Catholic theology that overly emphasized the subjective disposition of the recipient in order to account for the efficacy of the sacramental administrations. "The difference [between word and sacrament] is not to be defined in terms of the community's faith, nor in terms of the general sacramentality of the church. It can be derived only from a totally gratuitous initiative of the Blessed Trinity and of the risen Christ."[24] This graciousness on the part of God explains a feature of Catholic piety and devotion that counsels Catholics to thank him for the sacraments received. The "Thanksgiving after Mass" for priests and the thanksgiving after the reception of Holy Communion for laypeople afford some examples, whereas Catholic couples oftentimes make various consecrations to

20. Thus the provision of the *Code of Canon Law* that reserves the homily to clerics: "Among the forms of preaching, the homily, which is part of the liturgy itself and is reserved to a priest or deacon, is preeminent; in the homily the mysteries of faith and the norms of Christian life are to be explained from the sacred text during the course of the liturgical year" (can. 767 §1).

21. See, e.g., Thomas D. Rover, "The Sacramental Efficacy of the Act of Preaching," in *Proceedings of the Seventeenth Annual Convention*, by Catholic Theological Society of America, 241–47 (Washington DC: Catholic Theological Society of America, 1963).

22. According to Catholic teaching, in the conversion of the sinner, the first assent to the truths preached is not full-blown theological faith but what the tradition calls the *pius credulitatis affectus* (pious affect of credence).

23. See *CCC* no. 1128, citing the Council of Trent (1547), *DS* 1608: "If anyone says that through the sacraments of the New Law grace is not conferred by the performance of the rite itself but that faith alone in the divine promise is sufficient to obtain grace, let him be anathema." One may assume that the council fathers intended to counter certain opinions that circulated within the Church at that time.

24. O'Neill, *Sacramental Realism*, 78.

Our Lady after their celebration of Matrimony.[25] Likewise, after priestly ordinations, it has been customary that the newly ordained priests join the congregation in singing Mary's hymn of thanksgiving, the Magnificat (see Luke 1:46–55).

The third principle that governs Catholic sacramental practice concerns the true worship of the Father that the Church's liturgy fulfills. We find a succinct and trinitarian summary of what the sacramental dispensation accomplishes in the catechism: "The Father is acknowledged and adored as the source and the end of all the blessings of creation and salvation. In his Word who became incarnate, died, and rose for us, he fills us with his blessings. Through his Word, he pours into our hearts the Gift that contains all gifts, the Holy Spirit."[26] In the Christian tradition, the word *liturgy* means the participation of the baptized in the work of redemption. In the Church's enactment of the liturgy, which includes not only the sacraments but also the preaching of the gospel that both announces and explains them, all that God bestows on the human creature is fully revealed and communicated. The transformative power of the liturgy works itself out in the theological virtue of charity, whereby the baptized love God above all things on account of his own goodness and love their neighbors as themselves. Divine charity, of course, enables the believer to both manifest and express the image-perfection that describes his or her sanctification.

Catholic theology further emphasizes the global dimensions of liturgy: "In the liturgy the whole public worship is performed by the Mystical Body of Jesus Christ, that is, by the Head and His members."[27] Catholic theology also treats preaching and evangelization on its own terms as part of the Church's mission to draw all people to her embrace. Likewise, the workings of theological charity and its relationship to the grace that justifies fall under the heading of moral theology (at least in the Thomist schema of theology) or, in some Catholic authors, under the heading of dogmatic theology. All in all, however, liturgy mainly concerns the sacraments.[28]

The relationship between liturgy and sacraments becomes apparent when one considers the contents of part 2 of the catechism, which deals with the "sacramental dispensation."[29] The main division of part 2 splits it into two sections: section 1 is called "The Sacramental Economy," and section 2 is called "The Seven Sacraments of the Church." Section 1 is divided into two chapters. The second

25. The *Code of Canon Law* even urges the practice of thanksgiving for priests who celebrate the Eucharist. See can. 909: "A priest is not to neglect to prepare himself properly through prayer for the celebration of the eucharistic sacrifice and to offer thanks to God at its completion."

26. *CCC* no. 1082.

27. *Sacrosanctum Concilium*, no. 7 (VRL).

28. See *CCC* no. 1097: "In the *liturgy of the New Covenant* every liturgical action, especially the celebration of the Eucharist and the sacraments, is an encounter between Christ and the Church" (emphasis original).

29. See *CCC* no. 1076.

chapter discusses the general principles that govern Catholic liturgical celebrations. Chapter 1 sets forth the basic elements of sacramental theology under the heading "The Paschal Mystery in the Age of the Church." This same first chapter contains two articles that set forth what Catholic theology holds about liturgy in the global sense. The first article explains the cardinal principle of Catholic sacramental theology, which is discussed earlier under the heading "The Liturgy-Work of the Holy Trinity." The second article then focuses on the sacraments themselves under the general heading "The Paschal Mystery in the Church's Sacraments." Five subdivisions provide basic Catholic teaching on the following points: (1) the sacraments of Christ, (2) the sacraments of the Church, (3) the sacraments of faith, (4) the sacraments of salvation, (5) the sacraments of eternal life.[30]

To bring the global considerations of liturgy into specific sacramental focus, it is important to state that the Church definitively and authoritatively recognizes seven sacraments. The names of the sacred seven are as follows: Baptism, Confirmation (also known as Chrismation), Eucharist, Penance and Reconciliation, Anointing of the Sick, Holy Orders, and Matrimony.[31] As will be seen below, theologians have produced reasons that fittingly explain the number and the ordering of the sacraments that belong to the new dispensation.

30. These details are found in *CCC* nos. 1113–34.

31. The seven sacraments of the Church are often considered in relation to the seven gifts of the Holy Spirit, which also form a "sacred seven." See, for instance, Henry Foemby, *Sacrum Septenarium; or, The Seven Gifts of the Holy Ghost: As Exemplified in the Life and Person of the Blessed Virgin for the Guidance and Instruction of Her Children* (London: Burns, Oates, 1874). The same author earlier published a book on the seven sacraments.

7

Christ, Justification, and Faith

The emphasis that the Church places today on the global, even cosmic, dimensions of liturgy—namely, on the participation of her members in the work of God (John 17:4)—owes its place, broadly speaking, to the enthusiasm for *ressourcement* theology that developed in Europe, especially in France, during the first half of the twentieth century. This return-to-the-sources movement insisted on the importance of, among other resources from earlier centuries, the writings of the Church fathers from both the East and the West.

When one speaks of a global dimension to the liturgy, the purpose is to point out the all-embracing perspectives that many of the ancient Christian writers attached to the Church's liturgical celebrations. One text from *Sacrosanctum Concilium* captures this global dimension: "In the earthly liturgy we take part in a foretaste of that heavenly liturgy which is celebrated in the holy city of Jerusalem toward which we journey as pilgrims, where Christ is sitting at the right hand of God, a minister of the holies and of the true tabernacle."[1] Like the style employed by the author of the book of Revelation, the patristic use of biblically inspired symbolic language provides inspiration and sparks the imagination. At the same time, the images require proper interpretation and legitimate explanation in order to provide guidance for those who, precisely as pilgrims, require recognizable signposts to move them toward heaven.

The Person of Christ

In order to understand the central role that Christ plays in the liturgy both on earth and in heaven, one must recall the important truth that the Church

1. *Sacrosanctum Concilium*, no. 8 (VRL).

proclaimed at the Council of Chalcedon. The *Catechism of the Catholic Church* summarizes this truth about the Incarnate Word as follows: "There is but one hypostasis [or person], which is our Lord Jesus Christ, one of the Trinity."[2] This means that no independent subject exists in the human nature of Christ, which always remains an instrument of his divinity. When we say that Christ acts in the sacraments, the Catholic faith proclaims that one of the Trinity acts in the sacraments.

Saint Thomas Aquinas captures this mystery at the start of the third part (*tertia pars*) of his *Summa theologiae*: "Our Savior, the Lord Jesus Christ, as he was, according to the angel's witness, 'saving his people from their sin,' showed *in his own person* that path of truth which, in rising again, we can follow to the blessedness of eternal life."[3] It is fair to say that, while Aquinas uses language that can be understood analogically, he captures in the thirteenth century what in the twentieth century the Church affirms about her liturgy, even though his account may lack the poetic inspiration that sparks the imagination of some aesthetically trained readers. At the same time, his philosophically inspired terms require less literary criticism in order to explore their meaning than does, for example, the poetry found in the book of Revelation.[4]

To summarize: Christ the God-man works through the sacraments. The *Catechism of the Catholic Church* offers three reasons for this foundational tenet of Catholic and divine faith: "Christ's work in the liturgy is sacramental: because his mystery of salvation is made present there by the power of his Holy Spirit; because his Body, which is the Church, is like a sacrament (sign and instrument) in which the Holy Spirit dispenses the mystery of salvation; and because through her liturgical actions the pilgrim Church already participates, as by a foretaste, in the heavenly liturgy."[5]

What does it mean that God dispenses the mystery of salvation through the sacraments? On a personal level, the answer to this question is known experientially by those who observe what is required in order to embrace a complete Catholic life. However, theologians, oftentimes under the impetus of theological

2. The text comes from the Council of Constantinople II (553), as cited in CCC no. 468. For a catechetical presentation of what the Church holds in faith about the Incarnate Word, see CCC nos. 464–78, esp. 467–68, which summarize the conclusions of the fourth ecumenical council, held in 451 at Chalcedon, and also of the fifth ecumenical council, held at Constantinople in 553.

3. *Summa theologiae* III.prologue (emphasis added).

4. For further discussion, see Thomas G. Weinandy, "The Human Acts of Christ and the Acts That Are the Sacraments," in *Ressourcement Thomism: Sacred Doctrine, the Sacraments, and the Moral Life*, ed. Reinhard Hütter and Matthew Levering (Washington, DC: Catholic University of America Press, 2010), 150–68.

5. CCC no. 1111.

confusions and debates, have established some common features of how the mystery of salvation takes hold of an individual believer.

Justification and Faith

The practitioners of dogmatic theology fill volumes with their explanations of the gift of divine grace, the virtue of faith that accompanies it, and the justification that describes the person who is a beneficiary of God's predestining love. When we consider that the catechism describes justification as "the most excellent work of God's love," such a literary monument to the fruitfulness of Christian theology should come as no surprise.[6] Disputes about the true nature of biblical justification, how one achieves it, what it results in for the justified person, and what mediations are required in order to make a person justified before God continue to occupy Christian theologians.[7] The essentials of Catholic teaching may be found in the catechism.[8] In brief, "Justification establishes *cooperation between God's grace and man's freedom*."[9]

How one is to understand this cooperation has become a matter of dispute among Catholic theologians, especially since the late sixteenth-century *De Auxiliis* controversy. What has become known as the Dominican position—after the members of the Order of Friars Preachers who developed it in dialogue (so to speak) with theologians from the Society of Jesus (or Jesuits)—places emphasis on the divine omnipotence that manifests itself in the predestining love that God bears for his creatures.[10] One attempt to bridge the differences that divide Lutherans and Catholics on the workings of justification took place at the approach of the new millennium. Although some agreement on general principles was reached, the interested parties failed to produce agreement on the details of what constituted justified Christian existence within the Church of Christ.[11]

6. *CCC* no. 1994.

7. For a brief but comprehensive account of one reductionist position adopted at the time of the sixteenth-century Protestant Reform, see Steven Ozment, *Protestants: The Birth of a Revolution* (New York: Doubleday, 1993). Ozment reports on how the Reformation eliminated the sacraments as "empty ritual."

8. See esp. *CCC* nos. 1987–95 and the cross-references to these numbers.

9. *CCC* no. 1993 (emphasis original).

10. For further discussion, see Steven A. Long, "Providence, Freedom, and Natural Law," *Nova et Vetera* (English ed.) 4, no. 3 (2006): 557–606; and Romanus Cessario, "Molina and Aquinas," in *A Companion to Luis de Molina*, ed. Alexander Aichele and Matthias Kaufmann (Leiden: Brill, 2013), 291–323.

11. For a report on the official deliberations, see the discussion surrounding the "Joint Declaration," *L'Osservatore Romano*, January 26, 2000, 9–10. For a popular account of the failed effort to reach some consensus between Catholics and Lutherans on justification, see Daphne Hampson, "Whales and Elephants," *The Tablet*, March 23, 2001, 446–47.

Because justification occurs, insofar as the Catholic Church knows, only within the context of the sacraments of salvation, especially Baptism and Eucharist, we can speak of a "sacramentalized freedom."[12] When the Catholic Church stresses the connection between justification and the sacraments, she does not ignore that the grace of justification shapes human freedom in a way that disposes humans to act in accord with the moral requirements of the New Law. In other words, she does not shift the divine action away from its effect on human freedom and into a mysterious and possibly superstitious dependence on empty rituals.

Catholic teaching follows what Thomas Aquinas says about the coming into existence of the theological virtues. In his discussion of theological faith, Aquinas clearly holds for the priority of faith over hope and charity when he answers the question about whether, among the virtues, faith is first. Further, Aquinas recognizes that human involvement in a person's movement toward justification engages the affective powers of human nature. On this process that leads to justification, one commentator observes, "In the final act of an adult's complete conversion from non-belief and sin to belief and grace, the infusion of grace, including charity, and the active turning to God in belief and love are simultaneous; yet there is a pattern of priority in meaning among the various elements—thus knowing before loving."[13]

Why does the Church insist on this priority of faith in the nature of conversion? Again, Thomas Aquinas offers a reason: "Some will-act," he writes, "is prerequisite to faith, but not an act informed by charity. An act of charity does presuppose faith, since the will can respond to God in perfect love only if the mind has a right faith in him."[14] It goes without saying, of course, that the will-act that is prerequisite to faith does not fall outside the loving designs of divine providence. To hold otherwise would return the Christian believer to some form of the Pelagian heresy.

The Divine Intimacy

Catholic theology and Catholic practice view the saving work of Christ and the sacraments as an ensemble. Each of the seven sacraments contributes variously to the sanctification of God's people. Catholic theology puts such discreet emphasis on the mode of efficiency—that is, the role that efficient cause plays in the

12. See *CCC* no. 1257 on the necessity of Baptism.

13. T. C. O'Brien, *Faith*, vol. 31 of the Blackfriars edition of *Summa theologiae*, by Thomas Aquinas (New York: McGraw-Hill, 1974), 142, note *h*. O'Brien provides a helpful commentary on the engagement of the human will in the process of justification.

14. *Summa theologiae* II-II.4.7 ad 5.

administration of the sacraments—because it is deeply interested in the result that the sacraments promise to those who receive them worthily. In a word, the sacraments make us knowers and lovers of God—Father, Son, and Holy Spirit.

In the aforementioned biblical commentary where Saint Thomas Aquinas comments on chapter 6 of the Second Letter to the Corinthians, we learn how our being created differs from our being sanctified. In the text on which Aquinas comments, Saint Paul appeals to his audience "not to receive the grace of God in vain" (2 Cor. 6:1). Aquinas then takes the occasion to explain the divine indwelling in the souls of the justified and how it comes about in those to whom God gives his divinizing grace. Recall that Aquinas first distinguishes the relationship that God sustains with the human creature from that which he creates in those who are sanctified by grace. Aquinas writes, "While we say that God is present in all things by presence, power and essence, we do not say that he dwells in them, but only in those who are sanctified by grace."[15] How does God "dwell" in the souls of the sanctified? As already mentioned, Aquinas explains: "He [God] is in the sanctified through *their* own acts, whereby they reach God and in a certain sense take hold of him, i.e., they love him and know him, and one who loves and knows has what he loves and knows within him."[16] This text, of course, touches on the heart of Christian living.

The divine indwelling consists in the presence of the divine persons to the justified soul as objects known and loved. This union sometimes receives the qualification "intentional." However, one should not interpret *intentional* in a purely cerebral way, such as one finds in a great deal of modern philosophy. *Intention* in a scholastic context derives from the words "tending toward" (*intendere*). The gift of divine grace makes it possible for the Christian believer who is animated by divine charity to tend toward the three divine persons. In this supernatural "tending toward," there exists no split between subject and object. Rather, the gift of divine grace received establishes the believer in a relationship that tends toward an end. This movement reaches its finality when the same believer attains, within the limits set down by a created soul, the divine persons themselves and in their own way of being. This attainment, of course, is realized by the supernaturally elevated acts of knowledge and love that justification makes possible in the believer.

Catholic spiritual authors speak about the divine intimacy. Consider one fairly well-known example. Father Gabriel of St. Mary Magdalen was a Discalced

15. Thomas Aquinas, *Commentary on 2 Corinthians*, chap. 6, lect. 3, as quoted in T. C. O'Brien, *Father, Son, and Holy Ghost*, vol. 7 of the Blackfriars edition of *Summa theologiae*, by Thomas Aquinas, 260.

16. Aquinas, *Commentary on 2 Corinthians*, chap. 6, lect. 3, as quoted in O'Brien, *Father, Son, and Holy Ghost*, 260 (emphasis original).

Carmelite priest who became one of the most revered twentieth-century masters of the spiritual life. His signature publication, *Divine Intimacy*, provides meditations that are meant to assist the Catholic in drawing from the several seasons and feasts of the Church's liturgical year lessons that may help him or her to discover the divine intimacy.[17] The Discalced Carmelite Nuns of Boston arranged to make an English edition of this book available in the United States. The book received an uncommon blurb from a Pope who is now a saint. Pope Saint John XXIII said of Father Gabriel's work, "This book of meditations is meant for all priests, seminarians, religious, the devout laity, all who aspire to greater union with God: that is, to divine intimacy." Catholic theology refuses to make authentic teaching on the divine indwelling the private property of theologians.

17. Gabriel of St. Mary Magdalen and Discalced Carmelite Nuns of Boston, *Divine Intimacy: Meditations on the Interior Life for Every Day of the Liturgical Year* (Gastonia, NC: Tan Books, 1997).

8

Efficacy and Sacramental Character

When due consideration is given to the divine indwelling in the souls of the justified, it becomes clear that each of the sacraments of the Church possesses a permanent effectiveness. The kind and nature of the permanence that each sacrament confers differ among each of the sacred seven. Before consideration of the tripartite structure of each sacrament, which includes treatment of the sacramental character, can be suitably undertaken, some further reflection on how Christ enters into the administration of the sacraments proves useful.

Divine Action in History

To posit the role of the risen Christ in any theory of sacramental efficacy leaves open a question that saints and theologians have discussed since the earliest moments of the Church's history. Briefly put, How is this entry of Christ into the sacramental action to be envisaged? Truth to tell, various answers to this question have appeared throughout the course of that same history. In the twentieth century, the general question became a topic of discussion partly under the influence of certain modern thinkers who philosophized about history and partly as a result of a reprisal of the Neoplatonic heritage that accompanied the interest that *ressourcement*-minded theologians took in the Greek fathers. Those who engaged in these debates asked what sense can be made of the transhistorical significance of past events. In other words, how can something such as the passion, death, and resurrection of Christ that took place in the first century serve as a causal explanation for events that transpire in subsequent centuries?

One answer to this question was developed in the course of various efforts to reform the liturgical practices that had, by the twentieth century, largely gone unchanged since the baroque period. During the baroque period, especially in Europe, political structures, such as elaborate thrones for bishops, and cultural amenities, such as bowing and the doffing of birettas, exercised a certain influence on the liturgical customs of the Roman Church. The liturgy, as many handbooks of the period actually affirmed, was considered to be "the etiquette of the great King."[1]

As already explained, Father Leeming, in the mid-twentieth century, drew the attention of his specialized audience mainly composed of sacramental theologians to the work of the German Benedictine Dom Odo Casel (d. 1948). In the account of Colman O'Neill, Casel's "mystery presence" theory does not offer a completely satisfactory explanation for the divine causality at work in each of the sacraments. O'Neill's own words make this clear: "It cannot be legitimate to insist, as did those in the liturgical movement who accepted Dom Odo Casel's 'mystery-presence' theory, on the apparent realism of places such as *Romans*, ch. 6, and go on to assert that the historical death and resurrection of Christ are represented and reactualized in the action of baptism. The philosophical difficulties about this kind of telescoping of real events are too great."[2] Father O'Neill goes on to explain that Romans 6 becomes more readily understandable when the description of the baptismal effects is read "against the background of belief in the real union that exists between the risen Christ and his members."[3]

This opinion based on the principles of classical Thomism should provide comfort to those who receive the sacraments of the Catholic Church. What is more important, O'Neill's exegesis of Romans 6 becomes evidently correct when one recalls the affirmation that Saint Paul makes early in this chapter of Romans: "We were indeed buried with him through baptism into death, so that, just as Christ was raised from the dead by the glory of the Father, we too might live in newness of life" (Rom. 6:4). The newness of the administration of the sacraments requires a more satisfactory explanation than that made by an appeal to symbolic representations.

In short, Casel's reliance on Platonic realism to account for the liturgy's authenticity and his extreme emphasis on the subjective appropriation of the liturgical action requires a somewhat arcane philosophical frame of mind in order to appreciate its coherence. Casel's explanation appeals, in Father O'Neill's analysis,

1. See the observations made in Giles Dimock, "Revisiting the Baroque," *Antiphon: A Journal for Liturgical Renewal* 5, no. 3 (2000): 8–10. The author refers to a quotation on baroque liturgy taken from Louis Bouyer, *Liturgical Piety* (Notre Dame, IN: University of Notre Dame Press, 1954), 4.

2. Colman E. O'Neill, *Sacramental Realism* (Chicago: Midwest Theological Forum, 1998), 121.

3. O'Neill, *Sacramental Realism*, 121.

"only to those rooted in the neo-platonic heritage of the Greek Fathers."[4] It is one thing to construct a descriptive image of how the liturgy operates; it is another task to render an explanation of what real results the liturgical celebration of the sacraments brings about.

It is not difficult to grasp why the theologians of the Church found the Aristotelian account of efficient causality the best way to express what Saint Paul means when he describes Baptism as making it possible for the human person to "live in newness of life" (Rom. 6:4). Even when the several schools of theology that developed after the medieval period opted for different ways to account for the effects of the sacraments, they all agreed that the sacraments do accomplish something in the believer that touches upon the spiritual dimension of human existence.[5] This widespread acceptance of some version of causal action to explain the effectiveness of the sacraments did not, however, develop only on the basis of interpretations of biblical texts. And this even though the New Testament offers many texts that refer to the "new creation" that the sacraments create. For instance, see 2 Corinthians 5, where the author concludes, "So whoever is in Christ is a new creation: the old things have passed away; behold, new things have come" (2 Cor. 5:17). The Church authoritatively holds that this text teaches about the transformation of human nature that Christ works through the sacraments.

The Dogmatic Constitution on the Church, *Lumen Gentium*, makes the following explicit statement of Catholic and divine faith about the relationships that exist between the Blessed Trinity, the humanity of Christ, the Church, and her sacraments: "In the human nature united to Himself the Son of God, by overcoming death through his own death and resurrection, redeemed man and re-molded him [*transformavit*] into a new creation. . . . In that [mystical] Body the life of Christ is poured into the believers who, through the sacraments, are united in a hidden and real way to Christ who suffered and was glorified."[6] The Latin text employs the word *transformavit* to make it clear that the fallen human race exists in a state other than that of the redeemed or transformed. Were this not the case, then there would exist nothing to serve as the subject of the transformation.

Of course, twentieth-century Catholic theology went to great lengths to examine the disposition of unredeemed human nature that renders it suitable for

4. O'Neill, *Sacramental Realism*, 121.

5. For a comprehensive rehearsal of the various opinions that Catholic theologians have developed over the course of the centuries, see Emmanuel Doronzo, *Tractatus dogmaticus de sacramentis in genere* (Milwaukee: Bruce, 1946).

6. *Lumen Gentium*, no. 7 (VRL), citing Gal. 6:15; 2 Cor. 5:17.

the gift of justifying grace.[7] For the present purposes of this discussion of the sacraments of the Catholic Church, it is helpful to observe that the Second Vatican Council, in the above-quoted document, refers to an important text from the *Summa theologiae* of Saint Thomas Aquinas that summarizes the efficacy that attaches to the flesh of Christ. The text associates the creative power of the Word of God at creation with the "life of the soul" that comes about instrumentally through the mysteries accomplished in the flesh of the Incarnate Word. The relevant text comes from a reply to an objection posed in response to the question of whether the sacraments of the New Law derive their power from the passion of Christ. The objection rests on a text—attributed, perhaps mistakenly, to Saint Augustine—that comments on bodily resurrection. Nonetheless, as he so often does, Saint Thomas here finds a way to clarify theological matters without offending the received authority of so important a teacher in the Church as Saint Augustine: "As having been in the beginning with God, the Word acts as a principal agent in imparting life to souls, but at the same time his flesh and the mysteries enacted in this have an instrumental function in contributing to the life of the soul."[8] The reply goes on to observe that with respect to right moral conduct, the mysteries of Christ's life also exercise a "certain exemplarity" (*quandam exemplaritatem*).[9]

No wonder the Thomist tradition and other theologians who followed the Thomist commentators chose to speak about a perfective physical causality at work in the sacraments. They recognized not only that the sacraments of the New Law accomplish something positive in the individual who receives them but also that this accomplishment perfects the human being in the supernatural order.[10] Further, because, as the adage goes, grace perfects nature, the sacraments strengthen as well that which is properly human in the worthy recipient.

7. For a comprehensive discussion of these debates, written under the direction of professor Steven A. Long, see Taylor O'Neill, *Grace, Predestination, and the Permission of Sin: A Thomistic Analysis* (Washington, DC: Catholic University of America Press, 2019).

8. *Summa theologiae* III.62.5 ad 1.

9. Moral theologians should take note of the relationship that Aquinas establishes between being and acting. Those who have become the beneficiaries of the transformation that the sacraments communicate also find the wherewithal to fulfill the commandments of the New Law that Christ himself by his virtuous living exemplifies as well as teaches. This explains why the treatment of the sacraments in part 2 of the *Catechism of the Catholic Church* comes before instruction about the Christian moral life in part 3.

10. For a classic description of the thesis about perfective instrumental causality, see Doronzo, *Tractatus dogmaticus de sacramentis in genere*, 165–66: "Hoc systema intendit causalitatem sacramentorum in sensu pleno explicare, docens sacramenta habere realem et physicum influxum in ipsam gratiam, quatenus a Deo assumuntur et elevantur in instrumenta divinae virtutis, ipsis communicatae et in ipsis ac per ipsa operantis, eo analogico modo quo causae naturales per physica et naturalia instrumenta operari dicuntur."

Tripartite Structure of the Sacraments

Catholic theologians who defended the thesis that the sacraments of the New Law work by a perfective physical causality (*causalitatis physicae perfectivae*) were not misguided in plying their craft. This evaluation holds true, even though they made good use of categories that belong to philosophical systems whose origins in some cases antedate the Incarnation. Sound Catholic theologians do not hesitate before the question of whether Athens has anything to do with Jerusalem. Rather, such theologians appeal to an analogy with physical and natural instruments in order to safeguard what the Church teaches about sanctifying grace. *Sanctifying grace* means the grace of justification—what might be suitably described as "the whole organism of the Christian's supernatural life."[11]

In order to give a full account of the sign-action that describes the constitutive element of each sacrament, it is convenient to introduce categories that have become standard in Catholic sacramental theology. Catholic theologians are familiar with the tripartite structure of a sacrament. In this classical model, the three constituents of a sacrament are listed under the headings (1) *sacramentum tantum*, (2) *res et sacramentum*, and (3) *res tantum*.

Historical Background

The remote origin of this tripartite theological distinction that applies to each of the sacraments may be found in the eucharistic controversies of the early Middle Ages. At the same time, it also serves, in a seminal way, Saint Augustine's earlier distinction between the truth of a sacrament (its *validity*) and the personal appropriation of a sacrament (its *fruitfulness*). Emmanuel Doronzo traces the proximate origin of the expressions to Peter Lombard (d. 1160) and the theologians of his period. Thomas Aquinas and the other theologians of the golden age of scholastic speculation developed the tripartite distinction. Later doctors and teachers in the Church sought further to explain and apply the tripartite structure to the ensemble of sacramental practice.[12] The tripartite division serves to explain how the various elements that enter into the administration of a sacrament combine to produce the effects that the Catholic Church recognizes in each of her sacraments.

Saint Augustine's use of the distinction between a sacrament validly administered and a sacrament fruitfully received arose not from conceptual reflection

11. CCC no. 1266.

12. See Doronzo, *Tractatus dogmaticus de sacramentis*, 319: "Haec doctrina detegi potest veluti in semine apud S. Augustinum, originem habet a Petro Lombardo et doctoribus eiusdem aetatis, evolvitur a S. Thoma et theologis saec. 13, explicatur et applicatur a posterioribus doctoribus."

only. The distinction came into use in order to provide a resolution to one of the earliest controversies that developed among Christian believers. A crisis that emerged in northern Africa during a period of fierce persecution provided the occasion for the Church to explain authoritatively how the power inherent in her sacraments works. The subsequent heresy that was condemned at the fourth-century Synod of Arles goes by the name of Donatism, after a sectarian bishop who argued that the holiness of the Church must be shared in by her ministers in order for the sacraments that they administer to produce their effects. Saint Augustine, in his refutation of the wrongheadedness of these dissenters, "erected a landmark in the understanding of the sacraments."[13]

Within Catholic theology, this landmark has been expressed in theological shorthand as the distinction between a valid sacrament and a fruitful sacrament. In the sixteenth century, the Council of Trent found it necessary to reaffirm this distinction when it numbered among its canons on the sacraments in general this admonition: "If anyone says that the sacraments of the New Law do not contain the grace they signify or that they do not confer that grace on those who do not place an obstacle in the way, . . . let him be anathema."[14]

What Saint Augustine discovered from his study of the Church's early sacramental practice concerns those who do place an obstacle in the way of their receiving a communication of divine grace. Contrary to what one might call a commonsensical reaction to the spiritual viability of sinful Catholics, Saint Augustine came to realize and to explain that the sacraments of the Church, especially Baptism, produce an intermediate effect—what O'Neill refers to as an "abiding sacrament"—even when the spiritual state of the one who administers or receives them lacks the proper disposition for spiritual growth.[15] In short, because a person may receive a sacrament validly but not fruitfully, the Church acknowledges that the sacraments possess a tripartite structure that includes, in addition to the rite employed to administer the sacrament and the grace received in a worthy reception, an intermediate effect or something that abides even in the unworthy recipient.

The abiding sacrament is not a theological hypothesis that some Catholic theologians hold whereas others do not. Instead, this distinction is required to give a theological account of the fact that the Church does not repeat certain sacraments. The rebaptism controversy of the third century first brought the matter to the fore. A disagreement arose as a result of the practice of the Church in North Africa of not recognizing Baptisms administered by apostates. Saint

13. O'Neill, *Sacramental Realism*, 130.
14. Council of Trent, Session 7, Canons on the Sacraments in General, can. 6, *DS* 1606.
15. O'Neill, *Sacramental Realism*, 132–35.

Cyprian of Carthage defended the practice of baptizing (again, as it were) those Christians already baptized by apostates, whereas the Pope in Rome clearly affirmed that "it is not the personal sanctity of the minister which assures the validity of baptism, but the majesty of God which works through the names."[16]

The third century—which still found the Church under attack from alien political regimes, of course—did not afford the leisure required for theologians to formulate expressions of doctrine in the way that developed later in the history of the Church. To tell the truth, the third century witnessed the age of martyrs. Pope Saint Stephen I, the Roman Pontiff who corrected the views of Saint Cyprian, died a year before him, in 257. Cyprian himself was executed by the Roman authorities for his refusal to participate in pagan worship. Because of the primacy of the Roman See to which he adhered, Cyprian did defer to Pope Stephen's authority.

The opposing views of the two saints that surround the third-century rebaptism controversy reflect not so much their theological speculation or even their faith presuppositions as their differing fundamental outlooks on what the virtue of religion requires. Saint Cyprian, whose Roman obedience kept him from heretical formulations, and especially the later Donatists held to the intuition that the practice of religion should be accomplished by people who exhibit probity of life. In other words, by an altogether recognizable human instinct, those who initially subscribed to the propositions and practices of what would become identified as a heresy considered that religion and its exercise should belong properly only to the saints. They concluded, in simpler terms, that holy things belong to holy people.

What Pope Stephen taught, however, placed the theological emphasis, not on the dispositions of either those who administered the sacraments or those who received them, but on the power of God at work in the sacraments. In what might be called an inchoate attempt to explain the mode of efficiency, Pope Stephen I pointed not to human beings but upward toward "the majesty of God which works through the names." Eventually, the pronouncement of the Roman Church and the subsequent First Synod of Arles (314–35) inspired Saint Augustine to distinguish between the existence ("truth") of a sacrament and its fruitfulness. The difference comes down in Catholic practice to the distinction between a sacrament validly received and one worthily received with its full spiritual fruits.

16. Burkhard Neunheuser, *Baptism and Confirmation*, trans. John Jay Hughes, The Herder History of Dogma (New York: Herder & Herder, 1964), 102–3. For a scholarly discussion of this debate, see Neunheuser's treatment in chap. 4, "The First Theological Classifications; the Controversy over Heretic Baptism (Third Century)," 92–106.

Saint Augustine's writings are replete with refutations of the Donatists' errors, one of which insisted on the blamelessness of the minister. One especially poignant text comes from his commentary on John 1:33. There he shows why even sacraments administered by those who are sinners are sustained by Christ himself who, through them, continues his saving mission:[17]

> They then whom Judas baptized were not baptized again. And were those whom John baptized, baptized again? Clearly they were, but not with a repetition of the baptism they had before. For those whom John baptized, were baptized by John, but those whom Judas baptized, were baptized by Christ. In like manner, therefore, they whom a drunkard hath baptized, or a homicide, or an adulterer, if the baptism was Christ's, it was Christ who baptized them. I do not fear an adulterer, nor a drunkard, nor a murderer, for I harken to the Dove, through whom it is said to me, "This is he which baptized" (John 1:33).[18]

The tripartite distinction that Catholic theology employs to explain how the sacraments work takes full account of the active role of the risen Christ in the bestowal of each sacrament. In the quarrels generated by diverse pastoral practices and one-sided views about how to sustain a holy life, the Church learned a great lesson about the saving omnipotence of God. She came to express clearly what motivates God's love for his creatures. In short, God loves us because he is good, not because we are. A proper metaphysics could easily conclude that God could not suffer movement from a cause outside himself and still remain God. However, as Aquinas makes clear, human reason comes to conclusions about God only after a long time and with an admixture of error. Certain members of the Church of Christ, on the other hand, required correction on an important issue of sacramental administration, and this grace was given to her through the Roman Pontiffs and holy teachers like Saint Augustine.

Sacred Signs

As already discussed, the abiding sacrament, which is a kind of intermediate effect of the sacramental action, appears in the Latin usage as the *res et sacramentum*. In this phrase, the Latin word *sacramentum* refers to the sign-action that lies at the heart of each sacramental administration. The use of the word

17. For a lucid account of the development of doctrine that culminates in St. Augustine's distinction between a sacrament and the working out of a sacrament, see O'Neill, *Sacramental Realism*, 128–38.

18. Augustine, *Tractates on the Gospel of John* 5.18, in *Nicene and Post-Nicene Fathers*, series 1, vol. 7, ed. Philip Schaff, trans. John Gibb (Buffalo: Christian Literature, 1888). Slightly revised.

sign to describe a sacrament gained currency in Catholic theology largely under the impetus of Saint Augustine and the early medieval theologians who followed him.[19] Conceptual confusions arose. It is held that Aquinas put some order into the use of *sign* when he explained that the term *sacrament* may be "applied to that which is a sign of a sacred reality inasmuch as it has the property of sanctifying men."[20] Aquinas's premier interpreter, the sixteenth-century Dominican thinker Cardinal Cajetan, emphasized the importance of Aquinas's remark. He says that Aquinas took pains to make this definition of a sacrament not only to show reverence for Saint Augustine but also because it had become common in the practice of the Church to describe sacraments as signs.[21]

Of course, the sacred sign comes into existence only when the sacramental action is administered properly. Indeed, the sacraments require administration by an authorized minister who possesses a correct intention. The sacraments of the New Law employ everyday symbolic actions such as washing, anointing, eating and drinking, and so forth. The intention and the words that the minister brings to these actions make the sign-action an instrument of salvation. So the Church holds that the "visible rites by which the sacraments are celebrated signify and make present the graces proper to each sacrament."[22] In short, according to the catechetical formula, the sacraments are visible signs of invisible grace.

Catholic theology does not consider the sacraments as so many sacred objects that in themselves contain divine power. Aquinas clarified this important point when he corrected the view of some earlier theologians who held that a sacrament contains grace as a vessel contains liquid. "A sacrament," he says, "has a threefold function. It is at once commemorative of that which has gone before, namely the Passion of Christ, and demonstrative of that which is brought about in us through the Passion of Christ, namely grace, and prognostic, i.e., a foretelling of future glory."[23] This text locates the efficacy of the sacraments, as already discussed, within the overall saving mission of Christ.

19. For a classical locus for St. Augustine's use, see his *De doctrina Christiana*, book 2 and book 3, chaps. 6–9.

20. *Summa theologiae* III.60.2.

21. See Cajetan's *Commentary on the Summa* (*In Summam*), commenting on *Summa theologiae* III.60.2: "Scito . . . quod Auctor non solum pro reverentia sic definientium sacramentum, sed etiam pro firmando usu Ecclesiae, quo sacramentum dicimus, non cujusque rei sacrae signum, sed homines sanctificantis, descriptionem hanc in definitionem erexit" (Know . . . that Aquinas sets up this description in a definition not only for reverence toward those who define a sacrament so, but also for buttressing the usage of the Church, which says that a sacrament is not any sign of a sacred thing, but [only] of one that sanctifies men). My trans.

22. *CCC* no. 1131.

23. *Summa theologiae* III.60.3. This text is quoted in *CCC* no. 1130 as a conclusion to its instruction on the Church's sacraments.

The term *res* serves as the Latin shorthand for the reality of the sacrament. The reality of each sacrament appears in the fruit of the sacramental reception. "The fruit of the sacramental life," affirms the *Catechism of the Catholic Church*, "is that the Spirit of adoption makes the faithful partakers in the divine nature (see 1 Pet. 1:4) by uniting them in a living union with the only Son, the Savior."[24] The particular graces that each sacrament produces correspond to the nature and purpose of each of the sacred seven.

Abiding Sacrament

The expression *res et sacramentum* refers, as already explained, to an intermediary term of the sacramental action, a sort of "interior sacrament" that, in a word, accounts for the divine action at work in a duly administered sacrament. The sacrament, understood as *res et sacramentum*, always marks the one who receives it, except in the extreme case when either the minister or the recipient thwarts the ordering of divine causality by consciously and maliciously withholding the required intention. This extraordinary circumstance effectively makes for a parody of pastoral care and not for the administration of a sacrament of salvation. The subject of intention requires a full exposition, which follows when we discuss the origins of sacramental mediation.

While Catholic theology has developed views on the *res et sacramentum* for each of the seven sacraments of the Church, three of the sacraments possess this effect of sacramental action in a way that impedes a person from receiving the sacrament again. The *Catechism of the Catholic Church* explains this point with reference to the notion of character or seal: "The three sacraments of Baptism, Confirmation, and Holy Orders confer, in addition to grace, a sacramental *character* or 'seal' by which the Christian shares in Christ's priesthood and is made a member of the Church according to different states and function."[25]

The use of the word "character" to describe what happens in the conferral of Baptism, Confirmation, and Holy Orders owes its origin to the theological imagination of Saint Augustine. In his reflection on the aforementioned rebaptism controversy of the third century, Saint Augustine appealed to the image of a brand-mark on a sheep, a practice in shepherding that identified which sheep belonged to which shepherd. Baptism conferred by someone outside the bounds of the Church, as has been determined by an early Roman Pontiff, nonetheless does leave its mark or effect on the one baptized. "Even when a

24. CCC no. 1129.
25. CCC no. 1121.

wandering sheep has received the Lord's brand-mark at the hands of dishonest robbers," writes Saint Augustine in one of his anti-Donatist writings, "and then comes into the security of Christian unity, it is restored, freed, and healed; but the Lord's brand-mark is recognized, not disallowed."[26] The Greek word for brand-mark, *charaktēr*, comes into English as *character*.

As the abovementioned text of the catechism indicates, character brings with it membership in the Body of Christ and participation in the worship of the Church. Saint Augustine's analogy of the brand-mark can lead some to interpret the *res et sacramentum* of the sacraments that bestow character in a static or even material way. Indeed, the Church's description of character as "an indelible spiritual sign on the soul" often came to be explained popularly as "an indelible spiritual mark." However, Aquinas clarifies the true nature of the sacramental character when he describes the character as a spiritual power that consecrates, as it were, the practical intellect, one of the cognitive powers of the soul.[27] The sacraments that bestow character prepare the Christian, diversely in accordance with his or her vocation in the Church, for the acts that are associated with the worship of God: preaching, Eucharist, and service in charity. Some theological traditions employ the word *seal* (from the Greek, *sphragis*) to describe character.[28]

It is generally held that the thought that character comes about as a participation in the priesthood of Christ owes its best formulation to the work of Thomas Aquinas. In *Summa theologiae* III.63, Aquinas discusses the implications of what he states boldly and simply about sacramental characters which, in his account, "are nothing else than certain kinds of participations in the priesthood of Christ deriving from Christ himself."[29] Because this kind of participation occurs in a person only as the result of a divine power that even personal sin cannot obstruct, the character is considered indelible. For no matter how much human freedom acts against the sanctification of a person, "character," says Aquinas, "is not removed because of the changelessness of the principal power."[30] He means God. In order to explain the permanence of the divine creative act at work in the sacraments, Catholic theology refers in various ways to an ontological bond that the sacraments that bestow character establish between the recipient and Christ.[31]

26. Augustine, *On Baptism, against the Donatists* 6.1, in *The Later Christian Fathers*, ed. Henry Bettenson (Oxford: Oxford University Press, 1970), 241.

27. See *Summa theologiae* III.63.4.

28. See CCC no. 698 on the seal of the Holy Spirit.

29. *Summa theologiae* III.63.3.

30. *Summa theologiae* III.63.5 ad 2.

31. See, e.g., John Paul II, *Pastores dabo vobis*, no. 11.

The Ritual

The tripartite distinction also includes what is called the *sacramentum tantum*. The English translation may appear as the "sacrament only" or "just the sacrament." This element of the sacrament points to the liturgical ritual or visible sign that each sacrament possesses. "The visible rites by which the sacraments are celebrated signify and make present the graces proper to each sacrament."[32] So Catholic teaching holds about the sacred rites that accompany the administration of each sacrament.

As instruments of Christ's saving mysteries, the sacraments are not magic. The sign character of the sacraments serves the purpose of ensuring that meaningful words combine with identifiable gestures or elements to play the instrumental role that Christ ordained the sacraments to fulfill. The following commentary succinctly summarizes what is operative in the *sacramentum tantum*. A sign, writes one theologian, is "something pointing to a reality beyond itself, and rendering it present to the beholder." The author continues: "In the case of the sacrament, a meaningful form of words is combined with a material gesture or material element so as to reinforce the vaguer and less determinate significance which the gesture or element is conceived to have in itself. The two together then constitute a well-defined sign ordained by Christ and causing the reality which they signify."[33]

Because of the importance that words, gestures, and material elements play in the administration of the sacraments, it comes as no surprise that the Church safeguards the integrity of the sacramental actions. "No sacramental rite," she insists, "may be modified or manipulated at the will of the minister or the community."[34] Why? God has not confided this authority to them.

Grace

The final element in the tripartite structure of a sacrament that remains to be treated is called the *res tantum*. Again, the English translation can be rendered "just the reality" or "the reality only." *Res* in this context points to what the sacraments accomplish in the spiritual lives of worthy recipients. To determine the nature of such graces, one may consider what is signified by each of the sacraments—namely, the particular grace that each of the seven communicates to the worthy recipient. As has already been explained, since certain dispositions are required in the person who receives a sacrament, one who lacks the

32. CCC no. 1131.

33. David Bourke, *The Sacraments*, vol. 56 of the Blackfriars edition of *Summa theologiae*, by Thomas Aquinas (New York: McGraw-Hill, 1975), 160.

34. CCC no. 1125.

appropriate disposition can be deprived of the sacrament's fruitfulness. For example, a person who abides in serious sin may not be properly disposed to effectively receive a sacrament. So the *Catechism of the Catholic Church* states simply, "Celebrated worthily in faith, the sacraments confer the grace they signify."[35] Within the general teaching on the working of divine grace, the *res tantum* of each sacrament points to the participation in the divine nature that the sacraments cause. Other graces flow from this divinizing effect of the Church's sacraments.

Sacramental Graces

Catholic theology also recognizes a category of special *sacramental* graces proper to each sacrament.[36] As the catechism states, "There are *sacramental graces,* gifts proper to the different sacraments."[37] Theologians differ when they come to explain what these sacramental graces look like for each sacrament as well as how these *sacramental* graces differ from sanctifying or habitual grace.

A helpful explanation of the difference between common and sacramental grace holds that sacramental graces provide actual (as opposed to habitual) graces that assist the Christian to accomplish what each sacrament contributes to the building up of the Church. One obvious example concerns Matrimony. The sacramental graces that come with this sacrament assist the spouses to fulfill the obligations of fidelity and fecundity that the sacrament requires of them. Something similar happens with the other sacraments: Baptism confers the grace to remain faithful to the promises made at the time of the Baptism. Confirmation adds to the baptismal grace the strength required to profess the faith outside the family structure. The Eucharist strengthens the recipient's charity and communion among the members of Christ's Body. Penance and Reconciliation helps the forgiven sinner remain penitent. The Anointing of the Sick fortifies the dying Catholic against the temptations that death occasions. Lastly, Holy Orders strengthens men to remain faithful to the obligations of the clerical state.

35. CCC no. 1127.
36. See CCC no. 1129.
37. CCC no. 2003.

9

The Nature of a Sacrament

Some general statements can be made about the nature of a Christian sacrament and its structure. Saint Thomas Aquinas conveniently discusses these themes in the first question of his treatment of the sacraments in the *Summa theologiae*.[1] In that work, it proves useful to recall the transition that Aquinas makes from his discussion of the mysteries of Christ's life to his presentation of the sacraments of the Church. In the introduction that precedes question 60 of *Summa theologiae* III, Aquinas writes, "Now that we have completed our consideration of the mysteries of the Incarnate Word, our next field of investigation is the sacraments of the Church, seeing that it is from the same Incarnate Word that these derive their efficacy." The first three articles of question 60, the question in the *Summa*'s third part that explains what a sacrament is, examine the sign character of a sacrament. The very first article of the question asks simply "whether sacraments fall under the general category of signs." The discussion in these articles sets forth basic Catholic teaching on what makes a sacrament a sign, even though later theologians have fleshed out Aquinas's exposition in various ways.

Further Reflection on Signs

When we ask to what general category of things a sacrament belongs, the answer that Aquinas gives establishes the normative instruction for subsequent theological discussion. Alternative explanations had been proffered by theologians of earlier periods. The actual term *sacrament* probably was introduced into

1. See *Summa theologiae* III.60.1–8.

Christian theology by the early Christian writer Tertullian, who applied the term broadly to a whole range of things associated with the Christian religion.[2] However, the notion that the Christian religion uses external, visible things to conceal invisible, divine power dates from the earliest days of Christianity. Indeed, from the moment that the Word of God "was incarnate of the Virgin Mary, and became man," the Christian religion has been committed to recognizing invisible divine power at work in visible created things.[3] For his part, Aquinas develops Saint Augustine's notion of sacred sign, a thought that may have some connection to the philosophy that inspired Alexandrian theological reflection in general and that of Origen in particular. In sum, the first three articles of question 60 discuss the reasons that lead the Church to affirm that a sacrament is a sign of the redemptive mystery in action. Catholic theology does not make totems of the Church's sacraments.

When a general category is sought to identify a sacrament, some alternatives are excluded. For instance, it is wrong to conclude, as some have proposed, that sacrament provides the religious alternative to medicament. Sacrament makes holy, whereas medicaments make well. Or, if one identifies a sacrament after the Greek usage, *mysterion,* then perhaps, it has been argued, sacrament belongs to the general category of those things that remain hidden. On the other hand, such a designation only serves to indicate that the sacraments are not included in the common properties of the human race. Again, others have held that sacraments may fall into the category of oaths, since the usage appears in some ancient canonical literature. This usage, however, does not allow the analogical flexibility required by Catholic theology to relate the seven sacraments "to some one thing which is the sacred reality."[4] In other words, Christian thinkers familiar with the sacramental practice of the Church have conjured up explanations that do not always fit the requirements of a Christian sacrament. Such proposals fall into the category of speculation that does not conform to the givens of divine revelation.

Neither Aquinas nor the other great theologians of the thirteenth century have made the problem of identifying the nature of a sacrament go away. Questions about the nature of a Christian sacrament arose, for instance, at the time of the sixteenth-century reform. It is reported, for instance, that during the Dispute at Lausanne held in 1536, the Catholic side was challenged

2. For a short discussion of the history of the notion of sacrament in Catholic theology, see David Bourke, *The Sacraments,* vol. 56 of the Blackfriars edition of *Summa theologiae,* by Thomas Aquinas (New York: McGraw-Hill, 1975), xiii–xxiii.

3. The quoted text comes from the Niceno-Constantinopolitan Creed as found in the *Roman Missal,* "Profession of Faith."

4. *Summa theologiae* III.60.1 ad 3.

by certain scholars to find the word "sacrament" in the Bible. No Catholic cleric, so it was reported, was available or perhaps was able to respond to the challenge, so a Catholic physician took up the question. He admitted that the term *sacramentum* does not appear in the Vulgate Bible, but then he noted that *sacramentum* should be read to mean "holy mind" (*sacra mens*). Loyal but better instructed in Latin than in theology, this Catholic physician retorted that the Bible serves to make men's minds holy, and so it does in fact treat of the sacraments.[5]

This answer, of course, did not lay to rest the objections raised by Huldrych Zwingli (d. 1531) and others. On the contrary, skepticism about the sacraments continued, as the clarifications made at the Council of Trent illustrate.[6] One may conclude that in order to understand properly to which general category of reality sacraments belong requires close and reasoned examination.

Aquinas draws on Saint Augustine's general appeal to the visible and invisible elements of the Christian religion to settle the dialectical inquiry that ends by favoring signs. In short, one should consider the sacraments as signs. More technically, Aquinas concludes from the tradition: "We assign sacraments to the general category of signs."[7] Some three hundred years later, one of the bright stars of the baroque Thomist commentatorial tradition, an Iberian Dominican named João Poinsot, better known by his name in religion, John of Saint Thomas (d. 1644), provided a working definition of *sign*: "A sign is what presents to a cognitive faculty something other than itself, and for which the sign takes its place."[8] According to this definition, the sacraments belong to the intentional order—that is, to the order of human knowing. *Intentional* in this context means "reaching out toward," as when the knowing power, the intellect, goes out and toward that which it knows.

Aquinas and the ecclesiastical tradition that follows him help to canonize the expression that the sacraments are "efficacious signs of grace."[9] However, the category of sign can open up into an expansive treatment of not only the sacramental signs but also the religious symbolism that accompanies the administration of the sacraments. Aquinas greatly aids Western theological reflection when

5. For more information, see *La Dispute de Lausanne (1536)*, proceedings of the Colloque international sur la Dispute de Lausanne, Université de Lausanne, 1986 (Lausanne, Switzerland: Bibliothèque historique vaudoise, 1988).

6. For a discussion of how the thought of Aquinas exercised an influence on the deliberations and decisions of the council, see Romanus Cessario, "Sixteenth-Century Reception of Aquinas by the Council of Trent and Its Main Authors," in *The Oxford Handbook of the Reception of Aquinas*, ed. Matthew Levering and Marcus Plested (Oxford: Oxford University Press, 2021), 159–72.

7. *Summa theologiae* III.60.1.

8. John of St. Thomas, *Cursus theologiae*, tomus 1. My trans.

9. CCC no. 1131.

he teaches that the signs are always sign-actions—that is, that sacramental signs always employ both specific material objects and determinate spoken words.

To advance the discussion of sacraments as signs, some more distinctions are required. The sacraments appear as conventional signs rather than purely natural ones, such as smoke signaling fire. That said, the material elements that the sacraments employ show a natural resemblance to the graces that they bestow. So, for example, washing fits Baptism as a cleansing from sin. Anointing with oil suits sacraments that strengthen and heal. Foodstuffs become the Eucharist, which provides nourishment for the baptized.

Conventional signs count as a sort of language, as when a red light signals drivers to stop their vehicles. Saint Augustine emphasizes the importance of the sacraments as conventional signs when he writes, "A sign is something which, over and above the specific form which it impresses upon the senses, causes some further object to enter our cognition."[10] Baptism brings new life; Confirmation gives spiritual strength to the soul; Holy Anointing heals the sickness of soul and even of body; the Eucharist feeds those who receive it worthily with the body and blood of Christ, who draws them into himself, unlike ordinary food that the body absorbs.

While there are many signs of sacred reality (*sacra rei signum*), as the early thirteenth-century theologians held, so the Church holds, again following Saint Augustine, that the word *sacrament* is said properly of those signs that, in the words of Aquinas, "signify the perfection of human sanctity" (*significant perfectionem sanctitatis humanae*).[11] The *Catechism of the Catholic Church* takes up this theme when it affirms that the sacraments of the Church, each of the seven, "make actively present the salvation wrought by Christ."[12] The key word in this catechetical shorthand stands out as "actively." In other words, the sacraments are conventional signs that accomplish something in the recipient beyond the natural effects of material elements they employ.

In order to emphasize that the sacraments combine both sign and action, the Catholic tradition further recognizes that the sacraments are practical signs. That is, sacramental knowledge is ordered to some kind of action—namely, the sanctification of the human person. The third article of question 60 exhibits how Aquinas and the Catholic tradition break with a mechanical view of the sacraments. Critics of Catholic sacramental theology often allege that Catholics treat the sacraments as so many talismans—that is, as objects thought to possess magical power. It is true, of course, that presentations of Catholic

10. Augustine, *De doctrina Christiana* 2.1, as quoted in Bourke, *Sacraments*, 15.
11. *Summa theologiae* III.60.2 ad 3.
12. CCC no. 1152.

theology that lack finesse can succumb to the temptation to present the sacraments as so many mechanical operations to which Catholics must submit themselves. This view was sometimes unwittingly abetted by moral theologians who discussed the sacraments as so many casuistic exercises of personal responsibility—for example, by asking questions such as when a Catholic is obliged to receive this or that sacrament. In any case, Aquinas clearly avoids this kind of sacramental automatism when he discusses sacraments in terms of cause, form, and end.

Further Reflection on Cause

When the theologian examines properly the lines of causal explanation that unpack the sacramental economy, the result provides edification. One comes to appreciate the seven sacraments as moments in the drama of the Christian life that the administration of each sacrament signals.[13] For instance, Aquinas first points to the actual cause of the sanctification of the human person. As already explained, this consideration makes the sacrament a sign of the passion of Christ. Next, he describes the form of human sanctification, which Aquinas locates significantly in grace and the virtues. Briefly put, grace means the sanctification of the person, whereas the virtues provide for the sanctification of a person's actions. Finally, Aquinas places the signification of human sanctification within the context of its finality or overall completion, which—as the gospels make clear—happens in heaven, or the attainment of a blissful eternal life.

The theoretical knowledge of salvation that the Scriptures and the preaching of the Church provide grounds the practical knowledge of the sacraments. In other words, sacraments cannot be made to serve whatsoever purpose—as, for example, when some persons request sacramental administrations for their pet animals. The sacraments serve as signs of salvation as preached in the Church. "In the sacraments of Christ," says the catechism, "the Church already receives the guarantee of her inheritance, and even now shares in everlasting life."[14]

To put cause, form, and end differently, the sacraments are the cause of our sanctification (the passion of Christ), the form of our sanctification (grace and the virtues), and the ultimate end (eternal life). One may observe, as Aquinas in fact does in the third article of question 60, that this threefold signification centered on the effects of Christ's passion can be described as commemoration,

13. For further discussion, see Romanus Cessario, "Sacramental Causality: *Da capo!*," *Nova et Vetera* (English ed.) 11 (2013): 307–16.

14. CCC no. 1130.

demonstration, prognostication. This description of the practical significance of the sacramental signs appears also in his poetry—for example, in an antiphon that Aquinas composed for the liturgical Feast of Corpus Christi: "O sacred banquet, in which Christ is received, the memory of his Passion is renewed, the mind is filled with grace, and a pledge of future glory is given to us."[15]

It is possible to recognize the symbolic role of the Church's sacraments inasmuch as each possesses a certain likeness to that which it signifies. Indeed, Aquinas is so convinced of this feature of the sacraments that he argues for an isomorphic relationship between the matter of the sacrament and its effect: "In choosing which sensible realities are to constitute sacramental signs, we choose the ones most commonly employed in the activity in which the meaning of the sacramental effect is symbolized."[16] He then gives the example of water, which people most commonly employ for physical washing, as the appropriate sign of spiritual washing. Aquinas's words provide a salutary reminder that the liturgical celebrations within which the sacraments are usually administered must observe the prescriptions set down in the liturgical books. Efforts to make changes to the liturgical rites run the grave risk of disfiguring the resemblance that the sacraments should manifest with Christ's passion.

The *Catechism of the Catholic Church* makes a point of relating the sign character of a sacrament to the life of faith. "Because they are signs," the text says of the sacraments, "they also instruct."[17] Indeed, the sacraments may be considered a sign of the faith of the saved inasmuch as some instruction is required in order to prepare a person even to receive a sacrament. A paradigmatic moment in the New Testament illustrates this sequence of Word and sacrament. An Ethiopian court official was returning from Jerusalem to his home when he encountered a deacon named Philip, who—at the official's prompting—"opened his mouth and, beginning with this scripture passage [Isa. 53], . . . proclaimed Jesus to him" (Acts 8:35). The instruction clearly must have included something about the Church's teaching on the necessity of Baptism. For the Ethiopian "ordered the chariot to stop, and Philip and the eunuch both went down into the water, and he baptized him" (Acts 8:38). According to this account in the Acts of the Apostles, Philip's instruction based on Sacred Scriptures became the occasion for the Ethiopian official to make an act of faith.

15. The antiphon for the Magnificat at vespers for the Feast of Corpus Christi: "O Sacrum convivium, in quo Christus sumitur: recolitur memoria passionis eius; mens impletur gratia et futurae gloriae nobis pignus datur."

16. *Summa theologiae* III.60.7 ad 2.

17. CCC no. 1123.

The Relation of Sacraments to Faith

The place that faith holds in accounting for the efficacy of the sacraments as instruments of human sanctification requires careful examination. Catholic theology, for example, does not envisage that justification by faith can replace the efficacy of the sacraments as powers capable of sanctifying those who receive them. Likewise, the Church does not regard the sacraments as mere external protestations of a sanctification that comes about only as a result of an interior action such as belief. As the example of Philip and the Ethiopian court official illustrates, the New Testament construes Baptism as something more than a profession of faith. At the same time, the Church does not envisage the sacraments as being fruitfully administered apart from a profession of the Church's faith. In a clear exposition of the difficulties that the relationship of faith and Baptism brought out at the time of the sixteenth-century reform, Colman O'Neill writes as follows: "There is, nevertheless, a certain priority given to baptism, not as in any way contrasted with faith, but as a rite which in some way encompasses faith, even though it is well understood that faith owes its origin to the ministry of the word."[18] This explanation describes perfectly what the Acts of the Apostles records about Philip and the Ethiopian court official.

Some general remarks serve to capture standard Catholic teaching on the relationship to a person's interior dispositions and the reception of the sacraments. First, one can understand that a sacrament expresses the faith of the person who benefits from its reception. O'Neill makes the claim that "when Saint Paul speaks of faith, he understands it as the faith of one who has been baptized."[19] Still, it is possible to give lie to the sacramental action, as when the recipient consciously and purposefully withholds the intention to participate in the saving mystery. This species of fraudulent activity provides the default line for what is said about sacramental efficacy. Again, the sacraments are not magic acts that override the most serious of indispositions with regard to their very reality.

Second, the sacraments express the faith of the Church, and essentially so, since "when the Church elaborates the sacraments, she confesses the faith received from the apostles."[20] This ecclesial confession of faith finds a certain concretization in the person of the minister. As long as the minister of a sacrament does what the Church specifies and with the intention of doing that which Christ

18. Colman E. O'Neill, *Sacramental Realism* (Chicago: Midwest Theological Forum, 1998), 118. For the full dimensions of this issue, see the whole of O'Neill's chap. 5, "Baptism: Word and Sacrament."

19. O'Neill, *Sacramental Realism*, 118.

20. CCC no. 1124.

and the Church intend, the sacrament works its effect. Personal holiness or theological sophistication does not affect the minister's effective instrumentality.

Third, the catechism describes a sacramental celebration "as a meeting of God's children with their Father, in Christ and the Holy Spirit."[21] Sacramental mediation provides a place of meeting between the Christian and Christ in which a living, formed faith plays an obvious role. Otherwise the encounter would result in producing a strange anonymity that is foreign to revealed religion. Christ does not teach his followers to address an anonymous god. This encounter means that the sacraments may be thought of more as a meeting of Christ in the sacraments than as a dispensing of Christ, even though the communication of divine grace may rightly be considered a kind of dispensation.

Matter and Form

The remaining articles of *Summa theologiae* III.60 discuss the composition of the Church's sacraments. Traditional Catholic usage employs an analogy drawn from what Aristotelian philosophy considers the essential parts of a physical reality. Form and matter may be described simply as that which determines the nature of something (its form) and that which is determined (its matter). Physical reality is said to be composed of an intelligible form and a material component disposed to receive it. It does not require much reflection to see why theologians were drawn to make an application of this hylomorphic structure to the Christian sacraments. Each of the sacraments requires determined words and a specific kind of matter.

In an apostolic letter of 1896, Pope Leo XIII begins by making an important distinction—one, moreover, that shows how, by the nineteenth century, the teaching Church had become well accustomed to the use of the categories of matter and form in discussions of the sacraments. The question of the validity of Anglican ordinations provides the historical circumstance that prompted the letter, *Apostolicae curae et caritatis*. "In the rite of confecting and administering any sacrament," Pope Leo XIII affirms, "one rightly distinguishes between the ceremonial part and the essential part, which it is customary [*consuevit*] to call matter and form."[22]

The history of the various ways the Magisterium has employed this expression dates at least from the start of the fifteenth century. Pope Martin V (d. 1431) refers to "the proper matter and form" in a document dealing with the errors of the English cleric John Wycliffe (d. 1384) and the Czech reformer Jan Hus

21. *CCC* no. 1153.
22. *DS* 3315 (translation slightly altered).

(d. 1415).[23] Theologians, however, have employed the language of form and matter since Thomas Aquinas put forth the analogy in question 60: "From words and things as combined in the sacraments a certain unity is constituted similar to the unity constituted by form and matter, a unity namely which . . . exists in virtue of the fact that the power inherent in the materials to act as signs and convey meaning is brought to its fulness through the words."[24] After Aquinas, the practice of speaking about a sacramental hylomorphism also became commonplace, although variations on the theme were not unknown, notably among the followers of Duns Scotus (d. 1308).[25]

What purpose does the hylomorphic composition serve? The reason that Aquinas gives to explain matter-and-form composition in the sacraments rests on the fact that the human person comes to a knowledge of intelligible things, such as signs, precisely through such composed, sensible realities. So each of the seven sacraments must appear as sensible realities. For Aquinas, this arrangement is not something that theologians devised to further their utilization of Aristotle's philosophy. Rather, the fact that each sacrament possesses something that can be grasped by the sense powers of the human soul reflects the divine Wisdom that "governs all things well" (see Wis. 8:1). The Church adopts this line of argument: "As a being at once body and spirit, man expresses and perceives spiritual realities through physical signs and symbols."[26]

Briefly put, this rule concerning sensible realities holds true, as indicated above, for each of the seven sacraments. The sensible reality may appear as a substance, as in the unique case of the Eucharist, which uses bread and wine. Or it may appear as a gesture, which nonetheless requires something determined, as in Baptism, Confirmation, Anointing of the Sick, and Holy Orders. Or it may appear as a human act concretized by a gesture and a word, as in contrition for Penance and mutual consent for Marriage. These sensible or "perceptible realities" are required, much like the words of the Sacred Scriptures, because of the condition of human knowing.[27]

The resemblance of the sacraments and the Sacred Scriptures lies in the fact that both employ sensible realities to illustrate or communicate spiritual realities to the human race. Additionally, because the sacraments involve not only human sanctification but also divine worship—that is, what each creature owes God—determined sensible realities are required. Aquinas makes an astute

23. *DS* 1262.

24. *Summa theologiae* III.60.6 ad 2.

25. For further information, see Albert Michel, "Matière et forme dans les sacrements," in *Dictionnaire de théologie catholique*, vol. 10.1 (1928), cols. 335–55, esp. 339.

26. *CCC* no. 1146.

27. See *CCC* no. 1148.

observation about the use of determined things in divine worship when he replies to an objection that the New Testament seems to exclude things such as food and drink from the kingdom of God (see Rom. 14:17). "Considered in their intrinsic nature," Aquinas replies, "sensible things do not pertain to the worship or the kingdom of God, but do so only inasmuch as they are signs of those spiritual realities in which the kingdom of God consists."[28] Catholic theology eschews favoring the purely physical to explain divine things.

Determined Realities

The sensible realities that remain indispensable for the human person's worship of God and for his or her sanctification by God are not left to the personal choice of the Christian believer. The sacraments use prescribed materials, or what Aquinas calls determined things (*determinatae res*). Even in the Middle Ages, some thinkers demurred before this restriction. Since Christ came to save all men, they argued, it is not fitting that the well-being of the human race should be restricted by divine law, and more particularly by the law of Christ. Aquinas, however, quotes Saint Augustine, who accounts for the determined forms that the Church fixes for each sacrament by appeal both to the ignorance of sinful human beings, who might not know how to worship God properly, and—what is more important—to the surpassing dignity of the grace of Christ, by which the human race is sanctified.

At the same time, no persons should consider themselves inconvenienced by the need to use determined things in the sacraments. "For the materials which it is necessary for us to use in the sacraments are either such as people generally have in their possession or such as it costs little trouble to obtain."[29] The Church interprets the prescription for designated matter strictly, and therefore refuses to accommodate the materials used for the sacraments to the peculiar circumstances of various regions of the world. She still insists on both bread for the Eucharist in places where wheat agriculture is not possible and wine in places that do not cultivate vineyards.

The perceptible signs alone are not sufficient to accomplish what the sacraments do for the sanctification of human beings. The sacraments of the Church also require determined words to express the saving reality to which the material things are put. Not any water bath, not any anointing with oil, not any eating of bread and drinking of wine serves to introduce, strengthen, or sustain the participated life of divine grace in a human person. For many reasons, this principle of Catholic sacramental theology requires patient reflection at the start

28. *Summa theologiae* III.60.4 ad 2.
29. *Summa theologiae* III.60.5 ad 3.

of the twenty-first century. Various factors in modern culture have led many persons, even those who should know better, to hold that the adaptation of the sacramental words is legitimate when done for the reason of recognizing changing cultural and societal practices and outlooks. The Catholic Church, on the other hand, regards the administration of the sacraments, including the liturgical ceremonies that surround it, as an expression of divine truth, "a constitutive element of the holy and living Tradition," and so forbids the modification or manipulation of any sacramental rite.[30]

Specific Words

Among the reasons for the use of determined words in the administration of the sacraments, three arguments from the tradition stand out. Saint Augustine, in his *Tractates on the Gospel of John,* provides a groundwork for subsequent theological reflection when he writes that "the word is conjoined to the element and the sacrament is constituted."[31] The first argument may be described as the christological, or incarnational, principle. What makes the sacraments of the New Law—the sacraments of the Catholic Church, distinct from all other signs of sacred reality, even the divinely prescribed rites found in the Old Testament—is that the sacraments of the New Law spring from Christ himself and even bear a certain similarity to him.[32]

Theologians see a parallel between the mystery of the Incarnation, in which the Word of God takes on flesh in the womb of the Virgin Mary, and the constitution of a sacrament. One writes, "As prolongations and extensions of the incarnate Word it is fitting that the sacraments should correspond in structure to it and consist of both words and fleshly realities."[33] The reason for asserting this resemblance of a sacrament to the Incarnate Word rests on the foundational principle of efficacy—that is, the sacraments' sanctifying cause. Since the sacraments of the New Law derive their efficacy from the Incarnate Word, they should bear some similitude to his unique personal constitution—namely, "Jesus Christ is true God and true man."[34]

30. *CCC* no. 1124. See also *CCC* no. 1123.

31. See Augustine, *Tractates on the Gospel of John,* Tractate 80 (on John 15:3), in *Nicene and Post-Nicene Fathers,* series 1, vol. 7, ed. Philip Schaff, trans. John Gibb (Buffalo: Christian Literature, 1888). Aquinas cites this text in the *sed contra* ("on the other hand") of *Summa theologiae* III.60.6. The text from Augustine runs as follows: "The word is added to the element, and there results the Sacrament, as if itself also a kind of visible word."

32. This poignant expression is found in *Summa theologiae* III.60.6 ad 3: "The sacraments of the New Law . . . spring from Christ himself and . . . bear a certain similarity to him."

33. Bourke, *Sacraments,* 20na.

34. CCC no. 464.

One metaphor that finds formal expression in the liturgical texts of the *Roman Missal* captures what is at stake in the incarnational principle. In the votive Mass in honor of the Most Sacred Heart of Jesus, the preface, a prayer said by the priest before the start of the eucharistic prayer, contains these impressive lines (which were quoted above, in chap. 5):

> For raised up high on the Cross,
> he gave himself up for us with a wonderful love
> and poured out blood and water from his pierced side,
> the wellspring of the Church's Sacraments.[35]

So the sacraments look like the One who is the source of their efficacy, inasmuch as each sacrament comes about by the speaking of words that combine with a sensible element.

Since the second argument rests on the requirements that belong to the human person who is sanctified by the sacraments, it may be called the anthropological principle. In short, the sacraments have been designed to fit the nature of the persons that they sanctify. Aquinas argues that the sacramental medicine, as he refers to it, corresponds by divine design to the body-soul composite of the human person. By this the Common Doctor means that the "visible materials in [a sacrament] touch the body, while the word in it is accepted in faith by the soul."[36] The description of the sacraments as "sacramental medicine" (*sacramentalis medicina*) brings to the fore an important feature of Catholic theology, even though Aquinas, as already noted, rejects medicine as a primary category to explain the nature of a Christian sacrament. Still, Christ institutes the sacraments for the benefit of a human race that stands in need of transformation.

Recent emphasis—that is, from the late 1960s—on the sacramental celebrations that accompany each sacrament, especially the Eucharist, has created in some quarters the view that the sacraments have been designed to make good people better. While it is true that the frequent reception of the sacraments that allow for such repeated reception—for example, Penance and Reconciliation and the Eucharist—sustains those who confess their sins and communicates the grace of justification, the fact remains that each sacrament also accomplishes the work of image-restoration. Even the Blessed Eucharist serves to promote this aspect of the sacraments' work in the salvation of the world.

35. *Roman Missal*, "Preface for the Most Sacred Heart of Jesus, Celebrated on the Friday after the Second Sunday after Pentecost."

36. *Summa theologiae* III.60.6.

For instance, those who communicate worthily receive an increase of divine charity that brings about the remission of venial, though not mortal, sins. The catechism employs a slightly different metaphor to describe the medicinal effects of the sacraments. The text recalls the power of the Holy Spirit that each sacrament brings about in the recipient. "As fire transforms into itself everything it touches, so the Holy Spirit transforms into the divine life whatever is subjected to his power."[37] It follows that the divine life and sinful dispositions cannot coexist in the soul of a person who is transformed by the sacraments.

The third argument that Aquinas gives for the use of prescribed words in each sacramental administration derives from the sacrament itself, and it may be called the sacramental signification principle. Communication of sacramental meaning requires the use of words. Words give intelligibility to a sign-action, so that words and sign-action together make up a sacrament. We know that a particular water bath sanctifies because the minister says, "I baptize you." We know that an anointing with oil confirms the recipient in the outward profession of the Christian religion because the bishop says, "Be sealed with the Gift of the Holy Spirit." We know that the anointing given to the sick is a sacrament because the priest says, "Through this holy anointing may the Lord in his love and mercy help you with the grace of the Holy Spirit."[38]

The sacraments of the Catholic Church do not traffic in the enigmatic. While they may be called mysteries, the sacraments plainly announce the nature of the mystery that they communicate. Aquinas saw this clearly when he reflected on the several features of water that connote wetness and coolness—that is, cleansing and refreshing. However, "once the words 'I baptize you' are uttered it becomes manifest that we are using water in baptism to signify a spiritual healing."[39] Given the importance that the use of words plays in the administration of the sacraments, it comes as no surprise to discover that the words to be used with each sacrament are determined words.

Aquinas returns to the analogy of hylomorphism in order to explain the need for determined words in sacramental administration. He compares the words used in each sacrament with the form that gives identity to matter: "In all entities made up of matter and form it is the form which acts as the principle of determination."[40] Because determined words are required for valid sacramental administrations, no quarter is given to slovenly distortions of pronunciation, even though—as long as an innocent mispronunciation does not totally destroy

37. CCC no. 1127.
38. *Roman Ritual: The Rites of Anointing and Viaticum*, no. 141.
39. *Summa theologiae* III.60.6.
40. *Summa theologiae* III.60.7.

the sacramental formula—"the sacrament is still valid in its effects."[41] The words matter. The Church takes strict precautions against overly casual ministers who abuse the forms of the sacraments.

This watchfulness arguably traces its origin to the emphasis that the holy doctors and theologians have stressed since the time of Saint Augustine. To be specific, Aquinas's discussion of whether additions or subtractions can be made to the sacramental formula shows that the tradition of the Church dating back to at least the fourth century frowns on changing the prescribed words for the sacraments.[42] Indeed, serious alterations nullify the sacramental efficacy.

Today, the Church does not allow alterations to be made to the sacramental formulas, and indeed punishes those who willfully distort a sacramental administration by changing the meaning of the words used in performing it. The reasons for the seriousness that the Church exhibits when it comes to dealing with the words of the sacraments stem from what one might call the supreme finesse of the Catholic sacraments. They are signs that employ determined words and sensible realities. The determined words are essential for knowing what the sign means. When serious alterations, additions, and deletions succeed in changing the identity of the sacrament, then two things necessary for a sacrament are inescapably forfeited. First, the minister of the sacrament cannot form the right intention to administer a sacrament if his words indicate that he is doing something other than confecting the saving sign. Second, since the very identity of the sacrament rests on the words that give specification to the material reality, such that Baptism is not confused with ordinary bathing, the very meaning of the sacrament itself would disappear were the minister to distort the words prescribed by the Church. Once the necessity that the Church attaches to the reception of the sacraments of the New Law is properly grasped, the Church's insistence on proper sacramental administration appears perfectly reasonable.

41. *Summa theologiae* III.60.7 ad 3. It is interesting to note that in this reply, Aquinas gives the example of a minister of Baptism mumbling "In nomine matris" (in the name of the mother) instead of the required "In nomine patris" (in the name of the father) as a major distortion that would invalidate the sacrament. Note that this error was envisaged as arising not from ideological distortions but from sloppy enunciation.

42. See the reference to Didymus the Blind (d. ca. 398) in *Summa theologiae* III.60.8.

10

The Necessity of the Sacraments

The Council of Trent affirmed the necessity of the sacraments in accord with what Catholic life and practice had exhibited from the beginning of the Church. Why? The early sixteenth-century controversies about the nature of justification prompted this authoritative declaration. In fact, the *Decree on the Sacraments* issued on March 3, 1547, made this context clear and at the same time indicated in a general way the scope of the various erroneous positions on the sacraments that had been advanced during the sixteenth-century controversies.

Scholars estimate that the doctrinal points that the decree sets down formulated the Catholic responses to errors found in the documents of the Lutheran reform, including Luther's own 1520 *De captivitate Babylonica ecclesiae praeludium* (*Prelude on the Babylonian Captivity of the Church*); the *Confessio Augustana* (*Augsburg Confession*), a document formulated by Lutheran theologians and presented at the Diet of Augsburg in 1530; and, finally, a defense of this confession composed by Philip Melanchthon (d. 1560), one of the first major architects of Protestant theology. The 1531 edition of this *Apologia Confessionis Augustanae* (*Apology* [Defense] *of the Augsburg Confession*) is said to have held a particular significance for those charged with the formulation of the Tridentine canons.[1]

1. For information on Melanchthon's text, see Christian Peters, "*Apologia Confessionis Augustanae*": *Investigations into the Text History of a Lutheran Confession (1530–1584)* (Stuttgart: Calwer, 1997). See also the Ignatius Press edition of the *Enchiridion* (Freiburg: Herder, 1965), 388. This unnumbered historical material, which serves as a preface to Trent's canons on the sacraments, also exists in the earlier Latin editions of Denzinger.

Canon 4 of the 1547 decree makes the following statement, which presumably reflects how the fathers of Trent understood the objections raised by Luther and others: "If anyone says that the sacraments of the New Law are not necessary for salvation, but that they are superfluous; and that without the sacraments or the desire for them men obtain from God the grace of justification through faith alone (although it is true that not all the sacraments are necessary for each person), let him be anathema."[2] The *Catechism of the Catholic Church* refers to this canon as the grounds for its assertion that "the Church affirms that for believers the sacraments of the New Covenant are *necessary for salvation*."[3]

The fact that the catechism composed after the Second Vatican Council includes a qualification on the necessity of the sacraments for salvation—namely, that "for believers the sacraments . . . are necessary for salvation"—is explained by the manner in which the Second Vatican Council interpreted an affirmation that appears frequently in the writings of the fathers of the Church, including eminent ones such as Saint Augustine and Saint Ambrose of Milan (d. 397): "Outside the Church there is no salvation." The catechism devotes three numbers to explaining the doctrinal significance of the affirmation.[4] In short, the classic expression means that "all salvation comes from Christ the Head through the Church which is his Body."[5]

The Dogmatic Constitution on the Church, *Lumen Gentium*, provides the basis for the statement of the catechism.[6] This conciliar text clarified that, under certain conditions, "those also can attain to salvation who through no fault of their own do not know the Gospel of Christ or His Church."[7] Another document of the Second Vatican Council, the Decree on the Church's Missionary Activity, *Ad Gentes*, adds to this clarification the important assertion that "yet a necessity lies upon the Church (1 Cor. 9:16), and at the same time a sacred duty, to preach the Gospel."[8] In other words, whatever the situation of those who find themselves outside the visible structures of the Church, the Second Vatican Council offers no reason to relax the Church's efforts to evangelize. The goal *evangelization*, of course, appears in the language accompanying Baptism and the other sacraments that provide, for those who receive them, the best means available to realize the promises of eternal life.[9] The documents of the

2. *DS* 1604.
3. *CCC* no. 1129 (emphasis original).
4. See *CCC* nos. 846–48.
5. *CCC* no. 846.
6. See *CCC* no. 847.
7. *Lumen Gentium*, no. 16 (VRL).
8. *Ad Gentes*, no. 7 (VRL). See also *CCC* no. 848, which quotes this passage.
9. See *Dominus Iesus*, no. 22: "If it is true that the followers of other religions can receive divine grace, it is also certain that objectively speaking they are in a gravely deficient situation in

council and those that followed, such as the declaration issued at the turn of the new millennium, *Dominus Iesus,* express what the Church has always held formally about the necessity of the sacraments. One witness to this continuity is Saint Thomas Aquinas in his *Summa theologiae.*[10]

Ways of Explaining Necessity

When Aquinas turns to consider the necessity of the sacraments, he does so by addressing the theological history of the world, so to speak. In other words, he approaches the question of necessity by comparing the main epochs of human history according to the several relationships that obtained between God and the human race. First, he considers the necessity of sacraments in the state of innocence; second, he considers the necessity of sacraments for those who lived after sin but before Christ; and third, he turns to those who live after the coming of Christ.

This discussion, however, follows a general treatment of the necessity that the human race, for its own well-being and right ordering toward a common end, agree on and find true fellowship in the same outward and visible expressions of faith and worship. The impetus for this approach comes from Saint Augustine's influential writing *Against Faustus the Manichaean,* which provides refutations to the errors of a fierce opponent of orthodox Christianity, the fourth-century heresiarch Faustus of Mileve (d. 400). In any event, Aquinas quotes Saint Augustine's text at the very start of *Summa theologiae* III.61.1. Here, Aquinas inquires whether sacraments are indeed necessary for salvation. Saint Augustine's point, as Aquinas reads him, is that in order to maintain unity within any religious group, there needs to be some system of symbols or sacraments in which all the members share. For his part, Aquinas correctly interprets this general principle to show the necessity "for human salvation that men should be united in one denomination constituted by true religion."[11] The Latin text makes it clear that denomination does not refer to sectarian branches of Christianity. Rather, the expression "unum verae religionis nomen" simply means "one religious identity"—namely, the true one. Likewise, the phrase "ad humanum salutem hominis" explains the necessity of the sacraments in terms of their relationship to eternal life in the hereafter.

---

comparison with those who, in the Church, have the fullness of the means of salvation." This text refers the reader to the 1943 encyclical *Mystici corporis Christi,* which teaches that those who do not enjoy full communion with the Catholic Church "remain deprived of those many heavenly gifts and helps that can only be enjoyed in the Catholic Church" (*DS* 3821). Among these gifts and helps fall all the sacraments except Baptism.

10. See *Summa theologiae* III.61.1–4.

11. *Summa theologiae* III.61.1, *sed contra.*

At the same time, neither Saint Augustine nor Aquinas fails to point out that the sacraments also serve as instruments of social unity for life here below. Contemporary discussions on religious pluralism and inclusiveness sometimes obscure this ungainsayable truth of the Christian religion. Common religious practice unites, whereas diversity of cult divides.

When Aquinas says that "it is necessary for human salvation that men should be united in one denomination of true religion," he affirms the need not only for the sacraments of the Church but also for a divine instruction that governs human life. The Church abides as the great sacrament of divine communion within which God acts to create in the human person a communion both with the Holy Trinity and with other members of the race, or what the catechism calls "fraternal communion."[12] The relationship that exists between the sacraments of the Church and the commandments of God is not an artificial one. In fact, this relationship between right worship and right conduct finds its basis in the Creator.

All sin entails a kind of idolatry. In the first chapter of the Letter to the Romans, Saint Paul in fact laments those who "exchanged the truth of God for a lie and revered and worshiped the creature rather than the creator, who is blessed forever. Amen" (Rom. 1:25). Catholic theology regards the knowledge of God about which Saint Paul speaks as naturally knowable: "For what can be known about God is evident to them, because God made it evident to them" (Rom. 1:19). Although Catholic thought includes many authoritative statements about how to read the first chapter of Romans, most recently, the 1998 encyclical of Pope John Paul II, *Fides et ratio*, provides grounds for this claim.[13] Of course, within the ambit of the Catholic Church, knowledge of the moral law stands among the many heavenly gifts and helps that God provides for believers. Among these one also numbers the sacraments of the Church, which assist the same believers to observe the moral law.

12. *CCC* no. 1108.

13. See John Paul II, *Fides et ratio*, no. 22:

> In the first chapter of his Letter to the Romans, Saint Paul helps us to appreciate better the depth of insight of the Wisdom literature's reflection. Developing a philosophical argument in popular language, the Apostle declares a profound truth: through all that is created the "eyes of the mind" can come to know God. Through the medium of creatures, God stirs in reason an intuition of his "power" and his "divinity" (cf. *Rom* 1:20). This is to concede to human reason a capacity which seems almost to surpass its natural limitations. Not only is it not restricted to sensory knowledge, from the moment that it can reflect critically upon the data of the senses, but, by discoursing on the data provided by the senses, reason can reach the cause which lies at the origin of all perceptible reality. In philosophical terms, we could say that this important Pauline text affirms the human capacity for metaphysical enquiry. According to the Apostle, it was part of the original plan of the creation that reason should without difficulty reach beyond the sensory data to the origin of all things: the Creator.

The Human Condition

The first article of question 61 further expands on the reasons for which a sacramental dispensation is required. Three reasons emerge that have not lost their usefulness for Catholic theology. First of all, says Aquinas, God provides visible sacraments to respect our human way of knowing. One philosophical principle holds that all knowledge begins in the senses. Aquinas repeats this axiom that grounds an Aristotelian theory of knowledge. He views the sacraments of the Church as required on the grounds that a human person is led to knowledge of spiritual or intelligible realities through corporeal and sensible things.[14] Because human nature has been created to know in this way, God provides for the salvation of the human race in a way that best corresponds to the way that the human knowing power operates. Aquinas does not consider this divine benefit an accident. He explicitly ascribes the visible nature of the sacramental dispensation to a work of divine providence, with its connotations of both unsurpassed wisdom and supreme love. Wisdom "governs all things well" (Wis. 8:1).

The particular philosophical presupposition that Aquinas employs should not distract from the important truth enunciated in this first reason for the necessity of the sacraments. One could say as a corollary to this argument that the Christian religion excludes the bizarre and inappropriate—that is, those things that would strike those possessed of refined human sensibilities as esoteric or cultist. The Christian religion employs neither hidden realities, such as cabalistic codes or sibylline symbols, that most people would find unintelligible, nor various esotericisms, such as divination and seances, that depend on what is unseen or is claimed to be seen by only a few. No. Instead, as Aquinas puts it, the divine Wisdom made use of "certain physical and sensible signs called the sacraments" that Aquinas also describes elsewhere in his *Summa* as familiar objects, easy to obtain.[15]

Human Weaknesses

The second reason set forth to support the suitability of sacraments in the plan of salvation draws on the condition in which original sin leaves the human person. Original sin leaves a certain disordering in human persons that compromises the judgments that they make about material things. In short, human beings find themselves drawn inordinately to goods that please and repelled unreasonably

14. Aquinas's original Latin puts this principle in excruciatingly clear language: "per corporalia et sensibilia in spiritualia et intelligibilia deducatur."

15. *Summa theologiae* III.61.1. For the explanation about ease of attainment, see *Summa theologiae* III.60.4 ad 2.

from those things that endanger. Disordered human passions or emotions may be considered as even leaving the human person subject to material things. In order to clear the mind of the thought that this argument reflects an antiquated or negative outlook on the power of fleshly goods, one may usefully reflect on the statistics that indicate the widespread use of risqué images on the internet. Other ways in which material things seem to constrain or even capture human freedom provide talking points for both spiritual guides and psychologists.

The sacraments, one may argue, manifest the divine mercy inasmuch as they apply spiritual medicine by means of certain physical signs. Aquinas advances the view that, were God to have acted otherwise, the human race all too likely would find it difficult to accept purely spiritual realities. After all, human nature in its fallen state has lost the touch for seeking out spiritual realities alone. Even before the thirteenth century, the Catholic theological tradition made use of the second reason to explain the need for the sacraments. To insist on the use of material instruments to bring about the right exercise of religion gives warning to those who would turn Christianity into a purely mental exercise. For instance, one hears today the description of certain people as spiritual but not religious. The Catholic Church rightly warns against assertions of this kind inasmuch as they provide an excuse for avoiding the practice of the sacraments. They also run in the face of the clear evidence that efforts to heal the wounds of nature, especially with respect to movements of the sense powers of the soul, fail considerably unless wounded nature benefits from healing grace.

Truthful Worship

The third argument that Aquinas gives for the necessity of God-given sacraments builds on the notion that original sin has weakened human nature and its ability to appreciate the spiritual world and immaterial realities in general. Instead, as everyday experience makes clear, weakened human nature easily involves the human person unreasonably with the everyday material things that human existence requires or that humans can use. One has only to consider the excuses that people proffer for avoiding spiritual exercises such as prayer—for example, "I am too busy with my work." Such excuses almost always confirm that fallen people find themselves prone to distractions about material things.

To counteract this temptation, therefore, God provides for a salutary physical expression of man's religious instincts. The sacraments enjoy the power, by their hylomorphic construction, to capture the religious imaginations of Christian believers and others drawn to participate in them. Because the sacraments each provide the occasion for healthy activities, they direct the human imagination away from superstitious practices such as demon worship and other sinful activities that can appear in some quarters as religious rites. Human sacrifice is one shocking example of such deviations; the enigmatic practices of Mithraism, known mainly from archaeological records, probably constitute other examples.[16]

Aquinas summarizes at the end of the article this teaching on why the sacraments are needed—a teaching, moreover, that represents the corporate reflection of the Christian tradition. These general principles that argue for the necessity of the sacraments also provide helpful guidelines for explaining current sacramental practices of the Catholic Church. When Aquinas speaks of the necessity of the sacraments, he already knows that God has ordained the sacraments as necessary. As the teachings of the Catholic Church have made evident, the divine plan for the salvation of the human race includes the sacramental mediations. Reasons such as the three mentioned in *Summa theologiae* III.61.1 seek to offer some reasonable account of this divine plan without, however, pretending to exhaust the divine wisdom that has established the sacramental dispensation. Aquinas's summary emphasizes the need for the sacraments given the human person's situation in the context of the history of salvation—that is, the situation of a fallen human nature redeemed: "Through the sacraments, sensible things are used to instruct man in a manner appropriate to his own nature. He is humbled by being brought to recognize his own subjection to physical things, seeing that he has to rely on them for the help he needs. At the same time he is preserved by the health-giving practices made available to him in the sacraments from various kinds of harm in the physical order."[17]

The arguments given to explain why the sacraments fittingly serve the salvation of the human person in no way compromise the basic given of salvation that the passion of Christ supplies the sufficient cause of salvation. Rather, the sacraments participate in the passion of Christ, "for they produce their effects in virtue of the passion of Christ which is, in a certain manner, applied to men through the sacraments."[18] In sum, no competition should be envisaged between what Christ accomplishes for the human race on Calvary and what transpires in the properly administered sacraments of the Church.

16. For one account, see Leonard Boyle, *A Short Guide to St. Clement's, Rome* (Rome: Collegio San Clemente, 1987). In the cellar of this ancient Christian Church, one finds some indications of Mithraic rites.

17. *Summa theologiae* III.61.1.

18. *Summa theologiae* III.61.1 ad 3.

Sacraments and Sins' Wounds

The second article of question 62 should command the student of sacramental theology's particular attention. Aquinas sets forth classic Catholic teaching about the relationship of the sacraments to the healing of sins' wounds. The *Catechism of the Catholic Church* devotes a chapter to this subject: "The Sacraments of Healing."[19] This chapter treats the sacraments of Penance and Reconciliation and Anointing of the Sick. Truth to tell, however, each sacrament serves in some way to relieve the burden that sin imposes on the human person. This kind of forgiveness begins with Baptism, which, as a model for the other sacraments, forgives all sins (original sin and personal sin) and remits all the punishment due for sin.[20]

For a variety of reasons, the climate of postconciliar theology proves somewhat inhospitable to discussions about original sin and its effects. The 1993 encyclical of Pope John Paul II, *Veritatis splendor*, identifies a circumstance that grew widespread by the end of the twentieth century: "Today, however, it seems necessary to reflect on the whole of the Church's moral teaching, with the precise goal of recalling certain fundamental truths of Catholic doctrine which, in the present circumstances, risk being distorted or denied. In fact, a new situation has come about within the Christian community itself, which has experienced the spread of numerous doubts and objections of a human and psychological, social and cultural, religious and even properly theological nature, with regard to the Church's moral teachings."[21]

While *Veritatis splendor* provides guidance for bishops and moral theologians, this papal teaching did not consider, in a focused way, the effect that relaxed notions of moral responsibility work on sacramental theologians and those charged with the revision of liturgical texts. In any case, the relationship between sacraments and forgiveness for sins has not received prolonged attention in sacramental catechesis and other kinds of instruction that present and support the Church's sacramental dispensation. For his part, Aquinas could not express himself more clearly than in his response to the question of whether the sacraments were necessary before Adam sinned: "Sacraments were not necessary in the state of innocence."[22]

Those who advanced the opinions to which Aquinas responds in this article were misled by mistakes about the status of Adam before the fall. They

19. See CCC, part 2, § 2, chap. 2, nos. 1320–532.

20. See CCC no. 1263, which refers to declarations of the fifteenth-century Council of Florence (*DS* 1316).

21. John Paul II, *Veritatis splendor*, no. 4.

22. *Summa theologiae* III.61.2.

assumed, for instance, that since he required grace to live in friendship with God, Adam also required the sacraments; that since Adam's nature did not change (that is, was not destroyed), he still would have required the sacraments that suit human nature; and, finally, that since matrimony was instituted before the fall (see Gen. 2:22), and matrimony remains a sacrament, sacraments were therefore required in the state of innocence. Aquinas, of course, provides replies to these mistaken assumptions. The discussion is not purely hypothetical. By showing that sacraments were not necessary in the state of innocence, Aquinas the theologian, in fact, illuminates the nature of the Church's sacramental dispensation.

To take the abovementioned arguments in order: Aquinas replies that, while it is true that Adam required grace, he did not obtain it through sensible signs. Further, while it is also true that human nature remains the same before and after the fall, the state of human nature has changed such that fallen man requires sensible realities in order for Adam's sinful progeny to find the due perfection even of the higher powers of the soul. In short, this means that the human race relies on visible signs both to come to a knowledge of divine truth and to love with divine charity. As for matrimony, in the state of innocence, matrimony was instituted not as a sacrament but, Aquinas rightly observes, as a "natural institution."[23] So, in sum, the human person in the state of innocence had no need of the sacraments, not merely inasmuch as the sacraments are designed as a remedy for sin, but also inasmuch as they are designed for the perfecting of the human soul. Sin had not yet entered the world. God perfected the first couple without the instrumental work of visible signs.

These details offer more than some theological clarifications about the state of the first human being. They also reveal something of the effects of original sin—inescapable effects that befall every child born into this world. Original sin leaves human nature disordered but not destroyed. The disordering affects both body and soul. Sickness and death affect the right ordering of the body, whereas ignorance, weakness of will, and concupiscence in the broad sense disorder the powers of the soul. The sacraments of the Catholic Church are designed to counter these adverse factors to human well-being that leave the human person prone to sin and corruption.

In the state of innocence, on the other hand, just as Adam's "reason was subject to God, so the lower powers of his soul were subject to the higher and the body to the soul itself."[24] This ordering of man to God and the resulting harmony of soul and body that it produced "comprised the state called 'original

23. *Summa theologiae* III.61.2 ad 3.
24. *Summa theologiae* III.61.2.

justice.'"[25] In this state of original justice, the first parents required neither remedies for sin, as there was no sin, nor perfection of union with God, as they were established in the fullest friendship with the Creator. After the fall, however, things changed dramatically.

The fact that Aquinas approaches the necessity of the sacraments by rehearsing the theological stages of human development emphasizes one major and indisputable point of the Christian religion: salvation comes about as a free gift from God. The analysis of the several theological stages of human development with respect to the coming of Christ shows how much the Christian people should appreciate the gift of the sacraments as indispensable—that is, as necessary mediations. All the sacraments, though in diverse ways, work both to escape the limitations (to use a euphemistic term) that the sin of Adam and the Catholic's own sins impose and to achieve a perfection of soul that human exercise alone cannot produce. This appreciation comes into sharp focus when we turn to consider how Aquinas explains the place that sacraments hold in the period between the first sin and the coming of Christ.

Rites of the Old Dispensation

Aquinas grants the name *sacrament* to the visible signs that were instituted by the Mosaic Law. The reason for this assignation comes from the Christian conviction that the old dispensation points toward salvation by the Incarnate Word. Indeed, as the catechism states, "Already in the Old Testament God ordained or permitted the making of images that pointed symbolically toward salvation by the incarnate Word."[26] And in another place, the text makes an even clearer assertion—namely, that "in the [Church's] sacramental economy the Holy Spirit fulfills what was prefigured in *the Old Covenant*."[27]

In the thirteenth century, however, intellectual opinion varied among the doctors about what one might call the suitableness of the rituals prescribed in the Old Law. Aquinas, for his part, holds firmly to the view that salvation history enjoys a progressive continuity from Adam to Christ. He declines to register suspicions about the sacraments of the Old Law or to question their legitimacy. Rather, he argues, based in part on the third chapter of the Letter to the Romans, that "it was right that before Christ's coming there should be certain visible signs which man can use to attest his faith in the future coming

25. CCC no. 376, which describes man in paradise.
26. CCC no. 2130.
27. CCC no. 1093 (emphasis original).

of the Savior."[28] Aquinas guards the unity of the two covenants by holding that the two propositions—namely, Christ will suffer and Christ has suffered—differ only by the tense of the verb that they employ and not in the substance of the belief that the verb signifies. "The mystery of Christ's Incarnation," Aquinas concludes, "was to be believed in all ages and by all peoples in some fashion, but in ways differing with the differences of times and of peoples."[29]

In a reply to one of the objections raised against the fittingness of sacraments in the period of the Old Law, Aquinas provides a detailed analysis of how sacraments figure in the salvation of fallen man. First, he distinguishes between the unity of faith and the progressive sinfulness that overtakes the human race after Adam's sin:

> The state of the human race after sin and before Christ can be considered under two aspects: first from the point of view of the essential meaning of faith, and in relation to this it has always remained the same in the sense that it has always been through faith in the future coming of Christ that men have been justified. But we can consider the state of the human race under a different aspect, that namely of the greater or lesser intensity of sinfulness, and also of explicit knowledge of Christ prevailing within it.[30]

In sum, Aquinas presents the specification of the natural moral law and the specification of the kinds of worship that men offered God as expressions of divine benevolence toward a human race that became progressively confused about both God and the worship due him. Aquinas continues:

> For as the years passed sin began to gain an increasing hold upon man in virtue of the fact that as human reason was darkened by sin the precepts of the natural law were no longer adequate to enable him to live aright, making it necessary to define the precepts in the form of a written law, and together with these to institute certain sacraments of faith. It was also necessary that as the years passed the knowledge of faith should become increasingly explicit. For, as Gregory says, with the passing of the years knowledge about God grew and increased.[31] Hence it was also necessary under the Old Law to define certain specific sacraments of the faith which men had concerning the Christ who was to come. And in fact these sacraments are related to those which existed before the Law as that which is determinate is related to that which is indeterminate. For prior to the Law it was not specifically laid down for man which sacraments he should use, as it was

28. *Summa theologiae* III.61.3.
29. *Summa theologiae* II-II.2.7, which forms part of the treatise on the virtue of faith.
30. *Summa theologiae* III.61.3 ad 2.
31. See Gregory the Great, *Homilies on the Book of the Prophet Ezekiel* 2.4 (PL 76:980).

> laid down by the Law. This was necessary both because of the obscuring of the natural law and in order that the signs in which the faith was expressed might be more specific.[32]

What emerges from these considerations in *Summa theologiae* III.61.3 not only points to the place that Christ holds in the salvation of the world but also offers an indirect warning to safeguard the integrity of the sacraments of the New Law. These sacraments possess an ultimate specificity about the mystery of redemption in Christ—a specificity that those of the Old Law do not share.

Necessity and the Cross

The contrast between what the sacraments of the old dispensation do and what the sacraments of the New Law effect becomes apparent in the final article, article 4, of the *Summa* question on the necessity of the sacraments. In this article, Aquinas inquires whether sacraments are necessary after the coming of Christ. Why, indeed, does the Church propose sacraments for salvation only after the passion of Christ? Aquinas points to the specificness that the sacraments of the New Law possess inasmuch as they announce that Christ has died, not that he will die. "Hence," he concludes, "it is right that in addition to the sacraments of the Old Law which foretold realities that lay in the future there are certain other sacraments in the New Law to stand for realities which have taken place in Christ in the past."[33] This insistence on the Christ who has suffered (*Christus passus*) calls to mind the important principle of efficient causality that governs the approach that Catholic theology takes to the sacraments.

In fact, Aquinas argues against those who would want to discount the sacraments on the basis of a text in Galatians 4 that laments our having been "enslaved to the elemental powers of the world" (Gal. 4:3). These verses rather celebrate the fact that we have been liberated from such material powers by faith in Christ. The objector wrongly concludes that, for this reason, Christians should not make use of physical sacraments. Aquinas contrasts the sacraments of the Old Law, which were in fact mere elements of this world (e.g., the slaying of the paschal lamb and the destruction of holocausts), with the sacraments of the Church. "Our sacraments," he writes, "both contain and cause grace," and so do not fall under the category of elemental powers.[34]

32. *Summa theologiae* III.61.3 ad 2.
33. *Summa theologiae* III.61.4.
34. *Summa theologiae* III.61.3 ad 2.

Such a conclusion raises another question: Why do the sacraments of the New Law, in differing from those of the Old Law (e.g., no slaying of the paschal lamb and no offering of holocaust), not indicate that God vacillates? Has God changed his mind about what instruments to employ when it comes to arranging things for the salvation of the human race? In order to respond to this admittedly somewhat marginal query, Aquinas again returns to the efficacy that the sacraments of the New Law possess. Whereas the sacraments of the Old Law "appropriately fulfilled the function of prefiguring grace," the sacraments of the New Law "are appropriate as manifestations of a grace that is already given."[35] From these considerations, one may find the answer to why the *Catechism of the Catholic Church* remains reserved about the usefulness of the Mosaic practices: the sacraments of the Church "fulfill the types and figures of the Old Covenant."[36] In what does this fulfillment consist? The sacraments of the Church, so the catechism continues, "signify and make actively present the salvation wrought by Christ and prefigure and anticipate the glory of heaven."[37]

35. *Summa theologiae* III.61.4 ad 3.
36. CCC no. 1152.
37. CCC no. 1152.

11

How Sacramental Mediation Works

Catholic theology conceives of sacramental instrumentality after Aristotle's notion of principal and secondary causes. When it comes to inquiring whether the secondary or instrumental cause can produce the interior effect of the sacrament, an important affirmation remains common among all orthodox sacramental theologians. In a word, as Saint Thomas Aquinas puts it, "It is God alone who works actively to produce the interior effect of the sacrament."[1] The reason for this foundational principle of sacramental theology lies deep in what revealed teaching holds about the divine nature as creative as well as about every creature's dependence on the divine omnipotence for its existence. In the case of the human creature, each human person is dependent, in a causal way, for everything that he or she possesses in both the natural and supernatural orders. The *Catechism of the Catholic Church* expresses this truth clearly: "The truth that God is at work in all the actions of his creatures is inseparable from faith in God the Creator."[2] The same truth appears as a salutary warning in a document of the Second Vatican Council, *Gaudium et Spes*: "Without the Creator the creature would disappear."[3]

Divine Agency

It is also necessary to recall what is taught in the catechism about divine providence: just as the human person can do nothing if cut off from his or her origin,

1. *Summa theologiae* III.64.1.
2. *CCC* no. 308.
3. *Gaudium et Spes*, no. 36 (VRL).

"still less can a creature attain its ultimate end without the help of God's grace."[4] The nature of sacramental mediation finds a parallel, though obviously not an identical, expression in creation. The Church teaches this clearly: "Since God could create everything out of nothing, he can also, through the Holy Spirit, give spiritual life to sinners by creating a pure heart in them and bodily life to the dead through the Resurrection."[5] Only God, who created immediately every spiritual soul, can enter the human soul, which is the spiritual or immaterial element in the body-soul composite.[6] Likewise, because only God can make us worthy of his friendship, only God bestows grace on his human creatures. "Grace," as the catechism puts it, "is a *participation in the life of God*."[7] In sum, because the sacraments accomplish those effects that remain proper to God alone, it follows that the human minister of the sacrament participates in the sacraments' causal efficacy only as an instrument—that is, only with dependence on the principal cause, God.

The reference to God as the principal cause of the effects that the sacraments produce in the human person requires further elaboration. Of course, since the sacraments stand among those effects of God that come into existence outside of God, divine and Catholic faith makes the sacraments works of the Blessed Trinity together: "The whole divine economy is the common work of the three divine persons."[8] The reason for this assertion rests on the need to uphold the unity of the divine nature and to avoid identifying the divine persons by reference to that which they accomplish outside themselves. "For as the Trinity has only one and the same nature," says the catechism, "so too does it have only one and the same operation."[9]

At the same time, according to Aquinas, one can view the incarnational and sacramental mysteries as the concrete way of salvation under the trinitarian communication of grace. In order to differentiate between Christ and the sacraments, Aquinas makes a further distinction that remains essential for Catholic theology—namely, the distinction between a conjoined instrument and a separate instrument. So, with this distinction in mind, one may conclude that "the principal efficient cause of grace is God himself, and the humanity of Christ stands to him in relation of a conjoined instrument, whereas a sacrament stands

4. CCC no. 308.
5. CCC no. 298.
6. See CCC no. 366. For the catechism's statement on the unity of body and soul, see CCC no. 365.
7. CCC no. 1997 (emphasis original).
8. CCC no. 258.
9. CCC no. 258.

in the relation of a separate one."[10] The relationship of Christ to the sacraments raises a question other than that of a theoretical explanation of double agency. How does the Catholic Church account for the origin of the sacred seven?

To answer this question requires making an important distinction. Catholic theology rejects the view that the sacraments work in the same way that petitionary prayer seeks to obtain favors from God. Aquinas puts the matter bluntly: "The sacramental effect is not obtained in answer to the prayers of the Church or the minister but from the merit of Christ's passion, the power of which works actively in the sacraments."[11] To apply this principle to Catholic life, one may distinguish between the sacraments of the Church that Christ institutes and what Catholic theology and practice calls *sacramentals*. Approved Catholic sacramentals essentially give physical expression to a petitionary prayer for some blessing.

The pious use of medals with images of the saints, of the Blessed Virgin Mary, and even of the Lord himself express the user's prayerful communion with our Lord, his Mother, and the holy ones who have done the will of God throughout the ages. Other examples of sacramentals commonly in use among Catholic believers include various scapulars that seek the protection of Our Lady under one or another of her titles or of the saints, rosary beads that provide a means of numbering the *Paters* and *Aves* that make up the Rosary devotion, or candles that the faithful light before sacred images to prolong their spiritual presence at places of particular devotion. The Church herself exercises supervisory authority over the selection and use of sacramentals. These expressions of a believer's devotion do not function as efficient causes that mediate the power of Christ. For this kind of working of divine power, other instruments are required—ones instituted by Christ himself.

Divine Institution

Aquinas approaches the question of divine institution on the well-established assumption that Christ, in fact, instituted each of the seven sacraments. The second article of *Summa theologiae* III.64 explains why divine institution is required for what the Church holds about sacramental efficacy. Aquinas, of course, was writing in the thirteenth century. He names no heresy or opinion of a recognized authority that challenges the historical truth that Christ instituted the seven sacraments. The absence of such, one assumes, leaves Aquinas free to discuss the theoretical reasons for what later centuries would identify as dominical institution.

10. *Summa theologiae* III.62.5.
11. *Summa theologiae* III.64.1 ad 2.

The sixteenth century raised new questions about divine institution, questions that could serve to undermine the Church's faith in the sacred seven. In this regard, it is significant to note that the *Catechism of the Catholic Church* treats the question of divine institution by referring to the declaration of the Council of Trent and its *Decree on the Sacraments* of March 3, 1547. In keeping with twentieth-century sensibilities, the catechism text recasts Trent's anathema into a positive affirmation of divine institution for each of the seven sacraments. The text runs thus: "Adhering to the teaching of Holy Scriptures, to the apostolic tradition, and to the consensus of the Fathers," we profess that "the sacraments of the new law were . . . all instituted by Jesus Christ our Lord."[12]

Obviously, the fact that the Council of Trent saw the need to make this affirmation in the form of an anathema—that is, a condemnation of anyone who maintains the opposite—indicates that the question of divine institution arose with renewed vigor during the reform of the sixteenth century. The other canons that the council formulated after canon 1, which is the basis for the catechism's quotation, treat matters generally related to the question of how the sacramental economy works to bring about the instrumental production of spiritual effects. It is possible to suggest that those who drafted Trent's document at least recalled the structure of Aquinas's treatment of sacramental mediation.

The general principle that Aquinas employs to explain the necessity of divine institution recalls the fact that instruments draw their power from the principal agent. Then the Common Doctor introduces an important distinction that remains essential to the Catholic understanding of the sacraments: "Now an instrument derives its power from the principal agent, and with regard to the sacraments the agent is twofold, namely he who institutes the sacrament and he who uses the sacrament once instituted by applying it in order to cause it to take effect."[13] Then Aquinas notes the obvious: the minister of the sacrament—namely, the one who applies the sacrament—cannot serve as the cause of the power that works through the sacrament. So the one who institutes the sacrament—namely, God—alone accounts for the spiritual effects that the sacraments produce. So, concludes Aquinas (whose teaching clearly has influenced the fathers of Trent), the sacraments must come into existence as a result of a divine institution. This statement of a general principle does not exclude a consideration of the role that Christ plays in the actual, historical institution of the sacraments.

One objection that was raised even in the Middle Ages against the claim of the sacraments' divine origin argues that the apostles and their successors are able to institute new sacraments. In modern terms, proponents could argue that

12. CCC no. 1114.

13. *Summa theologiae* III.64.2.

the Church should devise sacraments to suit the changing needs of contemporary people. The Church, however, takes another view, one that recognizes that the incarnate Son also comes among us as incarnate Wisdom. The catechism explains that the sacraments "are 'for the Church' in the sense that 'the sacraments make the Church.'"[14] The expression "make the Church" comes from Saint Augustine's *City of God* (22.17). There Augustine draws a parallel between the creation of the first woman and the establishment of the Church—a parallel in which he compares the blood and water that flows from the side of Christ to the Church's sacraments:

> For, in the beginning when a rib was taken from Adam, being asleep, to make Eve, this was a plain prophecy of Christ and the Church. Adam's sleep was Christ's death, from whose side being opened with a spear as He hung upon the cross, came blood and water, the two sacraments whereby the Church is built up. For the word of the text is not *formavit,* nor *finxit,* but *Aedificavit eam in mulierem,* he built her up into a woman. So the Apostle calls the Church "the edification of the body of Christ." The woman therefore was God's creature as well as man: but made from man, for unity's sake, and in the manner thereof was a plain figure of Christ and His Church.[15]

Aquinas echoes this teaching in his reply to the proposal that would authorize the apostles and their successors to institute new sacraments.

The text from the *Summa theologiae* holds special value inasmuch as one finds an affirmation of the way that the Church regards both creeds and sacraments. In short, neither are put at the disposition of human authorities but rather are confided to their care. In fact, Aquinas, in his reply to the third argument found at *Summa theologiae* III.64.2, where he discusses divine institution of the sacraments, makes this comparison: "Just as it is not lawful for [the apostles and their successors] to constitute any other church so too it is not lawful for them either to hand down any other faith or to institute any other sacraments."[16] Then he draws upon the image that, subsequently, has become canonized in the Roman Liturgy for the Feast of the Most Sacred Heart of Jesus. "The Church of Christ," replies Aquinas, "is rather said to have been built up with *the sacraments which flowed from the side of Christ hanging on the Cross.*"[17] This text,

14. CCC no. 1118.

15. Augustine, *The City of God* (*De civitate Dei*), trans. John Healey (Edinburgh: John Grant, 1909), 22.17.

16. *Summa theologiae* III.64.2 ad 3.

17. *Summa theologiae* III.64.2 ad 3 (emphasis original). The editors of the *Summa theologiae* trace this expression to a collection of early biblical commentaries, the twelfth-century *Glossa ordinaria,* on Rom. 5:14.

which clearly indicates that there are limits on the Church's authority over the sacraments, aims to make the point that neither the formulation of a new creed nor the institution of new sacraments forms part of God's plan for the ministry exercised by the hierarchical structure of the Church.

The centrality given to Christ in the historical institution of the sacraments requires that one reconcile this obvious truth with the equally indispensable truth of the faith that holds that the interior effects of the sacraments come about as a result of divine power. In the sacraments of the Church, the Blessed Trinity is at work. Colman O'Neill expresses this mystery in a succinct and lucid fashion: "At beginning and end [of the economy of salvation] is the divine Trinity giving of itself to its human creature through such an excess of life that this human person, made in the image of God, can be brought to see God as he is, to know him in the Word and love him in the Spirit."[18]

How then does the Church see the relationship between the work of the Blessed Trinity and the mediation of the Incarnate Word? Does the infallible affirmation that the sacraments are instituted by Jesus Christ in the course of his earthly mission require some further distinction in order to ensure that the spiritual effects that the sacraments bring about in the human person originate effectively in God?

The Human Nature of Christ

In short, the answer that Aquinas gives to the above question is positive. He points out that the divine power that Christ exercises in the institution of the sacraments "is the power of Christ as God and not as man."[19] The qualification of Christ "as man" recalls the centrality of the mystery of the hypostatic union as worked out substantially by the fifth-century Council of Chalcedon. "The Church thus confesses," states the catechism, "that Jesus is inseparably true God and true man. He is truly the Son of God who, without ceasing to be God and Lord, became man and our brother."[20]

The expression *hypostatic union* refers to the truth of the faith that the two natures of Christ, the divine and the human, "come together in one person (*prosopon*) and one hypostasis," as the Council of Chalcedon puts it.[21] What the Church holds about the unity of the two natures of Christ in the one person

18. Colman E. O'Neill, *Sacramental Realism* (Chicago: Midwest Theological Forum, 1998), 66.
19. *Summa theologiae* III.64.3, *sed contra*.
20. *CCC* no. 469.
21. Council of Chalcedon (451), "Definition," *DS* 301, as quoted in *CCC* no. 467.

of the Word helps one to understand Aquinas's use of the term "conjoined" to explain the instrumentality that Christ exercises in the sacramental economy.

From this point of contact with the divine in the person of Jesus Christ, we can approach a response to the question of how Christ figures in production of the sacrament's interior effects. In a brilliant exercise of the sword of distinction, Aquinas acknowledges that Christ works these effects both as God and as man. However, he does so in different ways: "For as God he works in the sacraments by his power as their author. As man, however, he works to produce the interior effect of the sacraments through merit and by way of efficient causality, but still by a causality that is instrumental."[22] In brief, Christ as God is the author, whereas Christ as man is related to the sacraments by way of both merit and efficient instrumental causality. Catholic theology refers to the first as the "power of authority," whereas the second has become known as the "power of excellence."[23]

The way that Christ as man works in the sacramental economy harks back to the discussion of the way that the passion of Christ works in the whole economy of salvation. The passion's effect on the world can be explained by reference to five modes or ways of considering its effectiveness. These modes include the mode of merit and the mode of efficient causality. The discussion, it should be noted, does not prolong an unnecessarily sophisticated argument that holds the interest only of those who study medieval theology. On the contrary, this discussion of the role that Christ's humanity plays in the production of the interior effects of the sacraments brings us squarely up against the central point of orthodox Christology.[24] The earliest reflection on the reality of the Incarnation led the holy doctors and saints to hold that Christ's humanity served as an instrument of his divinity, a conjoined instrument.

The power of excellence sets forth the role that Christ's human nature plays in the saving work of the sacraments. For his part, Aquinas offers a fourfold consideration when he discusses this power of excellence. That is, he gives four elements that make up the power of Christ as man at work in the sacraments. First, one may consider the merit and the effects of the passion of Christ, which are applied to the recipients of the sacraments by the virtue of faith. Aquinas refers his readers to the Letter to the Romans (3:25), where Saint Paul exhorts his audience to repose salvific confidence in the expiation Jesus Christ accomplishes

22. *Summa theologiae* III.64.3.

23. In *Summa theologiae* III.64.3, Aquinas explains the terms in this fashion: "Just as Christ, as God, has the power of *authority* in the sacraments so too as man he has the power of principal minister or the power of *excellence*" (emphasis original).

24. For further discussion, see Jacques Maritain, *On the Grace and Humanity of Jesus*, trans. T. W. Evans (New York: Herder & Herder, 1969).

by his blood. In a significant remark, Aquinas adds that the justifying faith that appeals to the power of Christ's passion stands available to Christian believers "by invoking Christ's name."[25]

The second element at work in the power of excellence points to the fact that the sacraments indeed sanctify in the name of Christ. The third consideration points to the suitability that the one who, as God, gave the sacraments their power should also institute them as man. The final consideration of the power of excellence that attaches to Christ's humanity in the administration of the sacraments points out that Christ himself did not require use of the sacraments to cause their effect. A cause, after all, does not depend on its effect, but vice versa.

These four elements that illuminate the power of excellence provide so many points of meditation that help the Catholic to penetrate more deeply into the mystery of both Christ and the sacraments of his Church. One should observe the remark that Aquinas makes about the Letter to the Romans and its theme of justification by faith. By relating justifying faith in the blood of Christ to the sacramental realities, Aquinas establishes the basis for that proper understanding of the relationship between faith and sacrament. For his part, Colman O'Neill considers Aquinas's position a proper reading of what the Apostle to the Gentiles teaches: "When Saint Paul speaks of faith he is simply turning his attention to one aspect, an essential one because of its relation to the word, of that Christian existence which is formally initiated in baptism and which he elsewhere can speak of as a 'new creation' for which Christ alone can be responsible (cf. 2 Cor. 5:17)."[26] The distinction between the power of authority and the power of excellence as this relates to the unique constitution of the Incarnate Word helps greatly to present an accurate picture of how the Lord may be said to institute the sacraments of the New Law.

No Alternative Models

Although article 4 raises a hypothetical question—namely, whether Christ could have communicated the power of excellence to other human ministers—it does serve to highlight an important point about the relationship that human ministers could have had, but in fact do not enjoy, with respect to the power of excellence. In other words, the relationship that the humanity of Christ enjoys with the divine person of the Word—that is, the hypostatic union—made it possible for Christ to set up alternative sacramental models and structures. However, as Aquinas notes, such delegated power would have been counterproductive to

25. *Summa theologiae* III.64.3.

26. O'Neill, *Sacramental Realism*, 119.

the plan of divine wisdom that orders all things sweetly. Aquinas explains why: "Christ refrained from communicating the power of excellence to ministers . . . to help the faithful lest they should put their trust in men, and lest there should be different sacraments leading to divisions in the Church."[27] It is useful to note that the Catholic Church takes the fact that Christ did not do something as a sign of the divine will that prohibits such a thing.

This argument enjoys a long history in the Church, as the 1976 declaration on reserving priestly ordination to men reports:

> Even his Mother, who was so closely associated with the mystery of her Son, and whose incomparable role is emphasized by the Gospels of Luke and John, was not invested with the apostolic ministry. This fact was to lead the Fathers to present her as an example of Christ's will in this domain; as Pope Innocent III repeated later, at the beginning of the thirteenth century, "Although the Blessed Virgin Mary surpassed in dignity and in excellence all the Apostles, nevertheless it was not to her but to them that the Lord entrusted the keys of the Kingdom of Heaven."[28]

This fairly recent magisterial text, though without using the technical terminology of "power of excellence," indicates that the humanity of Christ, including the manifest decisions of his human will, alone enjoys divinely inspired prerogatives that govern the Church's sacramental practices.

Divine Omnipotence and Sinful Ministers

The next consideration returns the discussion of sacramental mediation to those human ministers who administer the sacraments. With the exception of Baptism administered in exceptional circumstances, the ministers of the seven sacraments of the Catholic Church are clerics—that is, deacons, priests, or bishops. The rebaptism controversy and other controversies of the early centuries of Christian history that Saint Augustine reports in his anti-Donatist writings occasioned the first orthodox response to the question of unworthy ministers. Aquinas again quotes Saint Augustine's *Tractates on the Gospel of John*: "What difference does a bad minister make to you when the Lord is good?"[29] This text sets the tone for the Church's teaching about evil and unworthy ministers of the sacraments. "From the moment that a sacrament is celebrated in accordance with the intention of the Church, the power of Christ

27. *Summa theologiae* III.64.4 ad 1.

28. *Inter insigniores*, §2. The text refers to Innocent III's epistle to the bishops of Palencia and Burgos, December 11, 1210.

29. *Summa theologiae* III.64.5, *sed contra*, quoting Augustine, *Tractates on the Gospel of John* 5.1.

and his Spirit acts in and through it, independently of the personal holiness of the minister."[30] No other response to the proposal to make the efficacy of the sacraments depend on the holiness of the minister is possible. Those who, in whatever age of the Church, are tempted to succumb to the temptation that such a proposal generates require instruction not about the sacraments but about the power of God.

Were an unworthy minister to hold the power of blocking the divine action that the sacraments communicate instrumentally, such an anomaly would result in granting to a creature the ability to thwart the outpouring of the divine omnipotence and mercy. Such a proposal strikes not only at the heart of what the Catholic Church holds about the efficacy of the sacraments but also at the central message of both Old and New Testaments. The *Catechism of the Catholic Church* makes this telling observation about the divine omnipotence: "Of all the divine attributes only God's omnipotence is named in the Creed: to confess this power has great bearing on our lives."[31] In the supernatural order, a most striking example of the divine omnipotence appears in the sacraments, even sacraments administered by those whose personal holiness does not measure up to the standard that Christ exhorts his followers to observe.

In order to illustrate why an unworthy minister can still operate effectively in the mediation of divine grace that the sacraments accomplish, Aquinas offers two examples drawn from everyday experience. One ought to read the examples in light of the everyday experiences of the thirteenth century, before the founding of microbiology and the later discovery that lead pipes can adversely affect drinking water. The principle, of course, is not affected by examples that may be unsuitable for present-day instruction. "It makes no difference," says Aquinas, "whether the body of the doctor, which is the instrument of a mind possessing certain skills, is healthy or infirm, or whether a tube through which water is passed is made of silver or lead."[32] Moral turpitude does not affect a minister's instrumentality inasmuch as a minister receives power from Christ. Aquinas makes the important observation that the sacraments do not assimilate the recipient to the person who administers the sacrament but rather configure the recipient to Christ himself.

Catholic theology retains the theme of configuration with its affinity to the language of Saint Paul (e.g., see Rom. 8:29). The word also appears in connection with the effects of the sacraments—for example, when the catechism speaks of those who have been "configured more deeply to Christ by Baptism."[33] For

30. CCC no. 1128.
31. CCC no. 268.
32. *Summa theologiae* III.64.5.
33. CCC no. 1322.

his part, Aquinas explains the reason for making Baptism necessary only after the death of Christ by reference to its effect of configuration to Christ's passion. "Through baptism," writes Aquinas, "a man is configured to the passion and resurrection of Christ inasmuch as he dies to sin and begins a new life of righteousness." And so, concludes Aquinas, "it was proper for Christ to suffer and rise before the necessity of being configured to his passion and death was imposed upon men."[34] In sum, given the dimensions of the supernatural mystery at work in the sacramental mediations, it would appear highly counterintuitive to allow something as ephemeral as human weakness and even sinfulness to obstruct the fulfillment of the divine plan.

The provision of the divine benevolence that does not allow the unworthiness of the minster to impede the effects of the sacraments does not, of course, issue a license to wayward clergy. On the contrary, "before the grandeur of the priestly grace and office," the catechism reminds all Catholics, "the holy doctors felt an urgent call to conversion in order to conform their whole lives to him whose sacrament had made them ministers."[35] It is possible that the wickedness of certain ministers can lead them to destroy the very sacrament itself. This occurs when "due form and due matter is lacking." Aquinas, of course, recognizes that both due form and due matter as well as "a certain fitness" in the minister becomes each sacramental administration.[36] In other words, the Catholic tradition holds that good men should administer the sacraments, and those who are not good sin grievously by committing a certain irreverence when they administer the sacraments. Such wicked ministers do not, however, as already explained, obstruct the divine action.

The theological provisions that ensure that no human actor impedes the divine plan of salvation and its sacramental economy do not cover exhaustively the way that the Catholic Church governs her clerics. The *Code of Canon Law* provides ample legislation that stipulates both delict and punishment as these may apply to the ministers of the Church. The insistence that even unworthy ministers can act validly in the administration of the sacrament ensures that those who receive the sacraments are not troubled by the spiritual condition of their ministers.

There remains the question of the intention of the minister to do what Christ and the Church do. Again, Aquinas offers the best and simplest explanation as to why the minister of the sacrament must possess the right intention in order for the sacrament to produce its effects. In the first instance where he discusses the

34. *Summa theologiae* III.66.2.

35. CCC no. 1589. The text continues with a long quotation from St. Gregory of Nazianzus (d. 390).

36. Aquinas discusses this issue in the reply to the third objection of *Summa theologiae* III.64.5.

intention of the minister, Aquinas explains the difference between an inanimate instrument and a living instrument:

> An inanimate instrument has no intention regarding the effect; but instead of the intention there is the motion whereby it is moved by the principal agent. But an animate instrument, such as a minister, is not only moved, but in a sense moves itself, in so far as by his will he moves his bodily members to act. Consequently, his intention is required, whereby he subjects himself to the principal agent; that is, it is necessary that he intend to do that which Christ and the Church do.[37]

The Church speaks of a minister's possessing the right intention when he administers a sacrament.[38] The history of sacramental theology exhibits a variety of explanations about the kind of intention that one must possess to administer validly a sacrament. The different views reflect the seriousness of one's possessing the right intention and at the same time take into account the different ways in which the human mind works.[39]

Graham Greene's 1940 novel *The Power and the Glory* tells the story of a "whiskey priest" who, though his faith wavers under the pressures of anticlerical 1930s Mexico and for personal reasons, continues nonetheless to fulfill his sacramental obligations by following the rules. The story illustrates that the faith of the minister does not figure in the administration of a sacrament. In fact, as Aquinas points out, "a person devoid of faith can confer a sacrament so long as the other conditions are fulfilled which are necessary for sacramental validity."[40] Among these other conditions, the Church includes a right intention, so that

37. *Summa theologiae* III.64.8 ad 1. In Latin: "Ad primum ergo dicendum quod instrumentum inanimatum non habet aliquam intentionem respectu effectus, sed loco intentionis est motus quo movetur a principali agente. Sed instrumentum animatum, sicut est minister, non solum movetur, sed etiam quodammodo movet seipsum, inquantum sua voluntate movet membra ad operandum. Et ideo requiritur eius intentio, qua se subiiciat principali agenti, ut scilicet intendat facere *quod facit Christus et Ecclesia*" (emphasis added). The phrase "quod facit Christus et Ecclesia" has deeply shaped official Catholic teaching.

38. For example, see CCC no. 1128. See also, in the *Code of Canon Law*, can. 861 §2: "When an ordinary minister is absent or impeded, a catechist or another person designated for this function by the local ordinary, or in a case of necessity any person with the right intention, confers baptism licitly."

39. Those interested in the details will find the following materials helpful: Bernard Leeming, *Principles of Sacramental Theology* (Westminster, MD: Newman, 1956), esp. 435–96. See also Nicholas Halligan, *The Administration of the Sacraments: Some Practical Guides for Priests and Seminarians* (Staten Island, NY: Alba House, 1963), esp. 11–23. Halligan published a revised version of his book that reflects theological opinion on intention as it developed after the Second Vatican Council. See Nicholas Halligan, *The Sacraments and Their Celebration* (Staten Island, NY: Alba House, 1986), 3–19, esp. 4–7, 10–11.

40. *Summa theologiae* III.64.9.

the perverse minister who withholds the intention of conferring a sacrament would invalidate the sacramental action.

This circumstance, it is expected, happens rarely. On the contrary, most ministers of the sacraments formulate their intention, especially when it comes to confecting the Blessed Eucharist. The *Roman Missal* contains a prayer that includes the following formulation of intention to be said by Catholic priests before they celebrate Mass: “My purpose is to celebrate Mass and to make present the Body and Blood of our Lord Jesus Christ according to the rite of the holy Roman Church to the praise of our all-powerful God and all his assembly in the glory of heaven, for my good and the good of all his pilgrim Church on earth, and for all who have asked me to pray for them in general and in particular, and for the good of the holy Roman Church.”[41] Each minister of a sacrament needs to formulate an intention to do what Christ and the Church intends; further elaboration on this requirement can indeed aid the devotion of the minister.

The final article that Aquinas composed on the origins of sacramental mediation considers two cases of perverse intentions. The first case is invalidating and comes about when a feigning of the sacrament occurs—that is, when a minister makes a show of administering a sacrament but does not intend to administer it. Feigning or withholding a right intention destroys the sacramental mediation. On the other hand, conflicting intentions held by a person who administers the sacraments—for example, administering a sacrament with an eye toward committing some reprehensible action with the person who receives the sacrament—do not invalidate a sacrament. This kind of perversity, says Aquinas, “does not deprive the sacrament of its truth [*veritatem sacrament*].”[42] Obviously, such disordered behavior results in the minister sinning gravely and in all likelihood will cause great scandal.

These considerations should not be considered excessive extravagances of religious casuistry. On the contrary, the various foregoing considerations about sacramental mediation and about the minister who performs the sacramental action aim to ensure what Aquinas calls the truth of the sacrament. Right thinking about mediation reveals that the Lord has confided to his Church and her ministers seven instruments of salvation that, because of the effects that each produces, require a conformity to the divine will as discovered in the words and deeds of Christ.

41. *Roman Missal*, “Preparation for Mass.”
42. *Summa theologiae* III.64.10.

12

The Number of the Sacraments

The Catholic Church authoritatively teaches about the number of the sacraments that belong to the New Law of grace. As already indicated, "these are seven: Baptism, Confirmation (or Chrismation), the Eucharist, Penance, the Anointing of the Sick, Holy Orders, and Matrimony."[1] No other option is possible.

Trent and Other Official Statements

In order to give some theological arguments that expose the reason for the sacred seven, the *Catechism of the Catholic Church* makes use of Saint Thomas Aquinas's treatment of this topic. In his *Summa theologiae*, the Common Doctor offers reasons to explain why God provides seven sacraments.[2] Aquinas has not been the only authority to undertake this investigation. The history of theologians' views on the number of the sacraments occupies pages in the standard manuals of theology. One fact, however, appears clearly from a review of these materials: even saints held divergent opinions about which rites of the Catholic Church qualified as true sacraments of the New Law. In fact, it was not until the twelfth century that the widespread influence of Peter Lombard's *Four Books of Sentences* helped to settle common opinion on the number seven.[3] His

1. CCC no. 1210.
2. *Summa theologiae* III.65.1–4.
3. For Lombard's text, see his *Libri quattuor sententiarum*, 1.4, dist. 2, n. 1, as found conveniently in PL 192:841–43.

ordering of the sacraments, according to the manualist Emmanuel Doronzo, also influenced the authoritative pronouncement made at the Council of Trent.[4]

We can see this assertion borne out in the official proceedings of the Council of Trent. In fact, canon 1 of the aforementioned 1547 *Decree on the Sacraments* could not make the point more clearly: "If anyone says that the sacraments of the New Law were not all instituted by Jesus Christ our Lord, or that there are more or fewer than seven, that is, baptism, confirmation, the Eucharist, penance, extreme unction, orders, and matrimony, or that any one of these seven is not truly and properly a sacrament, let him be anathema."[5] This text stands in substantial conformity both with what was stipulated earlier, in the fifteenth century during the Council of Florence (1439–45), and with what later would appear in the Tridentine Profession of Faith.[6]

The definitive statement on the number of the sacraments appears relatively late in the history of Christianity. The standard explanation for this occurrence argues that the Church moves to solemn pronouncement only in the face of serious and explicit challenges to revealed truth. The various circumstances of the sixteenth-century reform provided just such an occasion. The fathers at Trent made this purpose explicit in the foreword to the council's *Decree on the Sacraments* when they explained their intent in no uncertain terms: they issued a decree on the sacraments "in order to do away with errors and to root out heresies that in our turbulent age are directed against the most holy sacraments . . . and which are doing great harm to the purity of the Catholic Church and to the salvation of souls."[7]

In any event, when Aquinas set about to explain why it is fitting for the Church to recognize seven sacraments, he expressed the consensus of theologians as it existed in the thirteenth century.

Resemblance to Human Life Stages

In *Summa theologiae* III.65.1, Aquinas first supplies a helpful recall of the overall purposes that the sacraments serve. His accounting of these effects common to each of the sacraments reflects the work both of image-perfection and of image-restoration. Aquinas summarizes, "The sacraments of the Church are

4. See Emmanuel Doronzo, *Tractatus dogmaticus de sacramentis in genere* (Milwaukee: Bruce, 1946), 517.

5. *DS* 1601.

6. The earlier magisterial statement appears in Council of Florence, *Exsultate Deo* (*Bull of Union with the Armenians*), November 22, 1439 (*DS* 1310), whereas for the later text, see Pius IV in his 1564 bull *Iniunctam nobis*, which contains the Tridentine Profession of Faith (*DS* 1864).

7. *DS* 1600.

designed to achieve two effects: to render man perfect in all that pertains to the worship of God as expressed in the religion of Christian living, and also as a remedy to counteract the harmful effects of sin."

The expression "the religion of Christian living" (*secundum religionem Christianae vitae*) of course points to a way of life that includes the fulfillment of the two great commandments of the law (see Matt. 22:33–40), which the Church teaches form a "single commandment of love."[8] The seven sacraments serve, then, to provide, albeit diversely, divine aid for the whole of the Christian life. This explains why Aquinas introduces an analogy between what the sacraments provide for growth in the life of grace and what the human person requires for the perfection of his or her physical life. Both human nature and uplifted human nature require helps and healing.

Throughout *Summa theologiae* III.65 we find an explanation of how the number of the sacraments reflects the coherence that exists between the physical life and the spiritual life. This explanation does not purport to prove that there are seven sacraments. Like the Incarnation itself, those things that reflect the free choice of the divine benevolence can be shown only to possess a fittingness that exposes the purpose of the salvation of the human race. God could have acted otherwise, but he did not. Recall, as discussed in *Summa theologiae* III.64.4, that Christ did not extend the power of excellence to his apostles and their successors. The theologian, then, is left to find reasons of suitableness or fittingness for the number of sacraments that, at least since the twelfth century, the teachers of the Church commonly taught to be seven. It may be useful to observe that other rites that some theologians, even saints, may have held to qualify as sacraments became recognized as sacramentals (e.g., abbatial blessings and the consecration of churches).

The analogy of spiritual development to human development requires a distinction between the individual in him- or herself and the individual in relation to society. The individual requires growth in life, and this phase is served by Baptism, Confirmation, and the Eucharist. Further, an individual also requires remedies for noxious influences that may harm him or her, and these are found in Penance and Holy Anointing. In relation to society, the human person stands in need of governance, which is supplied by Holy Orders, and in the most apparent need for propagation, which finds its analogue in Matrimony.[9]

As mentioned earlier, an authoritative text from the Council of Florence (held in the fifteenth century) makes use of Aquinas's arguments and provides a convenient abbreviated version of these arguments for fittingness. The

8. CCC no. 2055.
9. See *Summa theologiae* III.65.1.

Florentine Council's adoption of Aquinas's arguments gives some indication of the familiarity that the sacramental theology presented in the *Summa theologiae* and elsewhere enjoyed among churchmen even before the Council of Trent. The Florence conciliar text that stipulates the number and names of the sacraments comes from the *Bull of Union with the Armenians* (*Exsultate Deo*), which was issued on November 22, 1439, under Pope Eugene IV (d. 1447).

Exsultate Deo shows the influence of Aquinas's writings on a magisterial pronouncement. The text of the bull first explains that "these sacraments of ours . . . both contain grace and communicate it to those who worthily receive them." The document goes on to explain how the ensemble of the seven sacraments sustains a Christian's life spread out over the ages:

> Of these [sacraments], the first five are ordered to the spiritual perfection of each person in himself, and the last two (are directed) to the governance and the increase of the whole Church. Through baptism, in fact, we are reborn spiritually, by confirmation we grow in grace and are strengthened in faith. Once reborn and strengthened, we are nourished by the food of the divine Eucharist. If through sin we incur an illness of the soul, we are spiritually healed through penance (and healed) spiritually and bodily as well through extreme unction, insofar as it befits the soul. By the sacrament of orders, however, the Church is governed and multiplied spiritually; through matrimony, she grows bodily.[10]

The best scholarship of the twentieth century identifies the precise source for this instruction on the sacraments in an *opuscula* or "little work" of Thomas Aquinas titled *De articulis fidei et Ecclesiae sacramentis*.[11] There are grounds to suppose that this thirteenth-century work of Aquinas, which after his death enjoyed a large circulation in Europe, captures the standard catechetical instruction about the sacraments given in the Catholic Church during the late Middle Ages.[12]

The conciliar text quoted above explains in a most succinct form the place that the sacraments of the Church hold in making her members saints—that is, in making them fit for heavenly bliss. It is a work that, as has been said, Christian anthropology considers to be a work of image-perfection. In other words, the sacraments are necessary in order to endow the human person with what is required to perfect the image of creation in which God created man so that each person can enjoy the divine friendship here below as well as hereafter.

10. Council of Florence, *Exsultate Deo*, *DS* 1311.

11. See Jean-Pierre Torrell, *Saint Thomas Aquinas*, vol. 1, *The Person and His Work*, rev. ed., trans. R. Royal (Washington, DC: Catholic University of America Press, 2005), 126–27.

12. See Torrell, *Thomas Aquinas*, 1:126–27.

The Number of the Sacraments and the Perfection of the Human Person

The sacraments serve the high purpose of image-perfection as separated instruments that find their legitimacy and their effectiveness in the conjoined instrument that remains the human nature of the Incarnate Word. Recall the ungainsayable principle of Catholic theology—namely, that it is one thing to be a creature and another to become a saint. The origin of these divine actions is the same (i.e., God—Father, Son, and Holy Spirit), but the *terms* of these actions differ. The divine creative act makes us creatures in the image of God, whereas the divine sanctifying act makes us friends of God, who enjoy proper relations of knowledge and love with each of the divine persons of the Trinity.

The Catholic Church clearly holds that the sin of Adam becomes the sin of all his descendants. "It is a sin," states the catechism, "which will be transmitted by propagation to all mankind, that is, by the transmission of a human nature deprived of original holiness and justice."[13] It should come as no surprise then that Aquinas also offers reasons of fittingness to explain the number of the sacraments on the basis of the way that each offers a remedy for the effects of sin. These include both the effects of original sin, a sin contracted and not committed by Adam's progeny, and actual sins, or those that each of his progeny freely commits.

In order to appreciate the importance of the sacraments as remedies for sin, it is necessary to realize that sinning involves more than the transgression of a law. It is true that during certain periods of the Church's history—for example, the era of moral casuistry that flourished during the seventeenth and eighteenth centuries—one could easily have received the impression that sinning entailed only a change of legal status before the Divine Judge. Within this conception of things, the sacrament of Penance and Reconciliation would have functioned as a court that, as it were, settled accounts with the Almighty. An overly juridical interpretation of sin and forgiveness, however, can both underplay and obscure the harm that sinning causes to the powers of the soul. For instance, the familiar penances that Catholics famously receive within the confessional became interpreted more as retributive than as remedial acts.

Inasmuch as all sinning strikes against the divine wisdom that orders all creation wisely, the sinner who becomes accustomed to this or that transgression suffers a diminishment of spiritual energy. In other words, the more that one violates the truth about the good of the human person, the more such a sinner forgets about the true good of the human person. In the divine plan, God has

13. *CCC* no. 404.

ordained that the sacraments of his Son's Church supply, as Aquinas puts it, "a remedy against the harmful effects of sin."[14]

To understand how each sacrament remedies some effect of sin, it is necessary to recall the absolute gratuity of the gift of salvation. "Grace is favor, the free and undeserved help that God gives" to a human person who is set on the way to eternal life.[15] Fallen human nature enjoys no purchase on eternal life. Baptism then provides a remedy for this circumstance—namely, the lack of a spiritual life (*contra carentiam vitae spiritualis*)—which in this context means a supernatural life.[16] Confirmation provides a remedy for the weakness of soul (*contra infirmitatem animi*) that, even shortly after the birth of a child, makes itself felt in concrete ways. In this context, Aquinas's use of the word "animus" points not to the principle of physical life, as in the body-and-soul composite, but rather to the soul as a principle of rational or reasoned human existence. The Eucharist strengthens the worthy recipient against the proneness to sin (*contra labilitatem animi ad peccandum*) that results from the disorders that original sin leaves in the person even after Baptism. These disorders sometimes are called the penalties of the present life. The Eucharist accomplishes this objective by bestowing an increase in charity that belongs uniquely to the sacrament of Christ's love.

To continue, the sacrament of Penance and Reconciliation provides a saving remedy for sins committed after Baptism (*contra actuale peccatum post baptismum commissum*). The sacrament of the Anointing of the Sick provides a remedy, in Aquinas's own words, "against those elements of sin [*contra reliquias peccatorum*] which remain, those namely which, whether through negligence or ignorance, are not sufficiently removed by penance."[17] These five sacraments supply remedies to the individual who receives them, whereas the last two sacraments provide remedies for sin in those who receive them inasmuch as these persons form part of a community of life. Holy Orders, with the right and duty that the sacrament imposes on men to teach, govern, and sanctify, acts as a preventive against the breakup of the community (*contra dissolutionem multitudinis*). Lastly, Matrimony acts as a remedy for concupiscence (*contra concupiscentiam*), insofar as the couple enjoy rights to each other's bodies, and it also protects against losses that death (*contra defectum multitudinis*) deals to the human community.[18]

14. *Summa theologiae* III.65.1.
15. CCC no. 1996.
16. The catechism places Baptism as a cause of man's justification (CCC no. 1987).
17. *Summa theologiae* III.65.1.
18. The Latin expressions for each of the remedies that the sacraments bring appear in *Summa theologiae* III.65.1.

In light of this classic teaching of Catholic theology, it is easy to understand why no quarter should be given to those who propose overly enthusiastic celebrations of the sacraments. Such an approach to the Mass and other sacraments can distract the recipient from those effects of the sacraments that serve the work of both image-restoration and image-perfection.

The satisfactory aspect of the sacraments—that is, how each sacrament provides a special remedy against the effects or remains of sin that the human family experiences each day—does not figure much in contemporary mainstream Catholic catechesis. An undue emphasis on the notion of liturgy as a celebration does not lend itself well to considerations of sins' effects in the lives of Catholics. Each sacrament nonetheless can be looked at from the point of view of supplying a remedy for the harmful results of sin. The Catholic doctrine on satisfaction provides the theological background necessary to grasp fully the implications of the image-restorative qualities of the seven sacraments. In short, satisfaction for sin makes up a perpetual part of a Christian's life.

This thought need not evoke sentiments of sadness or melancholy, as if the Christian life promoted a morose preoccupation with human faults and imperfections. Christian life does not center on sin. Instead, Christian life brings the virtues, the gifts of the Holy Spirit, and other graces that perfect the one who receives them. At the same time, like the tares and the wheat of the gospel parable (see Matt. 13:24–30), the weaknesses of sins continue to afflict even the most devout souls. Only in heaven does the saint exist without the tares of sin and its baneful effects. Or, to appeal to a less allegorical argument, no Catholic here on earth finds a reason to stop praying the Lord's Prayer: "Forgive us our trespasses, as we forgive those who trespass against us."[19] After death, the Catholic soul that finds itself imperfectly purified of sinful attachments undergoes a final purification in Purgatory.[20]

The Sacraments around the Eucharist

Catholic theologians have offered other reasons for why the Church recognizes seven sacraments as instituted by Christ.[21] Their explanations include proposals that relate the seven sacraments to the seven virtues of the Christian life (faith, hope, charity, prudence, justice, fortitude, and temperance) or to the harmful effects of the seven deadly sins (anger, envy, gluttony, greed, lust, pride, and

19. *Roman Missal*, "The Communion Rite."

20. See CCC no. 1030–31.

21. For further information, see Doronzo, *Tractatus dogmaticus de sacramentis*, chap. 8 (pp. 495–537). The author devotes this forty-three-page chapter to an exposition of the historical opinions about the number and ordering of the sacraments.

sloth).[22] All in all, it seems best to establish an ordering among the sacraments that follows according to the rationales for their existence. The wide diversity of opinion about how to account for the number and the ordering of the sacraments gives testimony to the fruitful reflection that Catholic theology has given to the sacramental mediation that the Church safeguards. The rationale that compares the evolution of physical life with the beginning and evolution of supernatural life provides one model that seems best to suit sound pedagogy—namely, to move from what is better known to what is lesser known.

At the same time, what might be described as a linear model for arranging the sacraments finds a complement in a circular model. Here we find an explanation that illustrates how each of the six sacraments serves the seventh, the Holy Eucharist, which, in Aquinas's opinion, holds the distinction of being "in an absolute sense, the greatest of all the sacraments."[23] The Common Doctor offers an alternative way to envisage the number, ordering, and, indeed, the necessity of the sacraments in relation to the great gift of the Eucharist. Holy Orders obviously is required for the consecration of the Eucharist, whereas Baptism is required for its reception. Confirmation, says Aquinas, strengthens an individual against the thought of being unworthy to receive the Eucharist. Penance and Reconciliation and the Anointing of the Sick make a person worthy to receive the Eucharist. Finally, Matrimony finds its place in the constellation of sacraments that surround the Eucharist from the text of Ephesians that speaks of marriage between a man and a woman as a "great mystery" of union: "This is a great mystery, but I speak in reference to Christ and the church" (Eph. 5:32).[24]

A Differentiated Necessity

As already discussed, the question of whether the sacraments are necessary for salvation receives treatment in the context of salvation history. In short, after the fall, God directs the spiritual destiny of the human race by various concrete helps, whether these signs appear in the natural realities that make up the visible,

22. A 1557 sacramentary in use in the Diocese of Como (Italy) includes several explanations—namely, the various circumstances of a person's life in the Church, the various virtues of the Christian life, and the several sins against which each sacrament offers a special help. See *Septem sacramenta ecclesiae secundum septem diversitates hominum in ecclesia*, originally published in Milan in 1557 and reprinted in facsimile (Como, Italy: Typographia Editrice Cesare Nani, 1998).

23. *Summa theologiae* III.65.3.

24. See *Summa theologiae* III.65.3. The reply to the first objection of this article supplies a text that can be used to support the claim that Holy Orders (which is indispensable for the Eucharist) exceeds Matrimony in dignity as a sacrament. "Matrimony," says Aquinas, "is designed to contribute to the common good at a physical level. But the common good at the spiritual level, and that of the whole Church, is, in its very substance, contained in the sacrament of the Eucharist."

created world or are stipulated by divine instructions. Given the disqualification for heavenly bliss that befell the human race as a result of Adam's sin, only those sacraments that happen after Christ's passion bring a restoration and perfection of the human race. The Church administered the sacraments throughout her existence, as any number of texts makes clear. In the sixteenth century, some reformers cast doubt on the necessity and indeed the usefulness of the sacraments, especially those whose institution the New Testament did not appear to report in a manner that met their criteria. So the Council of Trent, cited by the *Catechism of the Catholic Church*, affirms, as already noted, the necessity of the seven sacraments of the New Covenant "for salvation."[25]

To affirm the necessity of the sacraments, of course, requires certain distinctions. Aquinas cuts to the chase when he observes, in response to those who made arguments for an extensive view of necessity (that is, the view that everybody needs each sacrament), that "children attain to salvation through baptism without the other sacraments."[26] This should not lead to the conclusion that the other sacraments are not necessary for salvation. They are necessary, but the necessity does not apply in the same way to each of the seven for every person.

If we follow Aquinas's schema of distinction, we need to recall some different kinds of necessity that Aristotle identifies.[27] A basic distinction proposes that whereas some things are absolutely necessary, other things are necessary for the better attainment of an end. According to Aquinas, Baptism, Penance and Reconciliation, and Holy Orders are necessary absolutely for human salvation—that is, without them, the beatific end of the human race remains impossible to attain. The first two of these sacraments, Baptism and Penance, are necessary for the perfection of the individual, while the third, Holy Orders, is necessary for the sake of the community, which is the Church.

Of these three, Baptism enjoys the distinction of being "necessary absolutely and unconditionally."[28] The other two are necessary when certain conditions arise. "Penance is necessary whenever mortal sin has been committed after Baptism."[29] Holy Orders is necessary since, without it, the Church would lack due governance and fall apart. Note that Aquinas does not teach that the Church runs more smoothly with priests and bishops. He holds, rather, that without the pastors of the Church, there would be no Church.

25. CCC no. 1129.

26. *Summa theologiae* III.65.4, *sed contra*.

27. For a brief account, see Romanus Cessario, *The Godly Image: Christian Satisfaction in Aquinas* (Washington, DC: Catholic University of America Press, 2020), 26–29.

28. *Summa theologiae* III.65.4. The Latin runs "simpliciter et absolute."

29. *Summa theologiae* III.65.4.

The remaining three sacraments—Confirmation, Holy Anointing, and Matrimony—are those that are required for the better attainment of the end. In other words, these sacraments aid the Catholic throughout life's journey and at the termination of it.

Various theological ways to explain the inequality of the sacraments aim to show the special excellence that the Christian religion attaches to Baptism and, for those who reach the age of reason, the Holy Eucharist. Catholic orthodoxy does not impose a specific theological paradigm. It does, however, reject the view that denies the supreme necessity of Baptism and the supreme excellence of the Eucharist. Again, it was the sixteenth century that occasioned an authoritative formulation in response to such a rejection. Canon 3 of Trent's *Decree on the Sacraments* reads, "If anyone says that these seven sacraments are so equal to one another that one is not in any way of greater worth than another, let him be anathema."[30]

To defend the inequality of the sacraments with respect to their necessity for salvation does not gainsay the requirement that those who administer the sacraments should do so with generosity and indeed under obligation. Neither does the fact that the sacraments are unequal in the degrees of their necessity lead to the conclusion that a Catholic is free to avoid the sacramental mediations that he or she may require. Instead, the distinctions that differentiate the necessity that attaches to each sacrament serve to show how the sacraments benefit different people at different times and in various circumstances of their lives. At the same time, no claim is made that every member of the Church must receive every sacrament of the Church.

30. *DS* 1603.

PART 2

THE SEVEN SACRAMENTS

13

Baptism

The 2004 *Compendium of the Social Doctrine of the Church* aims to collect the various elements that compose the entire body of social teachings advanced by the Catholic Church. In it we find a convenient summary of what the Catholic Church holds about the Sacraments of Initiation. According to the *Catechism of the Catholic Church,* these three sacraments—Baptism, Confirmation, and the Eucharist—"lay the foundation of every Christian life."[1] The compendium explains further: "The identity of the lay faithful is born in and nourished by the sacraments of Baptism, Confirmation and the Eucharist. Baptism conforms the person to Christ, Son of the Father, first-born of every creature, sent to all as Teacher and Redeemer. Confirmation configures the individual to Christ, sent to give new life to creation and to every being through the outpouring of his Spirit. The Eucharist makes the believer a participant in the unique and perfect sacrifice that Christ offered to the Father, in his own flesh, for the salvation of the world."[2] The broadly inclusive description of the work of the Holy Spirit appears to suit the overall theme of the document that addresses the requirement to respect the whole of creation. At the same time, it serves to identify the proper concern that Christ's lay faithful should manifest by their engagement in "temporal affairs and ordering them according to the plan of God."[3] This charge finds explicit expression in the documents of the Second Vatican Council.[4]

1. CCC no. 1212.
2. *Social Doctrine,* no. 542.
3. *Lumen Gentium,* no. 31 (VRL).
4. *Lumen Gentium,* no. 31 (VRL): "Since they [the laity] are tightly bound up in all types of temporal affairs it is their special task to order and to throw light upon these affairs in such a way

Overview of the History of Baptism

What the Catholic Church teaches about Baptism also receives a convenient and complete exposition in the *Catechism of the Catholic Church*. Specifically, section 2 of part 2 presents Church teaching on each of the seven sacraments. This treatment assumes the general principles that have been discussed in the first part of the present volume. Many of these general principles, indeed some of the most important of them, have been clarified by the Church in the course of dealing with misunderstandings that arose throughout the Christian centuries about the sacrament of Baptism.

One of the most vexing challenges to sacramental efficacy involves the view held by certain non-Catholic biblical scholars and theologians that Baptism serves to announce in a public forum the Christian status of an individual who either already has made the necessary profession of faith or, in the case of infant Baptism, is expected to make it upon reaching the required age. Generally speaking (for there are many nuances raised by one authority or another), this view of Baptism makes of the liturgical rite a kind of proclamation of justification instead of a cause of it.[5]

The Council of Trent found it necessary to anathematize fourteen propositions that circulated before and during the sixteenth century. Many of the positions that this council rejected in its "Canons on the Sacrament of Baptism" had arisen in light of various interpretations of texts in the New Testament that humanist scholars, some of whom were Catholic, had begun to produce during the sixteenth-century Renaissance.[6]

Even a catalog of what biblical scholars have written since the sixteenth century about Baptism would require its own research and, most probably, a multivolume publication. It is, however, a fair generalization to observe that

---

that they may come into being and then continually increase according to Christ to the praise of the Creator and the Redeemer."

5. For a discussion of some biblical issues related to the status of Baptism in the New Testament, see Burkhard Neunheuser, *Baptism and Confirmation*, trans. John Jay Hughes, The Herder History of Dogma (New York: Herder & Herder, 1964), 27n27. Neunheuser refers the reader to the work of the Catholic exegete Rudolf Schnackenburg (d. 2002), whom Joseph Ratzinger later referred to as "probably the most prominent Catholic exegete writing in German during the second half of the twentieth century." Joseph Ratzinger, *Jesus of Nazareth: From the Baptism in the Jordan to the Transfiguration* (New York: Doubleday, 2007), xii–xiii.

6. See Guy Bedouelle, *The Reform of Catholicism, 1480–1620*, trans. J. K. Farge, in *Catholic and Recusant Texts of the Late Medieval & Early Modern Periods*, Studies and Texts 161 (Toronto: Pontifical Institute of Medieval Studies, 2008), 52–53, for a list of three such biblical exegetes: Jacques Lefèvre d'Étaples (d. 1536), Erasmus of Rotterdam (d. 1536), and the Italian Dominican Sante Pagnini (d. 1536), whose "Latin Bible, based on the study of Hebrew and Greek texts and published in 1528 in Lyons, is accompanied by a number of philological and historical appendices which were essential tools used by all biblical scholars of the sixteenth century."

differences of interpretations of the New Testament about Baptism reflect, at least broadly, the confessional standpoint of the exegete. One recognized Catholic scholar offers this summary of how Baptism was administered in the New Testament period: "In sum, one may conclude that the rationale knitting together Christianity's earliest initiatory structure is something like this: *Preceded by authentic proclamation of the risen and exalted* Christos-Messiah *and by conversion, Spirit baptism by water at apostolic hands initiates one into the full life of the community in which the gospel has begun to become praxis.* Here is the common ground that serves an articulation point for all the multivalent practices that enter the initiatory continuum."[7] Nothing in this description raises doubts about the legitimacy of what the Catholic Church holds about Baptism. At the same time, the Church throughout the ages has rejected misinterpretations about the place that Baptism holds in the Christian life. That such clarifications arose especially within the context of the sixteenth-century reform appears evident in the third canon of the seventh session of the Council of Trent: "If anyone says that the Roman Church (the mother and teacher of all churches) does not have the true doctrine concerning the sacrament of baptism, let him be anathema."[8]

Because of the important place that Baptism holds in the sacramental economy, some cursory remarks about the history of the sacrament can serve to illustrate how sacramental theology has developed throughout the Christian Church. The selection of texts is governed by the principle that the essentials of Catholic teaching on the sacraments enjoy continuity with the earliest expressions of Christian theology. Some early developments during the second century that appear in both East and West include the following figures and events.[9]

A first witness who may command consideration arises in Origen of Alexandria. For his part, Origen encountered and responded to three dangerous misconceptions about the Christian mysteries: the first advanced a magical conception of the mysteries; the second advanced the Gnostic tendency to turn grace into a natural and cosmological process; and the third advanced the abuse of performing a rite without a proper understanding on the part of either the officiant or the recipient. In response to these issues that suggest the need to purify cultural conceptions for use in Christian theology, Origen places stress in his instruction on both the nature of authentic baptismal regeneration and the "new nature" that the baptized receive.

7. Aidan Kavanagh, *The Shape of Baptism: The Rite of Christian Initiation* (New York: Pueblo, 1978), 22–23 (emphasis original).

8. Council of Trent, Session 7, Canons on the Sacrament of Baptism, can. 3, *DS* 1616.

9. The information that follows is drawn from Neunheuser, *Baptism and Confirmation*, chaps. 3–9.

All in all, three elements especially figure in Origen's catechesis on Baptism. He first of all points out the parallel between Christ's humanity and the sacraments of the Church. One recognizes in this first point a theme that later theology will develop with the help of Aristotle's teaching on natures. In other words, the sacraments participate in the truth of the Incarnate Word and so do not fall into the category of occult magic. Second, Origen further clarifies in opposition to all purely cosmological accounts of the Christian mystery that, even though the sacraments may be considered as physical events, they enjoy the power to produce an effect in the spiritual order. Significantly, this third-century theologian reminds his hearers that this spiritual effect always comes about in connection with the Word—that is, he expresses a principle of intelligibility. Third and finally, Origen associates what he calls the "divine power which effects salvation" with "the epiclesis in which the Trinity is adored."[10] To put it differently, Origen assumes that the administration of the sacraments proceeds from an informed consciousness.

The witness of Tertullian, a lay authority, also deserves mention because of his explicit treatment of the sacrament of Baptism. His *De baptismo* centers on the sacrament and its administration. In this text, the author refers to Baptism, in a Latin phrase charged with doctrine, as the "happy sacrament of our water" (*Felix sacramentum aquae nostrae*).[11] Why a happy sacrament? Tertullian explains that, once we are washed of the faults of our original blindness, we are liberated unto eternal life.

As happened with many early Christian thinkers who wrote during the period of persecution, a certain unevenness appears in the way that Tertullian's works capture some teachings. Scholars, for instance, explain his reported reluctance about the practice of infant Baptism by remarking on the emphasis that he puts on the actuality of Christian life. Tertullian appealed to military analogies to explain the difference between Christians and non-Christians, and so he compared an integral faith, which infants of course would appear not to possess, with a military oath. The analogy would run something like this: Christians join themselves to Christ as soldiers to a leader, though instead of an oath of allegiance, they make a profession of faith. Since infants appear to lack the capacity to make such a profession, they also lack what it takes to join the Christian "army," so to speak. On the other hand, Tertullian's emphasis on regeneration and forgiveness points toward the mystery of Christ's power at

10. Origen, *Commentary on the Gospel according to John* 6.23, as quoted in Neunheuser, *Baptism and Confirmation*, 75.

11. Tertullian, *De baptismo* 1: "Felix sacramentum aquae nostrae quia ablutis delictis pristinae caecitatis in vitam aeternam liberamur."

work in the baptismal bath. One Catholic scholar summarizes the achievement of the initial development of a theology of Baptism accomplished as early as the second Christian century as follows: "Errors are being discarded and the original deposit of faith is coming to be grasped more clearly."[12]

The controversies that arose during the third century reflect the different opinions that holy men, mainly bishops, held about the validity of Baptisms administered by heretics. These controversies figure largely in the theology of the sacraments, as already noted. In short, the diverse practices of the Africans and the Romans, which became occasions for public disagreements, nonetheless helped to clarify the instrumentality at work in the administration of Baptism. In a supportive letter sent to Cyprian of Carthage by another bishop, we find this terse expression of sacramental efficacy: "Baptisma esse sine Spiritu non potest."[13] Baptism without the Holy Spirit cannot exist. Saint Cyprian and his colleague, however, held a different view about how the Holy Spirit works through Baptism than did the Pope of Rome. In the midst of controversies about Baptisms performed by heretics, a clarification of terms emerged that served to establish the congruence between *sacramentum* and *mysterion*—that is, between *sacrament* and the New Testament term *mystery*. Even with Tertullian's military analogy, with its juridical overtones, standing in the background, theologians came to realize that each of these terms points to the concrete act of salvation. This realization led the early scholars and saints to appreciate the gift quality of Baptism, and so directed theological reflection to the Author of Baptism.

In the West, properly theological developments took place during the fourth and fifth centuries. In a somewhat parallel repristination of the earlier controversy, the Donatist heresy developed an exclusionist response to the broadening scope of evangelization. In his *Against the Donatists*, Optatus of Mileve (d. 397) provides a defense against the heretical Donatists when he defends the "sacrament principle" in the drama of salvation, which succinctly states that sanctity of the sacraments depends on the Trinity, when they are administered within the Church. Optatus writes the following against these Donatists:

> Here are sown heavenly and spiritual seeds, so that, for those who are born again, a new nature may be procreated from a holy germ, and he who had once

12. Neunheuser, *Baptism and Confirmation*, 91.

13. Neunheuser, *Baptism and Confirmation*, 104, citing Cyprian's *Epistola* 74, 8. The phrase appears in the course of Cyprian's defense of his proposal that Baptism conferred by heretics lacks efficacy: "And as Stephen and those who agree with him contend that putting away of sins and second birth may result from the baptism of heretics, among whom they themselves confess that the Holy Spirit is not; let them consider and understand that spiritual birth cannot be without the Spirit."

> been born to the world may, where the Trinity meets Faith, be spiritually newborn to God. In this way does God become the Father of men, thus does the Holy Church become their Mother. I perceive that all these things have been left unmentioned by you, on purpose, lest in them all, the true principles of Baptism might be recognised, in which there is nothing that the human minister may, after your fashion, claim for himself.[14]

The witness of Optatus may be summarized succinctly in this way: "The sacraments take their sanctity not from their human ministers but from themselves. Men are not their masters but their servants."[15] Therefore, the Church made it clear that her members always stand in need of the divine largesse.

This period of Catholic life after the Edict of Milan in 313 also witnesses the contributions to sacramental theology that Ambrose of Milan (d. 397) sets down in two treatises, *De mysteriis* (*The Mysteries*) and *De sacramentis* (*On the Sacraments*). Saint Ambrose shows that by the end of the fourth century the Church had begun to speak in terms that would permanently express what she held about the sacrament of initiation: "Baptism is the mystery or the water-bath of regeneration in the name of the Father and of the Son and of the Holy Spirit."[16] Ambrose's most famous convert, Augustine of Hippo, gives definition to the heritage of the Latin West. He provides for subsequent generations "a more profound substantiation of the fact that because of its objective and concrete nature baptism is valid in every case in which it is administered in accordance with the 'regula ecclesiastica.'"[17]

In the East, the canons of the First Council of Nicaea (325) admittedly allowed rebaptism under certain circumstances—namely, when the followers of the misguided Paul of Samosata returned to the practice of the Catholic Church. Why were Paul of Samosata's followers baptized after having received his putative baptism? Orthodox authorities pointed out that his baptismal formula evidenced the trinitarian errors of his third-century Monarchian theology and so invalidated the baptism.

Later, the witness of Cyril of Jerusalem (d. 386) supplies evidence of the basic lines of the baptismal theology taught in Jerusalem during Cyril's tenure as bishop, which covered the better part of the second half of the fourth century. Cyril's *Mystagogic Catechism* reveals "how deep was the knowledge of the mystery of baptism to which the simplest believers in Jerusalem were led."[18]

14. Optatus, *Against the Donatists*, trans. O. R. Vassall-Phillips (London: Longmans, Green, 1917), book 2, x.

15. Neunheuser, *Baptism and Confirmation*, 109.

16. Neunheuser, *Baptism and Confirmation*, 111.

17. Neunheuser, *Baptism and Confirmation*, 127.

18. Neunheuser, *Baptism and Confirmation*, 146.

Cyril stressed the reality of the Church's sacramental life, even going so far as to explain that "image" always reveals something real.

Theodore of Mopsuestia (d. ca. 428), for his part, explains the movement from Christ to us using a form of remembrance and by appeal to figure and sign. However, because of his controversial proposal to describe a spiritual existence without a spiritual ontology, Theodore's doctrine of the "Two Ages" to describe the before and after of Baptism has been judged to be flawed.

The close of the patristic period reveals efforts made to correlate theological explanations—theories, if you will—with the practice of the Christian community. In short, the later patristic authors consolidate the theology of the golden age. This accomplishment further illustrates how one ought to read Christian history in a providential or sapiential fashion and to not succumb to romantic and archaeological interpretations of the past. Of course, a providential account of history remains centered on the historical person of Jesus Christ. Though certain identifiable moments of resolution appear, the history of the sacraments does not lead to the conclusion that a provisional and dialectical account remains all that the history can surrender. In a word, the history of what the learned men of Christian faith have taught about the sacraments shows development but not evolution.

For example, the ancient Christian writers developed a clear explanation of the relationship that exists between the regeneration and illumination that Baptism accomplishes in the person who partakes of the water bath and the water that comes forth from the pierced side of Christ. As has been noted above, this christological affirmation gives precision to the sacraments as powers that flow from the passion and death of Christ. Take, as one example, Saint Isidore of Seville (d. 636): on one expert's account, "When dealing with the ecclesiastical states [of life he] . . . includes a short but still quite significant and systematic chapter on baptism. Its material is taken from the Fathers of the early period."[19] Modern scholarship regards Isidore as the last scholar of the ancient world.[20]

Carolingian theology belongs to the following era. The term refers to the work done, mostly in monasteries, from the start of the imperial reign of Charlemagne, and it may be dated from the late eighth and early ninth centuries. Some historians, in fact, speak of a Carolingian renaissance of learning. Scholars mainly agree, however, that early medieval theology lacks the development of refined philosophical concepts that would characterize the work done in the thirteenth century and after.

19. Neunheuser, *Baptism and Confirmation*, 178.

20. See Charles F. Montalembert, *Les Moines d'Occident depuis Saint Benoît jusquà Saint Bernard* (Paris: J. Lecoffre, 1860).

Still, the Carolingian theologians faced the problems that had arisen earlier among the patristic authors. What is the *votum sacramenti*? How does this teaching, which considers the explicit purpose to receive the sacraments, figure in the deliberations of the early scholastic theologians? For example, Bernard of Clairvaux (d. 1153) wrote to Hugh of Saint Victor (d. 1141) about how far water Baptism can be replaced by the desire for it.[21] What everyday experience, one may inquire, urges such a reflection upon the Catholic mind?

Contemporary witness to the usefulness of the *votum sacramenti* appears in a 2020 Vatican document that describes pastoral care in a period of international pandemic. The example given concerns the sacrament of Penance and Reconciliation:

> Individual confession is the ordinary way of celebrating this sacrament (cf. can. 960 *CIC*), whereas collective absolution, without prior individual confession, cannot be imparted except in situations where there is an imminent danger of death, as there is insufficient time to hear the confessions of the individual penitents (cf. can. 961, § 1 *CIC*), or when there is a grave necessity (cf. can. 961, § 1, 2 *CIC*), the consideration of which, is up to the diocesan bishop, after reviewing the criteria agreed upon with the other members of the Episcopal Conference (cf. can. 455, § 2 *CIC*) subject to the necessity of the *votum sacramenti* from each penitent to obtain valid absolution, that is, the intention to confess in due time the individual serious sins, which at the time they had no possibility of confessing (cf. can. 962, § 1 *CIC*).[22]

It should appear clearly that the development of such a sophisticated regulation of sacramental practice results from the fruit of careful reflection on fundamental givens of the Christian Church, a work that can continue over centuries.

Other examples of the development of sacramental theology during the late Middle Ages include the treatment of questions concerning the "objective efficacy" of the sacraments and the human person's subjective participation (cooperation) with them. In sum, the proper answer to a question such as this requires a refinement of thought that serves the faith and practice of the Church. Or, to take another example, How does theological understanding of the infused virtues emerge from the requirement that everyone who receives Baptism must confess the saving power of God? Finally, consider the contribution of Alexander of Hales (d. 1245), who relates the abiding effect of Baptism to the hypostatic union and the sacrifice of Calvary. Alexander of Hales brings

21. See Neunheuser, *Baptism and Confirmation*, 183–84.

22. "Reconciliation in the Current Pandemic." *CIC* stands for *Codex Iuris Canonici* (Code of Canon Law).

this chronicle to the period of the summists and a time when, under their attempts to set forth comprehensive summaries of Catholic theology, there appears in Western thought a heightened presentation of an organic view of theology.[23]

The period of the great doctors gives to theology the architecture that to a large extent continues to govern the presentation of sacred doctrine (*sacra doctrina*).[24] On some questions, the great schoolmen agree. For example, in answer to the question why no satisfactory works are required of the newly baptized, the medieval theologians overall point to the all-sufficiency of Christ's saving work. No less a figure than Saint Bonaventure (d. 1276) testifies to this fact: "As the authorities say and the masters together demonstrate, all guilt is expunged in the sacrament of baptism, when its efficacy and value for salvation are fully received, and man is restored, as far as concerns his soul, to original innocence."[25] This claim coheres, as Bonaventure notes, with the emphasis of the "authorities" who wrote during the early and high patristic periods on the superabundance of Christ's gifts.

On other questions, however, the scholastics could offer diverse explanations. For example, one may ask about the meaning of the "pactio" (i.e., the promise) that Duns Scotus (d. 1308) and William of Ockham (d. 1347) employed to account for the efficacy of Baptism. One author puts the matter clearly and makes an arguably proper evaluation: "In the question of sacramental causality Ockham reveals himself as an opponent of instrumental causality and adopts the pact theory of Duns Scotus. For him the sacrament is merely a 'causa sine qua non' for the dispensation of grace. His definition of baptism is purely nominalistic. He denies all reality to baptism."[26]

It is difficult to align the pact theory as interpreted by Ockham not only with the earlier tradition but also with the great medieval doctors, such as Bonaventure and Saint Thomas Aquinas. Ockham, of course, introduces a period in late medieval theology where nominalist thought vied for influence with the thicker metaphysics of both Aquinas and Scotus. Certain features of nominalism make it difficult to render an ontological account of divine grace and of the sacraments of the Church, which provide the visible signs of it. The work of the fifteenth-century Dominican John Capreolus (d. 1444) represents a retrieval of

23. Neunheuser, *Baptism and Confirmation*, 196–98.

24. For explanation of the expression *sacra doctrina*, see James A. Weisheipl, "The Meaning of *Sacra Doctrina* in *Summa theologiae* I, q. 1," *The Thomist* 38 (1974): 49–80.

25. St. Bonaventure, *Commentary on the Sentences*, book 4, dist. 4, part 1, art. 1, q. 1, conclusion, as quoted in Neunheuser, *Baptism and Confirmation*, 205.

26. Neunheuser, *Baptism and Confirmation*, 219–20.

Aquinas's metaphysical outlook that heralded its renewed importance during the early European Renaissance.[27]

Trent and Baptism

The Council of Trent (1545–63) marks a landmark in the setting forth of the Church's doctrine in an authoritative and magisterial way. The challenges posed by the sixteenth-century reform are met, substantially, in the findings of the council—issued, according to the custom of the times, in the form of anathemas. The rejection of the sacraments, especially of Baptism, as efficacious instruments of divine grace that even infants can receive for their salvation took, in some quarters, fairly radical expression.[28] Though the council was content to condemn the errors that had become widespread, the anathemas represent important elements of authoritative Catholic teaching.

At the heart of the Tridentine doctrine stands the Catholic truth that has been taught for centuries. The effectiveness of Baptism does not depend on the faith or the worthiness of the minister but on the proper carrying out of Christ's command. In other words, efficacy derives from the divine action itself. Likewise, the proposal that Baptism can have no effect on little children who have not reached the age of discretion so that they can accept and profess their Baptism merits the council's reprobation. After all, one cannot imagine a proposal, espoused by the Anabaptists, that more defiantly reverses the constant witness of the Christian Church to the effective instrumentality of the seven sacraments.

The canons of the General Council of Trent that deal with Baptism (seventh session, 1547) illustrate the concerns prompted by departures from Catholic teaching on the sacraments. The advantages of examining the canons include a focus on issues and not persons. The council never ascribes the anathematized positions to particular authors or figures. The Council of Trent did not set out a complete doctrinal description of the sacrament of Baptism but only condemned certain errors that had become especially widespread and publicly exhibited since the early decades of the sixteenth century. The canons, however, serve to give precision to Catholic teaching on Baptism.

27. For further information, see the articles in Romanus Cessario, Guy Bedouelle, and Kevin White, eds., *Jean Capreolus en son temps (1380–1444)*, Mémoire Dominicaine, numéro spécial, 1 (Paris: Cerf, 1997). For a sample of Capreolus's Thomist thought on the virtues of the Christian life, see Romanus Cessario and Kevin White, eds., *John Capreolus (1380–1444): Treatise on the Virtues* (Washington, DC: Catholic University of America Press, 2001).

28. See George Huntston Williams, *The Radical Reformation* (Philadelphia: Fortress, 1962).

For example, consider the first canon: "If anyone says that the baptism of John had the same force as the baptism of Christ, let him be anathema."[29] This error contradicts what the Catholic Church holds about the efficacy of the sacraments and the cause of that efficaciousness that is identified with the passion and death of Christ. In broader terms, the council rejects the notion that water baptism provides only an external sign of a repentance that has already taken place. To take another example, "If anyone says that true and natural water is not necessary for baptism and therefore reduces into some sort of metaphor the words of our Lord Jesus Christ, 'Unless one is reborn of water and the Spirit' [John 3:5], let him be anathema."[30] This canon addresses the general question of the matter of the sacrament, which the Catholic Church has always held to be the water bath. Recall the expression of Tertullian: "Felix sacramentum acquae nostrae." More broadly considered, the canon addresses any proposal that identifies Christian initiation with a purely internal action, such as solitary repentance or a confession of faith in the Savior. A radical expression of this view comes from the pen of the Dutch reformer Dirk Philips (d. 1568), who wrote, "The external baptism with water is a witness to spiritual baptism, a proof of true sorrow and a sign of faith."[31]

Consider this third example of the council giving precision to what, by the sixteenth century, had become long-standing Catholic teaching: "If anyone says that the Roman Church (the mother and teacher of all churches) does not have the true doctrine concerning the sacrament of baptism, let him be anathema."[32] This fairly comprehensive anathema addresses a view that a majority of the sixteenth-century reformers considered axiomatic—namely, that the Roman Church and her hierarchy had misrepresented the primitive teaching of Christ as found in the pages of the New Testament. From these three general principles, there follow canons that address specific points of Catholic teaching about the nature and the efficacy of the sacraments.

The fourth canon addresses a Catholic principle of sacramental efficacy that reaches back to the third century and the controversy between Pope Stephen I and Saint Cyprian of Carthage: "If anyone says that baptism, even that given by heretics in the name of the Father and of the Son and of the Holy Spirit, with the intention of doing what the Church does, is not true baptism, let him

29. Canon 1, *DS* 1614.

30. Canon 2, *DS* 1615.

31. Dirk Philips, *The Writings of Dirk Philips*, ed. C. Dyck et al. (Waterloo, ON: Herald, 1992), 373, as quoted in John D. Rempel, "Sacraments in the Radical Reformation," in *The Oxford Handbook of Sacramental Theology*, ed. Hans Boersma and Matthew Levering (Oxford: Oxford University Press, 2015), 308.

32. Canon 3, *DS* 1616.

be anathema."[33] It is important to understand the divine truth that stands behind this anathema as well as that which has guided the Church to determine that neither the worthiness nor the faith of the minister affects adversely the sanctifying effects of a properly administered sacrament.

Of course, if one focuses on the personal dispositions of a minister in order to ensure that the Church does not provide shelter for scoundrels, then one undertakes a praiseworthy initiative. However, the place for the personal formation of the Church's ministers is called a seminary, at least after the Council of Trent. For clerics who succumb to immorality or even defect from the true faith, the Church provides sanctions and penalties stipulated in her legislation and established in her practices. At the same time, to call into question the efficacy of a sacrament as important as Baptism on the grounds that the minister does not exhibit the qualities that virtue produces or the full allegiance owed to the true faith undermines the divine activity that Christ instituted the sacraments to achieve.

It is ironic that those who insist on the establishment of an undefiled membership in the Church at the same time call into question the very means that God has ordained for eliminating all defilement from his Body, which is the Church. The following canon offers another reason for recognizing even the Baptisms performed by heretics. The council affirms the necessity of Baptism for salvation, and so condemns those who claim that receiving the sacrament is left to the discretion of an individual: "If anyone says that baptism is optional, that is, not necessary for salvation, let him be anathema."[34] Given the premium that the Catholic Church puts on the reception of Baptism, it makes no sense to restrict the administration of the sacrament to a selected group of right-thinking and good-living ministers. If one did, eventually no one would be found worthy to provide what every human person needs in order to obtain eternal salvation.

Again, the fifth canon addresses the necessity of Baptism. This issue, of course, raises a perennial question that Catholic theologians face. The canon, however, leaves no room for any answer other than an affirmative response to the question, "Is Baptism necessary for salvation?" To repeat, the fifth canon states simply the condemnation of those who deny the necessity of Baptism for salvation: "If anyone says that baptism is optional, that is, not necessary for salvation, let him be anathema."[35] The *Catechism of the Catholic Church* repeats the teaching of this Tridentine canon and actually refers back to it.

33. Canon 4, *DS* 1617.
34. Canon 5, *DS* 1618.
35. Canon 5, *DS* 1618.

At the same time, the twentieth-century document devotes five numbers to what the Catholic Church teaches about the necessity of Baptism. These include affirmations of the Church's constant teaching that while water Baptism remains the norm, the Church also recognizes a Baptism of blood that cleanses those who die for the faith without their having received water Baptism. The desire for Baptism also "brings about the fruits of Baptism without being a sacrament."[36] The same text emphasizes a principle of Catholic theology that merits special attention when discussing the necessity of the sacraments, especially of Baptism: "God has bound salvation to the sacrament of Baptism, but he himself is not bound by his sacraments."[37] This recognition of the sovereignty of the divine will does not, however, compromise what the Catholic Church holds about the necessity of the sacraments in the present economy of Christian existence. It would be difficult to suppose that any person sufficiently well instructed to cite the above qualification could also remain ignorant of the necessity of Baptism that the Church proclaims.

Canons 6, 7, and 8 discuss issues that relate the sacrament of Baptism to the moral life of the one baptized. Canon 6 anathematizes those who misunderstand the relationship of the sacrament to one's subsequent actions. "If anyone says that one baptized cannot lose grace, even if he wishes to, no matter how much he sins, unless he is unwilling to believe, let him be anathema."[38] This condemnation points to two errors that must have appeared in some sixteenth-century heterodox teachings. Catholic teaching holds that the character of Baptism (*res et sacramentum*) remains even in the serious sinner, but the graces of the sacrament, the *res tantum*, do not, of course, survive mortal sin. Further, the sins against the theological virtue of faith are not the only sins that affect negatively the state of the Christian soul. This second point appears more explicitly in the next canon, which relates Baptism to the whole of the Christian moral life: "If anyone says that those baptized are by the fact of their baptism obliged merely to faith but not to the observance of the whole law of Christ, let him be anathema."[39] Baptism, of course, introduces the one baptized into a new way of living and provides the strength, through the baptized person's union with Christ, to walk according to the "new life" that Baptism bestows.[40]

The next authoritative declaration, canon 8, clarifies that the law of Christ also includes those precepts that the Church formulates for the benefit of Catholics with respect to those things that flow from the Ten Commandments—for

36. *CCC* no. 1258.
37. *CCC* no. 1257.
38. Canon 6, *DS* 1619.
39. Canon 7, *DS* 1620.
40. See *CCC* no. 1697, citing Rom. 6:4.

example, to "attend Mass on Sundays and on holy days of obligation and rest from servile labor."[41] The *Catechism of the Catholic Church* today lists five such precepts.[42] The Council of Trent understood these precepts of the Church as representing the minimum exercises of prayer and moral effort required to keep a person faithful to the baptismal graces that he or she has received. So the fathers of the council rejected the view that the Church's "precepts" are left to the personal discretion of the baptized Christian: "If anyone says that those baptized are free from all the precepts of holy Church, whether written or handed down, so that they are not bound to observe them unless, of their own accord, they wish to submit to them, let him be anathema."[43] It is possible to suppose that those who advanced the position that canon 8 anathematizes exhibited the tendency to reject the institutional structure of the Church in favor of a purely spiritual realization of Christ's mystical Body.

The following canon, canon 9, addresses those who rejected consecrated life as instantiating legitimate expressions of the Christian life. "If anyone says that the remembrance of the baptism they have received ought to be so impressed on men that they be brought to understand that all the vows taken after baptism are void in virtue of the promise already made in baptism, as if those vows detracted from the faith they have professed and from baptism itself, let him be anathema."[44] In some countries where the sixteenth-century Reform took hold, the despoliation of the monasteries and other dwellings of those who professed the evangelical counsels of poverty, chastity, and obedience had become emblematic of the movement. Three centuries later, the English Romantic poet William Wordsworth found inspiration for his 1798 poem "Tintern Abbey" from pondering the ruins of one such monastery, located in Wales.

Of course, what today the Church refers to as consecrated life still flourishes, even in those countries where religious conflict once laid waste to both consecrated persons and their sacred domiciles. The Church defines consecrated life as "one way of experiencing a 'more intimate' consecration, rooted in Baptism and dedicated totally to God."[45] In other words, the profession of the vows of religion intensifies the baptismal commitment instead of violating it.

The remaining canons address errors about the effects of Baptism. Canon 10, for instance, insists that the sacrament of Penance and Reconciliation is required of those who sin after their Baptism. "If anyone says that all sins committed after baptism are either remitted or made venial by the mere remembrance of

41. CCC no. 2042.
42. See CCC nos. 2042–43.
43. Canon 8, *DS* 1621.
44. Canon 9, *DS* 1622.
45. CCC no. 916, quoting *Perfectae Caritatis*, no. 5.

and faith in the baptism once received, let him be anathema."[46] The *Catechism of the Catholic Church* devotes two paragraphs to explaining this: "Why a Sacrament of Reconciliation after Baptism?"[47] These texts remind the baptized person that weaknesses of human nature and "inclination to sin" remain even in the baptized. The Church places the sacrament of Penance and Reconciliation within the context of the baptized person's need for conversion, which she also describes as a "struggle."[48]

Canon 11 again addresses the permanence of Baptism, its indelible character: "If anyone says that for those who have denied the faith of Christ before infidels, baptism truly and rightly conferred must be repeated when they are converted to repentance, let him be anathema."[49] The confusion that this anathematized position exhibits points up a failure in certain reform proposals to reflect the primacy of the divine action in all things that lead to salvation. At the same time, the position strikes at the heart of a basic Christian tenet: only God saves us. Too much concern for the subjective disposition of a recipient undermines the efficacy that God has committed to the sacraments. In the condemned position, the Church rejects the suggestion that apostasy nullifies the sacrament. In so doing, she reminds us that *Deus semper maior*—God is always greater than our foibles. So neither the faith of the minister nor the eventual sins against faith of the baptized can cancel the abiding effects of a properly administered Baptism. Of course the apostate's need for, indeed obligation to receive, the sacrament of Penance and Reconciliation remains a given.

The last three canons—12, 13, and 14—deal with mistakes about the age at which Baptism is to be administered. In a word, the errors place what the Church teaches about the necessity of Baptism in a subordinate position to the personal states (e.g., age) of the candidates. So the fathers of the council, in canon 12, respond, "If anyone says that no one is to be baptized except at the age at which Christ was baptized, or on the point of death, let him be anathema."[50] Or, as canon 13 further makes clear, "If anyone says that little children, because they do not have an act of faith, are not to be numbered among the faithful after receiving baptism and that, therefore, when they have reached the age of discretion, they are to be rebaptized; or that it is better to omit their baptism, [if] they do not believe by an act of faith of their own, rather than to baptize them solely in the faith of the Church, let him be anathema."[51] These condemned

46. Canon 10, *DS* 1623.
47. *CCC* nos. 1425–26.
48. *CCC* no. 1426.
49. Canon 11, *DS* 1624.
50. Canon 12, *DS* 1625.
51. Canon 13, *DS* 1626.

proposals obviously shift the center of focus in the sacramental administration from the divine action performed to the individual's subjective disposition with respect to the act of belief.

The issue of the propriety of infant Baptism recurs in the history of the Church. In the twentieth century, the Church had to clarify the matter in an authoritative document, *Pastoralis actio,* issued in 1980. Baptism, it says, "is not just a sign of faith but also a cause of faith."[52] Causality, of course, implies movement in the free creature. Children baptized by parents who promise to bring them up in the practice of the Catholic religion possess the cause that, as they develop their human capacities, blooms into a fully supernatural life in a way *analogically* parallel to their cultural development. As already discussed, the number of the sacraments traditionally has been explained by reference to the needs of human development and decline.

The basic truth of divine prevenient love also explains why canon 14 anathematizes the proposal that infant Baptism requires a ratification once the person has attained at least the age of discretion (*adoleverint*): "If anyone says that when the little children thus baptized have grown up, they are to be asked whether they wish to ratify what their sponsors promised in their name when they were baptized; and if they answer that they are unwilling, they are to be left to their own judgment and are not in the meantime to be compelled to a Christian life by any penalty other than the exclusion from receiving the Eucharist and the other sacraments until they repent, let him be anathema."[53]

Again, the error that the anathematized proposition rejects concerns the view that the divine action requires a kind of confirmation or posterior cooperation on the part of the recipient in order to become effective. While this last canon may also envisage certain civil penalties that may have been in vigor in some principalities of the sixteenth century, the theological view of justification merits the Church's disapproval. Baptism, whether of infants or adults, manifests "God's initiative and the gratuitous character of the love with which he surrounds our lives: 'not that we loved God but that he loved us. . . . We love, because he first loved us' (1 John 4:10, 19)."[54]

The canons of the Council of Trent concerning Baptism offer a glimpse of the common errors that can arise with respect to the nature of the sacraments. Admittedly, the interplay between an efficacious sacrament and a well-disposed recipient provides a large expanse for theological reflection. Two poles are to be avoided: (1) the idea that the sacraments perform magic and (2) the idea that

52. *Pastoralis actio,* no. 18.
53. Canon 14, *DS* 1627.
54. *Pastoralis actio,* no. 26.

any free human person could save himself or herself. Sound Catholic theology has managed to develop a practical resolution for Christian living that avoids both errors.

The canons of the Council of Trent reveal that a fairly persistent issue that arises when the Church treats the sacrament of Baptism centers on the role that faith plays in the act of justification and how an individual's faith then relates to the sacramental action. One truth emerges clearly from the sixteenth-century controversies. Catholic theology insists on the priority of the divine action in our salvation. The Christmas liturgy turns to the Letter to Titus 3:4–8 to emphasize this bedrock principle of Catholic teaching:

> But when the kindness and generous love
> of God our savior appeared,
> not because of any righteous deeds we had done
>   but because of his mercy,
> he saved us through the bath of rebirth
> and renewal by the holy Spirit,
>   whom he richly poured out on us
> through Jesus Christ our savior,
>   so that we might be justified by his grace
> and become heirs in hope of eternal life.
> This saying is trustworthy.

Sacramental causality provides a means to express the divine creative power that continues to work in the world so that each succeeding generation "might be justified by his grace and become heirs in hope of eternal life" (Titus 3:7).

The Baptismal Character

At this juncture, one may usefully recall the words of Father Colman O'Neill. When speaking of the intervention of Christ in the sacramental action, O'Neill states, "The realism attributed to the presence of Christ in baptism by the whole Catholic tradition can be accounted for only if appeal is made to the present reality of the risen Christ and the way he is at work in the world."[55] Again, when speaking about justification by his grace, O'Neill relates the sacramental realism operative in Baptism to the work of the Blessed Trinity: "The mystery of salvation is . . . a mystery of communion with the Blessed Trinity which is

55. Colman E. O'Neill, *Sacramental Realism* (Chicago: Midwest Theological Forum, 1998), 121–22.

brought about by the reaffirmation of all that flows from the creative love of that same Trinity."[56]

When Catholic theology looks to explain the efficacy of Baptism, its focus, while not neglecting the need for an assent to the mysteries into which Baptism introduces the one baptized, rests on the creative act of the Trinity, whose action achieves a permanence that only God can create. The comparison of the permanence of physical creation with that of Baptism finds expression in the indelible mark or character with which Baptism seals the one who receives it. "No sin can erase this mark, even if sin prevents Baptism from bearing the fruits of salvation."[57] This text from the *Catechism of the Catholic Church* cites the canons of the Council of Trent, moreover.

What abides in a properly administered sacrament occupies the attention of Catholic theologians. One textbook offers a representative summary of the ways in which Catholic theology describes an abiding sacrament when the spiritual mark qualifies as a "character."[58] The authors make the following descriptive remarks about sacramental character:[59] First, character embodies a *signum distinctivum*, a distinctive sign. By this is meant that the sacramental character brings about something newly created, something possessing special ontological status in the order of grace. Second, character appears as a *signum dispositivum*, a dispositive sign—that is, the indelible spiritual mark readies the person who receives it for growth in the Christian life and also disposes them to exercise an office (*munus*) in the Church. It is common sense that for a person to take up an official responsibility in the Church, they must have been baptized. Third, character imposes a *signum obligativum*—that is, the sign or indelible spiritual mark imposes on the one who has received it certain obligations (i.e., the responsibilities of the baptized).

The *Catechism of the Catholic Church* summarizes this aspect of the sacramental character in the following way: "The baptismal seal enables and commits Christians to serve God by a vital participation in the holy liturgy of the Church and to exercise their baptismal priesthood by the witness of holy lives and practical charity."[60] Christian living and service to the Church are personal expressions of one's baptismal consecration. The Church does not envisage service to the Church as the equivalent of what secular culture considers a set of professional duties.

56. O'Neill, *Sacramental Realism*, 123.
57. CCC no. 1272.
58. See CCC nos. 1272–74.
59. Johann Auer and Joseph Ratzinger, *Dogmatic Theology*, vol. 6, *A General Doctrine of the Sacraments and the Mystery of the Eucharist* by Johann Auer, trans. Erasmos Leiva-Merikakis (Washington, DC: Catholic University of America Press, 1995), 73–74.
60. CCC no. 1273.

Fourth, the abiding sacrament effects a *signum configurativum*—that is, Baptism unites the one baptized with the person of Jesus Christ. Thus one uses the colloquial expression "christening" to describe the baptismal ceremony. The one who belongs to Christ, who is "incorporated into Christ by Baptism," is thereby "configured" to Christ.[61] The person christened experiences in faith a "birth into the new life by which man becomes an adoptive son of the Father, a member of Christ and a temple of the Holy Spirit."[62] This mystery finds liturgical expression in the essential rite of Baptism, which requires the minister to "pronounce the invocation of the Most Holy Trinity, the Father, the Son, and the Holy Spirit."[63]

The Baptismal Formula

The use of the names of the persons of the Blessed Trinity in the administration of the sacrament of Baptism remains obligatory. The practice of the Church with respect to the essential rite of Baptism (*sacramentum tantum*) is set forth in the *Catechism of the Catholic Church* as follows: "In the Latin Church [the] triple infusion in water is accompanied by the minister's words: 'N., I baptize you in the name of the Father, and of the Son, and of the Holy Spirit.' In the Eastern liturgies the catechumen turns toward the East and the priest says: 'The servant of God, N., is baptized in the name of the Father, and of the Son, and of the Holy Spirit.' At the invocation of each person of the Most Holy Trinity, the priest immerses the candidate in the water and raises him up again."[64]

This practice now occasions controversy in some quarters. One may venture to say that the pressure to degenderize our references to the Holy Trinity in the administration of the sacrament of Baptism risks dissolving the unity of the Christian communion that, up to this moment, has survived the rupture of eucharistic communion in the Western Church that began at the time of the sixteenth-century Protestant Reform. The controversy centers on God-talk. Influenced by Protestant theologians such as Sallie McFague and Catholic theologians such as Elizabeth Johnson and Sandra Schneiders, many feminist theologians and those sympathetic to their concerns have mounted "a deliberate attempt to unseat those names as descriptions of God which will allow no supplements or alternatives."[65] The concern for maintaining the sacramental unity of the Church by use of a common baptismal formula reflects the views

61. CCC no. 1272.
62. CCC no. 1279.
63. CCC no. 1278.
64. CCC no. 1240.
65. Sallie McFague, *Models of God: Theology for an Ecological, Nuclear Age* (Philadelphia: Fortress, 1987), 181.

of a long tradition of classical theologians. It is common Catholic teaching that the sacramental signification of the sacramental sign-action requires determined words.[66] The words or sacramental formula both embody and express Christ's meaning and intention in instituting the sacraments.

As an alternative to changing the formula of Baptism, some irenic inquirers have asked whether supplementing the formula with a subsidiary, contextual, not canonically effectual addendum pronounced by the priest or minister might allow the Church to meet some of the feminist and inclusivist challenges. By adding something to the sacramental formula, the Church would avoid actually changing the personal names of the three persons of the Blessed Trinity or replacing them with functional descriptions such as *Creator*, *Redeemer*, and *Sanctifier*.

The history of theology helps us to respond to this moderating proposal. In *Summa theologiae* III.60.8, Aquinas asks, "Utrum aliquid liceat addere verbis in quibus consistit forma sacramentorum." That is, Do the words constituting the form of the sacrament admit of any additions or subtractions? As discussed above, two important points emerge from Aquinas's reply. The first consideration centers on the intention of the one who introduces the changes. Valid administration of the sacraments requires a proper intention on the part of the one who administers the sacrament. Aquinas then comments, "And because of this it seems that if [the minister's] intention in making additions or subtractions . . . is to introduce another rite that has not been accepted by the Church, the sacrament is invalid. For in that case he is apparently not intending to do what the Church does."[67] If, however, some addendum can be put on the baptismal formula, the "optional" words must not convey something other than what the Church intends. Aquinas gives as an example of a noninvalidating addition, "and may the Blessed Virgin help you." However, a noninvalidating addendum could not serve as an alternative "inclusivist" rite for those who do not intend to confess the triune God. The Trinity, after all, abides with the Christian community in grace. Indeed, the *Catechism of the Catholic Church* makes this explicit: "The Church's first purpose is to be the sacrament of the *inner union of men with God*."[68] Some theologians, however, have made proposals that appear to consider the trinitarian invocation more malleable than the Church allows.[69]

66. See, for example, CCC nos. 1155, 1125.

67. *Summa theologiae* III.60.8.

68. CCC no. 775 (emphasis original).

69. For a critique of one such author, see Robin Darling Young, "She Who Is: Who Is She?," review of *She Who Is: The Mystery of God in Feminist Theological Discourse*, by Elizabeth A. Johnson, *The Thomist* 58 (1994): 23–33.

Aquinas's second consideration raises the question of the actual meaning of the words themselves. The general principle of sacramental signification is that the words give intelligible meaning to the sacramental action. Aquinas employs the apt expression *veritas sacramenti* to describe this proclaimed meaning. In brief, the sense of the words should correspond to the truth of the sacrament. Since the words speak the truthfulness of the sacrament, it follows then that any addition or detraction that substantially affects this *veritas sacramenti* would render the sacrament invalid. This teaching, as noted above, figures prominently in giving an account of how sacramental mediation works in the Church. A considerable body of quite detailed canonical commentary on the validity and licitness of baptismal forms bears witness to the Church's perennial interest in the question of *veritas sacramenti*.[70]

One classical witness to the intimate relationship between word and truth comes to today's Magisterium through Saint Jerome (d. 420) from his teacher, the fourth-century Alexandrian theologian Didymus the Blind (d. ca. 398): "If there should be someone of so strange a mind that he would baptize while omitting one of the aforesaid names, viz., of the three Persons, such a one baptizes invalidly."[71] Aquinas, on the other hand, acknowledges that if an addition at the beginning, the middle, or the end does not "deprive the words of their due meaning the truth of the sacrament is not destroyed."[72] In any event, any supplementation that alters the truth of the sacrament renders the sacrament invalid. So if the subsidiary addendum introduces a substantial distortion of the Christian faith, then it cannot be allowed by the Church. As an example of such an abuse, Aquinas cites the Arian practice of baptizing "in the name of the Father, who is greater, and the Son, who is lesser."[73]

Baptism introduces a human person into a life of friendship with the persons of the Blessed Trinity. This friendship is lived out here below in the Church of Christian faith and sacraments. About the mystery of the Blessed Trinity, the catechism reminds us, "God alone can make it known to us by revealing himself as Father, Son, and Holy Spirit."[74] For someone who administers Baptism

70. See, for example, Felix M. Cappello, *Tractatus canonico-moralis de sacramentis*, vol. 1 (Rome-Turin: Marietti, 1945); and Edward F. Regatillo, *Jus sacramentarium* (Santander, Spain: Editorial Sal Terrae, 1964).

71. As quoted in *Summa theologiae* III.66.6, *sed contra*. One may also consult Athanasius the Great and Didymus the Blind, *Works on the Spirit: Athanasius the Great & Didymus the Blind*, trans. Mark DelCogliano, Andrew Radde-Gallwitz, and Lewis Ayres, Popular Patristics Series 43 (Yonkers, NY: St. Vladimir's Seminary Press, 2011). See also St. Jerome, *Interpretatio libri Dydimi de Spiritu Sancto*, PL 23:99–154.

72. *Summa theologiae* III.60.8.

73. *Summa theologiae* III.60.8.

74. CCC no. 261.

to change purposefully the revealed names of God amounts to committing a form of trinitarian heresy.[75] Such a change would directly affect the truth of the sacrament. A recent pronouncement by the Holy See supports this view.[76] The commentaries on the document opined that the basis for this decision is the substantially unitarian theology of Emanuel Swedenborg's *Vera Christi Religio* (1771). It is interesting to recall that Swedenborg advanced the view that the Trinity represents three *qualities* of the one person of God: love, wisdom, and action.

There exists a general agreement among serious theologians that some expressions espoused by feminist theology aim to compromise seriously the mystery of the most Holy Trinity as the central mystery of the Christian faith and of Christian life.[77] Secular feminism challenges not only what figures in the movement consider the patriarchal names for God but also the way traditional theology defines God's way of being with us and the God with whom we are involved. Their proposals seem to take the direction of a religious syncretism. On the other hand, one may also observe that some female theologians, and even some feminist theologians, have argued against the practice of changing the trinitarian names in the Church's worship.[78]

75. In the discussion of the baptismal formula, it is important to know that the personal names of the divine persons as found in the canonical Scriptures ground the trinitarian theology that distinguishes one divine person from another. First, for the Word/Son: because in God "to be" (*esse*) denotes simply "to know" and "to speak" (*intelligere/dicere*), there is an intelligible emanation or intellectual procession in God's self-knowledge. Formally taken, knowing entails the speaking of what is known. This procession terminates in the Word Spoken, which is not simply the Knower (although it is the actuality of the Knower, precisely as such, and consubstantial with him) nor the knowing-act itself (which, in this instance, is simply the divine nature itself) nor the content of the knowing (the Father's knowledge of the divine nature as Principle) but merely the formal concept or inner word whereby the Knower knows. Since what the Father knows is the divine nature (in its simplicity as unreceived act of being), this knowing-act is also simple. That is, the knowing-act is also the speaking-act of the being of what is known. Further, because knowing is a generation of a terminal likeness of what is known and because likeness is the ground of love, there is a further procession in God—i.e., of love. This term of immanent operation is neither the lover himself nor the love-act nor the object loved (all of which are identically the divine nature, saving only the relations of mutual opposition whereby the Father is the Unprincipled Principle and the Son the Principated Principle). Rather, the term of this procession is the very reality of love itself, whereby the beloved abides in the lover. It is the *impulsus* or *pondus amoris*—the being-in-love itself, the expansion of the intellectual nature abidingly in the direction of and after the shape of the beloved, the inner dynamic orientation the lover bears toward the beloved: thus, the one whom we call the Holy Spirit.

76. In 1992, the Congregation for the Doctrine of the Faith replied in the negative to a question about the validity of Swedenborgian baptisms. For the official text, see *Acta Apostolicae Sedis* 85 (1993): 179.

77. For an important study, see J. A. Di Noia, "Knowing and Naming the Triune God: The Grammar of Trinitarian Confession," in *Speaking the Christian God: The Holy Trinity and the Challenge of Feminism*, ed. Alvin F. Kimel Jr. (Grand Rapids: Eerdmans, 1992).

78. See, for instance, Catherine LaCugna, "The Baptismal Formula, Feminist Objections, and Trinitarian Theology," *Journal of Ecumenical Studies* 26 (1989): 235–51; and Deborah Belonick, "Revelation

Though it remains highly unlikely if not impossible that an acceptable and suitable addendum to the baptismal formula can be authorized by the Church to satisfy secular feminists and other inclusivist voices, those who warn about the dissolution of baptismal communion among the Christian Churches and ecclesial communities of the West merit attention. A document of the Second Vatican Council, *Unitatis Redintegratio*, offers the comforting assurance that grounds the ecumenical movement: "Whenever the Sacrament of Baptism is duly administered as Our Lord instituted it, and is received with the right dispositions, a person is truly incorporated into the crucified and glorified Christ, and reborn to a sharing of the divine life. . . . Baptism therefore establishes a sacramental bond of unity which links all who have been reborn by it."[79]

The New Life of Baptism

The Council of Trent dealt with specific issues that mainly arose within the context of the sixteenth-century reform. Much that the council determined was influenced by the teaching of Saint Thomas Aquinas. For example, a first question that Aquinas treats in his *Summa theologiae* when he comes to Baptism asks about the true effect of the sacrament. He enunciates a principle that governs the whole of Catholic theology about Christian justification and the sacraments: "The sacraments of the New Law work in us a certain sanctification."[80] From this principle, Aquinas argues that "the perfection of a sacrament will be realized wherever the perfection of sanctification is had."[81] In the case of Baptism, this sacrament finds its highest achievement in the *res et sacramentum*, the baptismal character, "the sacramental sign of interior justification."[82] O'Neill explains the character as "a lasting relationship with Christ [that] imposes a constant obligation that the reality of the person's life should correspond to this sacramental incorporation into Christ."[83] This justification, Aquinas continues to explain, is the *res tantum*, that which is signified but itself not a sign, which is essential to the definition of a sacrament.[84]

---

and Metaphors: The Significance of the Trinitarian Names, Father, Son, and Holy Spirit," *Union Seminary Quarterly Review* 40 (1985): 31–42. Further, the distinguished Protestant theologian Wolfhart Pannenberg defends the immemorial practice of the Christian church with respect to the baptismal formula. See Pannenberg, *Systematic Theology*, vol. 1 (Grand Rapids: Eerdmans, 1991), 260–62.

79. *Unitatis Redintegratio*, no. 22 (VRL).

80. *Summa theologiae* III.66.1.

81. *Summa theologiae* III.66.1.

82. *Summa theologiae* III.66.1.

83. O'Neill, *Sacramental Realism*, 135.

84. Character supplies the causative grounds for the *res tantum* or interior justification. This means that the internal finality of Baptism is the state of being justified by the blood of Christ,

The *Catechism of the Catholic Church* spells out the meaning of this justification in terms of the work of image-restoration and image-perfection. The work of image-restoration involves the full forgiveness of sins that Baptism brings. "By Baptism *all sins* are forgiven, original sin and all personal sins, as well as the punishment for sin."[85] One should not pass over lightly this work of the divine omnipotence. Baptism not only removes the fault of sin—that is, forgives the violation of the divine law that sin entails—but also absolves from the punishment for sin that the guilty person incurs. Baptism imposes no penance or satisfaction for sin.

The implication of the abovementioned effect of Baptism for those who are baptized as an adult should provide great incentive to the newly baptized to preserve their baptismal innocence. Likewise, children should be taught to appreciate what they have received as infants and so guard against developing those weaknesses of character that will not serve their spiritual or temporal well-being. The catechism also includes a paragraph that explains the obvious fact that even the baptized suffer from what Aquinas calls the penalties of the present life and what the catechism calls "certain temporal consequences of sin."[86] These include "suffering, illness, death, . . . weaknesses of character, and . . . an inclination to sin that Tradition calls *concupiscence*."[87] These circumstances of human life, however, should not lead the baptized Christian to think that Christ's work suffers defect, as if the passion of Christ were not in fact adequate to take away the sins of the world. On the contrary, as the resurrection of Christ and the hope of our own resurrection indicate, Christ has conquered these enemies of human happiness. It falls to the baptized person to live in hope of sharing ultimately in Christ's victory.

Image-perfection does not imply only a sort of ethical purification, as if Baptism introduces the candidate into a putative paradise of sinless inhabitants. Liberal ideologies often put forth this kind of Romanticism. Some versions of Christian doctrine even promote it. Christian perfection results from the union of the baptized with Christ, the Incarnate Word. Again, the *Catechism of the Catholic Church* rightly emphasizes that "Baptism makes us members of the Body of Christ."[88] The document then spells out what may be called the institutional effects of Baptism. These include membership in a transnational communion, a share in the common priesthood of all believers, and

---

though it is important to understand "state" in a dynamic way—that is, ordered to growth in the Christian life.

85. CCC no. 1263 (emphasis original).

86. CCC no. 1264.

87. CCC no. 1264.

88. CCC no. 1267.

the obligation to observe one's place within the hierarchical structure of the Church and to become missionary disciples.

The properly ecclesial effects of Baptism are important to ensure that the community of the baptized remains centered on the grace of the Petrine office—that is, the visible point of unity that the Bishop of Rome provides for the Church and eventually for the world.[89] This claim, that the baptized are united with the Bishop of Rome as the center of their unity, finds beautiful expression in the words of Pope Paul VI that have passed into several conciliar documents and the catechism: "The Church 'is the visible plan of God's love for humanity,' because God desires 'that the whole human race may become one People of God, form one body of Christ, and be built up into one temple of the Holy Spirit.'"[90] When, however, we inquire about the spiritual implications of becoming members of the Body of Christ, we discover that the tradition borrows heavily from Pauline teaching on adoptive sonship such as one finds so beautifully expressed in Ephesians 1:3–14. The sacred author locates this grace within the mystery of predestination—that is, within God's knowledge of the saved: "He destined us for adoption to himself through Jesus Christ, in accord with the favor of his will, for the praise of the glory of his grace that he granted us in the beloved" (Eph. 1:5–6).

When Aquinas affirms that the baptismal character "is itself the sacramental sign of interior justification," he refers the reader to the material earlier in the *Summa* about Christian sanctification, about redemption in Christ, indeed about membership in the Church. Recall that in the thirteenth century, the ecclesiological issues occasioned by the later divisions in the West did not exist. There was no need, for example, to qualify *Catholic* with the adjective *Roman*. For Western Christians, "the church" meant the Church. This circumstance left Aquinas free to focus on the meaning of interior justification. For this, he drew inspiration from the Pauline teaching about our being adopted sons and daughters in the one Son.[91]

In fact, the theme of adoptive sonship and its soteriological implications serves as the prime model that explains the union of head and members. The *Catechism of the Catholic Church* announces this theme when it presents Catholic teaching on the ultimate purpose of creation: "God made us 'to be his sons through Jesus Christ.'"[92] Baptism results, then, in a person's being "incorporated

89. For a brief statement of the Pope's place in the Church, see CCC no. 882.

90. CCC no. 776.

91. For further discussion, see Romanus Cessario, "Sonship, Sacrifice, and Satisfaction," in *Theology and Sanctity*, by Romanus Cessario, ed. C. Cuddy (Ave Maria, FL: Sapientia, 2014), 69–98.

92. CCC no. 294, citing Eph. 1:5–6.

into the Church, the Body of Christ," of which washing serves as the effective sign.[93] Contrary to the opinion held by some earlier theologians, Baptism and the other sacraments cannot be considered as things (e.g., blessed water, consecrated oil), though specific "things" are required to complete the sacramental action—that is, for the *sacramentum tantum*. The word *thing* is put in scare quotes to warn that for some of the sacraments, such as Penance and Matrimony, the "thing" required is something immaterial.

The long and large Christian tradition contains many ways to describe and to explain Baptism. Think only of the many catechetical instructions given by the great doctors and fathers of the Church. Indeed, the history of Baptism proves difficult to exhaust. One of the most recent efforts appears in the two volumes published by the French priest Jean-Philippe Revel.[94] The enterprising author devotes some 1,500 pages to what the tradition holds about Baptism. Aquinas, for his part, mentions two representative figures of the ancient East, John Damascene (d. 749) and the fifth–sixth-century figure who has come down to the West as Dionysius the Areopagite.[95] Aquinas mentions as contributions of the East the following descriptive names for Baptism: seal and safeguarding, rebirth, and illumination.[96] He then explains each of the terms within the tripartite structure of the sacrament: *seal and safeguarding* point to the character (*res et sacramentum*), *rebirth* and *illumination* to the reality signified (*res tantum*). Illumination, says Aquinas, "pertains especially to faith through which man receives spiritual life," such that one may even call Baptism the sacrament of faith (*fidei sacramentum*).

Christ Instituted Baptism

Aquinas offers some refinement about dominical institution, at least as this Catholic tenet applies to the sacrament of Baptism.[97] He introduces a distinction between institution, on the one hand, and necessity for use, on the other. In accord with a long tradition, Aquinas places institution at the Baptism of Christ in the Jordan (see Mark 1:9–11). However, he qualifies this by asserting that "the necessity of using this sacrament was placed on man after the passion

93. *CCC* no. 1267, heading.

94. See Jean-Philippe Revel, *Baptême et sacramentalité*, 2 vols, Traité des sacrements 1 (Paris: Cerf, 2004, 2005).

95. For more information on Dionysius, see Dionysius, *The Mystical Theology*, trans. W. Riordan (Ave Maria, FL: Sapientia, 2020), 5–10.

96. See *Summa theologiae* III.66.1 ad 1.

97. See *Summa theologiae* III.66.2.

and resurrection."[98] The Church recapitulates this teaching in her *Roman Ritual* when she puts these words in the mouth of the priest at the blessing of the water to be used in Baptism: "O God, whose Son, baptized by John in the waters of the Jordan, was anointed with the Holy Spirit, and, as he hung upon the Cross, gave forth water from his side along with blood, and after his Resurrection, commanded his disciples: 'Go forth, teach all nations, baptizing them in the name of the Father and of the Son and of the Holy Spirit,' look now, we pray, upon the face of your Church and graciously unseal for her the fountain of Baptism."[99]

Aquinas establishes a principle by which he makes a distinction between the sacrament's institution at the Baptism in the Jordan and its necessity after the Resurrection: "Sacraments are obligatory only when we are commanded to receive them."[100] This typically medieval preoccupation serves to stress the basic principle that the enactment of the new dispensation of divine mercy turns on the paschal mystery. The work of both image-restoration and image-perfection flows, as explained above, from the pierced side of the Savior. One may usefully contrast Catholic teaching with the outlook generated by liberal Protestantism: "A God without wrath brought men without sin into a kingdom without judgment through the ministrations of a Christ without a Cross."[101]

Another issue that Aquinas treats in his discussion of the sacramentality of Baptism concerns the appropriateness of water as the proper matter for Baptism. How may the theologian account for what, in effect, comes to the believer as a divine given? John 3:5 establishes the biblical basis for the claim: "Jesus answered, 'Amen, amen, I say to you, no one can enter the kingdom of God without being born of water and Spirit."[102]

First, Aquinas points to water as a necessary condition for the growth of such things as seeds, and so he proposes that water figures as an appropriate sign of a person's spiritual rebirth. He reminds his readers that some of the ancient philosophers even held that water serves as a principle of everything. Next, he looks at the effects of Baptism and finds congruence in the properties of water. For example, moistness evokes the washing away of the stain of sin (*ad . . . causandum ablutionem peccatorum*), coolness, and the tempering of the sparks of sin that Adam's sin passes on to his progeny (*ad mitigandum concupiscentiam fomitis*), and lastly, water's limpidity recalls that Baptism makes the baptized

98. *Summa theologiae* III.66.2.

99. *Roman Ritual: The Order of Baptism of Children*, no. 91.

100. *Summa theologiae* III.66.2 ad 3. Another presentation of the divine institution of Baptism appears in *Summa theologiae* III.73.5 ad 4.

101. See the work first published in 1937 by H. Richard Niebuhr, *The Kingdom of God in America* (New York: Harper & Row, 1959), 193.

102. The text forms the *sed contra* of *Summa theologiae* III.66.3.

see by faith. Third, especially when the Baptism is performed by immersion, water evokes the baptized person's being buried with Christ, as Saint Paul states plainly in Romans 6:3–4: "Or are you unaware that we who were baptized into Christ Jesus were baptized into his death? We were indeed buried with him through baptism into death, so that, just as Christ was raised from the dead by the glory of the Father, we too might live in newness of life." Finally, Aquinas offers a comment on the availability of water as a reason for its use in a sacrament that the Church holds as necessary for salvation.

What we learn from this brief review of medieval theology corresponds to a compendium of basic truths about Baptism. Aquinas shows Catholics and others (1) that Baptism is the sacrament of interior justification whose effect enjoys permanence, even when the fruits of Baptism may be lost by post-baptismal sin; (2) that Christ both instituted this sacrament and proclaimed its necessity for the whole world; and (3) that Baptism creates in the one who receives it a new life that leaves itself open to the person's further spiritual development.

The Life of the Baptized Catholic

Catholic theology advances a strong and rich view of what Baptism creates in the one who receives it. It takes its cue, one may argue, from the lapidary expression of 2 Corinthians 5:17: "So whoever is in Christ is a new creation: the old things have passed away; behold, new things have come." (See also Eph. 4:24.) As has already been established, Catholic theology affirms the sacramentality of Baptism and the essential connection between this sacramentality (*res, res et sacramentum, sacramentum tantum*) and dominical institution. In short, the sacraments of the Catholic Church fall within what *Fides et ratio* calls "the logic of the Incarnation."[103] What are the spiritual implications in the one who has "put on the new self" (Eph. 4:24)? It is true, of course, that the sacraments do something, but the question that remains is this: What does each sacrament do? The following points summarize standard theological instruction on the effects of Baptism and provide classic replies to some of the questions that Catholic teaching and practice raise.[104]

Baptism, as we have seen, brings the remission of the fault of sin (*culpa*), both actual and original. Likewise, the sacrament frees the person baptized from the liability for the punishment (*reatus poenae*) that results from sinful actions. Baptism brings freedom from the penalties of the present life, which

103. John Paul II, *Fides et ratio*, no. 94.

104. The list follows the articles in *Summa theologiae* III.69, "On the effects of Baptism."

is given effectively but not here and now. A text from Aquinas helps to explain this provision of the divine wisdom. How do we understand an effective but not immediate deliverance from all the effects of Adam's sin, especially in light of the exclamations about new life that appear in the Pauline letters? One must recall the distinction between person and nature, a distinction that achieves clarity in the doctrinal controversies about the hypostatic union.

> Original sin spread in such a way that a person first infected nature but afterwards nature infected the person. But, conversely, Christ first of all repairs what pertains to person and afterwards will repair, at the same time for all, what pertains to nature. Therefore, the guilt of original sin and even the punishment of being deprived of the vision of God, which pertains to the person, he takes away immediately by baptism. But the penalties of the present life, such as death, hunger, thirst and the like, pertain to nature, from which principles they arise in so far as nature is deprived of original justice. So, therefore, these defects are not taken away until the last healing of nature by the resurrection of glory.[105]

This precious text from Aquinas explains the mystery of human suffering within an altogether hopeful context. Why does God allow these "penalties" to weigh on the souls and the bodies of those who have been redeemed by Christ, on those who have been baptized into Christ and therefore have become "a new creation" (2 Cor. 5:17)?

The theological tradition offers three reasons for why the penalties of sin remain even in those baptized. First, since the one baptized has been incorporated into Christ, it is fitting that he or she find opportunities to suffer for Christ. Christ did not accomplish his mission of salvation without undergoing suffering. Likewise, Christians do not find themselves exempt from personal suffering. Since death comes as an inescapable circumstance of human life, this suffering obviously escapes no human being. To put it otherwise, if Christ, though sinless, nonetheless underwent his passion and death, should not we who are not sinless suffer for him? One could call this sanctified suffering a way to practice the true imitation of Christ.

Second, the divine wisdom allows the penalties of the present life and what provokes them as a way to remind the baptized that they have not been made exempt from the requirement to engage in the spiritual battle. Christians must undertake a life of "spiritual exercises" in which the baptized fight against the effects of sin and so merit a crown of glory.[106]

105. *Summa theologiae* III.69.3 ad 3.

106. In *Summa theologiae* III.69.3, Aquinas actually employs the Latin phrase "*spirituale exercitium.*"

Third, Aquinas offers an argument that sounds somewhat odd in an age that lacks strong faith. The divine wisdom leaves the penalties of the present life in place for the moment so that no person will be tempted to seek Baptism for purely temporal benefits. It is difficult to imagine a world in which the special prerogatives of nature would have been restored by Baptism. Were all disease, pain, and death eliminated by Baptism, who would not run to receive it? Such a picture of the world, however, does not conform to what the New Testament records about the life and death of Jesus Christ. On the contrary, it would present the Christian life as the equivalent of a mythological utopianism.

Baptism, of course, does more than remove the penalties attached to human sinning. The happy fault of Adam's sin brings the remedies only Christ can bestow. John Henry Newman captures the thought genially in his 1865 poem *The Dream of Gerontius*. There the then somewhat recent convert to the Catholic Church writes, "O loving wisdom of our God! / When all was sin and shame, / A second Adam to the fight / And to the rescue came."[107] The rescue comes in the form of the bestowal of the seven gifts of the Holy Spirit—wisdom, understanding, counsel, fortitude, knowledge, piety, fear of the Lord—and the seven virtues of the Christian life—faith, hope, charity, prudence, justice, fortitude, and temperance.[108] The *Catechism of the Catholic Church* rightly ascribes these gifts to the work of the Blessed Trinity, whereas Aquinas prefers to present them in terms of their mediation through the capital grace of Christ—that is, the grace that Christ possesses as head of the Church and from which all sanctification of the members of his Body flows.[109]

Aquinas further specifies in what these graces consist. Those who are baptized receive with the sacrament a spiritual sense, a knowledge of the truth (*cognitio veritatis*) that may also be described as an illumination, as well as a spiritual motion through a felt movement of grace (*per gratiae instinctum*). He usefully compares the role that the physical head plays in the control of the senses and motion in the human body with the way a spiritual head works in the members of his mystical Body. Aquinas summarizes his teaching: "The baptized are enlightened by Christ in the knowledge of truth, and made fruitful by him in the fruitfulness of good works by the infusion of grace."[110] This baptismal endowment merits special attention. It is easy to portray the Christian life as an exercise in human initiative or to consider it as a challenge to meet. Catholic teaching, rather, emphasizes the divine prevenient love—that is, the

107. John Henry Newman, *The Dream of Gerontius* (London: Longmans, Green, 1910), p. 60, lines 805–8.

108. See *CCC* no. 1266. For the gifts, see *CCC* no. 1831.

109. See *Summa theologiae* III.69.4.

110. *Summa theologiae* III.69.5.

initiative that God takes on our behalf, not only by teaching the baptized the full truth about human living but also by moving the baptized toward a loving embrace of this truth in their lives. The remarkable sign of the divine power to transform the human creature appears in the practice of the Church that bestows Baptism on infants.

Since Catholic teaching recognizes the supreme gift character of Baptism, it continues the practice—at least implicitly indicated in the New Testament—of infant Baptism.[111] It helps to explain how spiritual gifts can be given to those who, as yet, are unable to benefit from them. Aquinas employs the Aristotelian category of *habitus* to speak about the gifts and virtues of the Christian life.[112] This means that divine grace creates in the human soul the capacity to act according to the specific nature of the *habitus* acquired. Even in the natural order, the distinction between capacity (*habitus*) and action is easily recognized. The infant Michelangelo possessed the capacity to paint the Sistine Chapel's ceiling long before he was able to climb a scaffold or pick up a brush. Aquinas puts it this way: "An incapacity to act does not happen to children because they lack habits [*ex defectu habituum*], but because of a bodily impediment; just as those who sleep, although they have virtuous habits, are still impeded from acts of the same because of their sleep."[113]

Since the grace and virtues of Baptism are given even to infant children, though they are impeded from acting according to them, the Church declares, "Baptism which is necessary for salvation, is the sign and the means of God's prevenient love, which frees us from original sin and communicates to us a share in divine life. Considered in itself, the gift of these blessings to infants must not be delayed."[114] A cursory look at the baptismal registers for the nineteenth century in most Catholic parishes located in the Northeast of the United States will reveal that the pastoral practice of the period dictated that a newborn be brought to the Church for Baptism within a few days of its birth, if not sooner. The parish priests, one must conclude, understood the administration of Baptism as part of their daily routines.

To continue what Catholic teaching holds about the effects of Baptism, mention must be made of the possibility of gaining eternal beatitude. When the Church speaks of the necessity of Baptism for salvation, she means eternal

111. See Neunheuser, *Baptism and Confirmation*, 38n36. The Church, of course, considers the practice of infant Baptism an "immemorial" one. See *Pastoralis actio*, no. 4: "Both in the East and in the West the practice of baptizing infants is considered a rule of immemorial tradition."

112. For further discussion, see Romanus Cessario, *The Moral Virtues and Theological Ethics*, 2nd ed. (Notre Dame, IN: University of Notre Dame Press, 2008), chap. 2.

113. *Summa theologiae* III.69.6.

114. *Pastoralis actio*, no. 28.

salvation. A traditional metaphor speaks about entering into eternal life as a result of the opening of the gates of heaven. Aquinas explains what stands behind the metaphor: "Opening the gates of the kingdom of heaven means removing the obstacle which keeps a person from entering."[115] The remedial effects of Baptism—that is, the forgiveness of all sins and the remission of all punishment due to sin—leave the Christian poised for "a kingdom that will have no end," to quote the Nicene Creed.[116]

Like everything that the sacraments of the Church accomplish, this benefit flows from the baptized person's incorporation into the passion of Christ. The passion of Christ, which finds concrete expression in his pierced heart, the source of sacramental life in the Church, occurs in time. The just who died before the time of Christ's passion or who may have been baptized with his Baptism before Calvary "awaited with certain hope their entrance into the kingdom of heaven."[117] The *Catechism of the Catholic Church* summarizes with a certain restraint what Catholic teaching holds about the descent into hell: "In his human soul united to his divine person, the dead Christ went down to the realm of the dead. He opened heaven's gates for the just who had gone before him."[118]

Catholic theology stresses the essential or what one might call the objective effect of Baptism. The baptismal bath washes away all stain of sin in all who receive it. For infants, there is no need to distinguish further this effect from the subjective state of the child, although the Catholic Church lays great emphasis on the proper education of offspring in the Catholic religion. After an infant is baptized, the priest gives a lighted candle to the father or godfather and says, "Parents and godparents, this light is entrusted to you to be kept burning brightly, so that your child, enlightened by Christ, may walk always as a child of the light."[119]

In the case of the Baptism of an adult, the effect of Baptism remains the same for all, although the fruitfulness of baptismal grace depends on the measure of devotion that each recipient exhibits—"just as the one who draws more closely receives more warmth from a fire, even though the fire, of itself, radiates its heat to all in equal fashion."[120] Of course, another circumstance comes into play in order to explain why so many of the baptized fall away from their baptismal innocence, and even from the practice of religion. Those who receive equal grace in Baptism may not use the grace equally. Baptism

115. *Summa theologiae* III.69.7.
116. See CCC no. 664.
117. *Summa theologiae* III.69.7 ad 2.
118. CCC no. 637.
119. *Roman Ritual: The Order of Baptism of Children*, no. 100.
120. *Summa theologiae* III.69.8.

is not magic. No amount of sacramental realism eliminates the fact that in the bestowal of divine grace a mysterious alchemy comes into play in which God's prevenient love works efficaciously though contingently on man's fragile freedom.

Are there personal dispositions in the recipient of Baptism that would effectively nullify the *res tantum*—that is, the graces that flow from the baptismal character? In a word, the tradition recognizes certain subjective factors that impede the bestowal of the divine gifts that Baptism bestows, though not of the indelible seal—that is, the character (*res et sacramentum*). Aquinas points out a useful distinction that helps to identify these effects of Baptism. He says that one can identify a twofold meaning in the expression "to be baptized into Christ": it can mean that whoever is baptized into Christ enjoys "conformity with him through faith and charity and puts on Christ through grace,"[121] or it can mean "to receive the sacrament of Christ, and so the baptized puts on Christ through the configuration to him imparted by the baptismal character and not through the conformity of grace."[122] This distinction between conformity and configuration aids greatly in understanding the delicate alchemy of grace and freedom, while at the same time it protects the Church's teaching from an untoward subjectiveness.

Still, there exists a minimum of human activity that is required for Baptism to effect the configuration of a person to Christ. Aquinas expresses this condition as follows: "The will or intention of receiving the sacrament is required on the part of the one being baptized."[123] In other words, absent all choosing of the sacrament, the *sacramentum tantum*—that is, the sacramental rite—becomes a pretense or, in technical language, a *simulatio*, a simulation, of the sacrament. Such a mockery of Baptism constitutes a serious offence not only against the Church but also and especially against God.[124] However, simulation differs from what the theological tradition calls "deceit," and so Aquinas rightly reminds his students that "the sacrament of Baptism is God's work, not man's. Therefore, it is not a dead reality even in a man who is baptized without charity because of his deceitfulness."[125] The word "deceitfulness" points up the incongruity of seeking Baptism absent the proper dispositions, such as the resolve to cease undertaking seriously sinful behavior.

121. *Summa theologiae* III.69.9 ad 1.

122. *Summa theologiae* III.69.9 ad 1.

123. *Summa theologiae* III.68.7.

124. The temptation to simulate a sacrament such as Baptism can arise, for example, when parents or other relatives stipulate as a condition for a descendent to receive an inheritance the requirement that he or she receive Baptism.

125. *Summa theologiae* III.69.10 ad 1.

The *Catechism of the Catholic Church* explains the special case of the catechumens—that is, of those preparing to receive the sacrament—who, however, die before their Baptism. Saint Ambrose sets the tone for Catholic teaching. This father of the Church wrote of the emperor Valentinian II (d. 392), who died while still a catechumen, "Qui habuit spiritum tuum, quomodo non accepit gratiam tuam?" (How can one who has God's spirit, not receive God's grace?)[126] This testimony comes from the bishop who wrote most eloquently about the Sacraments of Initiation and their liturgical enactment.[127] The Church then holds that catechumens who die before Baptism, on account of "their explicit desire to receive it, together with repentance for their sins, and charity, assures them" of the salvation they did not receive through the administration of the sacrament.[128]

Other pastoral questions arise about how to fulfill the Lord's command to baptize the nations (see Matt. 28:19). The basic truth remains a stable principle of Christian life in both the West and the East: "Every person not yet baptized and only such a person is able to be baptized."[129] Aquinas captures what has been the custom and teaching of the Church with regard to children of those who do not believe: "It would be contrary to natural justice to baptize such children when their parents are unwilling."[130] At the same time, the Church requires the Baptism of any child in danger of death, even if the parents are unwilling.[131] In general, the pastoral practice of the Church favors the Baptism of all human beings, even of those whose delivery from the womb is accompanied by certain natural difficulties, provided that some indication of willingness to receive the sacrament is manifest in the parents of a child who, at birth, obviously has not attained the age of discretion.

For other members of the human race, the desire for the sacrament may be considered the beginning of a person's coming to Christian faith. Indeed, as the *Catechism of the Catholic Church* makes explicit, "It is only within the faith of the Church that each of the faithful can believe."[132] Anonymous Catholics do not exist. The importance of a person's being baptized does not take away

126. Ambrose, *De obitu Valentiniani consolatio*, PL 16:1375A.

127. See Ambrose, *The Mysteries* (*De mysteriis*), trans. H. de Romestin, E. de Romestin, and H. T. F. Duckworth, in *Nicene and Post-Nicene Fathers*, series 2, vol. 10, ed. Philip Schaff and Henry Wace (Buffalo: Christian Literature, 1896).

128. CCC no. 1259.

129. CCC no. 1246, which quotes the *Code of Canon Law*, can. 864.

130. *Summa theologiae* III.68.10.

131. For more information, see Romanus Cessario, review of *Kidnapped by the Vatican? The Unpublished Memoirs of Edgardo Mortara*, by Vittorio Messori, *First Things*, February 2018, 55–58, and April 2018, 4–5.

132. CCC no. 1253.

from the requirement that the grace of Baptism flourish in the one who has been bathed in the sacred font.

Parents and godparents enjoy an ecclesial function or *officium* that burdens them with the task of helping their children or godchildren sustain their Catholic life. Indeed, "the whole ecclesial community bears some responsibility for the development and safeguarding of the grace given at Baptism."[133] It hardly requires mentioning that this charge creates for many a very difficult responsibility to discharge successfully.

As the canons of the Council of Trent suggest, the sixteenth century witnessed a renewed interest in the relationship between personal faith and sacramental Baptism. The discussion did not begin with the sixteenth-century reformers. Similar discussions about the objective efficacy of the sacraments and the subjective disposition of the recipient haunted the Church's life from the earliest centuries. One need only recall the controversies about the repetition of Baptism in the case of those who had committed serious sin against the virtue of faith, such as apostasy.[134] The *Catechism of the Catholic Church* quotes the Council of Trent when it addresses the delicate question of "cooperation between God's grace and man's freedom" that justification establishes.[135] The Tridentine text from the *Decree on Justification* runs as follows: "When God touches man's heart through the illumination of the Holy Spirit, man himself is not inactive while receiving that inspiration, since he could reject it; and, yet, without God's grace, he cannot by his own free will move himself toward justice in God's sight."[136] No wonder the Church calls the justification of the sinner "the most excellent work of God's love."[137] When the Catholic Church teaches that Baptism is necessary for salvation, she clearly locates the justification of the sinner within this sacramental action.

The *Catechism of the Catholic Church* also explains that "the Holy Spirit is the master of the interior life. By giving birth to the 'inner man' [Rom. 7:22; Eph. 3:16], justification entails the *sanctification* of his whole being."[138] However, as the

133. *CCC* no. 1255.

134. *CCC* no. 2089.

135. *CCC* no. 1993: "Justification establishes *cooperation between God's grace and man's freedom.* On man's part it is expressed by the assent of faith to the Word of God, which invites him to conversion, and in the cooperation of charity with the prompting of the Holy Spirit who precedes and preserves his assent" (emphasis original).

136. Council of Trent, Session 6, Decree on Justification, chap. 5, "The Necessity for Adults to Prepare Themselves for Justification and the Origin of This Justification," *DS* 1525, as quoted in *CCC* no. 1993.

137. *CCC* no. 1994. For further commentary, see O'Neill, *Sacramental Realism*, 116–20.

138. *CCC* no. 1995 (emphasis original).

noted Episcopal priest and theologian Euan Cameron explains, "The reformers saw things differently." He goes on to explain in what ways this was so:

> Their God did not purify sinners in order to accept them: he accepted sinners, and forgave their sins, in spite of their continuing state of sin. The righteous, the "elect," were righteous only in the sense that God had chosen them for his favour. . . . The righteousness of the saints was a garment, a cloak draped over their continuing faults and imperfections. The draping of this cloak over human nature was what saved the soul; and the immensity of that gift was understood through faith—a trusting belief in God's mercy which was itself a divine gift. . . .
>
> "Good works" could not even help to purify, to undo the consequences of sin. . . . If voluntary actions could not make a person better, then ritual acts of piety, ceremonial actions to purify the soul or earn merit, were at best futile and at worst a blasphemy. Therefore, there remained no place in reformed teaching for the cycle of sin, sacramental confession, priestly absolution, and ritual penance. . . . If there was no penance, there was no purgatory: the souls of the saved "paid all their debts by their death," as Luther said. If the sacrifice of Christ was complete and all-sufficient, the sacrificial mass, especially the private masses performed for the benefit of a named soul, was an abomination. If the elect of God were saved despite their sins, not because of their virtues, then there could not be a communion of superabundantly holy "saints" to intercede: prayer should only be addressed to God. Not only that: the idea that there was surplus "merit" available to the papacy to dispense at will via indulgences was a grotesque fiction. By a feat of theological reasoning, all the most distinctive and popular rites of late medieval religion were simply blown away.[139]

The reformers, of course, did not succeed in blowing away everywhere the authentic sacramental practices of the Church. If something positive may be credited to these departures from Catholic teaching, the polemics of the sixteenth-century reform helped the Catholic Church to clarify revealed truth about the true nature of justification.

In the 1547 *Decree on Justification*, which many consider the Council of Trent's signal doctrinal achievement, the Church took account not only of errors that arose from the Reformers of the period but also of the mistakes that saints and Popes had warned against from earlier centuries—notably those of Jovinian (d. ca. 405), about whom Saint Jerome wrote, and those of Pelagius (d. after 418), each of whom in his own way compromised the relationship between human freedom and divine action in the lives of Christians.

139. Euan Cameron, "The Power of the Word: Renaissance and Reformation," in *Early Modern Europe: An Oxford History*, ed. Euan Cameron (Oxford: Oxford University Press, 1999), 91.

Today the Catholic Church offers a ritualized program of preparation for the reception of Baptism by adults. The Rite of Christian Initiation of Adults, or RCIA (as it is commonly called), prescribes the various steps that are required of an adult who seeks Baptism or who wishes to enter into full communion with the Catholic Church. When executed properly, the program ensures that candidates for Baptism learn what they are required to know in order to take up the practice of the Catholic faith. At the same time, "Preparation for Baptism," as the Church also reminds her members, "leads only to the threshold of new life. Baptism is the source of that new life in Christ from which the entire Christian life springs."[140]

140. *CCC* no. 1254.

14

Confirmation

The Church numbers among the sacraments of Christian initiation Baptism, Confirmation, and the Eucharist. As discussed previously, theologians like to establish a parallel between the development of the spiritual life and that which occurs in nature: "The faithful are born anew by Baptism, [and] strengthened by the sacrament of Confirmation."[1] The indefatigable Jean-Philippe Revel managed to assemble nearly eight hundred pages to recount both the history and the development of the theology of the sacrament of Confirmation.[2] Today the Church gives, in sum, this compact account of the sacramentality of Confirmation: this sacrament leaves the baptized "more perfectly bound to the Church and . . . enriched with a special strength of the Holy Spirit."[3] As a result of this sacramental enrichment, the Catholic Church expects the confirmed Christian to take seriously his or her obligation to act as a true witness of Christ. Confirmed Catholics fulfill this expectation when by both their words and their deeds they spread and defend the Catholic faith.

The Councils of Florence and Trent

Like the sacrament of Baptism, Confirmation leaves its own unique spiritual mark or character on the soul of the recipient of the sacrament. One may

1. *CCC* no. 1212.

2. Jean-Philippe Revel, *La confirmation: Plénitude du don baptismal de l'Esprit*, Traité des sacrements 2 (Paris: Cerf, 2006). A concise account is found in Burkhard Neunheuser, *Baptism and Confirmation*, trans. John Jay Hughes, The Herder History of Dogma (New York: Herder & Herder, 1964), chap. 11, "The Full Recognition of Confirmation as an Independent Sacrament in Its Own Right."

3. *CCC* no. 1285.

conclude that this abiding sacrament of Confirmation sustains the Christian in the fulfillment of the obligations that the sacrament imposes. Saint Thomas Aquinas, in turn, summarizes this effect of Confirmation somewhat elliptically as “maturity in the life of the spirit.”[4]

Since Confirmation imparts an abiding sacrament (*res et sacramentum*), one may be confirmed only once. The Council of Trent made this teaching explicit: “If anyone says that in three sacraments, namely, baptism, confirmation, and orders, a character is not imprinted on the soul, that is, a kind of indelible spiritual sign by reason of which these sacraments cannot be repeated, let him be anathema.”[5] The gift of maturity in the life of the spirit marks the confirmed Catholic forever, whether for woe or weal.

The same Council of Trent composed only three canons that concern specifically the sacrament of Confirmation. This does not mean that the sixteenth-century Reform did not raise serious issues about this sacrament. In the view of one author, they—that is, the Reformers—“no longer perceived in confirmation a sacrament but merely ‘rites taken over from the Fathers, without God’s command and without a clear guarantee of grace.’”[6] Indeed, to some of these same Reformers the sacrament of Confirmation appeared only as a burdensome ceremony.[7] One reason why the Council of Trent in 1547 was content to reject flatly the Reformers’ dismissal of Confirmation undoubtedly turns on the work of the earlier Council of Florence (1431–47), especially the *Bull of Union with the Armenians* that, as already noted, was published on November 22, 1439, under the title *Exsultate Deo*. This document set down in detail the form, matter, and minister of the sacrament of Confirmation. *Exsultate Deo* also describes the effects of Confirmation in these terms:

> The effect of this sacrament is that in it the Holy Spirit is given for strength, as he was given to the apostles on the day of Pentecost, in order that Christians may courageously defend the name of Christ. And, therefore, those to be confirmed are anointed on the forehead, which is the seat of shame, so that they may not be ashamed to confess the name of Christ and chiefly his Cross, which according to

4. *Summa theologiae* III.72.1.

5. *DS* 1609, quoted in *CCC* no. 1304.

6. Neunheuser, *Baptism and Confirmation*, 250. Neunheuser excerpts the 1531 *Apology of the Confessio Augustana*, art. 13, no. 6: “Confirmation and Extreme Unction are rites received from the Fathers which not even the Church requires as necessary to salvation, because they do not have God’s command. Therefore it is not useless to distinguish these rites from the former, which have God’s express command and a clear promise of grace.” This text arose within the context of early exchanges between Lutheran and Catholic authorities on disputed issues of the faith.

7. Burkhard Neunheuser attributes the description “*otiosa caeremonia*” to Philip Melanchthon (d. 1560), one of Luther’s best scholastics. Neunheuser, *Baptism and Confirmation*, 250.

> the apostle, is a stumbling block for the Jews and foolishness for the Gentiles (*cf* 1 Cor. 1:23). This is why they are signed with the sign of the cross.[8]

As noted above, this description fits perfectly with what the Catholic Church today holds about the grace of the sacrament of Confirmation (*res tantum*). Furthermore, the *Catechism of the Catholic Church* today makes explicit the relationship with the Catholic Church that Confirmation strengthens. In the fifteenth century, however, such explicitness was less necessary, especially in a document that was intended to unite the ancient Christian sees of Armenia with the Roman communion.

By the time of the sixteenth century, the Council of Trent was obliged to address again those who gainsaid the sacramentality of Confirmation. Indeed, the fathers accomplished this task by borrowing the very words that some reformers had used to denigrate Confirmation. For example, the first canon states, "If anyone says that the confirmation of those baptized is a useless ceremony (*otiosam cæremoniam*) and not a true and proper sacrament; or that of old, it was nothing more than a sort of catechesis in which those nearing adolescence gave an account of their faith before the Church, let him be anathema."[9] Thus did the Council of Trent affirm, against the challenges raised by reforming Christians who flourished during the council's period, the true sacramentality of Confirmation.

When one considers what the earlier Council of Florence declared about the grace of the sacrament, it becomes clear that the sacrament of Confirmation rightly is known by two names, one in the East and the other in the West. "The Eastern Churches call this sacrament *Chrismation*, anointing with chrism or *myron* which means 'chrism.'"[10] Here the emphasis falls on the gift of the Holy Spirit that derives from Christ himself, whom—as the New Testament attests—God anointed "with the holy Spirit and power" (Acts 10:38). In the West, on the other hand, the use of the name *Confirmation* brings out the truth that "this sacrament both confirms Baptism and strengthens baptismal grace."[11]

The second canon from Trent's *Decree on the Sacraments* that deals with Confirmation responds to an objection that, if allowed, would have dissolved the unity of the sacramental action and changed its nature. Within a broader scale of theological topics, this canon addresses those who would take umbrage on

8. Council of Florence, *Exsultate Deo* (*Bull of Union with the Armenians*), November 22, 1439, *DS* 1319.

9. Council of Trent, Session 7, Decree on the Sacraments, Canons on the Sacrament of Confirmation, can. 1, *DS* 1628.

10. *CCC* no. 1289.

11. *CCC* no. 1289.

account of a basic principle of all sacramental actions in the Church—namely, that God can use material and therefore visible things as instruments of bestowing immaterial and therefore invisible benefits on a human person. Ultimately, one may conclude, the objection that Trent responds to strikes at the very heart of a religion that centers on the ministry of an Incarnate Word of God. "If anyone says that those who ascribe any power to the sacred chrism of confirmation are offending the Holy Spirit, let him be anathema."[12] Chrism of course holds a place of central importance in the administration of the sacraments that employ it. The ceremonies required to both confect and consecrate the chrism can last days, at least in the Eastern rites.

It is evident to all who enter a Catholic Church or who follow the Latin liturgies of Holy Week that the Catholic Church ascribes an important place to the sacred oils that the bishop consecrates, in principle, on Holy Thursday. The sacred chrism or *myron* merits not only special veneration but also a designated place of reservation within the sanctuary of Catholic churches. Why such solemnity for providing blessed oils? As the *Catechism of the Catholic Church* indicates, the chrism, "used in anointing as the sacramental sign of the seal of the gift of the Spirit, is traditionally reserved and venerated in a secure place in the sanctuary. The oil of the catechumens and the oil of the sick may also be placed there."[13] The relationship between the chrism and the gift of the Holy Spirit enjoys significant support from the Catholic biblical tradition.[14] In the West, the sacred chrism is consecrated by adding aromatic balsam to the olive oil.[15] The perfumed balm reminds those anointed in Confirmation that they should conduct themselves so as to "give off 'the aroma of Christ.'"[16]

The third canon concerns the ordinary minister of Confirmation. One may again observe that this text refers explicitly to *Exsultate Deo*, the *Bull of Union with the Armenians*. The canon reads, "If anyone says that the ordinary minister of holy confirmation is not the bishop but any simple priest, let him be anathema."[17] The same principle applies today: "*In the Latin Rite*, the ordinary minister of Confirmation is the bishop."[18] Some qualifications to this principle—mainly meant to meet practical necessities—are provided for in the *Code of Canon Law*.[19] The practice of the East, where ordinarily

12. *DS* 1629.
13. *CCC* no. 1183.
14. See the explanatory note in *CCC* no. 695 and the explanation in *CCC* nos. 1293–94.
15. See *CCC* no. 1241.
16. *CCC* no. 1294, citing 2 Cor. 2:15.
17. *DS* 1630.
18. *CCC* no. 1313 (emphasis original).
19. See *CCC* nos. 1313–14.

"the priest who baptizes also immediately confers Confirmation in one and the same celebration," does not ignore the place that the bishop holds in the ceremony.[20] The priest can only confirm with the sacred chrism or *myron* consecrated by either the patriarch or the bishop. This provides a way to express the "apostolic unity of the Church whose bonds are strengthened by the sacrament of Confirmation."[21]

In a remarkable exercise of conciseness, the authors of the *Catechism of the Catholic Church* have summarized the history of the administration of the first two Sacraments of Initiation and so have provided a succinct account of the two traditions of the East and the West that still govern the time of the administration of the sacrament of Confirmation.[22]

The Graces Confirmation Brings

When one considers an analysis of the graces that spring from the "indelible spiritual mark" that Trent teaches the sacrament imprints on the soul of the confirmand, it becomes clear that Confirmation brings not only an increase but also a deepening of the graces that the confirmand first received at Baptism.[23] To put it differently, Jesus Christ has marked a Christian with the seal of his Spirit for witnessing in the world to the truthfulness of his very person. This witness ordinarily takes the form of one's choice of either a sacramentalized state of life—that is, Holy Orders or Matrimony—or a quasi-sacramental life, such as that of those who consecrate themselves by professing the vows of religion. Whatever state of life the confirmand chooses, all those confirmed become official witnesses to the truth of the Catholic faith.

Aquinas went so far as to describe this witnessing, which one may usefully identify with calls for Christians to become missionary disciples, as "*quasi ex officio*."[24] The Latin phrase can be read to mean that the confirmed person, by reason of his or her unique sealing, takes on the professional responsibility to defend and to profess the Catholic faith. Such witnessing, moreover, does not fall only on those especially devout Catholics who decide to take it up. All confirmed Catholics must witness to both Christ and his Church. Open hostility to the Catholic faith does not excuse Catholic believers from this "*quasi ex officio*" obligation, as so many martyrs for the Christian faith illustrate.

20. *CCC* no. 1312.
21. *CCC* no. 1312.
22. See *CCC* nos. 1290–92.
23. See *DS* 1609.
24. *Summa theologiae* III.72.5 ad 2, as quoted in *CCC* no. 1305.

Public witness stands at the heart of the grace of Confirmation. In a now abandoned liturgical usage, the confirming bishop would strike confirmands lightly on the cheek to remind them that readiness to suffer for Christ must characterize their moral lives. Aquinas further clarifies the difference between the grace of Baptism and that of Confirmation. The former enables the baptized person to perform "those things which pertain to one's own salvation in so far as one lives for himself," whereas the latter gives the power to engage "in the spiritual battle against the enemies of the faith."[25] To sum up, Aquinas taught that Confirmation enables the baptized person "to profess faith in Christ publicly and as it were officially (*quasi ex officio*)."[26]

This teaching also finds expression in the brief summary of Confirmation's nature and effects that introduces the topic in the *Catechism of the Catholic Church*: "Hence they are, as true witnesses of Christ, more strictly obliged to spread and defend the faith by word and deed."[27] This expectation is reasonably fulfilled by the confirmed Catholic's taking up seriously the life in the Spirit. Thus the Second Vatican Council made this explicit claim with reference to Ephesians 4:23: "He [Christ] has shared with us His Spirit who, existing as one and the same being in the Head and in the members, gives life to, unifies and moves through the whole body."[28] The council then observes the analogy that the early church fathers drew between the Holy Spirit and the human soul: "This He does in such a way that His work could be compared by the holy Fathers with the function which the principle of life, that is, the soul, fulfills in the human body."[29]

In order to explore further what the catechism calls the grace of Pentecost, one should turn first to the trinitarian motif that dominates Peter's speech on Pentecost. "God raised this Jesus; of this we are all witnesses. Exalted at the right hand of God, he received the promise of the holy Spirit from the Father and poured it forth, as you (both) see and hear" (Acts 2:32–33).[30] This trinitarian movement finds its term in us in the divine filiation whereby all human creatures, both men and women, become sons in the Son. Aquinas makes this point clearly in his *Commentary on the Letter of Saint Paul to the Romans*, lectura 6, which treats Romans 8:28–32. There Aquinas comments on verse 29, "For

25. *Summa theologiae* III.72.5.

26. *Summa theologiae* III.72.5 ad 2, as quoted in CCC no. 1305.

27. CCC no. 1285.

28. *Lumen Gentium*, no. 7 (VRL).

29. *Lumen Gentium*, no. 7 (VRL). A note refers to several authors of the patristic era as well as to the commentary of St. Thomas Aquinas on Colossians, *In Col. 1:18*, lectio 5: "As one body is constituted by the unity of the soul, so the Church is constituted by the unity of the Holy Spirit."

30. See CCC no. 1302.

those he foreknew he also predestined to be conformed to the image of his Son," as follows: "This conformity is not the reason for predestination, but its end or effect. For the Apostle says, *he destined us to be his adopted sons through Jesus Christ* (Eph. 1:5). For the adoption as sons is nothing more than that conformity, because a person adopted into the sonship of God is conformed to his true Son."[31]

This state of being sons in the Son makes the confirmed adept at making their own the prayer of adoption, as again Saint Paul expresses it in the Letter to the Romans: "You received a spirit of adoption, through which we cry, 'Abba, Father!'" (Rom. 8:15). The saints recognized by the Catholic Church have made the theme of adoptive sonship a central point of their spiritual instruction and writing. Most notably among those of the modern period, Saint Thérèse of Lisieux (d. 1897) explains the centrality of this grace in her doctrine of spiritual childhood.[32] In an age when secular-minded folks are given to drawing their personal identities from sources peripheral to their true natures, the need to stress the spiritual identity common to those who have been baptized and confirmed takes on a certain urgency.

Those Catholics of a certain age who remember the preparation that they received in order to present themselves for the sacrament of Confirmation know that they were required to memorize the names of the gifts of the Holy Spirit: "wisdom, understanding, counsel, fortitude, knowledge, piety, and fear of the Lord."[33] The pedagogical purpose for this catechetical exercise appeared during the ceremony itself, when the confirming bishop would interrogate randomly those to be confirmed about important features of the Catholic faith.[34] One or another bishop often asked a candidate to name the seven gifts of the Holy Spirit. The deeper purpose of this exercise, of course, arose from the recognition that these same gifts of the Holy Spirit form part of the ordinary spiritual life of every Christian.[35] As the *Catechism of the Catholic Church* today explains succinctly about the seven gifts, "These are permanent

31. Thomas Aquinas, *Commentary on the Letter of Saint Paul to the Romans*, Biblical Commentaries 37, trans. F. R. Larcher, ed. J. Mortenson and E. Alarcón (Lander, WY: The Aquinas Institute for the Study of Sacred Doctrine, 2012), lect. 6, nos. 703–4 (emphasis original).

32. For a readable and charming account of the spiritual teaching of the Little Flower, see Ida Friederike Görres, *The Hidden Face: A Study of St. Thérèse of Lisieux* (New York: Pantheon Books, 1959), esp. 328–48.

33. CCC no. 1831.

34. Today this practice has given way to the following instruction: "The Bishop . . . gives a brief homily, by which, shedding light on the readings, he leads, as if by hand, those to be confirmed, their sponsors and parents, and the whole gathering of the faithful to a deeper understanding of the mystery of Confirmation." See *Roman Ritual: The Order of Confirmation*, no. 22.

35. For a classic account of the gifts of the Holy Spirit and their role in the Christian life, see Robert Edward Brennan, *The Seven Horns of the Lamb* (Milwaukee: Bruce, 1966).

dispositions which make [Christians] docile in following the promptings of the Holy Spirit."[36]

For his part, Aquinas associates the gifts of the Holy Spirit with the virtues of the Christian life. Whereas the virtues, even the theological virtues, observe a norm of reason, the gifts of the Holy Spirit "perfect the powers of the soul in regard to the Holy Spirit as moving principle.'[37] This movement of grace—that is, the prompting of the Holy Spirit—equips the confirmed Catholic to meet the exigencies of everyday life. The Holy Spirit guides Catholics in a way that ensures that their virtuous life finds its overall orientation in the New Testament Beatitudes, the teachings of Jesus about both the meaning of and the way to obtain true happiness (see Matt. 5:1–12).

The Time for Reception of Confirmation

As the Second Vatican Council emphasized, when a confirmed Catholic receives the Holy Spirit, he or she also becomes bound closely to the Church of the Incarnate Word. In the model instruction that the Church provides for the bishop or other minister of Confirmation, we find these words: "Dearly beloved, the gift of the Holy Spirit, which you are about to receive, will be a spiritual seal, by which you will be conformed to Christ and will be made more fully members of this Church."[38] This bond with the Church that Confirmation establishes explains in part why bishops historically have considered the second anointing applied after Baptism to remain their own proper activity. As the Catholic Church teaches authoritatively, "The individual bishops . . . are the visible principle and foundation of unity in their particular churches."[39] The Christian who receives Confirmation commits him- or herself to contribute to the life of the particular Church according to his or her state in life or, if you will, according to his or her particular vocation.

The temptation to parochialize the sacrament of Confirmation can easily arise when Catholics forget that the local bishop remains the source of unity for the particular Church in which they dwell. Among the many reasons that one may assign to the importance of unity in the Church, the strength of corporate

36. *CCC* no. 1830.

37. *Summa theologiae* I-II.68.8. For a good summary of Catholic teaching on the gifts of the Holy Spirit, especially that of Aquinas, see Edward D. O'Connor, *The Gifts of the Holy Spirit*, vol. 24 of the Blackfriars edition of *Summa theologiae*, by Thomas Aquinas (New York: McGraw-Hill, 1973), 80–150.

38. *Roman Ritual: The Order of Confirmation*, no. 22.

39. *Lumen Gentium*, no. 23 (VRL). This text is quoted in *CCC* no. 886, on the role of bishops.

witness ranks high on the list. Confirmation, then, also prepares each Catholic to take up a recognized vocation in the Church.

As already mentioned, the Council of Florence explained the anointing on the forehead as proper to Confirmation: "Those to be confirmed are anointed on the forehead, which is the seat of shame, so that they may not be ashamed to confess the name of Christ and chiefly his Cross."[40] These words from the 1439 council emphasize that Confirmation prepares the Christian for a life of Christian witness.

The words also give rise to the question of when Confirmation should be received. Admittedly, local customs vary. The following considerations, however, appear opportune for Catholics to consider. First, the catechetical values that arise from a person's receiving this sacrament at a later time than immediately after Baptism seem clear. The Church, one may argue, in fact suggests this option when she prescribes the order for the Sacraments of Initiation as follows: Baptism, Eucharist, and Confirmation.[41]

A second consideration arises from the role that the local bishop plays in the administration of the sacrament of Confirmation. A general agreement among historians of the sacrament holds that one reason why Confirmation became temporally separated from Baptism hinges on the sociological fact that as the Church grew in numbers and territory, the bishop could not be present at every Baptism.[42] Still, the bishop remains the ordinary minister at times conveniently scheduled, even though provision is made for other ministers.[43] Witness to this practice appears early in the history of the Church. In fact, there exists the early magisterial teaching of Pope Innocent I (d. 417). In 416, Pope Innocent wrote to a certain Bishop Decentius of Gubbio about the proper minister of Confirmation.[44] The meaning of his communication could not be more clear: "For to presbyters it is permitted to anoint the baptized with chrism . . . ; nevertheless (it is) not (allowed) to sign the forehead with the same oil, that is due to bishops alone when they bestow the Spirit, the Paraclete."[45]

From the emphasis that the Church places on the bishop as the ordinary minister of Confirmation, one may infer a pedagogical purpose. Confirmation should provide a time for the confirmand to become acquainted with the local church in which he or she lives. For the most part, the local church is identified

40. *Exsultate Deo* (*DS* 1319).

41. See CCC no. 1285.

42. See CCC no.1290, which also takes account of the practice of the East.

43. For a short explanation, see CCC nos. 1312–14.

44. For a short account of this historical incident, see William J. Levada, "Reflections on the Age of Confirmation," *Theological Studies* 57 (1996): 302–12.

45. *DS* 215.

with the diocese or, in the Eastern rites, the eparchy. To put the matter differently, the administration of the sacrament of Confirmation should introduce young Catholics to the person of the bishop.

A third consideration that may affect the decision about when to administer (in the normal course of events) the sacrament of Confirmation takes account of the need for the candidate to receive some spiritual preparation. In the West at least, the Church's sacred pastors must ensure that those to be confirmed will receive catechetical instruction about the sacrament. Instruction, then, provides the first step in the process of properly disposing an individual for a fruitful reception of Confirmation. No one can fully appreciate what he or she does not understand, at least in a rudimentary way. In order to avoid giving the impression that the Church amounts to just another nongovernmental organization, those responsible for the pastoral care of the confirmands should see to it that those who instruct candidates for Confirmation explain the basics of the Catholic faith. The candidates should, for example, learn that charitable activity flows from the Eucharist and so is not a Catholic replacement for the social welfare assistance provided by secular organizations. On the assumption that, again in the Roman practice, Confirmation comes after the first reception of the Holy Eucharist, the confirmand should also prepare by having recourse to the sacrament of Penance and Reconciliation. While the character of the sacrament marks the soul of all those confirmed, the graces of the sacrament (*res tantum*) take root only in those who place themselves in the state of grace.

The phrase *the state of grace* today appears less frequently in catechetical materials than it once did. However, the phrase merely puts in simple terms what the *Catechism of the Catholic Church* says about our participation in the life of God: "Sanctifying grace is an habitual gift, a stable and supernatural disposition that perfects the soul itself to enable it to live with God, to act by his love."[46] Sound catechesis and sacramental confession prepare the Catholic believer to receive fruitfully the sacrament of Confirmation. This requirement, which finds explicit approval in the Church's official teaching, rightly insists on the proper order of image-restoration and image-perfection.[47]

Just as happens in the sacrament of Baptism, the sacrament of Confirmation requires that the confirmand enjoy the assistance of a sponsor. Sponsors for both sacraments assist those for whom they serve as sponsors in living out in fidelity the graces that each sacrament confers.[48]

46. CCC no. 2000.
47. See CCC nos. 1309–10.
48. See CCC no. 1311.

Confirmed Catholics Active in the Church

The Catholic Church encourages priests to confirm any baptized Catholic "in danger of death" who has not been already confirmed, "even the youngest."[49] However, in the ordinary course of events, the sacrament of Confirmation affords the graces that one needs to attain Christian maturity and, as already explained, to undertake Christian mission.[50] The Catholic Church recognizes three states of life in which these graces of Confirmation may unfold.

The first state of life, which counts the greatest number of Catholic people, goes by the appellation of Christ's lay faithful. The 1987 Synod of Bishops devoted its energies to a teasing out of the Second Vatican Council's proper teaching on the laity. Afterward, Pope John Paul II authorized the publication of an official document on the topic: *Christifideles laici*, Post-synodal Apostolic Exhortation on the Vocation and the Mission of the Lay Faithful in the Church and in the World.

In the life of the laity, so the Church officially teaches, Christ is glorified as the foundation from which all created reality draws value and meaning. Thus, the papal exhortation determines that "the vocation of the lay faithful to holiness implies that life according to the Spirit expresses itself in a particular way in their involvement in temporal affairs and in their participation in earthly activities."[51] The expression "temporal affairs" comes directly from the documents of the Second Vatican Council.[52] These temporal affairs are usually identified as engagement in politics and economics and with the family as part of the greater society.

Within the communion of the Church, a particular state of life finds a dwelling place, one dedicated by either a sacrament or another form of consecration. The laity dwell in the family (*familiaris consortio*), which can be identified with the domestic church.[53] Their special consecration remains marriage, whereas the status of the single person supposes involvement in ecclesial movements or some other form of dedication that serves the communion of the Church.[54]

49. *CCC* no. 1314.

50. For a commentary, see William J. O'Malley, "Confirmed and Confirming," *America* 172 (June 17, 1995).

51. John Paul II, *Christifideles laici*, no. 17.

52. See *Lumen Gentium*, no. 31 (VRL): "The laity, by their very vocation, seek the kingdom of God by engaging in temporal affairs and by ordering them according to the plan of God."

53. See *CCC* no. 1656.

54. See *Lumen Gentium*, no. 11 (VRL): "Christian spouses, in virtue of the sacrament of Matrimony, whereby they signify and partake of the mystery of that unity and fruitful love which exists between Christ and His Church, help each other to attain to holiness in their married life and in the rearing and education of their children." See also *Code of Canon Law*, can. 835 §4.

A second way in which a baptized Catholic man can live out the graces of Confirmation lies in the holy priesthood. In short, some Catholic men who are confirmed ought to consider the pursuit of the priestly office.[55] Another post-synodal exhortation, the 1992 *Pastores dabo vobis*, explains that in the life of the priest, Christ reveals himself as head and shepherd, who never ceases to concern himself with the good of the people redeemed by his blood. Priests exercise the ministry of pastoral charity, which the exhortation describes in this way: "By virtue of their consecration, priests are configured to Jesus the good shepherd and are called to imitate and to live out his own pastoral charity."[56] Diocesan priests dwell in the presbyterate and, in some cases, within other groupings that are related to the bishop in a particular church.[57] Their consecration lies in the one sacrament of Holy Orders, which "includes three degrees: episcopate, presbyterate, and diaconate."[58]

The third option for confirmed Catholics to give themselves to includes the broad and diverse expressions of consecrated life that the Catholic Church recognizes.[59] The Church, in fact, confesses that consecrated life forms the highest expression of Christian living.[60] Those who profess the vows of poverty, chastity, and obedience imitate the life of Christ in a way that surpasses both marriage and priesthood. The Church calls consecrated life the most excellent form of Christian living. At the same time, monks, nuns, and other consecrated persons lose many of the things that people consider most essential to their lives: personal finance, conjugal union, and, above all, the right to self-determination.

The 1996 exhortation *Vita consecrata* explains what the Church holds about consecrated life. Above all, those who take up the life of a consecrated person contemplate Christ as the eschatological goal to which all tends. Thus, consecrated persons become icons of the transfigured Christ who dedicate themselves to him with "undivided heart."[61] The Catholic Church holds that consecrated persons dwell in a circle of fraternal life in communion. Such persons may be monastics, virgins, hermits, or widows. They may form contemplative institutes, secular institutes, apostolic religious orders, societies of apostolic life, or newer

55. For a discussion of this vocation, see Romanus Cessario, *The Grace to Be a Priest* (Providence, RI: Cluny Media, 2017).

56. John Paul II, *Pastores dabo vobis*, no. 22.

57. John Paul II, *Pastores dabo vobis*, nos. 30–31.

58. CCC no. 1536.

59. The Vatican Congregation for Institutes of Consecrated Life and Societies of Apostolic Life is responsible for everything that concerns institutes of consecrated life (orders and religious congregations, both of men and of women, and secular institutes) and societies of apostolic life, including their government, discipline, studies, goods, rights, and privileges.

60. See John Paul II, *Vita consecrata*, no. 32.

61. *Lumen Gentium*, no. 42 (VRL).

forms of community that the Church recognizes from time to time. At the same time, "religious institutes and secular institutes are the two main categories which constitute the state of consecrated life through profession of the evangelical counsels in the Church."[62] The consecration of these institutes' members arises from some sacred bond by which they assume the evangelical counsels of chastity, poverty, and obedience. *Vita consecrata* explains straightforwardly: "The Consecrated Life, deeply rooted in the example and teaching of Christ the Lord, is a gift of God the Father to his Church. . . . By the profession of the evangelical counsels the characteristic features of Jesus—the chaste, poor and obedient one—are made constantly 'visible' in the midst of the world."[63]

The Rite Employed in Confirmation

Confirmation, then, brings its own rich source of grace for the Catholic. After the preparation mentioned above, the confirmand, having chosen a patron saint whom he or she wishes to emulate, approaches the bishop who will preside at the confirmation ceremony. Confirmation underwent minor changes in its ceremonial administration after the Second Vatican Council. These postconciliar changes were authorized in 1971 by Pope Paul VI.[64] Today, then, the administration of the sacrament ordinarily unfolds within the celebration of the Mass. The sacramental action, the *sacramentum tantum*, occurs at the following interaction between the bishop and the confirmand, as prescribed by the Church's liturgy. The *Order of Confirmation* gives this instruction: "The Bishop dips the tip of the thumb of his right hand in the Chrism and, with the thumb, makes the Sign of the Cross on the forehead of the one to be confirmed, as he says: N., BE SEALED WITH THE GIFT OF THE HOLY SPIRIT. The newly confirmed replies: Amen."[65] ("N." indicates that the bishop speaks the Confirmation name of the person about to be confirmed.)

Like Baptism, the sacrament of Confirmation commits again those who receive it to the baptismal promises that summarize the principal features of Christian belief and life. Accordingly, the above-mentioned order gives this further instruction about the Confirmation ceremony: "The bishop adds: Peace be with you. The newly confirmed [replies]: And with your spirit."[66] This exchange of

62. "The Congregation for Institutes of Consecrated Life and Societies of Apostolic Life," Vatican website, accessed May 18, 2022, https://www.vatican.va/roman_curia/congregations/ccscrlife/documents/rc_con_ccscrlife_profile_en.html.

63. John Paul II, *Vita consecrata*, no. 1.

64. See Paul VI, *Divinae consortium naturae*.

65. *Roman Ritual: The Order of Confirmation*, no. 27.

66. *Roman Ritual: The Order of Confirmation*, no. 27.

greetings occurs at important junctures in the liturgical life of Catholics. For the newly confirmed, the greeting signifies the tranquility of life that the observance of a Catholic sacramental order produces.

Those confirmed in a particular church receive from their local bishop teaching, guidance, and sanctification. The source and summit of ecclesial life, however, finds its concretization in the third sacrament of initiation, the sacrament of the Eucharist.[67]

67. See *CCC* nos. 1324–27.

15

Eucharist

Catholic life centers on the Sacrifice of the Mass and the Most Holy Eucharist. Countless Catholics—laypeople, consecrated persons, and clerics—have given their lives either in defense of the Eucharist or in witness to the reality of this sum and summary of Catholic faith. The Church maintains this opinion about the place that the Council of Trent holds in providing authentic instruction about the sacrament of the Eucharist: Whereas the documents of the Second Vatican Council refer to the Eucharist, the "doctrinal expositions of the Decrees on the Most Holy Eucharist and on the Holy Sacrifice of the Mass promulgated by the Council of Trent . . . are still a dogmatic reference-point for the continual renewal and growth of God's People in faith and in love for the Eucharist."[1] Of course, scholarly writings on the Holy Eucharist—its place in the Sacred Scriptures, in Sacred Tradition, and in magisterial statements about the Eucharist—fill many volumes. In addition, one would need also to take into consideration the countless spiritual books by saints and others on this most Blessed Sacrament. This present introductory treatment of the sacrament allows reference only to the major documents of the Magisterium, the ultimate determination for Catholic teaching.

Some Biblical Notes

Generally speaking, one may affirm that the research done by Catholic scholars before the Second Vatican Council has shaped the present-day Catholic approach to the Eucharist. For example, Louis Bouyer, CO (d. 2004), and Jean-Paul

1. John Paul II, *Ecclesia de Eucharistia*, no. 9.

Audet, OP (d. 1993), have hypothesized that *eucharistia* is related to *eulogia* and *exomologesis*—that is, blessing and praise for the great things of God (*magnalia Dei*).[2] On this basis, these French-speaking authors have argued that *berakah* represents an authentic antecedent of *eucharistia*. While this thesis remains a hypothesis, the Mass of the Second Vatican Council does prescribe for the presentation and preparation of the gifts (the bread and the wine) the expression "Blessed are you, Lord God of all creation."[3] Likewise, whether or not the Last Supper was "the paschal meal," it remains true and agreed by all that the First Eucharist is carried out in the context of the Pasch. This sacrament recalls the Passover of the Lord and all that this central event in Old Testament history means for the salvation of the world.

Of course, now this Eucharist is brought about in a person in history, not just in a historical event.[4] Other scholars, such as Father Marie-Émile Boismard (d. 2004), have shown that in the New Testament books that bear the name of Saint John and Saint Paul, one finds an emphasis on the sacramental realism of the Church that must set the stage for all true theological understanding of the sacrament itself.[5] On the other hand, some biblical scholarship has favored a rational-historicist view of the Eucharist, whereas other scholars have taken issue with this approach.[6]

The Gospel of John is a key place to inquire about how theological presuppositions can shape biblical exegesis. Catholic scholarship, such as that of Sulpician Father Raymond Brown (d. 1998) in his contribution to the Anchor Yale Bible commentary series, argues that John 6:25–59, the well-known Bread of Life discourse, refers clearly to the Eucharist.[7] For his part, Jesuit Father Edward Kilmartin (d. 1994) follows this same line of interpretation, though with some peculiarities.[8] In sum, the dominant Catholic exegetical tradition since the Council of Trent accepts this reading of John 6.

2. For further information, see Louis Bouyer, *Eucharist: Theology and Spirituality of the Eucharistic Prayer* (Notre Dame, IN: University of Notre Dame Press, 1968), 29–49.

3. *Roman Missal*, "The Order of Mass."

4. For further discussion, see Theological-Historical Commission for the Great Jubilee of the Year 2000, *Jesus Christ, Word of the Father*, trans. Adrian Walker (New York: Crossroad, 1997).

5. For further information, see Marie-Émile Boismard, "The Eucharist according to Saint Paul," in *The Eucharist in the New Testament: A Symposium*, ed. J. Delorme, trans. M. Stewart (Baltimore: Helicon, 1964), 125–39.

6. See, for example, the work of the Anglican Benedictine Gregory Dix, *The Shape of the Liturgy* (London: Dacre, 1945). See also the work of the Dominican Father Pierre Benoit and, especially, that of Father Louis Bouyer in his *Eucharist*.

7. Raymond Brown, *The Gospel according to John*, Anchor Yale Bible, 2 vols. (1966, 1970; repr. New Haven, CT: Yale University Press, 1995).

8. See his posthumous work: Edward J. Kilmartin, *The Eucharist in the West: History and Theology*, ed. Robert J. Daly (Collegeville, MN: Liturgical Press, 2015).

In an interesting article, "The Two Forms of the Bread of Life in the Gospel and Tradition," Dominican Yves Congar (d. 1995) explains the Protestant preference to exclude the sacramental principle from commentaries and to apply the Bread of Life discourse instead to ecclesiology and ministry.[9] The best exegesis, however, favors a sapiential and eucharistic reading of the discourse. The eating and drinking of Christ's body and blood (see John 6:54–55) is not simply a metaphor for one's accepting divine revelation. On the contrary, these verses provide a statement about what some theologians call "realized" and "final" eschatology—in other words, about the new life that the sacrament bestows on the worthy communicant.

The Early History of Eucharistic Theology

The tradition on the Eucharist exhibits the same uniformity that applies to what the early Church fathers teach about Baptism.[10] The witness of the earliest extant tradition associates the eucharistic mystery with communion and martyrdom. Saint Ignatius of Antioch (d. second century) stands out as a witness to the intrinsic relationship that binds together the eucharistic sacrament, Church order, and Christian realism. Major themes emerge: sacrifice, thanksgiving, the cause of unity, spiritual medicine, pledge of resurrection. To cite an early text of Ignatius that appears in the Roman *Liturgy of the Hours*: "Allow me to become food for the wild beasts, through whose instrumentality it will be granted me to attain to God. I am the wheat of God, and let me be ground by the teeth of the wild beasts, that I may be found the pure bread of Christ."[11]

Justin Martyr's *Apologia* appeals to the continuity between the sacrifices of the Old Law and the Eucharist—for example, consider Malachi 1:11: "For from the rising of the sun, even to its setting, my name is great among the nations; And everywhere they bring sacrifice to my name, and a pure offering." This text still captures the Catholic understanding of the Eucharist, which is destined to reach all over the world.[12] Irenaeus of Lyons (d. ca. 202), who combated the Gnosticism that threatened the early Church in the West, places the Eucharist squarely within the logic of the Incarnation. He develops Saint Paul's argument

9. Yves Congar, *A Gospel Priesthood*, trans. P. F. Hepburne-Scott (New York: Herder & Herder, 1967), chap. 7.

10. For a brief overview of the patristic age, see Aidan Nichols, *The Holy Eucharist: From the New Testament to Pope John Paul II* (Dublin: Veritas, 1991), chap. 2, "The Eucharist in the Age of the Fathers."

11. Ignatius, "Letter to the Romans" 4.1, in *Ante-Nicene Fathers*, vol. 1, trans. A. Roberts and J. Donaldson (Buffalo, NY: Christian Literature, 1885).

12. For further discussion of Justin Martyr's use of the Malachi text, see James T. O'Connor, *The Hidden Manna: A Theology of the Eucharist*, 2nd ed. (San Francisco: Ignatius, 2005), 18–22.

for the resurrection of the dead. In other words, the eucharistic transformation stands at the heart of the Church's mystery of general transformation: new life in this world (Baptism), eternal life (resurrection of the dead), and eucharistic life.[13]

By the fourth century, the fathers of the East had come to formulate a truth that derives from a basic Christian intuition about the Incarnation itself—namely, that when the Word became flesh, everything, including the nature of things, became changed. Take Gregory of Nyssa (d. 395), for example, who in his *Great Catechism* writes, "He gives these things through the power of the blessing by which he transelements [Gk. *metastoikeiosas*] the nature of the visible things."[14] *Transelements* points to the "substantial" character of the transformation. Note that *transelements* is an analogical term, not a "physical" one. The fathers of the East and the West dealt with common issues that faced Christian orthodoxy. They had to deal with objections to the Real Presence of Christ in the Eucharist. They, for example, were sensitive to the charge leveled by nonbelievers that what Christians took to be a sacred sign and mystery actually involved cannibalism. This led the fathers to seek a balance between two faith claims: first, the eucharistic elements really are the body and blood of the Lord; second, the eucharistic species should not be identified with the physical elements of Christ's human body. In the West, Saint Ambrose provides some strong language to explain the eucharistic conversion when he uses the term *transfigurantur*.[15]

The fathers of the Church recognize that the Eucharist requires spiritual sacrifices on the part of the communicant. In short, as the *Catechism of the Catholic Church* suggests by its very ordering of parts, the sacraments and the moral life go together. There exists a consensus that a connection exists between the spiritual offering of a holy life and the Eucharist. This relationship acknowledges that both Christian life and the Holy Eucharist depend on the cross of Christ.[16] In other words, the Eucharist serves as a source of communion among those who communicate. The rule of life that the Eucharist imposes is ordered toward charity so that those who engage, for example, in intemperance are no longer welcome into the eucharistic assembly precisely because of the disruption that sins of this kind cause in the communion of fraternal life. In other words, the

13. For further discussion, see O'Connor, *Hidden Manna*, 22–25.

14. Gregory of Nyssa, *The Great Catechism*, chap. 37, as quoted in O'Connor, *Hidden Manna*, 34.

15. Ambrose, *Exposition on the Christian Faith* (*De fide*), book 4, chap. 10. For a collection of texts from the fathers on the eucharistic conversion, see John R. Willis, ed., *The Teachings of the Church Fathers* (New York: Herder & Herder, 1966), 441–53.

16. For texts that show the relationship of the Eucharist as sacrifice to the life of Christians, see Willis, *Teachings*, 457–59. See esp. John Chrysostom, *On the Priesthood* 3.4, as quoted in Willis, *Teachings*, no. 906: "When you see . . . all the worshipers empurpled with that precious blood, can you then think that you are still among men, and standing upon earth?" (459).

early fathers recognized an intrinsic relation between the Eucharist and charity that cannot be reduced to merely disciplinary stipulations. The unity of the Eucharist and the moral life remains a Catholic intuition, even though the distribution of Holy Communion requires the exercise of a certain discretion.

When the fathers speak of the "Flesh born of Mary," they draw our attention to the continuity between the eucharistic body of the Lord, his historical body, and his glorious body. These three ways of looking at the body of Christ control the patristic convictions about the Eucharist. In his *The Mysteries* (*De mysteriis*), Saint Ambrose points to the virgin birth as a reason for the Christian not to wonder about the Real Presence. Both Christ and the Eucharist, he says, stand outside the order of nature.[17] The fathers, with their preference for allegorical interpretation of Sacred Scriptures, delighted to point out symbolic prefigurements of the Eucharist, such as they identified in the manna in the desert and the rock from which Moses obtained (also in the desert) water for Israel. No doubt, however, arises about the worth of the figures as compared with the reality that they prefigure. Again, Saint Ambrose teaches the Church: "It is said: 'For they drank of the rock that followed, and the rock was Christ; but with many of them God was not well pleased; for they were laid low in the desert. Now these things came to pass in a figure for us. You recognize the more excellent things; for the light is more powerful than the shade, truth than figure, the body of its author than manna from heaven."[18]

A final theme taken from the fathers concerns the Eucharist and community. Saint Augustine, for example, exclaims in the course of his commentary on the Gospel of John, chapter 6, the aforementioned Bread of Life discourse, "O Sacrament of devotion! O sign of unity! O bond of charity!"[19] One need only to observe that moral discipline, when animated by divine charity, unites people and creates a communion of love. This theme, of course, runs through the entirety of the Christian tradition. The 2003 papal encyclical *Ecclesia de Eucharistia* summarizes the relationship between moral comportment and the

17. See Ambrose, *De mysteriis*, book 1, chap. 9, no. 53: "Et hoc quod conficimus corpus, ex Virgine est: quid hic quaeris naturae ordinem in Christi corpore, cum praeter naturam sit ipse Dominus Jesus partus ex Virgine?" English translation: "Did the process of nature precede when the Lord Jesus was born of Mary? If we seek the usual course, a woman after mingling with a man usually conceives. It is clear then that the Virgin conceived contrary to the course of nature. Why do you seek here the course of nature in the body of Christ, when the Lord Jesus himself was born of the Virgin contrary to nature?" Ambrose, *St. Ambrose Theological and Dogmatic Works*, Fathers of the Church 44, trans. Roy J. DeFerrari (Washington, DC: Catholic University of America Press, 1963), 25–26.

18. Ambrose, *De mysteriis*, book 1, chap. 8, no. 49, as quoted in Ambrose, *Theological and Dogmatic Works*, 23. For more on the testimony that comes from St. Ambrose, see O'Connor, *Hidden Manna*, 37–44.

19. Augustine, *Tractates on the Gospel of John* 26.13 (PL 35:1613), as quoted in CCC no. 1398.

Eucharist when it states, citing the Church's governing legislation, "The *Code of Canon Law* refers to this situation of a manifest lack of proper moral disposition when it states that those who 'obstinately persist in manifest grave sin' are not to be admitted to Eucharistic communion."[20] When it comes to the distribution of Holy Communion, Catholics are taught to accept that discretion can apply only to a certain point.

The teachings of the early Church fathers became the workbook for the study of theology that unfolded in the monasteries, whose role in preserving both Christian and human culture in the West has been well studied.[21] Nonetheless, it appears noteworthy that what the Church holds about the Eucharist met certain challenges in early medieval disputes about the sacrament. These controversies mainly transpired within the monastic schools of theology. The first bout of exchanges took place between roughly the ninth century and the end of the eleventh century.[22] The list of main authors and their works includes the following figures of the ninth century and covers the first period of eucharistic controversies: Amalarius of Metz (d. 850/851) and his *De ecclesiasticus officiis* (823); Paschasius Radbertus (d. 860) and the two editions of his *De corpore et sanguine Domini* (831, 844); Ratramnus (d. 868) and his *De corpore et sanguine Domini* (ca. 859); and the well-known monk, theologian, poet, encyclopedist, and military writer Rabanus Maurus (d. 856) and his *De laudibus sanctae crucis* (810).

In short, these authors grappled with the question of how to interpret the sayings of the fathers about the Eucharist that include references to both symbol and reality. The role of standard-bearer for the ultrarealist position usually falls to Paschasius Radbertus, whereas the work of Ratramnus provides a theory that seeks to avoid some of the physicalist overtones to which Paschasius may have inadvertently left himself open. Ratramnus, however, advanced a view that emphasized the symbolic character of the Eucharist to such an extent that one could have interpreted the sacrament as a metaphor for interior renewal.

The second period of the controversy, which includes the eleventh century, again pits monk against monk. In this period, Berengarius of Tours (d. 1088) and his *De sacra coena* (or *Rescriptum contra Lanfrancum*) were pitted against the monk and archbishop of Canterbury Lanfranc (d. 1089). Berengarius sustained a long battle to win acceptance for his views on eucharistic symbolism. His efforts, however, met with rebuttal by the Church, and he himself ended his

20. John Paul II, *Ecclesia de Eucharistia*, no. 37.

21. For a classic exposition, see Jean Leclercq, *The Love of Learning and the Desire for God: A Study of Monastic Culture* (New York: Fordham University Press, 1961). The French original was published in 1957.

22. For a short presentation of this material, see Nichols, *Holy Eucharist*, 58–61.

life as a hermit on an island in the Loire River.[23] For her part, the Church took the occasion of Berengarius's theories to confirm authoritatively the reality of the Lord's presence in the Holy Eucharist. Further, Berengarius's condemnation reaffirms the truth that the Church regards the change in the eucharistic elements as irreversible.

The problems that these early eucharistic controversies expose include the problem that arises from a naive realism—that is, a realist perspective that makes Christ's presence in the Eucharist the same as his physical presence on earth. This extreme realism gives rise to bizarre questions. For example: What happens to Christ's body when a rat eats the consecrated host? Or, even more distressing: What happens to it during the bodily process of digestion and elimination? Members of the heretical sect called the Stercoranists actually looked for the presence of Christ in the excrement of those who had received the Eucharist.

Such physicalist interpretations of the Real Presence also raised questions about the conversion of the elements that, by way of reaction, led to an exaggerated concentration on the symbolic character of the Eucharist. Reactionaries inclined in this direction argued that one best understands the sacramental sign as working by means of a self-actualizing symbolism, an approach that effectively reduces the sacraments of the Church to mere aids to Christian belief. The radical followers of Berengarius earned for themselves the minimalist sobriquet of *umbratici* (shadowers).

Some systematic conclusions did emerge from these early eucharistic controversies. These examples of right thinking led to eventual dogmatic formulations on the Real Presence, on the use of the term *transubstantiation*, and on the permanent status of the eucharistic elements. One may also argue that the intellectual confusion led subsequent thinkers to reconsider the sources and method of doing theology.[24]

The twelfth-century West has earned the reputation among scholars as a period of intellectual and cultural renaissance. The anti-heretical polemics that engaged some of the priest-monks fueled the development of a systematic theology that better expressed the theology of the Eucharist than the theologies on offer during the last centuries of the first millennium were able to. This improvement appears, for instance, in the tradition of writings on the *Sentences* and in the compositions of the canonists. Take, for example, Pope Innocent III (d. 1213), who composed the six-volume *De sacro altaris mysterio*. This work

23. See Nichols, *Holy Eucharist*, 65. For a fairly complete summary of Berengarius's travails, see O'Connor, *Hidden Manna*, 97–116.

24. For further discussion, see Romanus Cessario, "Toward Understanding Aquinas' Theological Method: The Early Twelfth-Century Experience," in *Studies in Thomistic Theology*, ed. Paul Lockey (Notre Dame, IN: Center for Thomistic Studies, 1995), 17–89.

contains important material on the matter-and-form distinction as well as on the Real Presence.[25] The relationship of the Eucharist both to the Last Supper and to Calvary finds artistic expression in the decoration of churches. One fine example appears in the tympanum of the French Romanesque Church of Saint-Pierre in Champagne (Ardèche).[26]

Still, the provenance of the themes that emerged during the twelfth century requires clarification: Do these themes find their origin in Aristotle (with the matter-and-form distinction), or in Saint Augustine (with his use of *sacramentum*)? Likewise, some attention to Real Presence is required in order to avoid the earlier polemics that veered somewhat unpredictably between ultrarealist and purely symbolic interpretations. Finally, the twelfth century witnessed the introduction of the technical term *transubstantiation*. The bishop of Autun, Stephen of Baugé (d. 1139/40), ranks among the first to employ the term (in his *Tractatus de sacramento altaris*), but more than twenty-five authors followed suit between 1150/60 and 1215.[27]

The biblical and historical information that has been broadly sketched in the foregoing paragraphs should serve only to indicate that the effort to discover a proper language to express the Eucharist and, especially, the conversion of the bread and wine into the body and blood of Christ exhibits a dialectical development. This development, however, reached a point of authoritative determination. When the controversies of the sixteenth century arose, the resolutions offered by the Council of Trent show themselves in continuity with the expressed faith of the Church handed down by the apostles. Even before the fruitful deployment of Aristotelian categories by Saint Thomas Aquinas, the Church in her official documents had begun to rely on Aristotelian vocabulary to clarify what she held about the Blessed Sacrament of the Altar. The creed *Firmiter*, issued by the Fourth Lateran Council, made the following bold statement: "In the Sacrament of the Altar, under the species of bread and wine, his Body and Blood are truly contained, the bread having been transubstantiated into his Body and the wine into his Blood by the divine power."[28] This text dates from 1215. Thomas Aquinas was born about a decade later.

25. For the full Latin text, see *PL* 217:773–916, and *De sacro altaris mysterio: Libri VI* (Berlin: Nabu Press, 2013).

26. For an image of the tympanum, see https://commons.wikimedia.org/wiki/Category:%C3%89glise_Saint-Pierre_de_Champagne_(Ard%C3%A8che)#/media/File:Champagne_(Ard%C3%A8che)_Saint-Pierre_104.JPG. The damage was done during the course of the sixteenth-century wars of religion, presumably by those who rejected the sacrificial character of the Eucharist.

27. O'Connor, *Hidden Manna*, 183–84.

28. Quoted in O'Connor, *Hidden Manna*, 186.

Renaissance Challenges

Some issues around the sixteenth-century Reform will illuminate the elaboration of the Catholic theology of the Eucharist that has become and remains the standard for orthodoxy. The writings of Thomas Aquinas and the tradition that issues from his work arguably provide the best exemplar of this orthodoxy. Pope John Paul II brought *Ecclesia de Eucharistia,* his encyclical on the Eucharist, to a close with words from the last two verses of the *Lauda Sion,* which was composed by Aquinas for the Feast of Corpus Christi:

> Come then, good Shepherd, bread divine,
> Still show to us thy mercy sign;
> Oh, feed us, still keep us thine;
> So we may see thy glories shine
> in fields of immortality.[29]

Those who undertook the Protestant Reform in the sixteenth century were obliged to consider the Catholic doctrine of the Eucharist. They could not simply dismiss the Eucharist itself as a useless ritual invented by early Christians for whatsoever purpose. At the same time, as already noted, the animators of the Reform considered the Mass of the Roman rite something that distracted from justifying faith instead of fortifying it. The range of objections to Catholic teaching on the Eucharist and on the practices that surrounded its confection and distribution were manifested in the 1531 *Decree on the Sacrament of the Eucharist.*

The sixteenth-century controversies were adumbrated by two figures of the fourteenth and fifteenth centuries. The English priest John Wycliffe (d. 1384) bandied about in the English church a version of Berengarius's views. He seems to have withdrawn from the proposal that the "sign of the Body of Christ is really Christ himself."[30] The Council of Constance in 1418 found forty-five propositions from Wycliffe's writings to censure.[31] Subsequently, Jan Hus (d. 1415) brought Wycliffe's teachings to Bohemia. There Hus included the innovative call to allow the laity to communicate from the chalice. However, the Council of Constance reacted by explaining that the standard practice—in which only the priest consumed the precious blood—came into existence for "good reasons."[32]

29. John Paul II, *Ecclesia de Eucharistia,* no. 62.

30. See his work, John Wycliffe, *De Eucharistia tractatus major,* chap. 4, as cited in O'Connor, *Hidden Manna,* 125. O'Connor also provides a fairly complete account of Wycliffe's teaching in *Hidden Manna,* 123–30. (Note that various sources use different spellings of Wycliffe's name.)

31. *DS* 1151–95.

32. *DS* 1199.

By and large, these early departures from Catholic teaching on and practice of the Eucharist were contained within the institutional strictures of the late medieval Church. Wycliffe died a few days after suffering a stroke while he said Mass, although after his posthumous condemnation at the Council of Constance, his remains were exhumed and burned. Wycliffe's ashes were then thrown into the River Swift, a tributary of the River Avon. Hus, however, fared less well. His ashes were cast into the Rhine River after he had suffered execution by being burned alive at the stake.

The sixteenth-century, of course, resulted in organized withdrawals from the Catholic Church, whose authority, especially after 1555, suffered even political opposition in certain realms. Truth to tell, even a brief account of the positions held by the figures of the Protestant Reform risks making broad generalizations that may fail to do justice to the complexity of views and the development that one or another author underwent. Martin Luther, for example, undertook a critique of eucharistic practices, questioned the sacrificial character of the Eucharist, and engaged critically with another Reform figure, the Swiss priest Huldrych Zwingli (d. 1531). For his part, Zwingli, a humanist, held a view that prioritized the faith of the communicant over any transformation of the elements of the Eucharist themselves, a view to which Martin Luther is said to have demurred at the famous 1529 Marburg Colloquy. Martin Bucer (d. 1551) was the architect of the "Wittenberg Concord," which, after a period of strong dispute (1524–36), probably takes the responsibility for having set the Lutheran and Reformed traditions on their peaceful but separate ways with respect to the Real Presence in the Eucharist. Philip Melanchthon, who signed the aforementioned document for the Lutheran party, stressed, it is said, a moral meaning of the Eucharist and distinguished between a propitiatory sacrifice and a eucharistic sacrifice.

To turn to Reformed theology, John Calvin (d. 1564) is said to have held for a true spiritual impartation of Christ's body and so made the Eucharist an effective sign of grace received elsewhere than from the sacrament.[33] He clearly distanced himself from authentic Catholic teaching on the Real Presence. For example, in a 1539 letter to a cardinal located in France, near Geneva, Calvin explained that "there must be no fiction of transubstantiating the bread into Christ, and afterwards worshiping it as Christ."[34] Additionally, Calvin also expressed his movement away from the Eucharist as a sacrifice. In the same letter, he wrote,

33. See O'Connor, *Hidden Manna*, 147, where O'Connor writes of Calvin's views on the Eucharist, "The Supper is, in short, a powerful and effective sign, on the occasion of whose reception the Holy Spirit unites the heavenly Lord to us as our food, which we eat spiritually."

34. John Calvin to James Sadolet, Basle, September 1, 1539. For the text, see "Sadolet's Letter and Calvin's Reply," accessed November 26, 2021, https://www.monergism.com/thethreshold/sdg/calvin_sadolet.html.

"We are indignant, that in the room of the sacred Supper has been substituted a sacrifice, by which the death of Christ is emptied of its virtues."[35] Calvin was, in fact, responding to a request from James Sadolet (d. 1547), bishop of the Holy Roman Church at Carpentras, who was a cardinal and who had written to the citizenry of Geneva asking them to return to the Roman obedience.

The evolution of teaching on the Eucharist that took place in the Church of England proceeded in phases.[36] One indication of the uncertainty that characterized the early phase of the English Reformation comes from the lips of Queen Elizabeth I (d. 1603), daughter of Henry VIII. The queen gave this answer upon being asked her opinion of Christ's presence in the sacrament: "'Twas God the word that spake it, / He took the bread and brake it; / And what the word did make it; / That I believe, and take it."[37] Such indeterminacy, however, was fairly widespread in the Reformation period. Earlier, the highly acclaimed Christian humanist Desiderius Erasmus (d. 1536) voiced this view about the newly proposed accounts of the eucharistic conversion: "As an old man I did not change the opinion that I had when young, except to make the point that, under the force of different arguments, I could waver to either side of the question, were I not strengthened by the authority of the church."[38] He, of course, refers to the classic doctrine of the Real Presence and to the authority of the Roman Church.

Given the upheavals that occurred among both Protestants and Catholics with regard to how each described the sacrament of the Eucharist, it comes as no surprise that the Council of Trent devoted several sessions to this central issue of Catholic orthodoxy—session 13 (October 1551) and sessions 21 and 22 (July and September 1562). From the above, albeit sketchy, overview of sixteenth-century departures from the clear teaching of the Fourth Lateran Council (1215), one may conjecture that three principal theories emerged that would radically change received Catholic teaching about the sacrament of the Most Holy Eucharist. The first considers a "Real Presence" as a result of consubstantiation. That is, one finds an affirmation of the mystery explained as the coexistence of two substances in the bread and wine.[39] The second may be described as memorialism, in which Christ's circumscribed body remains in

35. Calvin to Sadolet, September 1, 1539.

36. For a brief overview, see Nichols, *Holy Eucharist*, 125–32.

37. This quotation comes from Samuel Clarke, *The Marrow of Ecclesiastical History* (1675), part 2, book 1: "The Life of Queen Elizabeth."

38. Desiderius Erasmus, *Detectio praestigiarum*, in Desiderius Erasmus, *Controversies*, Collected Works of Erasmus 78, ed. James D. Tracy and Manfred Hoffman (Toronto: University of Toronto Press, 2011), 177.

39. Luther himself never uses the word *consubstantiation*, nor has the Lutheran church accepted it officially at a later point. However, the doctrine of consubstantiation might be found in the 1577 Formula of Concord 7.37–38:

heaven with a presence here below caused by his divinity.[40] The third theory, which expresses the minimalist position, may be termed virtualism, which holds that there exists an effective power for the believer in the substantially unchanged bread and wine.[41] Of course, the Fourth Lateran Council, in 1215, summarized authentic Catholic teaching in one pregnant sentence: "His Body and Blood are truly contained in the sacrament of the altar under the appearances (*sub speciebus*) of bread and wine, the bread being transubstantiated into the body by the divine power and the wine into the blood, to the effect that we receive from what is his what he has received from what is ours in order that the mystery of unity may be accomplished."[42]

From this thirteenth-century affirmation of eucharistic realism, one may usefully consider the connection that the Catholic Church makes between the real transubstantiation of the substances of bread and wine and the real transformation of the worthy recipient that in turn brings about the "mystery of unity" that only a communion in divine charity effects. Unfortunately, the best of the Reformers considered this conciliar pronouncement an opinion that too

---

> Many prominent ancient teachers, like Justin, Cyprian, Augustine, Leo, Gelasius, Chrysostom, and others, have cited the personal union as an analogy to the words of Christ's testament, "This is my body." For as in Christ two distinct and untransformed natures are indivisibly united, so in the Holy Supper the two essences, the natural bread and the true, natural body of Christ, are present together here on earth in the ordered action of the sacrament, though the union of the body and blood of Christ with the bread and wine is not a personal union, like that of the two natures in Christ, but a sacramental union, as Dr. Luther and our theologians call it in the above-mentioned articles of agreement of 1536 and elsewhere. (*The Book of Concord: The Confessions of the Evangelical Lutheran Church*, trans. and ed. Theodore G. Tappert et al. [Philadelphia: Fortress, 1959], 575–76.)

I am indebted to Professor Reinhard Hütter for both the reference and the scholarly information contained in this note.

40. One contemporary author states, "'Symbolic memorialism' was the viewpoint of Zwingli [who] viewed the Supper as a visible word and a prompt for faithful remembrance." Michael Allen, "Sacraments in the Reformed and Anglican Traditions," in *The Oxford Handbook of Sacramental Theology*, ed. Hans Boersma and Matthew Levering (Oxford: Oxford University Press, 2015), 292. This commentator and others remark on the various nuances on the theme of memorialism held within the Reformed tradition.

41. This position is often attributed to John Calvin, who wrote, "Wherefore, inasmuch as the virtue of the Holy Spirit is conjoined with the sacraments when we duly receive them, we have reason to hope they will prove a good mean and aid to make us grow and advance in holiness of life, and specially in charity." Calvin, *Short Treatise on the Holy Supper of Our Lord Jesus Christ*, 19. http://hornes.org/theologia/john-calvin/short-treatise-on-the-holy-supper-of-our-lord-jesus-christ.

A twentieth-century theologian and New Testament scholar, Markus Barth, represents what may be called the minimalist position: "To summarize, eating bread that is and remains bread and drinking wine that is and remains plain wine—these material, bodily, palpable actions are not too little, too trite, too contemptible, to serve a magnificent purpose." Barth, *Rediscovering the Lord's Supper* (Atlanta: John Knox, 1988), 57.

42. *DS* 802.

much favored alien philosophical concepts that, as they saw things, had crept into the Christian religion by medieval scholastics such as Thomas Aquinas.[43]

Trent and the Eucharist

Because of the variety of proposals about the Holy Eucharist that emerged within the first half of the sixteenth century, the Council of Trent devoted, as already mentioned, several sessions to considering this central element of Catholic faith and practice.[44] The first decree appeared on October 11, 1551, during the thirteenth session of the council. A foreword and eight chapters preceded the anathemas issued by the council. The foreword acknowledges that the Church of God has been deeply affected by the eucharistic controversies and so "divided into many and diverse parts."[45]

Chapter 1 straightaway declares the authentic Catholic teaching, which, moreover, remains such: "After the consecration of the bread and the wine, our Lord Jesus Christ, true God and true man, is truly, really, and substantially contained under the appearances [*sub specie*] of those perceptible realities."[46] Chapter 2 gives a description of the *res* of the sacrament, the graces that it brings into the Church and that the worthy communicant receives. These include the forgiveness of venial sins, strength to live virtuously with an eye to an eternal reward, and the establishment of a eucharistic communion on earth under the bond of charity.

Chapter 3 deals with some technical features of the eucharistic conversion that explain the natural concomitance that puts the whole Christ in both the consecrated bread and the consecrated wine. The technical concepts employed

43. See, for example, the *Babylonian Captivity of the Church*, composed by Martin Luther in 1520: "Moreover, the church kept the true faith for more than twelve hundred years, during which time the holy fathers never, at any time or place, mentioned this transubstantiation (a monstrous word and a monstrous idea), until the pseudo philosophy of Aristotle began to make its inroads into the church in these last three hundred years." In the same part of the text that considers the eucharistic conversion with only the accidents of bread and wine remaining, Luther writes: "But this opinion of Thomas hangs so completely in the air without support of Scripture or reason that it seems to me he knows neither his philosophy nor his logic. For Aristotle speaks of subject and accidents so very differently from Saint Thomas that it seems to me this great man is to be pitied not only for attempting to draw his opinions in matters of faith from Aristotle, but also for attempting to base them upon a man whom he did not understand, thus building an unfortunate superstructure upon an unfortunate foundation." This translation of the sixteenth-century text is that of A. T. W. Steinhäuser, as revised by Frederick C. Ahrens and Abdel Ross Wentz, in *Luther's Works*, ed. J. Pelikan and T. Lehmann (St. Louis: Concordia, 1958).

44. These were session 13, October 11, 1551; session 21, July 16, 1562; and session 22, September 17, 1562.

45. *DS* 1635.

46. *DS* 1636. See *CCC* no. 1374, which cites canon 1 (*DS* 1651).

to describe the power of the words (*ex vi verborum*) and the power of concomitance (*vi naturalis illius connexionis et concomitantiae*) had precedents in the work of the medieval authors.[47] This canon also distinguishes the Eucharist from the other sacraments, inasmuch as "the Author of sanctity himself is present before the sacrament is used."[48]

Next, chapter 4 treats the Catholic doctrine of transubstantiation, which the council describes as a fitting way to refer to what transpires in the eucharistic conversion. Twice the council affirms the conversion "of the whole substance" of bread and of wine (*totius substantiae . . . totius substantiae*). Twice the same text refers to the conversion of the aforementioned into the substance (*in substantiam*) of the body and the blood of Christ our Lord. It would be difficult to propose a better word to describe this unique conversion than *transubstantiation*, a term that the Catholic Church has used in conciliar texts since the early thirteenth century. In fact, Abbot Vonier introduces his chapter on transubstantiation with these striking words: "Nothing could give us a clearer insight into the Eucharistic doctrine than the position that Transubstantiation holds in the Eucharist."[49]

Chapter 5 turns to consider practices that had become customary in the Catholic community. These include eucharistic adoration, processions, public celebrations of the Feast of Corpus Christi, and other forms of worship of the Holy Eucharist outside the Mass. The Council of Trent makes the following strong affirmation about the Holy Eucharist: "It is not to be less adored because it was instituted by Christ the Lord to be received."[50] This chapter especially corrects those who found the public worship of the Eucharist on the Feast of Corpus Christi a departure from what is proper. In places where Catholic practices receive political support, Corpus Christi processions still figure as important elements of both popular piety and local culture. In the Catholic canton of Fribourg in Switzerland, for instance, the day's festivities begin early in the morning by the firing of cannon volleys from a high place near the city. These serve to alert the population to the important events about to unfold within the city limits and also to warn anyone who may consider disrupting them.

Chapter 6 moves on to consider the reservation of the Holy Eucharist and to determine a suitable place, commonly known as a tabernacle, for doing so. Among the main benefits of reservation of the Blessed Sacrament is that it makes

47. For a clear explanation of these terms in the eucharistic theology of Aquinas, see Anscar Vonier, *A Key to the Doctrine of the Eucharist* (Westminster, MD: Newman Bookstore, 1946), chap. 19.

48. *DS* 1639.

49. Vonier, *Key*, 176.

50. *DS* 1643.

the Eucharist available to the sick and dying. This chapter also observes that the practice of thus reserving the Eucharist dates back at least to the Council of Nicaea (325). In fact, the fathers of the Council of Trent refer to the practice of reserving the Blessed Sacrament in the churches of the world as "a most salutary and necessary custom."[51]

Chapter 7 establishes a discipline that Catholics observe when they prepare to receive the Holy Eucharist. In short, those guilty of mortal sins should first receive the sacrament of Penance and Reconciliation before they approach the reception of Holy Communion. A special provision is made for priests in a sinful state who nevertheless must celebrate Mass for the faithful but lack a confessor: "If a priest should celebrate in urgent need without previous confession, let him confess at the first opportunity."[52] This rule reflects the priority that the Church places on priests' supplying the Mass for the Catholic faithful. It does not, however, condone unworthy priests who persist in serious sin without recourse to the sacrament of Penance and who still celebrate the Holy Sacrifice of the Mass.

Chapter 8 then turns to consider a particular feature of Catholic theology that forms the basis for practices still in vigor among devout Catholics. The chapter points to three ways of receiving the Eucharist from priests. The first applies to serious sinners—that is, to those who find themselves not well disposed to grow in charity and so do not receive the *res tantum* of the Eucharist. Were such persons to consume the sacred species, they would do so only "sacramentally" and to their spiritual impairment. This distinction obviously answers the objection of those who placed subjective conditions on the recipient of the Eucharist in order to explain its reality. For example, some teachers advanced the heterodox view that for those who do not believe the truth of the sacrament, no sacrament exists.

Other persons, by contrast, who are suitably prepared to receive Holy Communion but who are kept for whatever external reason from the actual reception of the Eucharist, may receive the sacrament "spiritually." This practice continues today under the rubric of a "Spiritual Communion." The fruit and benefit of such Spiritual Communions, of course, depends on the strength of the desire in the hearts of those who cannot communicate. Saints have composed prayers to help those who wish to make a Spiritual Communion. For example, the eighteenth-century doctor of the Church Saint Alphonsus Liguori (d. 1787) wrote,

51. *DS* 1645.
52. *DS* 1647.

> My Jesus, I believe that You are present in the Most Blessed Sacrament.
> I love You above all things,
> and I desire to receive You into my soul.
> Since I cannot now receive you sacramentally,
> come at least spiritually into my heart.
> I embrace You as if you were already there,
> and I unite myself wholly to You.
> Never permit me to be separated from You.[53]

In places where priests are scarce or where persecution and other adversities, such as confinement, prohibit Catholics from assisting at Mass, the practice of a Spiritual Communion affords Catholics great consolation.

The third way of receiving the Holy Eucharist represents the ordinary practice of most Catholics—the reception of the sacrament "sacramentally and spiritually" (*sacramentaliter simul et spiritaliter*).[54] When persons such as these receive Holy Communion, the graces associated with this sacrament become theirs. This last chapter closes with an exhortation that all Christians would return to eucharistic communion within the unity of the Church of God and that Catholics who are well disposed would take this "super-substantial bread" frequently.[55]

In order to alert Catholics about the heresies that should be avoided, the Council of Trent added eleven canons to what had been exposed in the chapters about "Catholic doctrine."[56] These canons capture the doctrinal points about the sacrament of the Holy Eucharist already set down with the addition of one disciplinary canon that stipulates what Catholics have come to know as the "Easter duty." That is, Catholics who have reached the age required for the reception of the sacrament should receive Holy Communion at least once "every year, at least during the Paschal Season."[57] The text that stipulates this commandment of the Church points back to an enactment by the Fourth Lateran Council. The requirement still holds for Catholics.[58]

The Council of Trent further considered in its twenty-first session certain questions related to Communion under both species and the Communion of young children. Three canons anathematized those who criticized the practice of distributing Holy Communion "in the one species of bread alone."[59] One canon

53. See Alphonsus Liguori, "The Spiritual Communion," available at *Vatican News*, accessed November 26, 2021, https://www.vaticannews.va/en/prayers/the-spiritual-communion.html.
54. *DS* 1648.
55. *DS* 1649.
56. See *DS* 1650.
57. Canon 9 (*DS* 1659).
58. See CCC no. 1389.
59. *DS* 1732.

anathematized those who held that children should receive Holy Communion before they have reached "the age of discernment."[60]

As an indication of the centrality of the Mass, the Council of Trent devotes a complete session to expounding the doctrine on the Sacrifice of the Mass, complete with nine canons on the same.[61] The length of the treatment indicates the breadth of the controversies that developed during the sixteenth-century Reform. The more radical positions that are anathematized reflect, for the most part, those minimalist positions advanced that deny the Real Presence.

One of the most neuralgic points that certain theologians of the period brought to the fore concerned what the Catholic Church teaches about the eucharistic sacrifice. The reluctance to acknowledge this mystery turned on an aversion to the Catholic notion of propitiation. So the council fathers addressed the issue in chapter 2, titled "The Visible Sacrifice Is Propitiatory for the Living and the Dead."[62] Canon 3 summarizes the teaching with concision: "If anyone says that the Sacrifice of the Mass is . . . not a propitiatory sacrifice, or that it benefits only those who communicate, and that it should not be offered for the living and the dead . . . , let him be anathema."[63]

How does Catholic theology understand the sacrificial character of the Holy Mass? In the eucharistic sacrifice, the Christian people offer to the Father what he has first given to us: the meritorious sacrifice of the incarnate Son.[64] This means that what we offer to the Father comes, in the words of the Roman Canon, "from the gifts that you have given us, this pure victim, this holy victim, this spotless victim" (de tuis donis ac datis hostiam puram, hostiam sanctam, hostiam immaculatam).[65] Or, as Father Colman O'Neill has expressed it, "The Father of Jesus Christ is not propitiated; on the contrary, he is the fount of mercy."[66]

Still, as the words of institution remind us (see Luke 22:19–20), the Eucharist remains a true sacrifice.[67] As introduced above, the Council of Trent solemnly defines this teaching by insisting that the unbloody Sacrifice of the Mass (1) is the same as the bloody sacrifice of Christ ("Only the manner of offering is

60. *DS* 1734.

61. This was session 22 on September 17, 1562.

62. *DS* 1743.

63. *DS* 1753.

64. Sacrifice is distinguished from simple oblation by reason of the fact that, when it is a case of sacrifice, something is done—e.g., slaying—to what is offered. For extensive discussion, see Romanus Cessario, "'Circa Res . . . Aliquid Fit' (*Summa theologiae* II-II, q. 85, a. 3, ad 3): Aquinas on New Law Sacrifice," *Nova et Vetera* (English ed.) 4 (2006): 295–312.

65. *Roman Missal*, "Prex Eucharistica I seu Canon Romanus."

66. Colman E. O'Neill, *Sacramental Realism* (Chicago: Midwest Theological Forum, 1998), 110. O'Neill provides one of the best postconciliar accounts of Catholic doctrine on the eucharistic sacrifice (pp. 101–15).

67. See *Sacrosanctum Concilium*, no. 47.

different"[68]) and (2) is not "a simple commemoration" of the bloody sacrifice of the cross[69] and that (3) the fruits of Christ's bloody sacrifice are received for the living and the dead through this unbloody oblation.[70]

As a sacrifice, the Eucharist belongs to the whole Church, and it must be understood from this perspective. For through Christ and in Christ and with Christ, the Church—in the first place, the Blessed Virgin Mary and then with her all other saints, both here on earth and in heaven above—offers her "spiritual worship" (see Rom. 12:1) to God.[71] Since the Eucharist becomes the sacrifice of the Church, it stands at the center of the Church's universal communion—that is, of her unity. For this reason, the Roman Pontiff and the local bishop of a particular church are associated necessarily with every celebration of the Eucharist.[72] In fact, the Council of Trent interprets the ritual that calls for water to be mixed with wine as a symbol of "the union of Christ the head with his faithful people."[73] Headship defines the first property of priest and bishop.

Essential Catholic Teachings

The Eucharist makes the Church. As noted above, Saint Augustine sang of this sacrament as one of unity and love.[74] The *Catechism of the Catholic Church* makes the ecclesial dimension of the Eucharist clear: "Those who receive the Eucharist are united more closely to Christ. Through it Christ unites them to all the faithful in one body—the Church. Communion renews, strengthens, and deepens this incorporation into the Church, already achieved by Baptism."[75] So reception of the Holy Eucharist follows Baptism in the order of the Sacraments of Initiation. In the renewal of the Church that followed the Council of Trent, devotion to the Holy Eucharist figured largely in the practices that characterized Catholic parishes and in the new religious institutes that began, especially, in the seventeenth and eighteenth centuries.

To take one example, the books by the founder of the Redemptorists, the aforementioned Saint Alphonsus Liguori, provided Catholics with practical

68. *DS* 1743.

69. *DS* 1753.

70. See *DS* 1739–49.

71. See Augustine, *The City of God* (*De civitate Dei*) 10.6, in *Nicene and Post-Nicene Fathers*, series 1, vol. 2, ed. Philip Schaff, trans. Marcus Dods (Grand Rapids: Eerdmans, 1979): "Thus a true sacrifice is every work which is done that we may be united to God in holy fellowship, and which has a reference to that supreme good and end in which alone we can be truly blessed."

72. For further development, see John Paul II, *Ecclesia de Eucharistia*, chap. 3.

73. *DS* 1747.

74. See CCC no. 1398.

75. CCC no. 1396.

instruction about the Holy Eucharist and other Catholic devotions that a bien-pensant native of the Enlightenment period might have found, well, odd-sounding. Notwithstanding the intellectual climate of his age, the saint's *Visits to the Blessed Sacrament* (*Visita al SS. Sacramento*), first published in 1745, went through forty editions during his lifetime. Subsequently, the practice of making a visit to the Blessed Sacrament became emblematic of Catholic devotion and remains so to this day.[76] In his 1965 encyclical *Mysterium fidei*, Pope Paul VI exhorted Catholics "not [to] forget about paying a visit during the day to the Most Blessed Sacrament in the very special place of honor where it is reserved in churches . . . , since this is a proof of gratitude and a pledge of love and a display of the adoration that is owed to Christ the Lord who is present there."[77] Today, eucharistic devotion in various forms, especially exposition of the most Blessed Sacrament, characterizes in many places authentic Catholic life.

The *Catechism of the Catholic Church* indicates that the "essential signs of the Eucharistic sacrament are wheat bread and grape wine."[78] The same text then states that "by the consecration the transubstantiation of the bread and wine into the Body and Blood of Christ is brought about."[79] The sacramental sign (*sacramentum tantum*) further and properly entails the twofold action of the sacramental oblation and the eating and drinking of the eucharistized elements. Aquinas helpfully observes that this eating and drinking "is several in a material sense, but in a formal and complete [*formaliter et perfective*] sense it is one."[80]

While the Church requires that the celebration of the Eucharist proceed in accord with the instructions set down in the *General Instruction of the Roman Missal*, the essential words that constitute the form of the sacrament of the Eucharist give specific determination to its *sacramentum tantum*. The double consecration proceeds as follows: within the eucharistic prayer, the priest says over the bread, "Take this, all of you, and eat of it, for this is my Body, which will be given up for you." Then, bowing slightly over the chalice, he says, "Take this, all of you, and drink from it, for this is the chalice of my Blood, the Blood of the new and eternal covenant, which will be poured out for you and for many for the forgiveness of sins. Do this in memory of me."[81]

The Jesuit theologian and Thomist scholar Louis Billot makes this trenchant observation about the double consecration: "The definition of a formal sacrifice is said to be preserved purely and simply in the mystical slaying, that is, in the

76. See *CCC* no. 1418.
77. Paul VI, *Mysterium fidei*, no. 66.
78. *CCC* no. 1412.
79. *CCC* no. 1413.
80. *Summa theologiae* III.73.2.
81. *Roman Missal*, "The Order of Mass."

sacramental separation of the Body from the Blood under the distinct species of bread and wine."[82] The thought actually enjoys a distinguished pedigree—for example, in the writings of the eminent French bishop Jacques-Bénigne Bossuet (d. 1704), who embellishes the rhetorical quality of this teaching by comparing the words of consecration spoken by priests to a "sword" that brings about the slaying ("mactation").[83] The Church of the Crucified One does not shy away from embracing his sacrifice under the sacramental signs of bread and wine.

What abides in this sacrament, the *res et sacramentum*, may be expressed simply as the Real Presence—in other words, Christ "Being-There" under the eucharistic species or appearances.[84] Indeed, as Saint Augustine intuited, Christian unity finds its origin in the Blessed Sacrament of the altar. The whole of Catholic teaching on the Eucharist promotes this sacrament's central place in the life of the Church. Pope John Paul II in a 1986 "Letter to All the Priests of the Church" explained this centrality by pointing to the example of Saint John Marie Vianney: "The Curé of Ars," writes the Pope, "was particularly mindful of the permanence of Christ's real presence in the Eucharist. It was . . . towards the tabernacle that he often turned during his homilies, saying with emotion: 'He is there!'"[85]

There remains to consider the *res tantum*, the grace or interior reality of the Eucharist. According to Thomas Aquinas, two elements, which are related to each other as part to the whole, make up the grace of the Holy Eucharist. These elements include the increase of charity in the individual and the promotion of unity within the Church.[86] One commentator succinctly explains this mystery of spiritual solidarity in charity: "The proper *locus* of charity is the Church. All in charity should be in the Church; all in the Church should be in charity. Charity is Church-unity in the deepest sense."[87]

82. Louis Billot, *De ecclesiae sacramentis: Commentarius in tertiam partem S. Thomae*, 5th ed. (Rome: Ex Typographia Pontificia in Istituto Pii X, 1914), 617.

83. See Jacques-Bénigne Bossuet (1627–1704), *Méditations, la Cène, 57ème jour* (Lyons, 1879), as cited in Billot, *Commentarius*, 629n1.

84. Theologians make a helpful distinction in the way that accidents are said of the Eucharist. On their account, a distinction exists between *inhering* accidents and *containing* accidents: in the Holy Eucharist, the accidents of bread and wine inhere in nothing, but they do contain the body and blood of Christ—not, however, like an empty envelope reaching up to heaven; rather, the Christ who is locally in heaven is really contained, although not naturally, but sacramentally, *within* the sacramental species.

85. Pope John Paul II, "Letter to All the Priests of the Church, for Holy Thursday 1986," Vatican Translation (Editions Paulines, 1986), available at Library, Catholic Culture, https://www.catholicculture.org/culture/library/view.cfm?recnum=5455.

86. See *Summa theologiae* III.73.4.

87. William Barden, *The Eucharistic Presence*, vol. 58 of the Blackfriars edition of *Summa theologiae*, by Thomas Aquinas (New York: McGraw-Hill, 1965), 15n*b*.

The spiritual unity of the Church finds sacramental signification and cause in the sacraments of Baptism and Eucharist. In the Eucharist, however, this unity derives from the sacrificial character of the sacrament and its subsequent incorporation into the life of the believer by Holy Communion. Saint Paul himself consciously relates his own experiences to Christ's sacrifice in this way: "In my flesh I am filling up what is lacking in the afflictions of Christ on behalf of his body, which is the church" (Col. 1:24). The Eucharist enjoys a special affinity with the passion of Christ.[88] Aquinas even states, provocatively, "The celebration of this sacrament is an image representing Christ's passion" (Celebratio huius sacramenti est imago repraesentativa passionis Chrisiti).[89]

Allied to this doctrine of the *res tantum* remains the following question: What kind of unity does the celebration of and participation in the Eucharist presuppose? The issue may be addressed from two different perspectives. First, the unity of faith centered on the person of the Roman Pontiff remains indispensable for an authentic celebration of the Eucharist. Second, the personal union of the believer with Christ requires concrete manifestation through a life of Christian virtue. The relationship of the Eucharist to growth in holiness includes the forgiveness of venial sins. Aquinas's teaching on this effect of the Eucharist by those who worthily receive Holy Communion gives a glimpse of his teaching on how the Catholic aims for moral perfection. "The reality [*res*] of this sacrament," writes Aquinas, "is charity, not merely in habit, but also in act."[90] The increase of charity, which consists in our loving God and neighbor more than before we have received the Eucharist, shakes off, as it were, venial sin. Recall that venial or lesser sins enter our lives when we fail to love completely as we should. Serious or grave sin, on the other hand, requires another sacrament.[91] The person attached to mortal sin separates himself or herself from Christ and therefore cannot increase in a virtue that is not possessed.[92]

To sum up: the *res* of the Eucharist centers on the gift of divine charity. In this caritative union with God, the ultimate fruit of Christ's sacrifice on the cross finds completion for the Christian believer. Indeed, no opposition exists between this personal element of the sacramental *res* and its ecclesial dimension, unity. For only in communicating personally with Christ through the Eucharist

88. See John Paul II, *Ecclesia de Eucharistia*, no. 11: "'The Lord Jesus on the night he was betrayed' (1 Cor 11:23) instituted the Eucharistic Sacrifice of his body and his blood. The words of the Apostle Paul bring us back to the dramatic setting in which the Eucharist was born. The Eucharist is indelibly marked by the event of the Lord's passion and death, of which it is not only a reminder but a sacramental re-presentation. It is the sacrifice of the Cross perpetuated down the ages."

89. *Summa theologiae* III.83.1 ad 2.

90. *Summa theologiae* III.79.4.

91. See CCC no. 1385.

92. For Aquinas's argument, see *Summa theologiae* III.79.3.

can the believer communicate in Christ with every other member of his Body, the Church. Finally, conformity to Christ remains the progressive fruit of this sacrament. Saint Augustine aptly summarizes the Eucharist as a work of image-perfection when he hears the eucharistic Christ say to him, "You will not change me into yourself, as you change food into your flesh; but you will be changed into me."[93] For most Catholics, this conversion proceeds over a lifetime.

93. Augustine, *Confessions*, in *The Confessions of St. Augustine*, trans. John K. Ryan (Garden City, NY: Image Books, 1960), 7.10. In Latin: "Nec tu me in te mutabis sicut cibum carnis tuae, sed tu mutaberis in me."

16

Penance and Reconciliation

After a treatment of the Sacraments of Initiation, the Church turns to another set of sacraments—namely, the Sacraments of Healing. She reminds Catholics that the Lord Jesus Christ forgave sins and restored bodily health. A dramatic account of this saving work that Christ carries out appears in the Gospel according to Matthew 8:5–11, where we learn of the Roman centurion's faith and the cure of his paralyzed servant. The two Sacraments of Healing continue this salvific work of Christ among those who are members of the Catholic Church. They include the sacrament of Penance and Reconciliation and the sacrament of the Anointing of the Sick.

Forgiveness and Truth

Philosophy seems a strange place to begin an instruction about the sacrament of Penance and Reconciliation. However, the 1998 papal encyclical *Fides et ratio* does explain that when the Church insists on the importance and true range of philosophical thought, she also promotes both the defense of human dignity and the proclamation of the gospel message. This service enables all people to discover both their capacity to know the truth and their yearning for the ultimate and definitive meaning of life. The Pope who authored the encyclical, John Paul II, further expresses the wish that through the mediation of a philosophy—which is also a true wisdom—people of our period will come to realize that their humanity is all the more affirmed the more they entrust themselves to the gospel and open themselves to Christ.[1]

Among the important places where, for Catholics, this entrustment and openness finds a concrete expression, the sacrament of Penance, commonly known as "Confession," ranks high, if not first. Those who embrace Christ embrace "Christ the power of God and the wisdom of God" (1 Cor. 1:24). This wisdom includes what is good for the human being. In fact, in the abovementioned encyclical, the Pope further points up the relationship between philosophy and the human good: "It should never be forgotten," he writes, "that the neglect of being inevitably leads to losing touch with objective truth and therefore with the very ground of human dignity."[2]

Confession offers Catholics an encounter with objective truth, a meeting that begins with an examination of conscience and ends with the graced resolve to sustain a life in accord with a respect for human dignity that suits a creature created in the image of God. This sacramental encounter unfolds in the dialogue that penitent and confessor together undertake. The confessional dialogue forms part of the invitation to conversion that the Catholic priest speaks continually not only to the people confided to his pastoral care but to all men and women of goodwill. Because of his conviction that the Church communicates authentic "moral discipline," the Catholic priest-confessor proceeds with confidence.[3] Pope John Paul II points out an advantage that conviction about moral truth holds out: "To believe it possible to know a universally valid truth is in no way to encourage intolerance; on the contrary, it is the essential condition for sincere and authentic dialogue between persons."[4] In the confessional, the dialogue helps the penitent to turn away from those activities that impair the human dignity of others and that diminish his or her own moral worth.

The papal encyclical *Fides et ratio* goes on to argue that the contemporary crisis of truth is linked to a crisis of the moral life.[5] When people feel trapped in some bad conduct, they tend to rationalize the deviant behavior, and this

1. John Paul II, *Fides et ratio*.
2. John Paul II, *Fides et ratio*, no. 90.
3. See CCC nos. 75, 88.
4. John Paul II, *Fides et ratio*, no. 92.
5. John Paul II, *Fides et ratio*, no. 98 (emphasis added):

> In order to fulfil its mission, moral theology must turn to a philosophical ethics which looks to the truth of the good, to an ethics which is neither subjectivist nor utilitarian. Such an ethics implies and *presupposes a philosophical anthropology and a metaphysics of the good*. Drawing on this organic vision, linked necessarily to Christian holiness and to the practice of the human and supernatural virtues, moral theology will be able to tackle the various problems in its competence, such as peace, social justice, the family, the defense of life and the natural environment, in a more appropriate and effective way.

kind of bad thinking proves detrimental to conversion of life. One can turn to the eighteenth-century English poet Alexander Pope (d. 1744) to see this axiom rendered in his classic verse:

> Vice is a monster of so frightful mien,
> As, to be hated, needs but to be seen;
> Yet seen too oft, familiar with her face,
> We first endure, then pity, then embrace.[6]

Thus one may aver that Alexander Pope's *An Essay on Man* (1734) very much expresses a classic Catholic tenet.

The poet Pope supports the Pope John Paul II, who has observed that the problems of the contemporary world stem from a crisis of truth. So the Pope encourages the development of a right moral theology. He in fact teaches that "moral theology requires a sound philosophical vision of human nature and society, as well as of the general principles of ethical decision-making."[7] Otherwise, moral theologians can aid people to embrace a lie, which in the moral life is called vice.

Some Recent Catholic Teaching

Fortunately, the Catholic Church, during the last quarter of the twentieth century, supplied a detailed presentation of the Catholic practice of Confession and the reasons for it. The 1984 Post-synodal Apostolic Exhortation on Reconciliation and Penance in the Mission of the Church Today (*Reconciliatio et paenitentia*) provides a summary of this Catholic teaching. This exhortation begins with an exegesis of the parable of the prodigal son (Luke 15:11–32), which, the Pope explains, offers the types of those persons who need to hear the story of the inexpressible love of a father, one who offers the gift of full reconciliation. They are two: first, the son who was lost and gave himself over to dissolute living; second, the son who stayed at home but whose heart became poisoned by envy and bitterness. In sum, the Pope insists that all Christians need to listen to this parable because they all seek the embrace of the Father.[8]

For her part, however, "the church promotes reconciliation *in the truth*, knowing well that neither reconciliation nor unity is possible outside or in

6. Alexander Pope, *An Essay on Man: Epistle II* (1734), 5, lines 1–4, The Poetry Foundation, https://www.poetryfoundation.org/poems/44900/an-essay-on-man-epistle-ii.

7. John Paul II, *Fides et ratio*, no. 68.

8. John Paul II, *Reconciliatio et paenitentia*, nos. 5–6.

opposition to the truth."[9] Indeed, the Church establishes the locale or place where this reconciliation occurs, and which is represented ultimately by the communion of saints (*communio sanctorum*). The teleology of the Church, which lies ultimately in heaven, dictates the teleology of the moral act. One may observe that both heaven and authentic virtue achieve the same beatifying end. Philosophies that promote skepticism about one's ability to know the truth avoid the teleological question, however. The saints, on the other hand, know exactly to where they are headed. In addition, all forms of moralizing (i.e., stipulating moral truth solely in terms of moral obligation) fail to achieve the full mystery of reconciliation. The saints are not defined by what they refrain from doing but by that which they love—that is, that which they do for the good. Because the communion of saints embodies the final reconciliation, the ministry of reconciliation becomes burdensome only when the priest exercises his ministry outside the framework of the universal call to holiness.

The reason for the impossibility of combining a bad life with a happy end lies in the very structure of what it means to be a human being. Sin represents an aversion from God (*aversio a Deo*) and a turning toward some creature (*conversio ad creaturam*). This means that there exists no middle way between life and death.[10] The loss of the sense of sin both erodes the human good and destroys the possibility of realizing the communion of the Church. On the other hand, the sacrament of Penance and Reconciliation holds out before the Catholic believer a *mysterium pietatis*, a mystery of the divine piety. This *mysterium pietatis* encompasses and overcomes the *mysterium iniquitatis*—that is, the existence of sin in the world. The rhythm of sin and forgiveness in the life of the Christian establishes the basis for all spiritual exercise and fruitfulness.

Consider the steps of humility found in the Rule of Saint Benedict.[11] This exercise, which forms the foundation for every form of Christian vocation, consecrated life, priesthood, and marriage, reminds us that growth in the Christian life never proceeds from better to best, but from our clinging to what turns away from God to our embracing the living God. "Then we exclaim in gratitude: 'Yes, the Lord is rich in mercy,' and even: 'The Lord is mercy.'"[12] Every Catholic

9. John Paul II, *Reconciliatio et paenitentia*, no. 9 (emphasis added).

10. See John Paul II, *Reconciliatio et paenitentia*, no. 17: "It still remains true that the essential and decisive distinction is between sin which destroys charity and sin which does not kill the supernatural life: There is no middle way between life and death."

11. St. Thomas Aquinas, who spent his early years of education as a resident of the Benedictine Abbey of Monte Cassino, includes reference to the feature of the Rule of St. Benedict in his treatment of the cardinal virtue of temperance. He explains each of the steps in terms of his definition of *humility* as a virtue that "lies in the appetite, and restrains its inordinate urge for things which are above us." See *Summa theologiae* II-II.161.6.

12. John Paul II, *Reconciliatio et paenitentia*, no. 22.

needs to hear these words spoken in love: "The Lord *is* mercy." Only the Virgin Mother of God enjoys the privilege of the immaculate conception.[13]

The Dynamics of Penance

We find a schema for exposing Catholic teaching on the structure of the sacrament of Penance in the three elements traditionally enumerated: First, the *res*, or grace that amounts to the remission of sins committed after Baptism. Second, the *sacramentum tantum*, or the common symbolic action of outward expression of sorrow, with confession of sinfulness and manifest readiness to make amends, together with the priest's words of absolution. Third, the *res et sacramentum*, or the penitent's sorrow for sin and renewed love for God, which leads to readmission to the eucharistic communion of the Church.[14] Theologians observe that the role past sins and sorrow for them play in the sacrament of Penance and Reconciliation offers a unique analogical instance of the sacrament's matter. Penance and Reconciliation creates a different dynamic than what the other sacraments set up in their administration.

The wonder of this dynamic lies in this: the acts of the sinner, acts from the same will that gave offense, now form part of the sacrament through which God works the mystery of reconciliation and atonement. Rather than on water, bread, oil, or the laying on of hands, in the sacrament of Penance and Reconciliation the *form* falls on the outward expression of the penitent's human acts. To make a proper judgment about the components of this sacrament, one must make a distinction between the sacrament's proximate matter and its remote matter. The sins that a person has committed provide the remote matter upon which the sacrament works. These are not brought forward for approval, however, but for detestation and destruction. The proximate matter, that which enters into the composition of the sacrament, consists in the sorrow for sin that has brought the sinner to the confessional.

To return to the tripartite structure of the sacrament of Penance, theologians describe the *sacramentum tantum* by appeal to three actions that sinners are prepared to bring to the sacrament of Penance: First, heartfelt sorrow for sin, *contritio cordis*, which includes the serious intention of the sinner to make amends—that is, to resolve to avoid both the sin and its near occasions. The near occasion of sinning refers to circumstances of everyday living that lead to one's

13. See CCC nos. 491–92.

14. See CCC no. 1469. For further discussion, see Colman E. O'Neill, *Sacramental Realism* (Chicago: Midwest Theological Forum, 1998), 171–84. Also see Pope John Paul II's March 22, 1996, letter to Cardinal William W. Baum, Major Penitentiary, where the Holy Father discusses the need of penitents to possess a theological trust.

committing a given sin. For instance, an avid and habitual gambler visits the gambling parlor for the purported aim only of engaging in genteel conversation. He does not avoid the near occasion of sin—namely, unreasonable gambling.

In addition to manifesting sorrow for sin, the penitent must demonstrate a willingness to confess orally (*confessio oris*) his or her sins according to both kind and number. By this oral narration, the so-called confession, the penitent submits to the judgment of the priest, who then offers suitable counsel about how to develop the virtues that will strengthen a person's resolve to avoid this or that sin. Finally, the *sacramentum tantum* includes the proposal to perform works of satisfaction (*satisfactio operis*) that contribute to both recompense for the sins committed and the reform of one's life.[15]

To these acts of the penitent the sacrament of Penance and Reconciliation joins the act of the minister, who is always a priest or a bishop, which is called *absolution*. As explained below, the Church includes the formula for absolution in the Rite of Penance.[16]

Saint Thomas Aquinas makes a point of introducing a consideration of the virtue of penitence between his account of the sacramentality of Penance and his explanation of the sacrament's effects. What might seem a distraction from the subject matter at hand in fact corresponds to what the sacrament of Penance and Reconciliation aims to accomplish in the penitent. In a word, this sacrament makes perpetual penitents of the former sinners who have received absolution worthily. Aquinas, then, first establishes that penitence as a virtue stands related to the cardinal virtue of justice. Penitence further qualifies as a specific virtue inasmuch as "the penitent grieves over sin committed as it is an offense against God and because he has the purpose of amendment."[17] Justice, however, without further qualification transpires between equals. Indeed, Aquinas observes that "justice is a kind of equality."[18] Penitence, on the other hand, involves a relationship between nonequals. To which Aquinas responds "that the penitent turns to God, with the purpose of amendment as a servant to his master."[19]

A consideration of the place that the virtue of penitence plays in the fruitful reception of the sacrament of Penance provides a helpful perspective on the sacrament's unique character and place in the life of the Catholic Church. One finds the matter for this sacrament not in concrete substances such as oil or bread and wine or even the imposition of hands. Instead, this sacrament finds its "matter" in actions that remain immaterial. The special virtue of penitence

15. See *Summa theologiae* III.90.2.
16. *The Roman Ritual: The Rite of Penance*, no. 46.
17. *Summa theologiae* III.85.3.
18. *Summa theologiae* III.85.3.
19. *Summa theologiae* III.85.3.

helps forgiven Catholics to hold on to this immaterial sorrow. So much is this the case that certain saints, especially after a conversion from a sinful way of life, have devoted the rest of their lives to penitential practices. Saint Mary Magdalen offers the iconic model, whereas Saint Charles de Foucauld (d. 1916) lived closer to our own period.

What does this sacrament achieve in the absolved sinner? First of all, once this sacramental action has been accomplished, God fully infuses the inner repentance of the sinner with his grace. The penitent is united to the saving work of the risen Christ, who, in the power of the Holy Spirit, abides in the world for the work of reconciliation. The fact of one's having been forgiven becomes a sign of the final effect of forgiveness of sins and of reconciliation with the Church of the Eucharist. Even after possible future sins, the experience of having been forgiven abides with the once-forgiven Catholic believer. This grace or the remembrance of this grace (depending on the gravity of the future sin) becomes the abiding sacrament (*res et sacramentum*) of Penance and Reconciliation.

The form of the sacrament, as indicated above, signifies what the sacrament accomplishes in correspondence with the matter of the sacrament. The sacrament of Penance deals with a matter to be removed—that is, the remote matter of personal sin. To express the abiding sacrament differently, one can say that Catholics who have been absolved of serious sin, even should they relapse, know that there exists in the world a source of authentic forgiveness to which they can return. Those who have never received the sacrament of Penance and Reconciliation need to discover this divine gift in the Church of Christ.

Relapse into serious sin, of course, deprives the sinner of the graces that the sacrament bestows. Why? The *res tantum* of Penance bestows or infuses the gift of forgiveness and peace. This grace should not be squeezed into psychological categories, as the colloquial expression "Confession is good for the soul" might indicate. The forgiveness and peace that Penance brings restores the sinner to the full exercise of all the infused virtues. Aquinas explains that the tradition discovers a sense in which the state of being forgiven surpasses the malice of sin, even in the recidivist and the great sinner. "Good," he says, "comes to [recidivists] from their fall, not because they always return to a higher degree of grace, but to a more lasting grace."[20]

Why is the grace of forgiveness more lasting? The forgiven sinner should proceed through life's struggles more cautiously and humbly. Something similar happens in the case of the outrageous sinner who repents wholeheartedly. Aquinas assures us, "They attain a deeper habit of grace and virtue, as is clear

20. *Summa theologiae* III.89.2 ad 1.

in the case of Mary Magdalen."[21] Even in sinners who do not relapse into the same sin, the remnants or aftereffects of sin remain even after they have received the sacrament of Penance. These dispositions, however, "continue in a weakened or diminished state, not having man in their grip."[22] Then Aquinas adds an illustrative comparison that illuminates the different graces of the sacraments as each affects those who receive it. The Common Doctor says that after Confession, certain bad dispositions from previous sinful acts remain, "just as the inclinations to evil do after Baptism."[23] Secular authors have observed the personal dramas that sinful inclinations, especially disordered sexual desires, commonly produce among many of their twenty-first-century contemporaries.[24] Aquinas's remarks about the effect of the sacrament of Penance should bring some comfort to all people of goodwill, even as his words urge Catholics to practice frequent Confession.

The Celebration of Penance and Reconciliation

The above précis drawn from the theological teaching that has been preserved within the Thomist commentatorial tradition captures the main elements of Catholic teaching on the sacrament of Penance and Reconciliation. As already noted, the *Catechism of the Catholic Church* introduces this sacrament under the heading "The Sacraments of Healing," which "continue [Christ's] work of healing and forgiveness."[25]

The text of the catechism acknowledges that this sacrament has undergone changes in both the discipline (e.g., the frequency of reception) and the mode of celebration (e.g., the requirement for a penitent to perform public penances). Still, one can identify a "fundamental structure" that remains. This structure, as Aquinas has outlined, "comprises two equally essential elements: on the one hand, the acts of a man who undergoes conversion through the action of the Holy Spirit: namely, contrition, confession, and satisfaction; on the other, God's action through the intervention of the Church."[26] This text from the *Catechism of the Catholic Church* goes on to explain that the Church acts through the

21. *Summa theologiae* III.89.2 ad 3.

22. *Summa theologiae* III.86.5. Aquinas observes the weakened condition of such after-effects of sinning: "Indeed they persist more as dispositions than as habits" (Et hoc magis per modum dispositionum quam per modum habituum).

23. *Summa theologiae* III.86.5.

24. For one short but well-written account of the present manner of handling what a person initially may consider untoward desires, see Alexandra Schwartz, "We're Shaped by Our Sexual Desires. Can We Shape Them?," *New Yorker*, October 4, 2021.

25. CCC no. 1421.

26. CCC no. 1448.

ministry of her bishops and his priests. These forgive sins in Christ's name and determine the manner of satisfaction. Then the catechism gives the formula of absolution in use in the Latin Church:

> God, the Father of mercies,
> through the death and resurrection of his Son
> has reconciled the world to himself
> and sent the Holy Spirit among us
> for the forgiveness of sins;
> through the ministry of the Church
> may God give you pardon and peace,
> and **I absolve you from your sins**
> **in the name of the Father, and of the Son, and of the Holy Spirit.**[27]

Sometimes a priest must administer this sacrament under pressing circumstances, such as to victims of an automobile accident or in the heat of battlefield combat. In these cases, the essential words of the formula (which are printed in bold) suffice for a valid administration of the sacrament.

The catechism describes the acts of the penitent in some detail. These numbers cite repeatedly the 1551 teaching of the Council of Trent. Thus the definition of *contrition* specifies this interior act as "sorrow of the soul and detestation for the sin committed, together with the resolution not to sin again."[28] The catechetical text also usefully describes the difference between contrition and attrition. The former is called perfect because the sorrow springs from a love of God whom one has offended by sinning, whereas the latter arises from a consideration of sin's deformity or a fear of eternal damnation and other penalties, such as civil punishments. When a sinner approaches the sacrament of Penance with only a contrition of fear (attrition), the sacrament itself elevates this disposition into a more perfect form of contrition. Why? Christ offers the answer when he says, "So I tell you, her many sins have been forgiven; hence, she has shown great love. But the one to whom little is forgiven, loves little" (Luke 7:47).

The catechism continues with some specification about the confession of sins. The text notes that accountability requires that a sinner face the wrongdoing squarely. Some people erroneously conclude that such a disclosure can remain within the secrecy of the sinner's heart. Such people underestimate the capacity of anyone, but especially a sinner, to rationalize bad behavior or to make unreasonable excuses for the same.

27. CCC no. 1449.
28. Council of Trent, Session 14, chap. 4, "Contrition" (*DS* 1673), as quoted in CCC no. 1451.

Why this self-disclosure to another human being—namely, the priest? Many persons find this requirement of the sacrament of Penance the most difficult to embrace. However, Pope John Paul II has beautifully explained the purposes of the confession of sins. Among the reasons that the Pope gives for making a complete confession of at least grievous sins, there appears this appeal to the social ramifications of bad actions, even of the most seemingly private of actions. "This confession," writes the Pope, "in a way forces sin out of the secret of the heart and thus out of the area of pure individuality, emphasizing its social character as well, for through the minister of penance it is the ecclesial community, which has been wounded by sin, that welcomes anew the repentant and forgiven sinner."[29] This text of Pope John Paul II's Magisterium merits a close reading by those who wish to develop their understanding of the sacrament of Penance and Reconciliation.

While the Church requires confession of grave or mortal sins, she also recommends, following the advice given by Saint Augustine in his *Tractates on the Gospel of John,* the confession of "everyday faults (venial sins)" in order to strengthen a person against greater temptations.[30]

The third of the penitent's actions that figures in the human side of the sacrament of Penance follows upon sorrow for and self-disclosure of sins. The forgiven sinner willingly takes on the satisfaction that the priest imposes on him or her. In everyday usage, Catholic people refer to this satisfaction as their penance. Sound theology does not limit the performance of a penance to the dimensions of a retributive exercise, although the notion that one expiates sins enjoys warrant in both the Scriptures and the tradition. What dominates in the performance of a satisfactory work appears as the restorative feature of good works. For example, the miserly and stingy person receives a penance to give alms to the poor. This action of charity, almsgiving, should open up the heart of the miser to recognize that helping the poor surpasses whatever contentment one obtains from the mere acquisition and even hoarding of wealth.

Oftentimes, the penance given in the confessional by the Catholic priest consists of the recitation of certain familiar prayers—for example, to say the Hail Mary so many times. This nominal penance achieves a meritorious status beyond what its simple execution may merit by reason of the superabundant meritoriousness of Christ's saving sacrifice that the sacrament of Penance communicates to the performance of a prescribed penance.[31]

29. John Paul II, *Reconciliatio et paenitentia,* no. 31.3.

30. CCC no. 1458.

31. For further discussion, see Romanus Cessario, "Saint Thomas Aquinas on Satisfaction, Indulgences, and Crusades," *Medieval Philosophy & Theology* 2 (1992): 74–96.

The *Catechism of the Catholic Church* continues its discussion of the sacrament by describing the role of the minister. Bishops and priests enjoy the power to forgive all sins, not—of course—by appeal to their own capacities but "in the name of the Father, and of the Son, and of the Holy Spirit."[32] The text goes on to assert that "the confessor is not the master of God's forgiveness, but the servant."[33] Perhaps no circumstance better proves this obvious truth of the Catholic religion than the very strict obligation to keep absolute secrecy about the sins that people confess in the sacrament of Penance. "This secret," the catechism explains, "which admits of no exceptions, is called the 'sacramental seal,' because what the penitent has made known to the priest remains 'sealed' by the sacrament."[34]

Throughout history, political and other authorities have sought to challenge this sacramental seal for their own purposes. Most recently political authorities have argued that child abuse amounts to such a grave offense that whoever learns of it should report it to public officials. The Church refuses to accede to such insistences, however. No one should be impeded from receiving divine forgiveness because of the fear that their confession will be used against them in forums other than that of the divine mercy. Further, when the sacrament of Penance works its effect, the rehabilitation of a sinner happens with greater assurance than can be had from retributive justice. "The whole power of the sacrament of Penance," so the Church professes, "consists in restoring us to God's grace and joining us with him in an intimate friendship."[35]

Sixteenth-Century Challenges and Replies

The sacrament of Penance and Reconciliation encountered challenges in the period that led up to the Council of Trent. In fact, Session 14 (held on November 25, 1551) issued some lengthy instructions about the sacrament, since, as the members expressed it, "so great is the accumulation of errors about that sacrament during our time that no small public advantage will come from giving a more detailed and full definition concerning this sacrament in which . . . the Catholic truth will become more clear and distinct."[36] There follow nine short chapters that expound the Catholic theology presently exhibited in the *Catechism*

32. CCC no. 1461.
33. CCC no 1466.
34. CCC no. 1467.
35. CCC no. 1468.
36. *DS* 1667.

of the Catholic Church, which cites the Council of Trent seventeen times within its teaching on the sacrament of Penance and Reconciliation.

Again, according to the literary style adopted by the Council of Trent, there then follows a series of anathemas that identify the major errors that prompted the conciliar reflection undertaken by the assembled bishops. These replies may be conveniently summarized as follows: Canon 1 addresses those who deny that Penance is a sacrament. Canon 2 warns against confusing the sacraments of Baptism and Penance. Canon 3 addresses those who ascribe the power of forgiveness of sins to preaching instead of to the sacramental action. Canon 4 affirms the "matter of the sacrament of penance, namely, contrition, confession, and satisfaction."[37] Canon 5 anathematizes those who dismiss true contrition as a harmful exercise that makes one a hypocrite and greater sinner. Canon 6 corrects those who deny the necessity of Penance or who consider the particular confession of sins to a priest a purely human invention. Canon 7 treats errors concerning what is known as an integral confession—that is, the confession of all mortal sins—and warns against specious arguments that would allow a selective confession of sin. Canon 8 anathematizes those who would dissuade others from the practice of confession at least once a year, as the earlier Fourth Lateran Council had stipulated. (Editors of these conciliar documents note texts where Luther, Melanchthon, and Calvin appear to have advanced such a view.)[38] Canons 9, 10, and 11 treat errors that pertain to the ministers of the sacrament of Penance and the exercise of their office. The final canons address errors about the temporal punishment due to sin and the role that satisfaction—that is, the satisfactory works that the priest assigns to the penitent—plays in the sanctification of the sinner.

The anathemas of the Council of Trent not only reveal the errors that began to circulate in the early sixteenth century but also, undoubtedly, point up the difficulties penitents experienced in their approach to the sacrament of Penance. Canon 10 responds to what must have been a pastoral concern of the time—namely, whether a confessor in the state of mortal sin himself possesses the power to forgive others' sins. Since such priests "exercise the office of forgiving sins as ministers of Christ through the power of the Holy Spirit conferred in ordination," the council responds in the affirmative.[39] The Council of Trent rightly, then, turned the attention of Catholics away from the minister of the sacrament and toward the lasting or abiding effect of the sacrament.

37. *DS* 1704.
38. See *DS* 1682n1.
39. *DS* 1684.

Father O'Neill makes an astute comment about this abiding sacrament that illuminates the place that the sacrament of Penance and Reconciliation holds even when administered by an unworthy, though duly authorized, priest. "The abiding sacrament of penance," O'Neill writes, "which in this case is identified with the personal sorrow of the absolved sinner, accords no new status in the church but it remains an inseparable component of the moral psychology of the member of Christ and imposes its own obligations."[40] Foremost among these obligations comes the resolve to avoid the near occasion of sin. The repeated reception of the sacrament of Penance contributes to the development of a moral tone in the Catholic believer. He or she comes to recognize that various areas of human life require the unique kind of perfecting that only the gift of divine grace can accomplish.

Indulgences

The *Catechism of the Catholic Church* attaches a treatment of what the Catholic Church teaches about indulgences to the section on the sacrament of Penance.[41] In sum, these numbers teach that "through indulgences the faithful can obtain the remission of temporal punishment resulting from sin for themselves and also for the souls in Purgatory."[42]

This punishment results from the very nature of sin itself. Saint Augustine sets the tone when he remarks that every disordered affection brings its own punishment. Saint Thomas Aquinas quotes this text: "In *Confessiones* 1, [12,] Augustine says, 'Every disordered affection (*inordinatus animus*) is its own punishment.'"[43] This punishment leaves the soul impaired in its capacity for love, and so unfit for entrance into the beatific vision. While the faithful remain on earth, penitential practices gradually ease the disorder that sin introduces into the movement of the soul. Those who die while still suffering under the temporal punishment of sin—for example, the thief who has made restitution for his theft but still clings to cupidity that prompted stealing in the first place—pass over into Purgatory. In either case, the Church can dispense from what she calls her treasury—which contains the merits of Christ, the Blessed Virgin Mary, and all the saints—an indulgence that remits the temporal punishment due to sin.[44]

40. O'Neill, *Sacramental Realism*, 183.

41. See CCC nos. 1471–84.

42. CCC no. 1498.

43. *Summa theologiae* I-II.87.1 arg. 3. This quotation was taken from the translation of Alfred J. Freddoso, https://www3.nd.edu/~afreddos/summa-translation/Part%201-2/st1-2-ques87.pdf.

44. See CCC nos. 1476–77.

An indulgence is obtained when the Church "intervenes in favor of individual Christians and opens for them the treasury . . . to obtain from the Father of mercies the remission of the temporal punishments due for their sins."[45] The Council of Trent made no apology for the Catholic practice of granting indulgences, which it described as "most salutary to the Christian people and approved by the authority of the holy councils."[46] At the same time, the council took note of the complaints that had been raised among reform figures in the early decades of the sixteenth century and so counseled that churchmen observe moderation in speaking about indulgences. Further, the council acknowledged that abuses also had occurred and that these aberrations gave the chance to "heretics to blaspheme the distinguished name of indulgences."[47] As a result, the same assembly decreed that "all base gain for the securing of an indulgence should be totally abolished."[48] The Catholic Church has faithfully executed this command of the Council of Trent, which finds its most recent exposition in the apostolic constitution of Pope Paul VI, *Indulgentiarium doctrina,* issued on January 1, 1967.

Holy Priest Confessors

Sometimes one learns important truths about the sacraments from the experience of those who administer them. The Italian cleric Saint Joseph Cafasso (d. 1860) was known as the "Priest of the Gallows." His biography includes a touching episode in which he was trying to persuade a hardened criminal, who was very much impenitent, to receive the sacrament of Penance. It is reported that, although Joseph Cafasso was small of stature and curved of spine, he seized this very large inmate's beard and told him he would not let go until the man confessed. The saint's insistence worked. The prisoner confessed his sins, and with tears. The convict then left Cafasso's confessional giving praise to God.[49]

A somewhat less dramatic but still very informative lesson from the saint's ministry to prisoners reveals why he earned the sobriquet "Priest of the Gallows." It happened that the saint escorted sixty converted inmates who had been condemned to death by hanging. The majority of these Catholic prisoners were hanged straight after they had confessed and received absolution from Father Cafasso. He, in turn and with just cause, referred to these good "thieves" as his "hanged saints."

45. *CCC* no. 1478.
46. *DS* 1835.
47. *DS* 1835.
48. *DS* 1835.
49. See Meg Hunter-Kilmer, "The Holy Priest Who Left Hardened Sinners 'Weeping for Joy,'" *Aleteia,* June 22, 2017, https://aleteia.org/2017/06/22/the-holy-priest-who-left-hardened-sinners-weeping-for-joy/.

In 2010, Pope Benedict XVI gave a public teaching on this saint that captures the genius of Joseph Cafasso and shows his devotion to the sacrament of Penance and Reconciliation. "His teaching was never abstract, nor based exclusively on the books that were used in that period," said the Pope. "Rather, it was born from the living experience of God's mercy and the profound knowledge of the human soul that he acquired in the long hours he spent in the confessional and in spiritual direction: his was a real school of priestly life."[50] It should be evident from this Pope's words and from countless other examples of holy priest confessors who have helped the Catholic people to put sins behind them and to grow in Christian holiness that the sacrament of Penance and Reconciliation holds an indispensable place in a pilgrim Church.

"Repent, for the kingdom of heaven is at hand" (Matt. 4:17). With these words, Jesus announces that reformation of life remains the indispensable condition for realizing the new order that his coming introduces into a sin-marked world. For the human person, as Saint Paul clearly teaches, the new order means that "whoever is in Christ is a new creation" (2 Cor. 5:17). Now, it is a general rule of the Christian gospel that God never requires a person to do something that he himself does not supply the strength to fulfill. So, whereas reformation of life remains indispensable for participation in God's kingdom, it never presents a condition that a Catholic must fulfill alone.

Indeed, Catholics learn this great mystery of God's providence and predestination in the sacrament of Penance and Reconciliation. For when anyone has failed in his or her efforts at reform of life, Christ waits to forgive that sinner. As already noted, each Catholic needs to hear this comforting truth spoken personally—that is, by the priest, the same person who also has heard the sins that cry out for mercy and reconciliation. So again, the Church insists that "confession to a priest is an essential part of the sacrament of Penance."[51]

Further, it bears repetition that the Catholic Church, following the aforementioned instruction given by Saint Augustine, recommends even the confession of venial sins.[52] As explained above, besides auricular confession, the Church also requires in ordinary circumstances a particular confession of sins, "for if the sick is ashamed to lay open his wound before the physician, the medicine does not heal what it does not know."[53] That is, the Church asks

50. Benedict XVI, General Audience, St. Peter's Square, June 30, 2010 (VRL).

51. CCC no. 1456.

52. CCC no. 1458.

53. This quotation from St. Jerome's *Commentary on Ecclesiastes* (PL 23:1152A) appears in the Council of Trent, Session 14, Doctrine on the Sacrament of Penance, chap. 5, "On Confession," *DS* 1680.

that penitents entrust themselves with honesty and courage to the divine mercy that forgives.

Recall too that Pope John Paul II has explained that Confession brings sin out of both the secret of the heart and the individual's own (perhaps misguided) conscience. Experience shows that this feature of sacramental Reconciliation causes considerable difficulty for not a few Catholics. Many of them may imagine a form of forgiveness that dispenses with the need to examine their lives as well as their consciences. So it is important to see that God provides something much better for sinners than the chance to hide behind their own pride and excuses. He gives sinners pardon and peace. The Catholic penitent learns that a few acts of confidence and love are worth more than a thousand evasions and maybes.

No Catholic ever outgrows the need for frequent confession. And what about those who themselves exercise the ministry of reconciliation? Each priest must also frequent the confessional of another priest.

Finally, the Church celebrates the Feast of the Immaculate Conception during the season of Advent, the season of expectation for the Messiah. This Marian feast arouses confidence in Catholics that their sins will not overcome them. By the grace of her sanctification, Mary, conceived without original sin, reveals the power of God's transforming love that stands ready to embrace all who seek forgiveness for their sins.

17

Anointing of the Sick

The second sacrament that the *Catechism of the Catholic Church* lists under the heading "The Sacraments of Healing" appears as the "Anointing of the Sick." This appellation represents a change from the name for this sacrament that had been in common use prior to the early 1970s. When in 1972 Pope Paul VI officially changed the name of the sacrament of Extreme Unction,[1] he acted in response to a proposal of the Second Vatican Council found in *Sacrosanctum Concilium*, the Constitution on the Sacred Liturgy. This document makes the following assertion: "'Extreme unction,' which may also and more fittingly be called 'anointing of the sick,' is not a sacrament for those only who are at the point of death."[2] In other words, this sacrament does not help only those in extremis—that is, at the point of death. The change of name, the Pope further notes, also indicates a slight change of practice in the administration of this sacrament. Those of the faithful who have begun to confront the danger of death from sickness or old age are eligible to receive this sacrament. It is not, as I have said, necessary to wait until the moment of death is imminent.

Basic Truths about Anointing

Although the name of this sacrament was modified along with a broadening of the circumstances that allow for the proper administration of this sacrament, the nature of the sacrament has remained the same. In *Sacram unctione infirmorum*,

1. Paul VI, *Sacram unctione infirmorum*.
2. *Sacrosanctum Concilium*, no. 73 (VRL).

the apostolic constitution that authorizes the aforementioned changes, Pope Paul VI refers to the teachings of the Councils of Florence and Trent. The fathers of Trent explain that "the Catholic Church professes and teaches that the Sacred Anointing of the Sick is one of the seven Sacraments of the New Testament, that it was instituted by Christ and that it is 'alluded to in Mark (Mark 6:13) and recommended and promulgated to the faithful by James the apostle and brother of the Lord.'"[3] Thus, according to Catholic teaching, this sacrament fortifies the Catholic against the debilitating effects on human life caused by illness and suffering.[4] When theologians explain the number of the sacraments by associating each with some moment of human development, the Anointing of the Sick obviously comes last, just as Baptism must come first.[5]

The following general statements capture the essence of Catholic teaching about this sacrament of healing. The sacrament of the Anointing of the Sick intervenes in the life of a Christian believer at the moment when the temptations caused by human sufferings are most likely to tempt the believer to doubt and despair.[6] Catholic theological reflection recognizes that the sacrament strengthens the irascible or contending emotions that have been weakened by the effects of original sin.[7] Consecration to the compassionate blood of Christ offers an alternative to such a dreadful end such as would result from a dying person's turning away from God. The anointed believer, on the other hand, can enter personally into the mystery of the suffering Christ and bear witness to his victory.

Father Colman O'Neill captures well the drama of this moment and of the sacrament instituted to sanctify it: "It is perhaps the ultimate and unavoidable outcome of Christian life, where salvation alone can give meaning, that justifies numbering anointing among the sacraments."[8] When, however, one considers prevailing secular attitudes toward death, the wisdom behind the Anointing of the Sick comes into full relief. To describe what abides in the sacrament of the Anointing of the Sick—that is, the *res et sacramentum*—Catholic teaching

3. Council of Trent, Session 14, Doctrine on the Sacrament of Extreme Unction, chap. 1, "The Institution of the Sacrament of Extreme Unction," *DS* 1695.

4. See CCC no. 1500.

5. See *Summa theologiae* III.65.1. Aquinas bases his analysis on the principle that "just as physical things have a certain resemblance to spiritual realities, so too there is a certain correspondence between spiritual living and physical living."

6. See CCC no. 1501.

7. See Aquinas's discussion of original sin in *Summa theologiae* I-II.82.3, where he writes that "the disorder of the other powers of the soul [other than the will, that is] is chiefly noticeable in an unruled turning to goods that pass away, which disorder can be designated by the term 'concupiscence.'"

8. Colman E. O'Neill, *Sacramental Realism* (Chicago: Midwest Theological Forum, 1998), 203.

holds that grave illness that leads to the ultimate and unavoidable outcome of Christian life presents a moment when the intervention of Christ can restore bodily health or reveal the ultimately "satisfactory" character of human life (or both), thus sacramentalizing the dying process. The restoration of bodily health can result from the administration of this sacrament, although this lasting effect comes with the provision "if it is conducive to the salvation of the soul."[9]

The above considerations about the primary effect of Anointing raise the question of how Penance and Anointing complement each other in the life of the sinful and sick Catholic believer.[10] Saint Thomas Aquinas enunciates a general principle when he says that God provides a cure for a person's sins that contains two elements, just as he provides two cures for physical illness or disease. The first remedy, says Aquinas, provides an actual healing by which health is restored. Penance fulfills this purpose in the spiritual order. The second element entails the restoration of the sufferer's former strength by means of a suitable diet and exercise. In the spiritual order, the Anointing of the Sick matches this restorative work by removing the remaining effects of sin.[11]

The *Roman Ritual* stipulates the order of the sacraments in what is called a continuous celebration of Penance, Holy Anointing, and Viaticum for those who unexpectedly find themselves in danger of death. This official text also urges the priest to be very attentive to the desire of the dying person to make a confession.[12] If we wonder why Penance and Holy Anointing should be administered together, the answer lies in the distinctive sacramental graces that each sacrament mediates through the instrumentality of the priest. As I have said, Aquinas explains the difference by analogy with bodily health. One may be without illness but still not be in good shape. Penance is ordered to spiritual health inasmuch as this sacrament brings healing from the illness of sin, whereas the Anointing of the Sick restores robustness to a fatigued spiritual life. The sacrament's medicinal effects attend to the various remains of sin that weaken or limit a healthy but not vigorous spiritual life.[13]

Note that what Aquinas says about the Anointing of the Sick conforms to his overall vision of the spiritual—that is, the Christian—life. "Now the aim and

9. *CCC* no.1532.

10. Some material in this section has appeared in Romanus Cessario, "Anointing of the Sick: The Sanctification of Human Suffering," *Nova et Vetera* (English ed.) 17 (2019): 1–11.

11. See *Summa theologiae* III.65.1 for the text that presents Aquinas's argument for the seven sacraments.

12. *Roman Ritual: The Rites of Anointing and Viaticum*, no. 237.

13. See John F. Boyle, "Saint Thomas Aquinas on the Anointing of the Sick (Extreme Unction)," in *Rediscovering Aquinas and the Sacraments: Studies in Sacramental Theology*, ed. Matthew Levering and Michael Dauphinais (Chicago: Hillenbrand Books, 2009), 76–84.

end of the spiritual life," the Common Doctor says, "is that man be united to God, which union is achieved through charity."[14] Holy Anointing strengthens charity in the Catholic whose personal energies have begun to flag as a result of illness and suffering.[15]

In light of Aquinas's teaching, it would be difficult to argue that the Anointing of the Sick forgives grave sins when the sick person still is able to obtain forgiveness through the sacrament of Penance.[16] As mentioned above, the *Roman Ritual* makes provision for a priest's administering consecutively both Sacraments of Healing. This provision, however, leaves open a case that occurs with some frequency—that is, the administration of the sacrament of the Anointing of the Sick in cases of emergency. What about the case of someone who was not able to obtain forgiveness through the sacrament of Penance—a circumstance mentioned in the catechism, moreover? There we read that the effects of the sacrament of the Anointing of the Sick include "the forgiveness of sins, if the sick person was not able to obtain it through the sacrament of Penance."[17]

In his standard textbook of sacramental theology, *Meeting Christ in the Sacraments*, Father O'Neill offers an explanation of this provision that recognizes the difference in the sacramental causality exercised by each of the Sacraments of Healing. He writes, "Should the recipient be in a state of grave sin, and granted that he has such sorrow as is compatible with this state—that is, attrition—anointing will bring him absolution."[18] However, O'Neill goes on to signal the difference between what is required for the valid reception of Penance and what Anointing requires. He even speaks of a certain advantage that Anointing enjoys over Penance. "It is not certain," O'Neill observes, "that penance can benefit an unconscious person since, although the required imperfect sorrow may be present, it is not clear that it can be externally manifested as the sacrament requires."[19] Anointing, on the other hand, does not require such active external participation. Anointing requires only that one suffer from a serious illness and have exhibited at least an implicit desire to receive the sacrament of the Anointing of the Sick.

14. *Summa theologiae* II-II.44.1.

15. This essential feature of the Anointing of the Sick raises a question of pastoral practice—namely, whether the sacrament can be validly administered to persons who do not experience illness and suffering.

16. However, see what is said about the necessity of Baptism in CCC no. 1257.

17. CCC no. 1532.

18. Colman E. O'Neill, *Meeting Christ in the Sacraments*, rev. ed., ed. Romanus Cessario (Staten Island, NY: Alba House, 1991), 287.

19. O'Neill, *Meeting Christ*, 287–88.

The Ceremony for the Anointing of the Sick

The normal order of celebrating the sacraments that prepare the sick person for death include Penance, Viaticum, and Anointing. Oftentimes, priests do not enjoy the leisure or circumstances to conduct the full liturgical rites associated with these sacraments. The *Roman Ritual* allows the priest to make a judgment about the status of the moribund person and use the form for emergencies, which consists in the essential forms for the sacraments of Penance and Anointing.[20]

The inversion of the order of giving the Eucharist as Viaticum and subsequently of administering the sacrament of the Anointing of the Sick occurs in cases where the person's condition dictates. In the Rite for Emergencies, this inversion is explained as follows: "Because of the emergency situation, viaticum follows immediately [after a requested confession]. Christians in danger of death are bound by the precept to receive communion."[21]

The provision that the Church makes for the administration of the sacrament in emergency circumstances draws one's attention to something unique about the sacrament of the Anointing of the Sick. Unlike the sacraments that usually take place within a church or other sacred space, the Anointing of the Sick happens wherever a sick person suffers from a grave illness—that is, when the Catholic "begins to be in danger of death from sickness or old age."[22] Today, at least in the developed countries, the hospital becomes a place where priests frequently administer the Anointing of the Sick. However, other venues—such as battlefields, private homes, automobile crash sites, execution chambers in prisons—also can serve as places where priests must bring the comfort and strength of the sacraments to persons in danger of death.

The aforementioned account of the ministry of Saint Joseph Cafasso, the "Priest of the Gallows," offers a praiseworthy example of how Catholic priests meet dying Catholics wherever they may be found. This practice of the saint does not mention him administering the sacrament of the Anointing of the Sick to those sentenced to death. Why? The condemned prisoners were not in fact sick. The old *Catholic Encyclopedia* explains the protocol that dictates this sacramental discipline as follows: "Nor will danger, or even certainty, of death from any other cause than sickness qualify a person for extreme unction. Hence criminals or martyrs about to suffer death and other [persons] similarly circumstanced may not be validly anointed unless they should happen to be

20. *Roman Ritual: The Rites of Anointing and Viaticum*, no. 237.
21. *Roman Ritual: The Rites of Anointing and Viaticum*, no. 261.
22. CCC no. 1514.

seriously ill."[23] Prison chaplains in France regularly anointed those sentenced to the guillotine, but only after their heads had been severed from their bodies.

Indeed, many priests have shown heroic bravery in fulfilling their sacred duties to those suffering from communicable diseases, such as when a pandemic occurs. Joseph Benedict Cottolengo (d. 1842), an Italian priest of the nineteenth century, contracted typhoid while bringing the sacraments to poor and disease-ridden Catholics near Turin, Italy. In 2005, Pope Benedict XVI included him in a list of saints who demonstrated the social dimensions of theological charity. Saint Joseph Benedict Cottolengo, said the Pope, is numbered among the "lasting models of social charity for all people of good will."[24] The saint discovered his mission when he administered Extreme Unction to a woman who had been refused treatment in Turin's hospitals because she was tubercular. He also baptized the child with which the woman was pregnant before it died. The Anointing of the Sick remains a sacrament of divine comfort when all the various secular interventions fail, for whatever reasons, to care for the dying.

Saints Joseph Cafasso and Joseph Benedict Cottolengo exhibit the ideal of priestly service. Throughout history, however, various social circumstances have affected the way that some clerics have approached the administration of the sacrament for the dying. Historians, then, can cite examples of less praiseworthy clerics. In the thirteenth century, for instance, Extreme Unction was known in some places as the sacrament for the rich. Parish priests would claim, as a particular sort of in-kind stole fee (the monetary stipend customarily given to priests when they administer certain sacraments), ownership of the linen sheets upon which the sick person had been anointed or of the candles that had been lit during the ceremony. One piece of evidence from Germany in 1260 reports that only those "worth at least two cows" should bother asking for the sacrament.[25]

However, these reports should not be read as indications of widespread abuses. It suffices to point to an individual's human weakness to explain why a minister of the sacraments would hesitate before approaching to anoint a suspected plague victim but not before baptizing a newborn infant. At the same time, the nineteenth century gives us the aforementioned examples of holy priests who risked everything to serve sacramentally the sick and the dying.

23. *The Catholic Encyclopedia*, ed. Charles G. Hebermann et al. (New York: The Encyclopedia Press, 1913), s.v. "Extreme Unction."

24. Benedict XVI, *Deus caritas est* (*Encyclical Letter on Christian Love*), December 25, 2005, no. 40.

25. Bernhard Poschmann, *Penance and the Anointing of the Sick*, trans. F. Courtney (New York: Herder & Herder, 1964), 244n30.

The twenty-first century does not lack similar examples. In a photo-journal essay, the *New York Times* printed this remarkable account of priestly devotion to the sacrament of the Anointing of the Sick:

> Beyond the glass lay a man, unconscious in the electric blue light, shrouded in tubes. His family was not allowed to visit. His body could not be touched. Father Ryan Connors stood at the door watching, his Roman collar barely visible beneath his face shield. Since the coronavirus pandemic began, he had gone to the bedsides of Covid-19 patients across the Boston area to perform one of the oldest religious rituals for the dying: the Roman Catholic practice commonly called last rites. For centuries, priests have physically anointed the dying with oil to heal body and soul, if not in this life, in the next. Many Catholics have spent their entire lives trusting that in their most difficult hours a priest, and through him God, would come to their aid.

The journalist goes on to recount a first-hand experience of how devoted priests learn quickly to navigate the sometimes complicated protocols enacted by health care centers.

> On this Tuesday morning, in the intensive care unit at St. Elizabeth's Medical Center, west of the city, all that Father Connors knew about the patient was his name, and that his family had called for a priest. He had a clear plastic bag with a cotton ball containing a few drops of holy oil. He carried a photocopy of pages from a liturgical book. At 10:18 a.m., he slid open the door. He walked over to the bed, careful to avoid the tubes on the ground. He stretched out his hand, and began to pray.[26]

This human-interest story goes on to explain the extraordinary measures that one Catholic diocese employed to ensure that those dying during the height of the COVID-19 pandemic would not die deprived of the graces that the Anointing of the Sick brings.

Official Teaching on the Anointing of the Sick

It is noteworthy that the sixteenth-century Council of Trent makes no mention of blameworthy clerical practices surrounding the administration of the sacrament of the Anointing of the Sick. Instead, the four canons that deal with

26. Elizabeth Dias (text) and Ryan Christopher Jones (photographs), "The Last Anointing," *New York Times*, June 6, 2020, https://www.nytimes.com/interactive/2020/06/06/us/coronavirus-priests-last-rites.html?smid=wa-share.

the sacrament of "Extreme Unction"—or what Trent also called the "sacrament of those going forth/departing" (*sacramentum exeuntium*)—treat only arguments made against the sacramentality of the Anointing of the Sick.[27] Canon 1 anathematizes those who argue that the sacrament of Extreme Unction is "only a rite received from the Fathers or a human invention."[28] The editors, in a footnote, cite places in the works of both Melanchthon and Calvin where they assert that this claim is made. Canon 2 also condemns those who argue that the administration of the sacrament produces no effects, since it wrongly mimics the grace of healing reported to have occurred in the early Church. Canon 3 addresses its anathema against those who hold in contempt the rites and usage of the Roman Church under the pretext that such practices do not find support in the "doctrine of the blessed apostle James."[29] In fact, the Tridentine council gives an authoritative interpretation of James 5:14–15—namely, that the apostle "teaches the matter, the form, the proper minister, and the effects of this salutary sacrament."[30] The fourth canon condemns those who argue that James ordered the senior members of each community to come to the sick person and not "priests ordained by a bishop."[31] In order to present Catholic teaching about the sacrament of Anointing of the Sick, the *Catechism of the Catholic Church* today refers seven times to these key affirmations of the Council of Trent.

Confusion about who can administer the sacrament of the Anointing of the Sick still raises questions among some members of the Catholic Church. In a note dated February 11, 2005, the Congregation for the Doctrine of the Faith was obliged to clarify what had become a widespread misconception about the suitable minister for the sacrament of the Anointing of the Sick. In brief, the congregation reaffirmed that only priests and bishops can administer this sacrament.[32]

In a commentary on the note published shortly thereafter by two Dominican priests, the authors explain that the reasons for this determination pertain directly to the theological meaning of the sacrament—that is, to its sacramental efficacy. What does Holy Anointing do? It confers, declare the authors, a "radically personal configuration to Christ on the part of a faithful Christian in the

27. See *CCC* no. 1523 and *DS* 1698.
28. *DS* 1716.
29. *DS* 1718.
30. *DS* 1695.
31. *DS* 1719.
32. "Note on the Minister of the Sacrament of the Anointing of the Sick (February 11, 2005)," Vatican website, accessed September 6, 2022, https://www.vatican.va/roman_curia/congregations/cfaith/documents/rc_con_cfaith_doc_20050211_unzione-infermi_en.html.

final moment of earthly existence."[33] The authors conclude that this kind of consecration and the remedy for sin that accompanies it argues for the necessity that the minister of the Anointing of the Sick must possess the priestly character, which establishes a man as "Christ's instrument for his Church."[34] What is more, in the sacrament of the Anointing of the Sick, there occurs, as in each sacrament, both a distinctive form of divine worship and a distinctive form of rescue from man's fallen state. Only priests and bishops can validly bring about these effects through their administration of the sacraments.[35]

The *sacramentum tantum* or the action performed by the priest together with the words prescribed for the "form" of the sacrament find their authoritative description in the apostolic constitution of Pope Paul VI, mentioned above. In this document, the Pope sets down instructions for the administration of the sacrament by a priest or bishop: "The Sacrament of the Anointing of the Sick is administered to those who are dangerously ill, by anointing them on the forehead and hands with olive oil, or, if opportune, with another vegetable oil, properly blessed, and saying once only the following words: 'Per istam Sanctam Unctionem et suam piissimam misericordiam adiuvet te Dominus gratia Spiritus Sancti, ut a peccatis liberatum te salvet atque propitius alleviet.'"[36] The approved English translation of this sacramental form appears as follows: "Through this holy anointing may the Lord in his love and mercy help you with the grace of the Holy Spirit." These words are said while the priest anoints the sick person's forehead. Then he anoints the hands, saying, "May the Lord who frees you from sin save you and raise you up." The response to this prayer, "Amen," follows.[37]

As the name of this sacrament suggests, "the proper matter for the sacrament is olive oil or, according to circumstances other oil derived from plants."[38] The Church requires that a bishop or priest bless the oil used in the administration of the Anointing of the Sick. Priests, however, may bless the oil only under certain conditions. The Catholic Church identifies Holy Thursday, the Thursday of Holy Week—that is, before Easter Sunday—as the time for bishops to bless the holy oils used in their dioceses during the course of a year. One of the

33. J. A. Di Noia and Joseph Fox, "Priestly Dimensions of the Sacrament of the Anointing of the Sick," *The Priest* 62 (2006): 10–13. One may take this consecration as a description of what abides in the Anointing of the Sick, the *res et sacramentum*. When the anointed Catholic returns to physical health, the consecration takes on a different complexion.

34. CCC no. 1581.

35. The *Code of Canon Law* was modified to make this point. Can. 1003 §1: "Every priest and a priest alone validly administers the anointing of the sick."

36. Paul VI, *Sacram unctione infirmorum*.

37. *Roman Ritual: The Rites of Anointing and Viaticum*, no. 141.

38. *Roman Ritual: The Rites of Anointing and Viaticum*, no. 20.

three traditional oils blessed, in addition to the sacred chrism and the oil of catechumens, serves for the administration of the Anointing of the Sick. Like the other oils, the oil of the sick, *oleum infirmorum,* is kept in a special vessel and preserved ordinarily in a locked container within the church.[39]

In order to explain the sacredness that the Catholic Church attaches to the holy oils, one may usefully advert to a theological teaching mentioned in the *Catechism of the Catholic Church.* The symbols of the Holy Spirit that find currency in the practice of the Church include, so the catechism affirms, anointing. In fact, "the symbolism of anointing with oil . . . signifies the Holy Spirit to the point of becoming a synonym for the Holy Spirit."[40] The significance of this symbolism for the sacrament of the Anointing of the Sick appears when it is recalled that Christ ("messiah") means the one anointed by God's Spirit. From this exegesis, one may conclude that the holy oils used in the administration of the sacraments refer the Catholic believer back to the Blessed Trinity, the source of all saving grace in the world.

The sacraments enact the salvation won by Jesus Christ, the Messiah. Admittedly, the sacrament of the Anointing of the Sick mainly effects a work of image-restoration. This explains why, as already noted, the Church refers to it as a sacrament of healing.[41] Because, however, the anointed Christian unites him- or herself to Christ's passion, Anointing also fosters image-perfection. The one anointed in a certain way is "consecrated to bear fruit by configuration to the Savior's redemptive Passion."[42]

The old terminology, Extreme Unction, captured something lost in the present usage. The word *extreme* in fact referred to a final consecration to Christ, not to the end of life (*in extremis*).[43] In any event, whoever draws close to Christ in charity receives growth in the virtues and gifts. These virtues and gifts perfect the human soul by making the sick person grow in charity. Within the context of Anointing, this perfection arises from the participation of the believer in the sufferings of Christ. In fact, the *Catechism of the Catholic Church* explicitly specifies that this configuration makes even the most severe physical sufferings fruitful: "Suffering, a consequence of original sin, acquires a new meaning: it becomes a participation in the saving work of Jesus."[44] Herein lies the *res* or the grace of the sacrament of the Anointing of the Sick.

39. *Roman Ritual: The Rites of Anointing and Viaticum,* nos. 20–22.

40. CCC no. 695.

41. See CCC nos. 1420–21.

42. CCC no. 1521.

43. This meaning remains in the description of the sacrament that appears in the *Catechism of the Catholic Church.* See CCC no. 1535.

44. CCC no. 1521.

Infused Fortitude and the "Remains" of Sin

When theologians look at the graces that the sacrament of the Anointing of the Sick brings to the suffering Catholic, the virtue of fortitude or courage comes to their minds. Aquinas, for example, includes under the parts of cardinal fortitude subordinate virtues such as patience, longanimity, perseverance, and constancy.[45] He also explains the gift of the Holy Spirit that he associates with the virtue of fortitude and that bears the name of the gift of courage. This gift of the Holy Spirit comes to the aid of the Catholic "for sometimes it does not lie within human power to attain the end of one's work, or to escape evils or dangers, since these [difficulties] sometimes press in upon us to the point of death."[46] To this, Aquinas adds a description of the gift of courage: "But the Holy Spirit achieves this in us when he leads us to eternal life, which is the end of all good works and the escape from all dangers."[47] These words supply a commentary on the graces of the Anointing of the Sick and also explain the urgency that Catholic priests have attached to their administration of this sacrament, even under circumstances that could bring risk to their own physical well-being.

Further, Catholic teaching on this sacrament of healing places it within the context of the Church's life, especially that of the pilgrim Church. This "ecclesial grace" works in two ways. The communion of saints, both on earth and in heaven, intercedes for the sick person, whereas the recipient of the sacrament "contributes to the sanctification of the Church and to the good of all men for whom the Church suffers."[48] One is reminded of the enigmatic utterance of Saint Paul: "Now I rejoice in my sufferings for your sake, and in my flesh I am filling up what is lacking in the afflictions of Christ on behalf of his body, which is the church" (Col. 1:24).

Catholic priests and teachers oftentimes face the formidable challenge of explaining to their people and students why suffering sanctifies the Christian believer. Or to reassure them, as Father O'Neill laconically puts it, that "suffering has clearly a special significance in the church of the crucified Christ."[49] It may be observed at this juncture that the Catholic Church encourages that the sacrament of the Anointing of the Sick "should be celebrated with members of the family and other representatives of the Christian community whenever this

45. See *Summa theologiae* II-II.136–37.
46. *Summa theologiae* II-II.139.1.
47. *Summa theologiae* II-II.139.1.
48. CCC no. 1522.
49. O'Neill, *Sacramental Realism*, 202.

is possible."[50] The administration of each sacrament offers the opportunity to evangelize those who have either fallen away from the practice of the Catholic faith or have not yet been exposed to Catholic teaching about salvation. These reminders become all the more reasonable when one recalls that secular culture proposes expedient measures to the dying that make Christian fortitude or courage completely unnecessary.

Within this perspective of the sacrament as one of strengthening and witness, Aquinas correctly summarizes the effect of the Anointing of the Sick when he says that the sacrament "removes the remaining effects of sin and renders man ready for final glory."[51] Aquinas further explains his meaning when he gives an account of the number of the sacraments by reference to the remedies they bring against the harmful effects of sin. Recall that, as already mentioned, in his general treatment on the sacraments, the Common Doctor explains the Anointing of the Sick as a sacrament that supplies a remedy "against those elements of sin which remain, those namely which, whether through negligence or ignorance, are not sufficiently removed by penance."[52]

When the *Catechism of the Catholic Church* refers to what the Anointing of the Sick effects, it mentions more generally "the forgiveness of sins."[53] The reason for this broader description of the special effects of Anointing lies in the practice of the Church not to take sides in theological debates. In fact, Aquinas throughout his career denied that Anointing "is ordered to the forgiveness of venial sins."[54] Why? For his part, Aquinas held that contrition suffices for the remission of venial sins and that Anointing remains ordered to the elimination of the "remains" (the *reliquiae*) of original and personal sins.[55]

By "remains," he means the dying person's weaknesses and unfitness as well as his or her lack of strength and vigor—spiritual conditions that are rendered more acute by bodily infirmity. Think of the impatience that the Little Flower, Saint Thérèse of Lisieux, exhibited on her deathbed when she was given the wrong dose of medicine.[56] One may conclude from this experience of a dying

50. *Roman Ritual: The Rites of Anointing and Viaticum*, no. 99.

51. *Summa theologiae* III.65.1.

52. *Summa theologiae* III.65.1.

53. CCC no. 1532.

54. For a discussion, see the very informative article by Boyle, "Anointing of the Sick (Extreme Unction)," 76–84.

55. On the other hand, St. Bonaventure and Duns Scotus and his school after him "saw," in the words of one expert, "the principal effect [of Anointing] in the remission of venial sins which weigh on the soul of the dying man and prevent his complete abandonment to God." Poschmann, *Penance and the Anointing of the Sick*, 253.

56. Thérèse of Lisieux, *The Story of a Soul: The Autobiography of St. Thérèse of Lisieux*, trans. J. Clarke (Washington, DC: ICS Publications, 1975), 267.

saint that the "remains" of sin may segue easily into what one might call light or venial sins.[57] In order to forestall unwarranted speculation about where venial sin begins and the "remains" of sin end, the eighteenth-century papal Magisterium warned against overanalyzing the nature of the *reliquiae peccati*.[58] No serious person, however, may contest their existence—that is, that there are harmful psychological dispositions that remain even within the most disciplined of Christian souls.[59]

Life Everlasting

From all that has been said, it becomes clear that this sacrament of forgiveness and healing prepares the sick Catholic for everlasting life. The sacrament of the Anointing of the Sick does not provide a Catholic replacement for proper palliative care. Truth to tell, the reception of this sacrament makes little sense without a firm faith in the final articles of the Apostles' Creed: "I believe in . . . the resurrection of the body and life everlasting. Amen."[60]

Present-day cultural forces do not create a psychological environment that favors belief in life after death. For instance, funeral rites being abbreviated (or, in some cases, forgone altogether) contributes to the impression that dead bodies hold no purchase on sacred places, whether churches or cemeteries, or on sacred rites. In addition, dechristianized outlooks and even some Catholic funeral practices urge people to reduce the dearly departed to a cherished memory of a life once lived. Legitimate Catholic devotion to the faithful departed that suffuses so much of the Church's official liturgy can easily suffer marginalization or even fall into oblivion altogether. In short, this tenet of the Catholic faith, "I believe in . . . life everlasting," requires renewed catechesis and preaching.

Some similarly negative views have developed about how to care for moribund bodies. In general, popular psychological speculations make it difficult to imagine life outside of an active consciousness as experienced by the living. A Cartesian anthropology and other expressions of mind-body dualism also make it difficult to talk about the vision of God. Talk of beatific vision requires

57. The category of the imperfection remains foreign to Thomist thought. It represents a juridical way of speaking about the "remains" of sin. For further discussion, see James C. Osbourn, *The Morality of Imperfections*, Thomistic Studies 1 (Washington, DC: Pontifical Faculty of Theology, Dominican House of Studies, 1943).

58. Pope Benedict XIV (1740–1758) issued the warning. See Poschmann, *Penance and the Anointing of the Sick*, 254.

59. For a discussion of Catholic teaching on Purgatory, see Romanus Cessario, "Purgatory: The Place of Christian Satisfaction," in *Hope & Death: Christian Responses*, ed. M. Dauphinais and R. Nutt (Steubenville, OH: Emmaus Academic, 2022), 165–78.

60. See CCC no. 185 overleaf.

persuading people that they can "see" something without bodily organs. The Church's anthropology, which acknowledges that the powers of knowledge and love are rooted in the immortal soul, escapes the comprehension of many Christian believers.[61] In short, as the growing enthusiasm for euthanasia indicates, people prefer to make short work of death instead of preparing patiently for death to happen according to the designs of divine providence. Few, in fact, remark on how much so-called mercy killing sins against the requirement that each creature submit to the wise and loving plan of divine providence. Euthanasia, as the practice makes evident, suppresses the good effects that the sanctification of human suffering can bring to the Church on earth.

How many Catholics today would grasp the pathos of these lines from Jesuit poet Gerard Manley Hopkins's (d. 1889) "The Wreck of the Deutschland," subtitled "To the happy memory of five Franciscan Nuns, exiles by the Falk Laws, drowned between midnight and morning of Dec. 7th, 1875"?

> And they the prey of the gales;
> She to the black-about air, to the breaker, the thickly
> Falling flakes, to the throng that catches and quails
> Was calling "O Christ, Christ, come quickly":
> The cross to her she calls Christ to her.[62]

By the sacrament of the Anointing of the Sick, Catholics receive the grace to accept the dying process, even under the most dramatic circumstances. Catholics should recognize the death agony as a period of time set aside in order to wait for Christ to come and escort them home. At the appointed time, they should call out, "O Christ, Christ, come quickly." No human power should intervene to alter this divinely scheduled rendezvous.

61. See *CCC* no. 367: the "soul can be gratuitously raised beyond all it deserves to communion with God."

62. Gerard Manley Hopkins, "The Wreck of the Deutschland," in *Poems of Gerard Manley Hopkins Now First Published*, ed. Robert Bridges (London: Humphry Milford, 1918), lines 188–92.

18

Holy Orders

The *Catechism of the Catholic Church* presents the last two sacraments of the sacred seven under the heading "The Sacraments at the Service of Communion." The rationale for this division is given as follows: "Two other sacraments, Holy Orders and Matrimony, are directed toward the salvation of others; if they contribute as well to personal salvation, it is through service to others that they do so."[1] This categorization of the sacraments does not prejudice the Catholic teaching on the sacraments as true causes of grace. Father Colman O'Neill reminds us that certain specified sign-actions qualify as sacraments "in the strict sense when the risen Christ intervenes personally in the symbolic activity of the community."[2] O'Neill goes on to explain that "the words and symbols of each sacrament, together with the way of life, the human realism, that each one implies, give to each its own special significance in the mystery."[3]

The service that the ordained priest renders to the community becomes apparent primarily in his relation to the Eucharist. Again, Father O'Neill expresses this relationship clearly: "The abiding sacrament [*res et sacramentum*], even more clearly than in the case of baptism, can only be given by the risen Christ who, through it, brings the priest into a permanent relationship with himself in view of his own personal entry into the community in the Eucharist."[4] As has already been discussed in an earlier chapter, the Eucharist remains the center

1. *CCC* no. 1533.
2. Colman E. O'Neill, *Sacramental Realism* (Chicago: Midwest Theological Forum, 1998), 186.
3. O'Neill, *Sacramental Realism*, 209.
4. O'Neill, *Sacramental Realism*, 195.

point of the sacramental Church that priests serve by their ministry of Word and sacrament.

Official Teaching on the Catholic Priesthood

Catholic teaching on the priesthood comes forward as fulsome and complete. Those tempted to think about the Catholic priest primarily in functional terms may usefully recall the words of Saint Irenaeus of Lyons (d. ca. 202), who defended the realism of the Christian gospel against the anti-material mythologies that populated Gnostic literature: "Our teaching is in accord with the Eucharist, and the Eucharist in turn confirms the teaching."[5] The Catholic priest and the Eucharist stand together as visible icons of divine salvation. As often as priests consecrate the eucharistic species they are in "physical" contact with Christ, who moves them and elevates them to perform the act of transubstantiation.[6]

We can explain this presence of the transubstantiating Christ only in "physical" terms. The idiom of a merely moral or symbolic presence fails to express the realism of the Eucharist, in which Christ is really, truly, and substantially present.[7] Throughout its history, the Catholic Church has set forth the realism of the priest. Within recent memory, Pope John Paul II explained this realism when he set down his reflections on the fiftieth anniversary of his own priestly ordination: "For in every priest it is Christ himself who comes. If, as Saint Cyprian said, the Christian is 'another Christ'—*Christianus alter Christus*—with all the more reason it can be said: *Sacerdos alter Christus*."[8] The priest is another Christ.

When he composed the above reflection, Pope John Paul II drew on the teaching of the Second Vatican Council. Catholic teaching on the priesthood received a contemporary exposition during the course of this ecumenical council. The principal document appears as the Decree on the Ministry and Life of Priests, *Presbyterorum Ordinis*, promulgated by Pope Paul VI on December 7, 1965. This document's initial presentation of the identity of the Catholic priest clearly supports the catechism's employment of the description "service to the communion." As has become familiar in talk among Catholics, the Church teaches that the Catholic priest enters the world as a man for others. As the 1965 conciliar text puts it, "Priests by sacred ordination and mission which

5. Irenaeus, *Adversus haereses* book 4, 18, as quoted in O'Neill, *Sacramental Realism*, 218.

6. The use of the term "physical" in this context is meant to underline the reality of the divine motion in the world. It distinguishes this movement from descriptions that remain merely moral or symbolic.

7. See O'Neill, *Sacramental Realism*, 196.

8. John Paul II, *Gift and Mystery: On the Fiftieth Anniversary of My Priestly Ordination* (New York: Doubleday, 1996), 99.

they receive from the bishops are promoted to the service of Christ the Teacher, Priest and King. They share in his ministry, a ministry whereby the Church here on earth is unceasingly built up into the People of God, the Body of Christ and the Temple of the Holy Spirit."[9]

The decree continues, providing further specification of how the Catholic priest serves the ecclesial communion.[10] The salient points indicate the relationship of the ordained priest to the administration of the sacraments: the Lord "has established ministers among his faithful . . . able by the sacred power of orders to offer sacrifice and to forgive sins, and they perform their priestly office [*officio*] publicly for men in the name of Christ."[11] The references to sacrifice and forgiveness obviously evoke in a primary way the sacraments of the Eucharist and of Penance and Reconciliation.

The abovementioned stipulated functions of the priestly ministry do not entail inequality among the members of the Church. Priests come into the communion of the Church as brothers who enjoy differentiated powers to fulfill their divinely appointed mission. Some comparison, albeit imperfect, can be made between priests and laity and the processions of origin that distinguish the persons in the Trinity itself.[12] Indeed, the Church recognizes a differentiation of the vocations that flourish within the one communion. As already mentioned, the priestly office requires of the ordained priest a commitment to both sacrificing and forgiving, ministries that serve the whole membership of the Church. In performing these and other priestly works, the Catholic priest acts in the person of Christ.[13]

What sacred actions then differentiate the priest from both the laity and consecrated persons? Common teaching holds that Catholic priests—by their

9. *Presbyterorum Ordinis*, no. 1 (VRL).

10. See also another Vatican document that treats the holy priesthood: "Indeed, the priest, by virtue of the consecration which he receives in the sacrament of orders, is sent forth by the Father through the mediatorship of Jesus Christ, to whom he is configured in a special way as head and shepherd of his people, in order to live and work by the power of the Holy Spirit in service of the Church and for the salvation of the world." John Paul II, *Pastores dabo vobis*, no. 12.

11. *Presbyterorum Ordinis*, no. 2 (VRL).

12. For further discussion, see the work of Sister Sara Butler, "In Persona Christi," *Proceedings* (Catholic Theological Society of America) 50 (1995): 146–55; Sara Butler, "Woman's Ordination and the Development of Doctrine," *The Thomist* 61 (1997): 501–24.

13. *Presbyterorum Ordinis*, no. 2. Because of the central place this teaching holds in subsequent documents of the Magisterium, the normative text merits quotation: "peculiari tamen illo sacramento confertur, quo presbyteri, unctione Spiritus Sancti, speciali charactere signantur et sic Christo sacerdoti configurantur, ita ut in persona Christi capitis agere valeant." The English is rendered thus: The priesthood "is conferred by that special sacrament; through it priests, by the anointing of the Holy Spirit, are signed with a special character and are conformed to Christ the Priest in such a way that they can act in the person of Christ the Head" (VRL).

preaching of the gospel, their forgiving of sins, and their offering of the eucharistic sacrifice—constitute the community of the Church as they act in the person and name of Christ. The conciliar decree expresses this central feature of the priest's proper responsibilities in these terms: "Exercising the office of Christ, the Shepherd and Head, and according to their share of his authority, priests, in the name of the bishop, gather the family of God together as a brotherhood enlivened by one spirit. Through Christ they lead them in the Holy Spirit to God the Father."[14] Like each of the sacraments, Holy Orders provides concrete expressions of the sanctifying power that flows from the Blessed Trinity.

Priests gather people together. For this reason, the Church looks at teaching, sanctifying, and governing such that they combine to form a single act of pastoral care. These obligations are designated also as the burdens of the priest. As another and later Vatican document explains, the "teaching, sanctifying, and governing" (munus docendi, sanctificandi et regendi) form an "indivisible unity."[15] That is, teaching, sanctifying, and governing serve a single supernatural end or purpose.

At the same time, what Pope Paul VI wrote in his 1964 encyclical, *Ecclesiam suam*, finds a special resonance when we consider the distinctiveness of the Catholic priest. "The fact that we [priests] are distinct from the world does not mean that we are entirely separated from it. . . . When the Church distinguishes itself from humanity, it does so not in order to oppose it, but to come closer to it."[16] Perhaps there is no better way to express the closeness that the Catholic priest should exhibit to the members of Christ's Church than with the designation used by spiritual authors of the priest as a spiritual father.[17]

Catholic teaching, in its official exposition, identifies the priest's paternity with the celibacy required of the priests in the Latin Church. *Presbyterorum Ordinis* expresses this relationship in a way that shows the kind of dedication required of the Catholic priest: "Through virginity, then, or celibacy observed for the Kingdom of Heaven, priests are consecrated to Christ by a new and exceptional reason."[18] The reference for this teaching includes a raft of authorities that reach back to the earliest centuries of the Christian era. The conciliar teaching continues by associating an undivided heart, which finds a reference

14. *Presbyterorum Ordinis*, no. 6 (VRL).

15. See *Ecclesiae de mysterio*, §2: "Therefore, since the exercise of the munus docendi, sanctificandi et regendi by the sacred minister constitute the essence of pastoral ministry, the diverse functions proper to ordained ministers form an indivisible unity and cannot be understood if separated, one from the other."

16. Paul VI, *Ecclesiam suam*, no. 3.

17. For instance, see T. E. D. Hennessy, "The Fatherhood of the Priest," *The Thomist* 10 (1947): 271–306.

18. *Presbyterorum Ordinis*, no. 16 (VRL).

in the Second Vatican Council's Dogmatic Constitution on the Church, *Lumen Gentium*,[19] with the ministry of priests, which includes the work of sacramental regeneration. "They [priests] adhere to him more easily with an undivided heart, they dedicate themselves more freely in him and through him to the service of God and men, and they more expeditiously minister to his Kingdom and the work of heavenly regeneration, and thus they are apt to accept, in a broad sense, paternity in Christ."[20] Furthermore, it is within this context of spiritual fatherhood that the reservation of priestly consecration to men may be understood.[21]

The Catholic Priest Represents Christ

The 1994 apostolic letter of Pope John Paul II *Ordinatio sacerdotalis* provides official Catholic teaching about ordination to the priesthood being reserved for men. The pertinent passage of this document runs as follows: "In order that all doubt may be removed regarding a matter of great importance, a matter which pertains to the Church's divine constitution itself, in virtue of my ministry of confirming the brethren (cf. Lk 22:32) I declare that the Church has no authority whatsoever to confer priestly ordination on women and that this judgment is to be definitively held by all the Church's faithful."[22] This authoritative teaching relies on an account of salvation history and on the value of natural symbols as two theological reasons for determining the matter of the sacraments.

Various factors, mostly from outside the Christian tradition, have made the reception of this teaching a matter of controversy. These factors include the practices of other Christian communities that have rejected the notion of sacramental character, the scandal of particularity (or exclusiveness) as a complaint first raised by Enlightenment thought against Christianity in general, and various liberation movements that developed during the twentieth century. These and other cultural factors have contributed to making this Catholic teaching on the priesthood difficult for some Catholics and others to accept with equanimity. Although constructive dialogue often proves difficult to undertake,

19. *Lumen Gentium*, no. 42.

20. *Presbyterorum Ordinis*, no. 16 (VRL).

21. For discussion on this question, see Benedict M. Ashley, "Gender and the Priesthood of Christ: A Theological Reflection," *The Thomist* 57 (1993): 343–79.

22. John Paul II, *Ordinatio sacerdotalis*, no. 4. An earlier document, *Inter insigniores*, recalled the teaching of the Council of Trent: "In the Church there has always existed this power, that in the administration of the sacraments, *provided that their substance remains unaltered*, she can lay down or modify what she considers more fitting either for the benefit of those who receive them or for respect towards those same sacraments, according to varying circumstances, times or places." *DS* 1728 (emphasis added).

Catholics need to recall basic Catholic teaching that the infallibility of faith rests on God's truthfulness, not on human judgments.[23]

The Catholic Church identifies the Catholic priest in many ways. One theological description that helps to establish the priest in his proper role within the Church borrows from the philosophical notion of instrument. As use of this concept to describe the relationship of the humanity of Christ to his divine person indicates, instrument emphasizes the relational dimension of priestly identity. In fact, the Second Vatican Council sounded this note when the fathers of the council spoke about the Catholic Church as a mediator of ultimate communion with the Blessed Trinity.[24] Again, we find in the Second Vatican Council implicit references to the way that the Catholic priest serves the Church "now sojourning on earth as an exile"; he serves "the pilgrim Church," if you will.[25]

As an instrument of salvation, the Catholic priest makes Christ present as male head of the community. In sum, the priest finds his identity and his job description as a servant of the Church as mystery, communion, and mission. In this sense, one can understand why the Catholic Church regards each of her priests as a servant and not as an undifferentiated officeholder. This leads the Church to insist on the humility of the priest, who stands in the person of the only begotten Son. Christ's redemptive death on Calvary represents an act of submission without, however, qualifying as an abuse, a distinction that would be more difficult to make were Christ not a Son (see Heb. 5:8). The Catholic Church expects the Catholic priest to follow in his own life this kind of self-abnegation.

In order to appreciate the fittingness of an all-male priesthood, it helps also to grasp the nuptial meaning of the priesthood. One official text puts it this way: "The Church, as the Spouse of Jesus Christ, wishes to be loved by the priest in the total and exclusive manner in which Jesus Christ her Head and Spouse loved her."[26] How does this love manifest itself? We return to the spiritual paternity of the Catholic priest, his spiritual fatherhood. Indeed, each of the dimensions of the priestly office—prophetic, kingly, and priestly—may be understood as so many ways of spiritual begetting: preaching emerges as an act of bringing forth the Word; the exercise of authority becomes an exercise of spiritual development; and the celebration of sacramental worship, especially the eucharistic sacrifice, serves to beget and nourish divine charity in the

23. One of the best treatments of this issue appears in a book that received, unfortunately, little public notice. For an embellishment of theological principles that undergird *Ordinatio sacerdotalis*, see Benedict M. Ashley, *Justice in the Church: Gender and Participation* (Washington, DC: Catholic University of America Press, 1996).

24. *Lumen Gentium*, no. 2.

25. *Lumen Gentium*, nos. 14, 48 (VRL).

26. John Paul II, *Pastores dabo vobis*, no. 29.

baptized and, ultimately, in the world.[27] No wonder, then, that the Church seeks, according to one formulation, to prepare future priests to "live the sacrament of holy orders, which configures them to Christ the head and shepherd, the servant and spouse of the Church."[28]

Controversies and Remedies

As has happened with the other sacraments of the Catholic Church, misunderstandings about Holy Orders have arisen over the course of the centuries. The Council of Trent devoted four chapters to "the true and Catholic doctrine on the sacrament of orders."[29] These chapters were followed by eight doctrinal canons that treat the following eight points. First, the council affirmed the nature of the priesthood as other than the "bare ministry of preaching."[30] Second, it upheld the legitimacy of the existence of "other orders, major and minor."[31] Third, it defended the true sacramental nature of Holy Orders against those who hold that this sacrament is a "kind of human invention devised by men experienced in ecclesiastical matters."[32] Fourth, it asserted that the sacramental character of Holy Orders is permanent, and so anathematized those who argue that "he who has once been a priest can again become a layman."[33] Fifth, the council defended the validity of the rites used in the ceremony of ordination, especially the anointing of the ordinand's hands.[34] Sixth, it addressed the reality of the Church's sacramental hierarchy, and so anathematized those who affirm that

27. These themes find a concise expression in John Paul II, *Pastores dabo vobis*, no. 15:

> In the Church and on behalf of the Church, priests are a sacramental representation of Jesus Christ—the head and shepherd—authoritatively proclaiming his word, repeating his acts of forgiveness and his offer of salvation—particularly in baptism, penance and the Eucharist, showing his loving concern to the point of a total gift of self for the flock, which they gather into unity and lead to the Father through Christ and in the Spirit. In a word, priests exist and act in order to proclaim the Gospel to the world and to build up the Church in the name and person of Christ the head and shepherd.

28. John Paul II, *Pastores dabo vobis*, no. 3.

29. See *DS* 1763–70.

30. *DS* 1771.

31. *DS* 1772. One may note here that Pope Paul VI's 1972 apostolic letter, *Ministeria quaedam*, made certain adjustments to this practice of distinguishing between major and minor orders, which had prescribed a series of preliminary steps—each ordination related in some way to the celebration of the liturgy—that an ordinand in the Latin Church was required to take before the seventh step, priestly ordination.

32. *DS* 1773.

33. *DS* 1774.

34. *DS* 1775. One may also note here that the identification of the essential rites in the administration of Holy Orders later received clarification in Pope Pius XII's 1948 apostolic constitution *Sacramentum ordinis* (see *DS* 3857–61).

the Catholic Church lacks a hierarchical organization "that consists of bishops, priests, and ministers."[35] Seventh, it addressed the proper relationship of bishop to priest and the conditions necessary and not necessary for receiving Holy Orders, such as the "call of the people or of the civil authority."[36] And eighth, the council spoke about the relationship of bishops to the Pope who chooses them.[37]

The reforms initiated by the Council of Trent bore special fruit in the formation of priests and in the affirmation of their pastoral ministry. One can cite certain sixteenth-century figures of the Catholic reform who exhibited an exemplary practice of the priestly ideal as the Council of Trent described it: Saint Cajetan (Italian, d. 1547); Saint John of Avila (Spanish, d. 1569); Saint Philip Neri (Italian, d. 1595); Saint Charles Borromeo (Italian, d. 1584); Saint Robert Bellarmine (Italian, d. 1621). In response to the introduction of professional, academic training for ministers active in Reformation circles, the Catholic Church also established seminaries that provided focused attention on priestly formation. In countries where the Reformation took complete hold, such as England, these seminaries were established in other places where the Catholic Church enjoyed civil standing, such as the English College at Douai, then in the Spanish Low Countries.

The post-Tridentine reforms of priestly formation and life found special exposition in the seventeenth-century French School, the *école francaise*. Among the many figures who represent this French School, one may cite François de La Rochefoucauld (d. 1645), who stressed that the priest must appear as a man of prayer, and Pierre de Bérulle (d. 1629), who guided the foundation of the French Oratory, an innovative arrangement for diocesan priests to live in community. In addition, Bérulle—also a cardinal and spiritual author—placed the Catholic priest within the logic of the Incarnation, stressed the priest's role in both giving spiritual instruction and administering the sacraments, and even began to speak about the Christian perfection of the priest.[38]

During this very fecund century for French Catholicism, societies dedicated to the formation of candidates for the priesthood were instituted by saints and holy priests such as Saint Vincent de Paul (d. 1660), founder of the Congregation of the Mission or Vincentians; Charles de Condren (d. 1641), who succeeded Bérulle at the French Oratory; and Jean Jacques Olier (d. 1657), who gave direction and organization to the Sulpicians. These institutes still continue their work within the Catholic Church. All in all, the French School introduced as its

35. *DS* 1776.
36. *DS* 1777.
37. *DS* 1778.
38. For further discussion, see Aidan Nichols, *Holy Orders* (Dublin: Veritas, 1990), 112–14.

main themes for priestly renewal the notion of the priest as another Christ (*alter Christus*), the priest's central work as that of offering the eucharistic sacrifice, and the priest's spiritual support as being from his practice of Marian devotion (including invoking the Virgin Mary as *Regina cleri*, Queen of Clerics). These themes, moreover, continue to dominate official Catholic teaching, especially in *Pastores dabo vobis*, the last fully developed articulation about the priesthood from the Roman Magisterium.

The renewal of priestly life and ministry that the seventeenth-century French School made popular spread outside France, particularly in the anglophone parts of the world. This expansion of influence occurred thanks especially to the missionary work of both Sulpician and Vincentian priests. Sulpician teachers specially drew on classical texts from the patristic and scholastic periods. Although no full treatment of the sacrament of Holy Orders appears in the *Summa theologiae*, the thought of Saint Thomas Aquinas on this sacrament does appear in various places throughout the *Summa*. Aquinas's thought, drawn also from his commentary on the Letter to the Hebrews, offers a convenient summary of the main emphases that the Catholic Church still employs in her official statements on priests. The Church's practices with respect to regulating the life and ministry of her priests also betray the influence of Aquinas.

Take, for example, Aquinas's understanding of participation. Participation serves as a key philosophical principle that undergirds the Common Doctor's understanding of priesthood. He holds that the most perfect representative of any given kind exercises a causal influence on all participants in that kind.[39] So in *Summa theologiae* III.22.4, Aquinas writes, "Christus est fons totius sacerdotii" (Christ is the source of all priesthood). Formal causality operates in this affirmation. This notion of participation, a favorite of Aquinas's, one with backgrounds both Aristotelian and Platonic, further implies that there exists a direct relationship between a man *being* a Catholic priest and a man *functioning* as a Catholic priest. For this reason, sound theology speaks more about the grace to be a priest than it does about the process of discernment that seeks to determine whether a man can adjust his personal dispositions to accommodate what a Catholic priest does.[40]

Once Holy Orders seals a man with the priestly character, the Catholic priest finds himself inserted into a world where the virtue of religion emerges as the dominant setting. Why? The acts of the virtue of religion encompass

39. See *Summa theologiae* III.22.4: "For any given order the first agent influences others, while it is itself subject to no influence within the limits of that order."

40. See Romanus Cessario, *The Grace to Be a Priest* (Providence, RI: Cluny Media, 2017).

the important features of the life and the duties of a priest.[41] The Letter to the Hebrews, especially its description of Christ's prayers and supplications—"He was heard because of his reverence" (Heb. 5:7)—places reverence among the features of Christ's priestly identity. Christ, in any case, embodies the eminently religious man. This means that Christ both receives everything from God and gives to God the one sacrifice that pleases him. Hebrews continues to explain that Christ preeminently possesses the fullness of priestly power—that is, "he became the source of eternal salvation for all who obey him" (Heb. 5:9). From this christological principle, the conclusion follows that the communication of grace requires that the person who serves as an instrument himself be established as such through a specific sacramental grace. What Christ possesses by nature, the Catholic priest receives by reason of his priestly ordination, his reception of the sacrament of Holy Orders.

Ordination and Ministry of Priests

The sacramentality of Holy Orders lies in a spiritual power that is conferred by a visible, external rite, which today includes the laying on of hands as the essential action, though at one time the handing over of cultic instruments, the *traditio instrumentorum*—namely, a filled chalice and a paten with bread—held a place of special significance.[42] The *Catechism of the Catholic Church* sets forth the *sacramentum tantum* of Holy Orders in this way: "The essential rite of the sacrament of Holy Orders for all three degrees consists in the bishop's imposition of hands on the head of the ordinand and in the bishop's specific consecratory prayer asking God for the outpouring of the Holy Spirit and his gifts proper to the ministry to which the candidate is being ordained."[43]

The priestly character of Christ forms the foundation for the spiritual power that the Catholic priest exercises unto the sanctification of Christ's members. As the Church expressed this mystery in the fifteenth century, "The effect [of Holy Orders] is an increase of grace, so that one may be a suitable minister of Christ."[44] Just as Baptism and Confirmation open up the way for the Catholic believer to participate in Christ's redemptive worship of the Father, so the

41. For an overview of these acts properly associated with the virtue of religion, see *Summa theologiae* II-II.82–91.

42. Pope Pius XII explains this shift of emphasis clearly: "In the ordination of priests, the matter is the first imposition of the bishop's hands, which is done in silence." Pius XII, *Sacramentum ordinis, DS* 3860.

43. *CCC* nos. 1573, 1542.

44. "Effectus est augmentum gratiae, ut quis sit idoneus Christi minister." Council of Florence, *Exsultate Deo* (*Bull of Union with the Armenians*), November 22, 1439, *DS* 1326.

indelible spiritual character of Holy Orders imparts a focused and distinct participation in the priesthood of Christ.[45]

The most clear teaching on differentiation without inequality appears in a document of the Second Vatican Council. The Dogmatic Constitution on the Church, *Lumen Gentium*, insists that the difference between the ministerial and the royal priesthood is one of kind and not simply of degree.[46] This means that priesthood does constitute a special vocation for Catholics, one distinguished from the vocations of both laity and consecrated persons.

Another way to approach this differentiation may be found in what Aquinas teaches about sacramental character. In short, the sacramental character works with special effect in those established in Holy Orders. Recall that Aquinas holds that, in general, character "is a sign by which someone or something is made to be configured to the principal figure which is vested with the necessary authority for that which the individual is deputed."[47] The Common Doctor then applies this definition to the character imprinted by the Catholic sacraments: "And in this way those deputed to Christian worship, the author of which is Christ, receive a character by which they are brought into configuration to Christ."[48] In sum, the ministerial priesthood—that is, the priesthood exercised by those in Holy Orders—provides "a *means* by which Christ unceasingly builds up and leads his Church."[49]

The 1992 exhortation *Pastores dabo vobis* summarizes the very Catholic understanding of the priesthood as a ministry of service to the sanctification of Catholics. "There can be no doubt," the document says, "that the exercise of the priestly ministry, especially in the celebration of the sacraments, receives its saving effects from the action of Christ himself, who becomes present in the sacraments."[50] Catholic teaching on the priesthood continues to associate inseparably priestly ministry with Christ's own priesthood. When Aquinas discusses Christ's priesthood, he recalls that Christ is the one mediator between humans and God and that, as a priest, Christ accomplishes this task within the context of his filial relationship with the heavenly Father.[51]

Three elements in Christ's relationship to the Father hold special meaning for priestly life and mission. The first is his submission to the Father, which implies that Christ recognizes that only the Father is good (see Matt. 19:17; Mark 10:18;

45. See *CCC* nos. 1581–82, which refers to the Council of Trent, *DS* 1767.

46. *Lumen Gentium*, no. 10.

47. *Summa theologiae* III.63.3 ad 2.

48. *Summa theologiae* III.63.3 ad 2. For discussion of the sacramental character as it applies to bishops, see Guy Mansini, "The Character of Episcopal Orders," *The Thomist* 66 (2002): 369–94.

49. *CCC* no. 1547 (emphasis original).

50. John Paul II, *Pastores dabo vobis*, no. 25.

51. See *Summa theologiae* III.22.

Luke 18:19). Christ is entirely given over to living with divine providence, even as a slave (see Phil. 2:7). His obedience extends even unto death (Phil. 2:8).[52] The Catholic Church, in turn, sets forth this summary spiritual guidance to her priests: "Only the person who knows how to obey in Christ is really able to require obedience from others in accordance with the Gospel."[53] Priestly obedience presupposes the conviction that a good and provident God ordains all things sweetly.

The second element of Christ's relationship with the Father is prayer, which implies a communication between Christ and the Father that disposes Christ to surrender his own will to that of the heavenly Father, trusting that God will accomplish his purposes.[54] The Church, then, urges her priests to maintain their own communication with God: "It is above all in the celebration of the sacraments and in the celebration of the Liturgy of the Hours that the priest is called to live and witness to the deep unity between the exercise of his ministry and his spiritual life."[55] The *Liturgy of the Hours*, also known as the Divine Office, contains the prayers or "work" (*officium*) Catholic clerics promise to pray or better fulfill daily.

The third element of this relationship is Christ's own priesthood—namely, the office that Christ assumes in order to fulfill his saving mission. As already noted, the following tasks belong to the office of the ministerial priesthood, for just as Christ fulfills these in a perfect way, so the ordained priest accomplishes them by reason of his ordination. In brief, the Catholic priest exercises his mediation when he communicates sacred doctrine (see Mal. 2:7), performs the perfect satisfaction (Heb. 5:1), communicates divine life (2 Pet. 1:3–4), and mediates these graces because he enjoys possession of a sacramental identity (Col. 1:19–20). The biblical references cited in this discussion of Christ's priesthood are those employed by Saint Thomas Aquinas in his treatment of Christ's submission to the Father, his prayer, and his priesthood.[56]

Saint John Vianney

To return to a central theme of Catholic teaching on Holy Orders, one may trust that official Catholic teaching on the priesthood always revolves around the

52. See *Summa theologiae* III.20.1–2.

53. John Paul II, *Pastores dabo vobis*, no. 28.

54. See *Summa theologiae* III.21.1–4. See also the treatise on prayer in *Summa theologiae* II-II.83.

55. John Paul II, *Pastores dabo vobis*, no. 26.

56. For further expert discussion of this important feature of Catholic theology, see the English translation, introduction, appendixes, and glossary in Colman E. O'Neill, *The One Mediator*, vol. 50 of the Blackfriars edition of *Summa theologiae*, by Thomas Aquinas (New York: McGraw-Hill, 1965).

identity of the priest as another Christ. In a homily delivered before some five thousand priests, Pope John Paul II made this point with exquisite clarity: "Beloved," the Pope addressed the priests, "through ordination, you have received the same Spirit of Christ, who makes you like him, so that you can act in his name and so that his very mind and heart might live in you."[57] Then the Pope applied the principle of *in persona Christi* to the personal comportment of the Catholic priest: "This intimate communion with the Spirit of Christ," he said, "while guaranteeing the efficacy of the sacramental actions which you perform *in persona Christi*, seeks to be expressed in fervent prayer, in integrity of life, in the pastoral charity of a ministry tirelessly spending itself for the salvation of the brethren. In a word, it calls for your personal sanctification."[58] Though even sinful priests can effectively administer the sacraments, especially to those in danger of death, nothing replaces the witness of a holy, Christlike priest.

No wonder saints have demurred from trying to explain fully the true nature of the Catholic priesthood. Take the holy Curé of Ars in France. He affirms that "the priesthood is the love of the Heart of Jesus." However, this same Saint John Marie Vianney (d. 1859) goes on to inform us, "Only in heaven shall we know what a priest is. If we were to know this on earth, we would die, not of grief, but of love."[59] What, then, does Catholic teaching conclude about the work of the Catholic priest? The truth appears clearly: only the Catholic priest readies us for this kind of heaven, this heaven that the loving vision of God creates. Why? Without the Catholic priest, no transformations divinize, no sacraments effect what they signify, no saving premotions reach their term, no human love survives the grave, and, as far as we know, no one sees God "face to face" (see 1 Cor. 13:12). Small wonder Saint John Marie Vianney proclaims that only from the vantage point of heaven do the blessed discover what a Catholic priest is.

Catholics clearly see that the "sacred power" given to the priest benefits the world just as paternal authority ensures good ordering within a family.[60] What deep Catholic instinct prompts Christ's lay faithful, at least in English-speaking countries, to address their priests, "Father"! The "sacred power" given to priests does not enable facile oppression, as critics often opine. The "sacred power" Christ confides to his priests rather causes people to flourish, making them lovers of God and neighbor.

57. As quoted in John Paul II, *Pastores dabo vobis*, no. 33.

58. John Paul II, *Pastores dabo vobis*, no. 33.

59. St. John Vianney, as quoted in Bernard Nodet, *Jean-Marie Vianney, Curé d'Ars, sa pensée, son coeur* (Le Puy, France: Mappus, 1958), 100. These words have been quoted subsequently both in *CCC* no. 1589 and by Pope Benedict XVI in his 2009 "Year for Priests."

60. *Presbyterorum Ordinis*, no. 2 (VRL).

The priest teaches and nourishes; he strengthens and sustains; he heals and forgives. No substitute exists for the indispensable work of the priest. Without the priest, no one would emerge to preach authoritatively revealed truth. Folks would be obliged to figure out for themselves God and the things of God. Without the priest, no Christian community would flourish. Catholics would be left without the Sacraments of Initiation: Baptism, Confirmation, Holy Eucharist. Without the priest, no sinner would find forgiveness for faults or release from punishments. Catholics would seek vainly for the Sacraments of Healing: Penance and Reconciliation, Anointing of the Sick. Without the priest, husband and wife could receive no blessing to strengthen their communion of persons. Spouses would find themselves left to their own cleaving, and so susceptible to the hardness of heart that the sacrament of Matrimony softens. In sum, without the Catholic priest, human life would fall apart under the weight of its own disorders.

No wonder Pope John Paul II never tired of recalling a central teaching of the Second Vatican Council: "The truth is that only in the mystery of the incarnate Word does the mystery of man take on light."[61] The Catholic priest comes among his people as another Christ in order to proclaim this mystery to the world.

61. *Gaudium et Spes*, no. 22 (VRL). Pope John Paul II quotes this text in his first encyclical, *Redemptor hominis*, no. 8.

19

Matrimony

As the Catholic Church teaches, a Catholic marriage celebrates a "mystery," a conjunction of wills, at once human and divine.[1] The *Catechism of the Catholic Church* makes this astonishing claim: "The covenant between the spouses is integrated into God's covenant with man. 'Authentic married love is caught up into divine love.'"[2] To put it differently, the sacrament of Matrimony places a man and a woman into the realm of the supernaturally sacred. "Marriage," so the catechism further affirms, "is not a purely human institution despite the many variations it may have undergone through the centuries."[3] For, in addition to the consent of the spouses, the "I do" of bride and groom, Almighty God adds his own "Amen," making a Catholic marriage an occasion of grace and of power.[4] "Since it signifies and communicates grace, marriage between baptized persons is a true sacrament of the New Covenant."[5]

Three to Get Married

The holy time of Matrimony necessitates a holy place. "In the Latin Rite the celebration of marriage between two Catholic faithful normally takes place during Holy Mass."[6] This sacrament, the sacrament of wedded love, points to a change, a transformation. Indeed, as one of the "rites of passage," sanctioned

1. See *CCC* no. 1602.
2. *CCC* no. 1639. The quotation within the quotation comes from *Gaudium et Spes*, no. 48.
3. *CCC* no. 1603.
4. See *CCC* nos. 1631–32.
5. *CCC* no. 1617, which cites the Council of Trent, *DS* 1800.
6. *CCC* no. 1621.

and blessed by the Lord himself, it imparts a new vocation and a higher dignity. Indeed, Matrimony, like all the sacraments of the Catholic Church, enjoys a connection with the paschal mystery of Christ. The Second Vatican Council expressed in its own words this fundamental principle of Catholic sacramental theology: "Thus, for well-disposed members of the faithful, the liturgy of the sacraments . . . sanctifies almost every event in their lives; they are given access to the stream of divine grace which flows from the paschal mystery of the passion, death, the resurrection of Christ, the font from which all sacraments . . . draw their power."[7]

Further, the eucharistic sacrifice that unites heaven and earth reminds both bride and groom that they form "one body" in Christ. The couple realize at the deepest level of human commitment that "whoever is joined to the Lord becomes one spirit with him" (1 Cor. 6:17). This realization takes on a eucharistic dimension when, by reason of their receiving Holy Communion, they grasp that as the Eucharist remains one, a married couple who "partake of the one loaf" themselves become "one body."[8]

The grace of Matrimony, like every divine grace given to human beings, flows from the Incarnate Word. Because in the mystery of the Incarnation the Son of God acquired a human heart, thereby making each one of our hearts capable of divine love, the love that husband and wife bear toward each other takes on its own particular christological character. Venerable Fulton Sheen (d. 1979) used to speak about "Three to Get Married."[9] Nowhere is this great mystery of Christ's union with the Church made more visible than in the sacrament of wedded love.

Pope John Paul II made this theme an explicit part of his widely acclaimed teaching on marriage and family. "The spouses," writes the Pope, "participate in [marriage] as spouses, together, as a couple, so that the first and immediate effect of marriage (res et sacramentum) is not supernatural grace itself, but the Christian conjugal bond, a typically Christian communion of two persons because it represents the mystery of Christ's Incarnation and the mystery of His covenant."[10] From this teaching, it becomes clear to Catholic married couples that their sacrament not only transforms their love, but it carries with it the responsibilities of a new vocation.

7. *Sacrosanctum Concilium*, no. 61 (VRL).

8. See 1 Cor. 10:17 and *CCC* no. 1621.

9. See Fulton J. Sheen, *Three to Get Married* (Strongsville, OH: Scepter, 2005). Sheen first published his book in 1951.

10. This text comes from an address that Pope John Paul II gave to the delegates of the Centre de Liaison des Équipes de Recherche on November 3, 1979. It later appeared in, and is here quoted from, John Paul II, *Familiaris consortio*, no. 13.

Matrimony as a Sacrament

How can one describe this change, this metamorphosis? Christian marriage presents an occasion when the mystery of God's love is realized in a special and extraordinary way. As mentioned above, the Church teaches that in this sacrament of the new dispensation, God has raised human love to the dignity of divine love.[11] Every other sacrament uses material things to achieve an end greater than such things as bread and wine, oil and water, even sorrow for sin. However, in Holy Matrimony, wherein a man and a woman are united in Christ, their human love and its manifold expressions become the very sacrament. This explains why in the Western tradition, the Catholic Church considers groom and bride to be the principal celebrants of their own sacrament.[12] Before the Church's minister, a cleric, or a representative, they promise to love each other.[13] And these promises constitute a covenant that no human power can put asunder.

Accordingly, Pope John Paul II penned these powerful words to explain the indissolubility of a Catholic marriage. "The content of participation in Christ's life is also specific," writes the Pope, such that "conjugal love involves a totality in which all the elements of the person enter—appeal of the body and instinct, power of feeling and affectivity, aspiration of the spirit and of will. It aims at a deeply personal unity, the unity that, beyond union in one flesh, leads to forming one heart and soul."[14] And so the conclusion follows that this unity of a married couple "demands indissolubility and faithfulness in definitive mutual giving; and it is open to fertility (cf. *Humanae vitae*, 9)."[15] More recently, Pope Francis has joined this train of thought when he recalls other themes that Pope John Paul II

11. See *Gaudium et Spes*, no. 48.

12. See CCC no. 1623: "According to the Latin tradition, the spouses as ministers of Christ's grace mutually confer upon each other the sacrament of Matrimony by expressing their consent before the Church." The Church is ordinarily represented by a cleric, deacon, priest, or bishop. However, a Catholic can request a dispensation from canonical form. So any Catholic who receives such a dispensation can marry in a ceremony officiated by a non-Catholic. This dispensation, however, would not be given to two Catholics, but to a Catholic marrying a non-Catholic—baptized or not. A bishop can designate a lay Catholic to officiate at a marriage between two Catholics (but would not designate a non-Catholic minister). Further, if it is truly impossible to find any such delegation, Catholics can marry before two witnesses, although this concession obviously envisages very remote parts of the world. I acknowledge the help of Reverend Ryan Wilson Connors, professor of theology at Saint John's Seminary, Boston, who supplied this technical information.

13. A slightly different understanding prevails in "the traditions of the Eastern Churches, [where] the priests (bishops or presbyters) are witnesses to the mutual consent given by the spouses, but for the validity of the sacrament their blessing is also necessary." CCC no. 1623.

14. John Paul II, Address to the Delegates of the Centre de Liaison des Équipes de Recherche, as quoted in *Familiaris consortio*, no. 13.

15. John Paul II, Address to the Delegates of the Centre de Liaison des Équipes de Recherche, as quoted in *Familiaris consortio*, no. 13.

had developed: "The procreative meaning of sexuality," writes Pope Francis, "the language of the body, and the signs of love shown throughout married life, all become an 'uninterrupted continuity of liturgical language' and 'conjugal life becomes in a certain sense liturgical.'"[16]

No wonder Saint Paul speaks about marriage as "a great mystery" (Eph. 5:32).[17] God takes something as ordinary as the love that occurs between man and woman and makes it a sacrament of salvation. Everything is transformed: human biology, human emotions, the whole structure of man and woman living together. "In a word," to return to Pope John Paul II's testimony, "it is a question of the normal characteristics of all natural conjugal love, but with a new significance which not only purifies and strengthens them, but raises them to the extent of making them the expression of specifically Christian values."[18]

Catholic spouses form a communion of persons that will serve as a source of blessing for themselves, their children, their friends, and the whole Church. This grace reminds us that the Church urges that everyone respect the nuptial meaning of the body. Father Colman O'Neill makes an astute commentary on the *res et sacramentum* of Matrimony when he says that Christ's saving work becomes manifest in the lives of two members of Christ, at the very sources of human life, where love and abiding fidelity represent one of the most striking instances of a sacrament of the Blessed Trinity precisely because marriage, like death, remains an unavoidable circumstance of the human race.[19]

The grace that the sacrament of Matrimony bestows on the couple, the *res* of the sacrament of Matrimony, finds the best succinct expression in the Catholic Church's teaching on her own reality, *Lumen Gentium*. In short, the grace of Matrimony helps each member of the couple to sustain the goods of marriage: indissolubility, fidelity, and fecundity.[20] So the Church teaches that the "grace proper to the sacrament of Matrimony is intended to perfect the couple's love and to strengthen their indissoluble unity. By this grace they 'help one another to attain holiness in

16. Francis, *Amoris lætitia*, no. 215.

17. Pope John Paul II drew on this theme when he established the Institute for Studies on Marriage and Family in 1982: "The Church has always shown her special pastoral concern for the great sacrament of Matrimony (cf. Eph 5:32), since she is 'conscious that marriage and the family are one of the greatest goods belonging to the human race' (*Familiaris consortio* §1)." See also John Paul II, *Magnum matrimonii sacramentum*, no. 1. Interestingly, the Wycliffe Bible renders Eph. 5:32 as "This sacrament is great; yea, I say in Christ, and in the church."

18. John Paul II, Address to the Delegates of the Centre de Liaison des Équipes de Recherche, as quoted in *Familiaris consortio*, no. 13.

19. Colman E. O'Neill, *Sacramental Realism* (Chicago: Midwest Theological Forum, 1998), 187–92.

20. See CCC no. 1643. The catechism discusses these goods under three headings: the unity and indissolubility of marriage, the fidelity of conjugal love, and the openness to fertility. See CCC nos. 1644–54.

their married life and in welcoming and educating their children.'"[21] Sometimes married Catholics speak about the graces they derive from their state of life.

In addition to a work of grace, every Catholic marriage celebrates another triumph: a triumph of the human spirit. For each partner, bride and groom, put away all their fears and suspicions, they put aside their doubts and hesitations, in order to declare before God and man their willingness to belong to one another for as long as they both shall live. Despite the dubieties of an age and the perils of a culture, the Catholic bride and Catholic groom are willing to confront these common ambiguities together, to take in hand the direction of their own lives. Moreover, by affirming their own mutual love, they receive from the Lord a new dignity, a new office—and that is the holy estate of Matrimony.

The Domestic Church

As mentioned above, the Church speaks about a new office, a new vocation—one that puts spouses in continuity with the chain of generations that the Lord causes to come and go to his great glory until he comes again (see 1 Cor. 11:26). As the smallest microcosm of his Church, Catholic spouses bear witness not only to the reality of his love but also to the imminence of his kingdom. As "the domestic Church," they enact in their daily lives the sacramental character of the Church, a witness for all to see.[22] And by pledging their determination to live out the meaning of Emmanuel, God-with-us, they make the Church more of what she already is.

Indeed, bride and groom, their lives and their loves, enhance the Church. So the ecclesial community in attendance, sharing the same Baptism, the same Catholic faith, the same Lord, mission, and destiny, rejoice with the couple, as the two of them disclose for us another variation on the theme of human possibility. And in this context of Church and witness, of community and love, the married couple become, as the poet says, "a constant sacrament of praise."[23]

Catholic teaching on Matrimony summons to mind Jesus's words: "I have told you this so that my joy may be in you and your joy may be complete" (John 15:11). And the papal teaching on marriage and the family stands out as an extraordinary witness to the Church's love of this truth. Indeed, Pope Francis has confirmed the view that "the Joy of Love experienced by families is also the joy of the Church."[24] Since the love of husband for wife and of wife for husband

21. CCC no. 1641, quoting *Lumen Gentium*, no. 11.

22. See CCC no. 1666.

23. Wallace Stevens, "Peter Quince at the Clavier," 4, The Poetry Foundation, https://www.poetryfoundation.org/poems/47430/peter-quince-at-the-clavier.

24. *Amoris lætitia*, no. 1.

makes this sacrament efficacious and consecrates their lives in this common joy, the rest of the community surrenders to its attraction. Recognizing the gift of married love, the Catholic people thank spouses for this sharing in a common heart. And they pray that the Lord will remain with the couple always and that they will be solicitous for his claims and desires.

This high purpose, of course, requires missionary zeal, especially today. Our own culture has forgotten that venereal pleasure according to God's plan knits together only the unique friendship that we find expressed in the chaste love of husband and wife. However, the Catholic Church refuses to acknowledge any friendship other than that between a man and a woman lawfully married where procured venereal pleasure can sanctify the persons who enter into sexual congress with one another.[25]

Newly married couples leave the church of their wedding as witnesses to Christ's saving power active at the very sources of human life. Their vocation together helps others to glimpse something of the Church's revelation of the Trinity, and their communion points others to the broader communion that unites the whole Church. For these reasons, the Second Vatican Council, as already mentioned, refers to the Christian family as "the domestic church."[26] Gladly, then, do Catholics offer themselves—their experience, talents, wisdom—in good times and in bad, so that the spouses can realize the fullness of the mystery that they enact on their wedding day.

Like all Catholics, bride and groom too must be confident that the Lord will bring to a successful conclusion the good work that he has already begun in them on their wedding day. The joy that all who celebrate a Catholic marriage know on a wedding day anticipates the happiness of heaven that will one day unite all the redeemed again in the communion of saints, a society of blessed friends. Again, poets best grasp the hidden meaning of a Catholic wedding:

> St. John tells how, at Cana's wedding-feast,
> The water-pots poured wine in such amount
> That by his sober count
> There were a hundred gallons at the least.
>
> It made no earthly sense, unless to show
> How whatsoever love elects to bless

25. The *Catechism of the Catholic Church* describes the moral evil of fornication as "gravely contrary to the dignity of persons and of human sexuality which is *naturally* ordered to the good of spouses and the generation and education of children." CCC no. 2353 (emphasis added).

26. *Lumen Gentium*, no. 11 (VRL).

Brims to a sweet excess
That can without depletion overflow.[27]

The poet draws on Catholic sensibilities. "The Church," so affirms the *Catechism of the Catholic Church*, "attaches great importance to Jesus's presence at the wedding at Cana."[28] So poet Richard Wilbur is right to extol how blessed love "brims to a sweet excess." The catechism goes on to explain that the Church sees in Christ's presence at the Cana wedding feast "the confirmation of the goodness of marriage and the proclamation that thenceforth marriage will be an efficacious sign of Christ's presence."[29]

The wedding at Cana as recorded in the Gospel of John introduces many biblical themes that Catholic theology develops. Not the least of these themes centers on the role that the mother of Jesus plays in the multiplication of the wine: "Do whatever he tells you" (John 2:5). In *Amoris lætitia,* Pope Francis sees this gospel event as a determining factor in establishing the dignity and centrality of marriage and family for the Church. "The example of Jesus," he writes, "is a paradigm for the Church. He began his public ministry with the miracle at the wedding feast of Cana (see John 2:1–11)."[30]

Pope Francis continues to summarize fundamental Catholic teaching on Catholic marriage: "The spousal covenant, originating in creation and revealed in the history of salvation, takes on its full meaning in Christ and his Church. Through his Church, Christ bestows on marriage and the family the grace necessary to bear witness to the love of God and to live the life of communion."[31] Further, the Pope restates the traditional Catholic teaching concerning the origin of the sacrament of Matrimony. "The sacrament of marriage," he says, "flows from the incarnation and the paschal mystery, whereby God showed the fullness of his love for humanity by becoming one with us."[32]

Challenges to the Sacramentality of Marriage

To return to the sixteenth century and the Council of Trent, we learn that throughout history not everyone has accepted Catholic teaching about the sacramentality of Matrimony. The fathers of the Council of Trent did not mince their words when it came to describing those who denigrated Matrimony:

27. Richard Wilbur, "Wedding Toast," in *The Mind-Reader* (New York: Harcourt Brace Jovanovich, 1976), 12.

28. CCC no. 1613.

29. CCC no. 1613.

30. *Amoris lætitia,* no. 63.

31. *Amoris lætitia,* no. 64.

32. *Amoris lætitia,* no. 74.

"Impious men of this age, in their foolishness, not only have entertained false ideas about this venerable sacrament, but, as is their custom, they have given freedom to the flesh under the pretext of the Gospel."[33] Later, the text refers to these impious men as both "schismatics" and "heretics"—without, of course, naming such individuals personally. This sad announcement, which comes at the end of the four short statements that summarize Catholic doctrine on the sacrament of Matrimony, leads into the setting forth of twelve canons that anathematize certain of the major errors that the council chooses to rectify.

The anathemas of Trent deal mainly with various technical aspects of Church law and practice regarding the sacrament of Matrimony. Only four of the twelve anathemas treat matters that may be considered directly related to doctrine. These, moreover, the Catholic Church still professes as sound doctrine. The first of these anathemas concerns a fundamental tenet of Catholic and divine faith—namely, that Christ instituted Matrimony as a sacrament. "If anyone says that matrimony is not truly and properly one of the seven sacraments of the law of the Gospel, instituted by Christ the Lord, but that it was devised in the Church by men and does not confer grace, let him be anathema."[34]

The *Catechism of the Catholic Church* sets this teaching as the preface to its treatment of the sacrament of Matrimony.[35] The references given are those of the *Code of Canon Law*, canon 1055, section 1, and the Second Vatican Council's *Gaudium et Spes*, number 48, section 1. This Pastoral Constitution on the Church in the Modern World in turn refers four times to *Casti connubii*, a 1930 encyclical of Pope Pius XI on the topic of Christian marriage. Among the pertinent references, the following reflects back on the first anathema of Trent. After the turmoil caused by World War I had settled, Pope Pius XI wrote the following expression of Catholic truth: "But in this good of the sacrament, besides the firmness and indissolubility, there are also much higher advantages, as the word 'sacrament' itself very aptly indicates; for to Christians this is not a meaningless and empty name. Christ the Lord, the Institutor and 'Perfecter' of the holy sacraments, by raising the matrimony of his faithful to the dignity of a true sacrament of the New Law, made it a sign and source of that special internal grace by which 'it perfects natural love, it confirms an indissoluble union, and it sanctifies both man and wife.'"[36] The citations from the Council of Trent come from a paragraph that refers to Saint Paul's teaching in Ephesians 5:25: "Husbands, love your wives, even as Christ loved the Church and handed himself over for her."

33. *DS* 1800.
34. *DS* 1801.
35. See CCC no. 1601.
36. Pius XI, *Casti connubii*, *DS* 3713.

The next canon of Trent that treats a doctrinal matter concerning Matrimony, canon 5, deals with the binding character of marriage. "If anyone says that the marriage bond can be dissolved because of heresy or difficulties in cohabitation or because of the willful absence of one of the spouses, let him be anathema."[37] The *Catechism of the Catholic Church* explains the permanence of the marriage bond in these words: "*The marriage bond* has been established by God himself in such a way that a marriage concluded and consummated between baptized persons can never be dissolved."[38] The same number continues to affirm the classic Catholic teaching on the marriage bond—namely, "The Church does not have the power to contravene this disposition of divine wisdom."[39]

Another canon with doctrinal emphasis, canon 7, renders a judgment on those biblical passages (Matt. 5:32; 19:9; Mark 10:11–12; Luke 16:18; 1 Cor. 7:11) that may be read to grant an exception to indissolubility in the case of adultery on the part of one of the partners. Trent addresses sternly anyone who "says that the Church is in error for having taught and for still teaching that in accordance with evangelical and apostolic doctrine . . . the marriage bond cannot be dissolved because of adultery on the part of one of the spouses."[40] The text refers to the New Testament passages mentioned above. The *Catechism of the Catholic Church* upholds the indissolubility of marriage (quoting Mark 10:11–12).[41] At the same time, however, the reaffirmation of the indissolubility of marriage is placed within a set of pastoral principles that include calling on the support of the Christian community for couples who face difficult marital situations, encouraging priests to "manifest an attentive solicitude" toward couples in strained marriages, and directing such couples to maintain as appropriate their obligation to practice the virtue of religion.[42]

The final canon to address doctrinal principles is canon 10: "If anyone says that the married state surpasses that of virginity or celibacy and that it is not better and happier to remain in virginity or celibacy than to be united in matrimony . . . , let him be anathema."[43] The *Catechism of the Catholic Church* actually includes three numbers within the treatment of Matrimony that discuss virginity for the sake of the kingdom and its legitimacy.[44] The 1996 Post-synodal Apostolic Exhortation on the Consecrated Life and Its Mission in the Church and in

37. *DS* 1805.
38. *CCC* no. 1640 (emphasis original).
39. *CCC* no. 1640.
40. *DS* 1807.
41. *CCC* no. 1650.
42. *CCC* no. 1651; see also nos. 1646–51 for what the catechism says about "the fidelity of conjugal love."
43. *DS* 1810.
44. See *CCC* nos. 1618–20.

the World (*Vita consecrata*) makes the point that this "way of living in chastity, poverty and obedience appears as the most radical way of living the Gospel on this earth. . . . This is why Christian tradition has always spoken of the objective superiority of the consecrated life."[45] And later in the document, the Pope, John Paul II, makes an even more explicit statement about the special value of consecrated life in the Church: "As a way of showing forth the Church's holiness, *it is to be recognized that the consecrated life*, which mirrors Christ's own way of life, *has an objective superiority*."[46]

The same can be said of priestly celibacy. *Pastores dabo vobis* devotes considerable attention to explaining the special value of priestly celibacy. In short, the Church holds that "celibacy is to be considered as a special grace, as a gift, for 'not all men can receive this saying, but only those to whom it is given' (Mt. 19:11)."[47] For his part, Saint Thomas Aquinas says that the "sacrament of order is designed for the consecration of the Eucharist" and that therein Holy Orders finds its relative excellence among the other sacraments.[48] So the Catholic Church still holds to the Tridentine assertion that the married state does not surpass that of virginity or celibacy.

The remaining canons on the sacrament of Matrimony fall under the heading of disciplinary matters. Canon 2, for instance, addresses those who propose to legitimize bigamy. Canons 3 and 4 address the Church's determinations concerning diriment impediments to marriage as well as those that arise from consanguinity and affinity. Canon 6 speaks to the effect that solemn vows of religion have on an unconsummated marriage. Canon 8 concerns the permission given to married couples to separate from bed and board for a period of time.

Canon 9 speaks to the circumstances of clerics in sacred orders or religious who have made a solemn profession of chastity and who attempt marriage. The council answers an objection that holds that said cleric or religious should be free to marry when he no longer feels able to sustain celibate chastity because he lacks the "gift of chastity."[49] To the ninth canon, which anathematizes this claim, the council attaches a reason drawn from the New Testament that explains what otherwise may appear to be an unreasonable expectation. To the one who feels that he no longer possesses the "gift" necessary to observe his promise or vow, the council declares that "God does not refuse that gift to those who ask for it rightly, and 'he will not let you be tempted beyond your strength' (1 Cor. 10:13)."

45. John Paul II, *Vita consecrata*, no. 18.
46. John Paul II, *Vita consecrata*, no. 32 (emphasis original).
47. John Paul II, *Pastores dabo vobis*, no. 50.
48. *Summa theologiae* III.65.3.
49. *DS* 1809.

Canon 11 addresses those who criticize the Church's practice of prohibiting the solemnization of marriage during certain liturgical seasons or who condemn the blessings and ceremonies used in such solemn nuptials. Current Church practice counsels pastors to remind couples who celebrate their marriage on a day having a special penitential character to take account of the special nature of the day. The only prohibited days for celebrating a marriage are Good Friday and Holy Saturday.[50]

The last canon, number 12, defends the legitimacy of the ecclesiastical judges and courts that treat cases dealing with marriage. This practice, of course, continues to this day.

Regulation of Clandestine Marriages

One other significant act that issues from the Council of Trent appears in the "Canons on a Reform of Marriage: The Decree *Tametsi*."[51] In a word, the council took note of various abuses, usually against women, that have resulted from the authorization of clandestine or secret marriages—that is, marriages "entered by free consent of the parties" but without witnesses.[52] At the same time, the council also went on record saying that "the holy Church of God has always detested and prohibited such marriages for the best of reasons."[53] To put an end to such clandestine marriages, the decree *Tametsi* orders that public announcements of a couple's intention to marry be made in the parish church in a convenient manner. After the announcements, a priest is to question both parties to the marriage about their consent and then bless the marriage using an approved formula.[54] The decree then issues a "Sanction." The text runs thus: "The holy council now renders incapable of marriage any who attempt to contract marriage otherwise than in the presence of the parish priest . . . and two or three witnesses, and it decrees that such contracts are null and invalid and renders them so by this decree."[55]

Professor Mary Ann Glendon has repeatedly acknowledged what she calls the Church's "countercultural accomplishments where women and the family were concerned. It still boggles the mind," Glendon says, "as a student of law and society, to think that the Church succeeded in gaining wide acceptance for the novel idea that marriage was indissoluble—in cultures where men had always

50. *The Roman Ritual: The Order of Celebrating Matrimony*, no. 32.
51. See *DS* 1813–16.
52. *DS* 1813.
53. *DS* 1813.
54. See *DS* 1814–15.
55. *DS* 1816.

been permitted by custom to put aside their wives!"[56] Glendon then observes the singular accomplishment of *Tametsi*: "Despite pressures from princes and merchants, the Council of Trent stood firm against marriages arranged without the consent of the spouses."[57] Obviously, clandestine marriage made it easy to coerce the weaker party in the marriage, usually the bride. No one was present to witness the consent, and so no one could challenge the claims of the stronger party, usually the husband.

The contributions that the Catholic Church has made to the refinement of marriage practices receive recognition from recognized scholars of the history of marriage. John Witte Jr., for example, has made a fairly explicit evaluation of the achievement of the Council of Trent. Speaking of the "comprehensive canon law of marriage" that the Catholic Church developed, this distinguished professor has observed that "this canon law of marriage, grounded in a rich sacramental theology and ecclesiastical jurisprudence, was formalized and systematized by the Council of Trent in 1563 and greatly influenced Western marriage law for centuries thereafter."[58]

Preparation for Matrimony

This achievement of the Catholic Church with respect to marriage law and custom merits recognition. However, the Catholic Church first looks to make saints of her members, so that these holy men and women can take up temporal affairs—government, economy, and domestic life—in accord with the help they receive from God through the sacraments. Therefore, the Church encourages those who are about to marry to prepare themselves for their reception of the *res*, the graces of the sacrament.

Because the liturgical celebration of marriage brings about a sacramental action of sanctification, the *Catechism of the Catholic Church* offers this salutary counsel: "It is . . . appropriate for the bride and groom to prepare themselves for the celebration of their marriage by receiving the sacrament of penance."[59] When one considers that the sacrament of Matrimony confers on spouses the ability to love each other as Christ loves the Church, so that they remain faithful to each other in all that married life requires of them, it becomes evident why both bride and groom should remove through the sacrament of Penance and

56. Mary Ann Glendon, *Traditions in Turmoil* (Ave Maria, FL: Sapientia, 2006), 404.

57. Glendon, *Traditions in Turmoil*, 404.

58. John Witte Jr., *From Sacrament to Contract: Marriage, Religion, and Law in the Western Tradition* (Louisville: Westminster John Knox, 1997), 4. For the author's detailed account of what he calls the "Tridentine synthesis," see pp. 36–41.

59. CCC no. 1622.

Reconciliation whatever may obstruct the bestowal of the grace of the Blessed Trinity destined to support them in their marriage.

To sum up: Pope John Paul II laid bare the importance of Matrimony within the order of creation. In his apostolic exhortation on marriage, the Pope writes, "The institution of marriage is not an undue interference by society or authority, nor the extrinsic imposition of a form. Rather it is an interior requirement of the covenant of conjugal love which is publicly affirmed as unique and exclusive, in order to live in complete fidelity to the plan of God, the Creator. A person's freedom, far from being restricted by this fidelity, is secured against every form of subjectivism or relativism and is made a sharer in creative Wisdom."[60] How much the more does this truth shine forth within the sacrament that Christ instituted at a wedding feast in Cana of Galilee.

60. *Familiaris consortio*, no. 11.

Conclusion

The *Catechism of the Catholic Church* draws on a theme that Saint Thomas Aquinas aptly summarizes when he calls the sign value of a sacrament "prognostic, that is, a foretaste of future glory."[1] Elsewhere—namely, in an antiphon to the Magnificat for Corpus Christi vespers—the Common Doctor proclaims the Holy Eucharist as a "pledge given to us of future glory" (*futurae gloriae nobis pignus datur*). So the catechism in turn announces to the world that "in the sacraments of Christ the Church already receives the guarantee of her inheritance and even now shares in everlasting life."[2] What better incentive can one imagine for embracing the sacramental rhythms of Catholic life?

Sometimes making a close study of the sacraments of the Catholic Church can lead a person to seek their reception. Study in fact has led some people into full communion with the Catholic Church. At the same time, it also happens, and perhaps more frequently, that people, whether Catholics or not, encounter a sacramental celebration. This personal experience may produce something powerful in a person's soul such that they seek either Baptism or, if they are already baptized, a conversion of life. Consider the experience of the French poet Paul Claudel (d. 1955) on Christmas Day 1886. During the singing of the Magnificat in the Cathedral of Notre Dame, this gifted Frenchman was moved to start a journey back to full participation in the sacramental life of the Catholic Church. His acclaimed literary output remains a testimony to the supernatural graces that he received.

Or consider the unexpected encounter of another Frenchman, Charles de Foucauld (d. 1916), with a certain Catholic priest, M. L'Abbé Huvelin, in the

1. *Summa theologiae* III.60.3.
2. CCC no. 1130.

confessional of a Paris church. Foucauld, then a self-reliant and debonair man-about-town, approached the priest to seek information. God, however, wanted to provide him with something more excellent than mere instruction. The priest responded by telling Foucauld to kneel down and confess his sins. A somewhat startled Foucauld did, and he subsequently embraced a complete change of life. By the time this book reaches the general public, the Church will have canonized Saint Charles de Foucauld, who spent the better part of his converted public life as a missionary in French Algeria. Many other examples of this kind of sacramental persuasion exist.

While extraordinary examples of conversion may edify the Christian people, the Catholic Church also provides for the ordinary. In countless parishes, churches, and chapels throughout the world, her ministers provide the sacraments of salvation to those who seek them. One can speak of the rhythms of Catholic life as punctuated by the reception of the sacraments that each Catholic requires to enter and to remain in God's good grace. The foregoing presentation of the pattern of sacramental life in the Catholic Church aims to encourage everyone to embrace these rhythms of salvation unto everlasting life.

Bibliography

Patristic Sources

Ambrose. *De obitu Valentiniani consolatio*. PL 16:1357–84.

———. *Exposition on the Christian Faith* (*De fide*).

———. *The Mysteries* (*De mysteriis*). In *St. Ambrose Theological and Dogmatic Works*. Fathers of the Church 44. Translated by Roy J. DeFerrari. Washington, DC: Catholic University of America Press, 1963.

Athanasius the Great and Didymus the Blind. *Works on the Spirit: Athanasius the Great & Didymus the Blind*. Translated by Mark DelCogliano, Andrew Radde-Gallwitz, and Lewis Ayres. Popular Patristics Series 43. Yonkers, NY: St. Vladimir's Seminary Press, 2011.

Augustine. *The City of God* (*De civitate Dei*). Translated by John Healey. Edinburgh: John Grant, 1909.

———. *Confessions*. In *The Confessions of St. Augustine*. Translated by John K. Ryan. Garden City, NY: Image Books, 1960.

———. *Contra Faustum*.

———. *De doctrina Christiana*.

———. *Epistula* 108.

———. *On Baptism, against the Donatists*. In *The Later Christian Fathers*, edited by Henry Bettenson, 241–42. Oxford: Oxford University Press, 1970.

———. *Tractates on the Gospel of John*. In *Nicene and Post-Nicene Fathers*, series 1, vol. 7. Edited by Philip Schaff. Translated by John Gibb. Buffalo: Christian Literature, 1888.

Cyprian. *On the Unity of the Catholic Church* (*De catholicae ecclesiae unitate*).

Gregory of Nyssa. *The Great Catechism*.

Gregory the Great. *Homilies on the Book of the Prophet Ezekiel*.

Ignatius. "Letter to the Romans." In *Ante-Nicene Fathers*. Vol. 1. Translated by A. Roberts and J. Donaldson. Buffalo: Christian Literature, 1885.

Jerome. *Commentary on Ecclesiastes*. PL 23:1009–116.

———. *Interpretatio libri Dydimi de Spiritu Sancto*. PL 23:99–154.

John Chrysostom. *On the Priesthood.*
Origen. *Commentary on the Gospel according to John.*
Tertullian. *De baptismo.*

Medieval Sources

Aquinas, Thomas. *Commentary on Aristotle's Physics.* Translated by R. Blackwell et al. New Haven, CT: Yale University Press, 1963.
———. *The Pocket Aquinas.* Edited by Vernon J. Bourke. New York: Pocket Books, 1960.
———. *Summa theologiae.* Blackfriars edition. 60 vols. Translated by Thomas Gilby et al. New York: McGraw-Hill, 1964–73.
Bonaventure. *Commentary on the Sentences.*
Dionysius. *The Mystical Theology.* Translated by W. Riordan. Ave Maria, FL: Sapientia, 2020.
Innocent III. *De Sacro altaris mysterio libri VI.* Berlin: Nabu Press, 2013.
Septem sacramenta ecclesiae secundum septem diversitates hominum in ecclesia. Originally published in Milan in 1557 and reprinted in facsimile. Como, Italy: Typographia Editrice Cesare Nani, 1998.

Modern Sources

Allen, Michael. "Sacraments in the Reformed and Anglican Traditions." In *The Oxford Handbook of Sacramental Theology*, edited by Hans Boersma and Matthew Levering, 283–97. Oxford: Oxford University Press, 2015.
Ashley, Benedict M. "Gender and the Priesthood of Christ: A Theological Reflection." *The Thomist* 57 (1993): 343–79.
———. *Justice in the Church: Gender and Participation.* Washington, DC: Catholic University of America Press, 1996.
———. *The Way toward Wisdom: An Interdisciplinary and Intercultural Introduction to Metaphysics.* South Bend, IN: University of Notre Dame Press, 2006.
Auer, Johann. *A General Doctrine of the Sacraments and the Mystery of the Eucharist.* Translated by Erasmos Leiva-Merikakis. Vol. 6 of *Dogmatic Theology*, edited by Johann Auer and Joseph Ratzinger. Washington, DC: Catholic University of America Press, 1995.
Barden, William. *The Eucharistic Presence.* Vol. 58 of the Blackfriars edition of *Summa theologiae*, by Thomas Aquinas. New York: McGraw-Hill, 1965.
Bedouelle, Guy. *The Reform of Catholicism, 1480–1620.* Translated by J. K. Farge. In *Catholic and Recusant Texts of the Late Medieval & Early Modern Periods.* Studies and Texts 161. Toronto: Pontifical Institute of Medieval Studies, 2008.
Belonick, Deborah. "Revelation and Metaphors: The Significance of the Trinitarian Names, Father, Son, and Holy Spirit." *Union Seminary Quarterly Review* 40 (1985): 31–42.

Benedict XVI. "Ad Romanam Curiam ob omnia natalicia." *Acta Apostolicae Sedis* 98 (January 6, 2006): 40–53.

Billot, Louis. *De ecclesiae sacramentis: Commentarius in tertiam partem S. Thomae*. 5th ed. Rome: Ex Typographia Pontificia Istituto Pii X, 1914.

Boismard, Marie-Émile. "The Eucharist according to Saint Paul." In *The Eucharist in the New Testament: A Symposium*, edited by J. Delorme, translated by M. Stewart, 125–39. Baltimore: Helicon, 1964.

Bossuet, Jacques-Bénigne. *Méditations, la Cène, 57ème jour*. Lyons, 1879.

Bourke, David. *The Sacraments*. Vol. 56 of the Blackfriars edition of *Summa theologiae*, by Thomas Aquinas. New York: McGraw-Hill, 1975.

Bouyer, Louis. *Eucharist: Theology and Spirituality of the Eucharistic Prayer*. Notre Dame, IN: University of Notre Dame Press, 1968.

Boyle, John F. "Saint Thomas Aquinas on the Anointing of the Sick (Extreme Unction)." In *Rediscovering Aquinas and the Sacraments: Studies in Sacramental Theology*, edited by Matthew Levering and Michael Dauphinais, 76–84. Chicago: Hillenbrand Books, 2009.

Boyle, Leonard. *A Short Guide to St. Clement's, Rome*. Rome: Collegio San Clemente, 1987.

Brennan, Robert Edward. *The Seven Horns of the Lamb*. Milwaukee: Bruce, 1966.

Brouillard, René. "Sacramenta propter homines." *Nouvelle revue théologique* 50, no. 9 (1923): 464–73.

Brown, Raymond. *The Gospel according to John*. Anchor Yale Bible. 2 vols. 1966 and 1970. Reprint, New Haven, CT: Yale University Press, 1995.

Butler, Sara. "In Persona Christi." *Proceedings* (Catholic Theological Society of America) 50 (1995): 146–55.

———. "Woman's Ordination and the Development of Doctrine." *The Thomist* 61 (1997): 501–24.

Cameron, Euan. "The Power of the Word: Renaissance and Reformation." In *Early Modern Europe: An Oxford History*, edited by Euan Cameron, 63–104. Oxford: Oxford University Press, 1999.

Cappello, Felix M. *Tractatus canonico-moralis de sacramentis*. Vol. 1. Rome-Turin: Marietti, 1945.

Carol, Juniper B. *Why Jesus Christ?* Manassas, VA: Trinity Communications, 1987.

Cessario, Romanus. "Anointing of the Sick: The Sanctification of Human Suffering." *Nova et Vetera* (English ed.) 17 (2019): 1–11.

———. "'Circa Res . . . Aliquid Fit' (*Summa theologiae* II-II, q. 85, a. 3, ad 3): Aquinas on New Law Sacrifice." *Nova et Vetera* (English ed.) 4 (2006): 295–312.

———. "Duplex Ordo Cognitionis." In *Reason and the Reasons of Faith*, edited by Paul J. Griffiths and Reinhard Hütter, 327–38. New York: T&T Clark, 2005.

———. *The Godly Image: Christian Satisfaction in Aquinas*. Washington, DC: Catholic University of America Press, 2020.

———. *The Grace to Be a Priest*. Providence, RI: Cluny Media, 2017.

———. "Molina and Aquinas." In *A Companion to Luis de Molina*, edited by Alexander Aichele and Matthias Kaufmann, 291–323. Leiden: Brill, 2014.

———. *The Moral Virtues and Theological Ethics*. 2nd ed. Notre Dame, IN: University of Notre Dame Press, 2008.

———. "An Observation on Robert Lauder's Review of G. A. McCool, S.J." *The Thomist* 56 (1992): 701–10.

———. Review of *Kidnapped by the Vatican? The Unpublished Memoirs of Edgardo Mortara*, by Vittorio Messori. *First Things*, February 2018, 55–58, and April 2018, 4–5.

———. "Sacramental Causality: *Da capo*!" *Nova et Vetera* (English ed.) 11 (2013): 307–16.

———. "The Sacraments of the Church." In *Vatican II: Renewal within Tradition*, edited by Matthew L. Lamb and Matthew Levering, 129–46. Oxford: Oxford University Press, 2008.

———. "Saint Thomas Aquinas on Satisfaction, Indulgences, and Crusades." *Medieval Philosophy & Theology* 2 (1992): 74–96.

———. "Scripture as the Soul of Moral Theology: Reflections on Vatican II and *Ressourcement* Thomism." *The Thomist* 76 (2012): 165–88.

———. "Sixteenth-Century Reception of Aquinas by the Council of Trent and Its Main Authors." In *The Oxford Handbook of the Reception of Aquinas*, edited by Matthew Levering and Marcus Plested, 159–72. Oxford: Oxford University Press, 2021.

———. "Sonship, Sacrifice, and Satisfaction." In *Theology and Sanctity*, by Romanus Cessario, edited by C. Cuddy, 69–98. Ave Maria, FL: Sapientia, 2014.

———. "Toward Understanding Aquinas' Theological Method: The Early Twelfth-Century Experience." In *Studies in Thomistic Theology*, edited by Paul Lockey, 17–89. Notre Dame, IN: Center for Thomistic Studies, 1995.

Cessario, Romanus, Guy Bedouelle, and Kevin White, eds. *Jean Capreolus en son temps (1380–1444)*. Mémoire Dominicaine, numéro spécial, 1. Paris: Cerf, 1997.

Cessario, Romanus, and Kevin White. *John Capreolus (1380–1444): Treatise on the Virtues*. Washington, DC: Catholic University of America Press, 2001.

Clarke, Samuel. *The Marrow of Ecclesiastical History* (London: Printed for W. B., 1675).

Congar, Yves. *A Gospel Priesthood*. Translated by P. F. Hepburne-Scott. New York: Herder & Herder, 1967.

Danneels, Godfried. "Current Challenges for Sacramental Theology." *Antiphon* 5, no. 2 (2000): 44–45.

Darling Young, Robin. "She Who Is: Who Is She?" Review of *She Who Is: The Mystery of God in Feminist Theological Discourse*, by Elizabeth A. Johnson. *The Thomist* 58 (1994): 23–33.

de Vio (Cajetan), Thomas. *Commentary on the Summa* (*In Summam*).

Dias, Elizabeth, with photographs by Ryan Christopher Jones. "The Last Anointing." *New York Times*, June 6, 2020. https://www.nytimes.com/interactive/2020/06/06/us/coronavirus-priests-last-rites.html?smid=wa-share.

Dimock, Giles. "Revisiting the Baroque." *Antiphon: A Journal for Liturgical Renewal* 5, no. 3 (2000): 8–10.

Di Noia, J. A. "Communion and Magisterium: Teaching Authority and the Culture of Grace." *Modern Theology* 9 (1993): 403–18.

———. "Knowing and Naming the Triune God: The Grammar of Trinitarian Confession." In *Speaking the Christian God: The Holy Trinity and the Challenge of Feminism*, edited by Alvin F. Kimel Jr., 162–87. Grand Rapids: Eerdmans, 1992.

Di Noia, J. A., and Joseph Fox. "Priestly Dimensions of the Sacrament of the Anointing of the Sick." *The Priest* 62 (2006): 10–13.

Dix, Gregory. *The Shape of the Liturgy*. London: Dacre, 1945.

Doronzo, Emmanuel. *Tractatus dogmaticus de sacramentis in genere*. Milwaukee: Bruce, 1946.

Dulles, Avery. "Criteria of Catholic Theology." *Communio* 22, no. 2 (1995): 303–15.

Erasmus, Desiderius. *Detectio praestigiarum*. In Desiderius Erasmus, *Controversies*. Collected Works of Erasmus 78. Edited by James D. Tracy and Manfred Hoffman. Toronto: University of Toronto Press, 2011.

Farley, Edward. *Theologia: The Fragmentation and Unity of Theological Education*. Philadelphia: Fortress, 1983.

Farrell, Walter, and Dominic Hughes. *Swift Victory: Essays on the Gifts of the Holy Spirit*. New York: Sheed & Ward, 1955.

Foemby, Henry. *Sacrum Septenarium; or, The Seven Gifts of the Holy Ghost: As Exemplified in the Life and Person of the Blessed Virgin for the Guidance and Instruction of Her Children*. London: Burns, Oates, 1874.

Gabriel of St. Mary Magdalen and Discalced Carmelite Nuns of Boston. *Divine Intimacy: Meditations on the Interior Life for Every Day of the Liturgical Year*. Gastonia, NC: Tan Books, 1997.

Gardeil, H. D. *Introduction to the Philosophy of St. Thomas Aquinas*. Vol. 2, *Cosmology*. Translated by John A. Otto. St. Louis: B. Herder, 1958.

Garrigou-Lagrange, Reginald. *De Eucharistia et Paenitentia*. Turin: Marietti, 1948.

Gilson, Etienne. *The Christian Philosophy of St. Thomas Aquinas*. Translated by L. K. Shook. New York: Random House, 1966.

Glendon, Mary Ann. *Traditions in Turmoil*. Ave Maria, FL: Sapientia, 2006.

Görres, Ida Friederike. *The Hidden Face: A Study of St. Thérèse of Lisieux*. New York: Pantheon Books, 1959.

Gray, Mark M., and Paul M. Perl. "Sacraments Today: Belief and Practice among U.S. Catholics." Report, Center for Applied Research in the Apostolate, Georgetown University, Washington, DC, April 2008.

Grillmeier, Aloys. *Christ in Christian Tradition*. Translated by J. Bowden. Vol. 1, *From the Apostolic Age to Chalcedon (451)*. Atlanta: John Knox, 1975.

Halligan, Nicholas. *The Administration of the Sacraments: Some Practical Guides for Priests and Seminarians*. Staten Island, NY: Alba House, 1963.

———. *The Sacraments and Their Celebration*. Staten Island, NY: Alba House, 1986.

Hampson, Daphne. "Whales and Elephants." *The Tablet*, March 23, 2001.

Hennessy, T. E. D. "The Fatherhood of the Priest." *The Thomist* 10 (1947): 271–306.

Hill, William J. *Proper Relations to the Indwelling Divine Persons*. Washington, DC: Thomist, 1952.

Hunter-Kilmer, Meg. "The Holy Priest Who Left Hardened Sinners 'Weeping for Joy.'" *Aleteia*, June 22, 2017. https://aleteia.org/2017/06/22/the-holy-priest-who-left-hardened-sinners-weeping-for-joy/.

Irwin, Kevin. "Recent Sacramental Theology: A Review Discussion." *The Thomist* 47 (1983), 52 (1988), 53 (1989).

John Paul II. *Gift and Mystery: On the Fiftieth Anniversary of My Priestly Ordination*. New York: Doubleday, 1996.

Kavanagh, Aidan. *The Shape of Baptism: The Rite of Christian Initiation*. New York: Pueblo, 1978.

Kilmartin, Edward J. *The Eucharist in the West: History and Theology*. Edited by Robert J. Daly. Collegeville, MN: Liturgical Press, 2015.

LaCugna, Catherine. "The Baptismal Formula, Feminist Objections, and Trinitarian Theology." *Journal of Ecumenical Studies* 26 (1989): 235–51.

La Dispute de Lausanne (1536). Proceedings of the Colloque international sur la Dispute de Lausanne. Université de Lausanne, 1986. Lausanne, Switzerland: Bibliothèque historique vaudoise, 1988.

Leclercq, Jean. *The Love of Learning and the Desire for God: A Study of Monastic Culture*. New York: Fordham University Press, 1961.

Leeming, Bernard. *Principles of Sacramental Theology*. Westminster, MD: Newman, 1956.

———. "Recent Trends in Sacramental Theology." *Irish Theological Quarterly* 23 (1956): 195–217.

Levada, William J. "Reflections on the Age of Confirmation." *Theological Studies* 57 (1996): 302–12.

Long, Steven A. "Providence, Freedom, and Natural Law." *Nova et Vetera* (English ed.) 4, no. 3 (2006): 557–606.

Luther, Martin. *Babylonian Captivity of the Church*. Translated by A. T. W. Steinhäuser. Revised by Frederick C. Ahrens and Abdel Ross Wentz. In *Luther's Works*. Edited by J. Pelikan and T. Lehmann. St. Louis: Concordia, 1958.

Lynch, Reginald. *The Cleansing of the Heart: The Sacraments as Instrumental Causes in the Thomistic Tradition*. Washington, DC: Catholic University of America Press, 2017.

———. "Domingo Bañez on Moral and Physical Causality: Christic Merit and Sacramental Realism." *Angelicum* 91 (2014): 105–25.

Mansini, Guy. "The Character of Episcopal Orders." *The Thomist* 66 (2002): 369–94.

Maritain, Jacques. *On the Grace and Humanity of Jesus*. Translated by T. W. Evans. New York: Herder & Herder, 1969.

McFague, Sallie. *Models of God: Theology for an Ecological, Nuclear Age*. Philadelphia: Fortress, 1987.

Michel, Albert. "Matière et forme dans les sacrements." In *Dictionnaire de théologie catholique*. Vol. 10.1, cols. 335–55. 1928.

———. "Sacrements." In *Dictionnaire de théologie catholique*. Vol. 14.1, cols. 485–644. 1939.

Moiser, Jeremy. "Why Did the Son of God Become Man?" *The Thomist* 37 (1973): 288–305.

Montalembert, Charles F. *Les Moines d'Occident depuis Saint Benoît jusqu'à Saint Bernard*. Paris: J. Lecoffre, 1860.

Neunheuser, Burkhard. *Baptism and Confirmation*. Translated by John Jay Hughes. The Herder History of Dogma. New York: Herder & Herder, 1964.

Newman, John Henry. *The Dream of Gerontius*. London: Longmans, Green, 1910.

Nichols, Aidan. *The Holy Eucharist: From the New Testament to Pope John Paul II*. Dublin: Veritas, 1991.

———. *Holy Orders*. Dublin: Veritas, 1990.

Nicolas, Jean-Hervé. "La grâce sacramentelle." *Revue Thomiste* 61 (1961): 165–92, 522–38.

Niebuhr, H. Richard. *The Kingdom of God in America*. New York: Harper & Row, 1959.

Nodet, Bernard. *Jean-Marie Vianney, Curé d'Ars, sa pensée, son coeur*. Le Puy, France: Mappus, 1958.

Nutt, Roger W. *General Principles of Sacramental Theology*. Washington, DC: Catholic University of America Press, 2017.

O'Brien, T. C. *Father, Son, and Holy Ghost*. Vol. 7 of the Blackfriars edition of *Summa theologiae*, by Thomas Aquinas. New York: McGraw-Hill, 1976.

O'Connell, Matthew. "New Perspectives in Sacramental Theology." *Worship* 39 (1965): 195–206.

O'Connor, Edward D. *The Gifts of the Holy Spirit*. Vol. 24 of the Blackfriars edition of *Summa theologiae*, by Thomas Aquinas. New York: McGraw-Hill, 1973.

O'Connor, James T. *The Hidden Manna: A Theology of the Eucharist*. 2nd ed. San Francisco: Ignatius, 2005.

O'Malley, William J. "Confirmed and Confirming." *America* 172. June 17, 1995.

O'Neill, Colman E. *Meeting Christ in the Sacraments*. Rev. ed. Edited by Romanus Cessario. Staten Island, NY: Alba House, 1991.

———. *The One Mediator*. Vol. 50 of the Blackfriars edition of *Summa theologiae*, by Thomas Aquinas. New York: McGraw-Hill, 1965.

———. *Sacramental Realism*. Chicago: Midwest Theological Forum, 1998.

O'Neill, Taylor. *Grace, Predestination, and the Permission of Sin: A Thomistic Analysis*. Washington, DC: Catholic University of America Press, 2019.

Osbourn, James C. *The Morality of Imperfections*. Thomistic Studies 1. Washington, DC: Pontifical Faculty of Theology, Dominican House of Studies, 1943.

Ozment, Steven. *Protestants: The Birth of a Revolution*. New York: Doubleday, 1993.

Pannenberg, Wolfhart. *Systematic Theology*. Vol. 1. Grand Rapids: Eerdmans, 1991.

Peters, Christian. *"Apologia Confessionis Augustanae": Investigations into the Text History of a Lutheran Confession (1530–1584)*. Stuttgart: Calwer, 1997.

Philips, Dirk. *The Writings of Dirk Philips*. Edited by C. Dyck et al. Waterloo, ON: Herald, 1992.

Pope, Alexander. *An Essay on Man: Epistle II* (1734). The Poetry Foundation, https://www.poetryfoundation.org/poems/44900/an-essay-on-man-epistle-ii.

Poschmann, Bernhard. *Penance and the Anointing of the Sick*. Translated by F. Courtney. New York: Herder & Herder, 1964.

Power, David N., Regis Duffy, and Kevin Irwin. "Sacramental Theology: A Review of Literature." *Theological Studies* 55 (1994): 657–705.

Regatillo, Edward F. *Jus sacramentarium*. Santander, Spain: Editorial Sal Terrae, 1964.

Rempel, John D. "Sacraments in the Radical Reformation." In *The Oxford Handbook of Sacramental Theology*, edited by Hans Boersma and Matthew Levering, 298–312. Oxford: Oxford University Press, 2015.

Revel, Jean-Philippe. *Baptême et sacramentalité*. 2 Vols. Traité des sacrements 1. Paris: Cerf, 2004, 2005.

———. *La confirmation: Plénitude du don baptismal de l'Esprit*. Traité des sacrements 2. Paris: Cerf, 2006.

Rover, Thomas D. "The Sacramental Efficacy of the Act of Preaching." In *Proceedings of the Seventeenth Annual Convention*, by Catholic Theological Society of America, 241–47. Washington, DC: Catholic Theological Society of America, 1963.

Schillebeeckx, Edward. *Christ the Sacrament of the Encounter with God*. New York: Sheed & Ward, 1963.

Sheen, Fulton J. *Three to Get Married*. Strongsville, OH: Scepter, 2005.

Stevens, Wallace. "Peter Quince at the Clavier." The Poetry Foundation, https://www.poetryfoundation.org/poems/47430/peter-quince-at-the-clavier.

Thérèse of Lisieux. *The Story of a Soul: The Autobiography of St. Thérèse of Lisieux*. Translated by J. Clarke. Washington, DC: ICS Publications, 1975.

Torrell, Jean-Pierre. *Saint Thomas Aquinas*. Vol. 1, *The Person and His Work*. Rev. ed. Translated by R. Royal. Washington, DC: Catholic University of America Press, 2005.

Vonier, Anscar. *A Key to the Doctrine of the Eucharist*. Westminster, MD: Newman Bookstore, 1946.

Wallace, William A. *Causality and Scientific Explanation*. 2 Vols. Ann Arbor, MI: University of Michigan Press, 1972–74.

———. "Cause and Effect: Temporal Relationships." In *From a Realist Point of View: Essays on the Philosophy of Science*, 115–30. Washington, DC: University Press of America, 1979.

Weinandy, Thomas G. "The Human Acts of Christ and the Acts That Are the Sacraments." In *Ressourcement Thomism: Sacred Doctrine, the Sacraments, and the Moral Life*, edited by Reinhard Hütter and Matthew Levering, 150–68. Washington, DC: Catholic University of America Press, 2010.

Weisheipl, James A. "The Meaning of *Sacra Doctrina* in *Summa theologiae* I, q. 1." *The Thomist* 38 (1974): 49–80.

Williams, George Huntston. *The Radical Reformation*. Philadelphia: Fortress, 1962.

Willis, John R., ed. *The Teachings of the Church Fathers*. New York: Herder & Herder, 1966.

Witte, John, Jr. *From Sacrament to Contract: Marriage, Religion, and Law in the Western Tradition*. Louisville: Westminster John Knox, 1997.

Name Index

Subject Index